SEX, RACE, AND SCIENCE

EDWARD J. LARSON

Sex, Race, and Science

Eugenics in the Deep South

The Johns Hopkins University Press
Baltimore & London

FOR LUCY

This book was originally brought to publication with the generous assistance of the Karl and Edith Pribram Endowment.

Johns Hopkins Paperbacks edition, 1996
05 04 03 02 01 00 99 98 97 96   5 4 3 2 1

The Johns Hopkins University Press
2715 North Charles Street
Baltimore, Maryland 21218-4319
The Johns Hopkins Press Ltd., London

ISBN 0-8018-4938-1
ISBN 0-8018-5467-9 (pbk.)

Library of Congress Cataloging-in-Publication Data will be found at the end of this book.

A catalog record for this book is available from the British Library.

Contents

Preface & Acknowledgments

Almost every day the media report another breakthrough in human gene therapy or reproductive technology. If we are to believe these reports, the potential for "designer children" lies just around the corner. The discoveries of the Human Genome Project, coupled with recombinant-DNA research and new techniques of *in vitro* fertilization, promise the power to correct unwanted inherited defects and to enhance desired hereditary traits in our offspring. The questions raised by ethicists and commentators about the implications that these developments have for our future led me to look back into our past for some answers about how Americans responded to a similar promise earlier in this century. At that time, conceptual advances in evolutionary biology and Mendelian genetics led many respected scientists to believe that human heredity could readily be manipulated through selective breeding. As these ideas filtered from the scientific journals into the popular press, and spread from eugenics experts to the general public, Americans changed the way we thought about and treated each another. Now that we again believe that we hold the promise of shaping our genetic future, I sought to review, and to learn from, what that promise once led us to do to our fellow citizens.

This study was made possible by the help of many friends. In my historical research, I benefited from the advice and counsel of my colleagues in the history department at the University of Georgia, particularly B. Phinizy Spalding, Lester D. Stephens, Peter C. Hoffer, John C. Inscoe, William F. Holmes, and Emory M. Thomas. There simply is no better place to study southern history. I also owe a special debt to the historians Daniel J. Kevles, who encouraged me in the early stages of this project, and Steven Noll, who lent me some of his materials on the founding of facilities for the mentally retarded in Florida and throughout the South. Further in the background stand other historians who have helped teach me how to write and think history. These include Ronald L. Numbers,

David C. Lindberg, Donald DeB. Beaver, and James MacGregor Burns.

With regard to my legal research, I wish to thank my deans, C. Ronald Ellington and Edward D. Spurgeon of the University of Georgia School of Law, and the geneticist Wyatt W. Anderson of the University of Georgia, Franklin College of Arts and Sciences, for their support during this project, and Thomas A. Eaton, my colleague in teaching health care law, for his encouragement and advice. The health-law expert at Alabama's Cumberland Law School, Leonard J. Nelson III, also provided valuable counsel and a place to stay while in the Birmingham area. Finally, the attorney-physician Philip R. Reilly graciously shared some of his research materials on this topic with me. Next to these scholars stand the many attorneys and law professors who have helped me learn how to analyze and understand the legal process, most notably Thomas E. Petri, Phillip Areeda, John Hart Ely, Robert E. Keeton, Malcolm A. Moore, Robert J. Nordstrom, and Robert M. O'Neil.

In conducting the research for this book, I had the privilege of traveling throughout the Deep South, from Whitten Village for the mentally retarded, in rural South Carolina, to Tulane's medical school in downtown New Orleans; and from the headquarters of the Florida Federation of Women's Clubs, in suburban Lakeland, to Mississippi's venerable state law school, in the shadow of Faulkner's home at Oxford. I am deeply indebted to scores of people and institutions that I encountered in these travels—far more that I can identify here.

Southerners treasure their history, and my research benefited from the willing and able assistance provided by countless librarians and archivists working in institutions throughout the Deep South to preserve the record of the region's past. I especially want to thank the staffs of the Alabama Department of Archives and History, the New Orleans Public Library, the South Caroliniana Library, and the South Carolina State Hospital, where Woodrow Harris went out of his way to help. I also wish to note my use of collections maintained by Auburn University; the Children's Home Society of Florida; the Florida Federation of Women's Clubs; the Louisiana Supreme Court Library; the Medical Association of the State of Alabama; Georgia's Central State Hospital in Milledgeville; Mississippi State University; Spring Hill College; the South Carolina Medical Association; the state archives of Florida, Georgia, and South Carolina; Tulane University; Tuskegee Institute; and the Universities of Alabama, Florida, Georgia, Mississippi, and South Carolina. From outside the region, materials from the Library of Congress in Washington, D.C., the medical and science libraries at the University of Washington, and the Social Welfare History Archives at the University of Minnesota significantly contributed to my research. Useful information not available at any institution came from Ilouise Partlow Hill, Eleanor Hoernle, and Charles F. Zukoski, among others, to whom I am deeply grateful.

Some portions of this book first appeared in articles of mine published in academic journals, and reappear here with the permission of those journals or their editors. These articles are "Belated Progress: The Enactment of Eugenic Legislation in Georgia," *Journal of the History of Medicine and Allied Sciences* 46 (1991): 44–64; "Involuntary Sexual Sterilization of Incompetents in Alabama: Past, Present, and Future," *Alabama Law Review* 43 (1992): 399–444; and "In the Finest, Most Womanly Way: Women in the Southern Eugenics Movement," forthcoming in *American Journal of Legal History* 38 (1994). My thanks go to those journals, their editors, and their manuscript readers.

The University of Georgia has generously sustained my work on these articles and this book through a Junior Faculty Research Grant, a Senior Faculty Research Grant, a Humanities Center Fellowship, and summer research grants from the School of Law and Department of History. I would have accomplished much less without this support. Research assistance for these publications came from several University of Georgia graduate students, including Kim Dawson, John Eglin, and Wendy Wickham. A word of thanks goes to each of them, and to Julie Palmer and Kathy Burkes, who assisted in some word-processing tasks.

Three final notes of appreciation. First, at Johns Hopkins University Press, I want to thank my editor, Bob Brugger, for his early interest and ongoing help in this project, and Miriam Kleiger for copyediting the manuscript. Second, I must acknowledge the companionship provided by our dog, Rusty, who faithfully lay at my side day after day as I wrote this book, only interrupting me for walks about once every five hours. Finally, I wish to express my thanks to and my love for my wife, Lucy, who gracefully endured this entire project.

SEX, RACE, AND SCIENCE

A well drawn sterilization law, to be operative through the institutions dealing with defectives whose propagation would be a menace to society. Hereditary imbeciles and low grade morons should not be allowed to marry and reproduce their kind. These are the promoters of pauperism, crime, prostitution, and veneral disease. They are the miser-

CHOPPING COTTON

ables and the majority finally are supported in some fashion by the taxpayers or by private charity. These should be recognized as children and brought under the supervision of the state, to be trained and in such cases as would be advisable, paroled after being sterilized.

Photograph and text from the 1927–29 biennial report of the Mississippi School and Colony for the Feebleminded. The photograph shows colony patients at work in the facility's cotton fields. Mississippi School and Colony for the Feebleminded, *Fifth Biennial Report* (Jackson: Tucker, 1929), 22.

Surveying the Land

"The South's 'poor white trash,' so aptly named by the Negro, is no doubt the product of the physical and mental unfit, left in the wake of the War Between the States," a respected Atlanta pediatrician observed in the 1930s. "Let us take stock of this rubbish." He then tallied the staggering toll of human delinquency, dependency, and deformity allegedly afflicting the state and the nation during that decade of the Great Depression, and prescribed his remedy: "Sterilize all individuals who are not physically, mentally or emotionally capable of reproducing normal offspring."[1] Thirty years earlier, an Alabama physician advised colleagues at a state medical convention, "People who have [dysgenic] hereditary traits ought not to be allowed to get married, and men who persist in [degenerate behavior] ought to be confined in reformatory institutions, or have their testicles removed, so that it would be impossible for them to propagate."[2]

These two public comments by practicing physicians from the Deep South effectively bracketed the period of greatest eugenic activism in the region and raised several of the issues in question. First, concern focused on protecting and purifying the Caucasian race. Second, the eugenically unfit—particularly the "insane" and "feeble-minded"—were blamed for a multitude of social problems. Third, eugenic marriage restrictions, sexual segregation, and compulsory sterilization (though usually not castration) became the proposed solution for these problems. Fourth, physicians and others from within the region's professional elite championed the cause of eugenics. These issues play out in the pages that follow, as suggested by this book's title, *Sex, Race, and Science: Eugenics in the Deep South.*

Sex. Certainly eugenicists were preoccupied with sex, or at least with the consequences of sexual activity. They typically believed that the mentally retarded were oversexed, and so utterly irresponsible that they threatened to swamp society with their defective offspring. The natural struggle for survival had once kept their numbers in check, eugenicists reasoned, but advances in modern medical science and Progressive Era reforms now allowed the "unfit" to survive and propagate. "I tell you we are swamped today from the charity standpoint due to feebleminded men and women, particularly women," a prominent southern feminist warned during the 1920s. "We cannot go on having women each bringing into the world eight and ten feebleminded children."[3] Thus, on the one hand, controlling the sexual activity of the mentally retarded became the primary goal of many southern eugenicists. On the other hand, the fact that both the speaker and her primary target were females suggested a second meaning for the term *sex* in this account—an alternative word for *gender*. Upper-middle-class women, acting individually and through their associations, played a significant part in the politics of eugenics across the Deep South. Significantly, this activity began before the ratification of the Nineteenth Amendment. Therefore, it provided an example of women's role in government prior to female suffrage, and illustrated that political participation included more than voting. Both issues stand as significant subjects of this study.

Race. Southern eugenicists were also preoccupied with race, but at least initially they worried more about the deterioration of the Caucasian race than about any threat from the African race. "What language can express the humiliation we should feel at seeing [our] race, physically, mentally and morally, slowly going to decay?" a White Louisiana physician asked in 1917, "a race, proud of its lineage, boastful of its achievement, . . . and withal rotting at its roots!" He blamed this decay on "the steadily increasing ratio of the insane to the balance of the population," resulting from excessive reproduction by White "degenerates."[4] Only later, after the civil rights movement began dismantling the machinery by which southern Whites controlled local Blacks, did regional eugenic practices turn against African Americans. This account explores these two ways in which race influenced eugenics in the Deep South.

Science. Eugenicists everywhere based their demands squarely on the authority of modern science. Those in the Deep South followed suit, albeit with the soft edge and common touch befitting a society that valued tradition. "The subject of eugenics is now attracting widespread attention, and many societies of scientific men are making research regarding the question of heredity," a Mississippi mental health official explained in 1912. "The societies of eugenics are trying to teach us, under the Mendelian law, how we may do for the human race . . . what stock breeders are doing in evolving thoroughbred horses."[5] Such analogies carried weight in the agrarian South, and appear throughout the following narrative.

Eugenics. During the late nineteenth and early twentieth centuries, geneticists and social scientists in America and western Europe developed the technical theories of human heredity that encouraged (or even demanded) the adoption of eugenic social practices and public health policies. These scientific theories did not develop in the Deep South, however. Their primary significance for this study follows from their influence on regional practices and policies. Further, such historians as Garland Allen, Linda Gordon, Mark Haller, Daniel Kevles, Kenneth Ludmerer, Donald Perkins, and Philip Reilly have ably examined the development of these theories far beyond the scope of this book. Therefore, I focus on the impact of those broad intellectual developments on the people and events of one particular region. Even though I introduce the technical theories of eugenics at the outset, most southerners understood the concept in simpler terms. In 1913, the Legislation Committee of the Florida State Federation of Women's Clubs clearly summed up this common understanding of eugenics with the words "Every State wishes to eliminate as many delinquent, defective wards as possible. In order to decrease the number of feeble-minded, insane and blind, defectives of these classes must be prevented from reproducing their kind."[6] This book traces the influence of such thinking.

The Deep South. No certain boundaries delineated the "Deep South" and isolated it from the rest of the country. The phrase described a state of mind as much as a geographic entity. Nevertheless, in objective terms, the six southeastern states of the United States responded to eugenics in a distinctive way, and eugenicists recognized it. For example, at the time when the region held back from adopting the eugenic reforms then sweeping most of the nation, a South Carolina physician exhorted his colleagues on the matter, "Read what some of the Northern and Western states are doing."[7] Another physician, who later sought to gauge regional eugenics practices, singled out colleagues in Alabama, Florida, Georgia, Louisiana, and Mississippi to receive his questionnaire.[8] The geographic boundaries of this study follow the lines suggested by these two physicians. Significantly, African Americans then comprised a higher percentage of the population of these six states than of any other state—more than 30 percent in each case. These demographics facilitate an exploration of the influence of racism on public policy, which represents a critical issue in any study of eugenics. Further, the regional analysis fills a gap in the existing historical scholarship, which mainly looked at eugenics as a national phenomenon, or at pioneering programs in the North and the West. Large-scale sterilization efforts in the border states Virginia and North Carolina have also received considerable attention from scholars, but the Deep South has largely been ignored.

The structure of this book reflects its contents and subject matter. Chapter 1 provides a brief introduction to the Deep South at the dawn of the eugenics movement—a place and time unfamiliar to many current readers. Chapter 2 adds an overview of eugenic doctrines and practices, including a case study of their application in California, to provide a context and perspective for events in the Deep South. These two introductory chapters rely heavily on source material familiar to other scholars, yet serve to present a framework for what follows. In particular, chapter 1 draws on sources well known to southern historians but often foreign to those outside the field. Similarly, chapter 2 retells the story of eugenics primarily to provide a background for readers not acquainted with that episode in the history of science and society. The narrative begins with chapter 3, which deals with the introduction of eugenics in the Deep South. Chapter 4 continues the story through 1920, and the enactment of laws to provide for eugenic segregation. Two long chapters cover events in the 1920s and 1930s, respectively, when southern eugenicists pushed for further restrictions, leading to major battles over eugenic sterilization in several states. Chapter 7 carries the narrative through the post–World War II era, and the repudiation of eugenics. A concluding section adds some personal reflections on these events in light of the recent developments in both human genetics and contraceptive technology.

Throughout, I weave brief quotations from participants into the narrative as a means to convey the tenor of the eugenics movement. Some of these quotations may seem unduly cruel or derogatory today, even though they sounded quite acceptable in an era before the civil rights movements for African Americans, women, and the handicapped raised the public consciousness regarding the treatment of minorities. Nevertheless, my goal in using these quotations was not to embarrass or offend anyone, least of all the speakers or their descendants, but rather to learn from our shared past so as to enlighten our collective future. Eugenicists, of course, also sought this objective.

CHAPTER ONE

Southern Soil

"There is power in the blood." This affirmation, which millions of southern Protestants regularly sang throughout the first half of the twentieth century, suggested much about the response of the Deep South to eugenics. As the title and key line of a hymn from the 1890s, it struck a chord with southern congregations. The song quickly became a fixture in southern Protestant hymnals at a time when Protestantism dominated southern society.[1] As a concept, the affirmation evoked complex images both of the power of the blood relationships that tied individuals into families, and of the power of the religious blood sacrifice that freed individuals from sin. Both images appealed to southerners and influenced their response to eugenics. This chapter introduces these images and explores the extent of southern distinctiveness, as background for examining the regional response to eugenics.

This analysis of southern families and religion assumes that the South was somehow distinctive during the years 1895–1945, which included the principal time covered by this book and represented the period when eugenic doctrines commanded the greatest national influence. This assumption bears examination. The nature and extent of southern distinctiveness has been debated for decades. Reviewing this debate, the historian David L. Smiley observed, "Local and state historians, students of regionalism and sectionalism, along with authors of American history surveys, have agreed in accepting the hypothesis that there is an American South and that it has had, historically, a unifying focus at its center." Indeed, Smiley added, "The man on the street, though his views may be hazy or overemotional, is confident that there are distinctive social and political patterns, perhaps traceable to a unique agricultural base, which combine to make the regions below the Potomac a recognizable entity."[2] Disagreements center on the unifying focus or central theme that distinguishes the South from other regions.

Countless explanations for this distinctiveness appear in the works of southern novelists, historians, and other writers. During the colonial period, Virginia's scholarly planter William Byrd contrasted the easygoing settlers of Jamestown with the stern, industrious colonists in Massachusetts and attributed the difference to religion.[3] In the early national period, Thomas Jefferson drew a similar distinction between southerners and northerners, but lay the blame for southern indolence on "that warmth of their climate which unnerves and unmans both body and mind."[4] During the 1920s, the first great modern historian of the South, Ulrich B. Phillips, offered his controversial "plantation legend" to account for the southern character. The climate, Phillips reasoned, led to a plantation system of agriculture that imported large numbers of Africans to work the soil. The continued presence of these African Americans forged a common resolve among White southerners to maintain White racial supremacy. This resolve, Phillips claimed, "whether expressed with the frenzy of a demagogue or maintained with a patrician's quietude, . . . [was] the cardinal test of a Southerner and the central theme of Southern history."[5] Even as some commentators followed Phillips in stressing the role of race in shaping southern character, others cited the impact of such diverse factors as the region's relative poverty, its rural agrarianism, its White ethnic homogeneity, its severe political and economic disruptions, and its high rate of disease.[6]

Regardless of the original cause or causes, the American South remained distinct so long as southerners viewed themselves as different from other Americans. Self-image is self-realizing. In 1941, during the waning days of eugenics in America, the Carolina journalist Wilbur J. Cash could still assert in his landmark book *The Mind of the South,* "The peculiar history of the South has so greatly modified it from the general American norm that, when viewed as a whole, it decisively justifies the notion that the country is—not quite a nation within a nation, but the next thing to it."[7] Three prominent current historians of the American South, C. Vann Woodward, George Brown Tindall, and Carl N. Degler, have identified sources for the region's persistent distinctiveness that derive from the minds of southerners. In particular, Woodward attributed it to the "collective experience of the Southern people"; Tindall suggested that it arose from "various mythical images of the South"; and Degler linked it to the "enduring sense of personal and regional identity born from a history no other American shares."[8]

"The American South is therefore not a place or a thing," Smiley concluded. "It is an idea. Those of whatever persuasion or tradition who believe themselves to be Southern are indeed Southern, and the South exists wherever Southerners form the predominant portion of the population."[9] During the period when eugenic doctrines swept across America, southerners viewed their commitment to their families and their God as two of the ways in which they differed from other Americans. These perceptions, along with various other differences from and similarities to the American norm, helped shape the region's distinct response to eugenics.

The Southern Family

The family was a revered institution throughout the Deep South during the early twentieth century. Indeed, the nature of family ties in the South constituted one of the region's chief claims to distinctiveness. At the time, this was reflected in the writings of both the conservative Vanderbilt Agrarians and the liberal school of sociological regionalism led by Howard W. Odum at the University of North Carolina. Taken together, these two sources provided a revealing glimpse into the mind of the South.[10]

The Vanderbilt Agrarians produced the most significant manifesto of southern distinctiveness in 1930, when they published *I'll Take My Stand: The South and the Agrarian Tradition,* a collection of articles by twelve noted southern writers and academics. "All the articles bear in the same sense upon the book's title-subject," the authors declared in their introductory statement of principles, "all tend to support a Southern way of life against what may be called the American or prevailing way; and all as much as agree that the best terms in which to represent the distinction are contained in the phrase, Agrarian *versus* Industrial."[11] They typically credited this agrarian way of life with fostering strong family ties.[12] Expanding on this theme, one article explained that "the family is the natural biological group, the normal milieu of shared experiences, community of interests, integration of personality. The segmentation of both adult and child activities which has accompanied the corporate age leaves little to the family beyond the details of finance and the primary sexual function." It added that, as northern ways crept southward, "the moral and educational functions of the family are more and more entrusted to depersonalized external agencies which simulate the form of familial function but which are entirely devoid of its content."[13] According to the Vanderbilt Agrarians, southerners should take their stand against such trends.

To an extent, statistics from the era documented a southern distinctiveness of the type described by the Vanderbilt Agrarians. In the South, for example, families were larger and divorce was less common than in the nation as a whole. A smaller proportion of southern children than of American youth in general went to school for their education, and those who went typically stayed for a shorter time. A greater percentage of southern women and children than of their northern counterparts worked at home or on the family farm, and a smaller percentage labored outside the homestead in manufacturing and service jobs. These departures from the national norm held true for both southern Whites and southern Blacks, though the contrasts were greater for Blacks. Howard Odum compiled and analyzed such statistics in his monumental 1936 publication *Southern Regions of the United States,* and concluded that there was a "regional emphasis upon the family."[14]

Resistance to the idea of changing the traditional family structure appeared in the region's relative reluctance to join such popular national crusades as those for compulsory school attendance, child labor laws, and women's suffrage.[15] The National Child Labor Committee observed this in a 1914 report on prospects for reform in the South: "The doctrine that social justice and human rights rise above parental and property rights does not yet determine either the law or custom of these states."[16] Commenting on the same issue two decades later, the noted Louisiana State University political scientist Charles W. Pipkin could still report with regard to southern attitudes, "The public has an aversion to legislative interference with parental rights except in cases of extreme neglect."[17] From his study of the resistance by southern mill workers to the child labor restrictions proposed by progressive reformers, the historian William A. Link concluded, "At the root of the matter lay conflicting conceptions of the family" that divided the workers and the reformers.[18] Of course, these statistics and statements reflected a difference of degree, not of kind. Further, as Odum reported, the South was moving toward the national norm with respect to the family and social reform.[19] Yet a stubborn sense of distinctiveness remained.

The doctrine of eugenics, which swept through the northern and western states during the first quarter of the twentieth century, directly challenged southern concepts of the family and parental rights. First, eugenicists sought to move mentally retarded and other eugenically unfit children from their homes to state institutions where they would be segregated by sex. Later, they advocated the forced sterilization of such children so as to remove permanently the ability to create a family. Throughout, they favored eugenic restrictions on the freedom to marry. If the Agrarians truly opposed national movements toward entrusting familial functions to "depersonalized external agencies," then eugenics should have aroused their deepest enmity.[20] In apparent contrast to the eugenicists' scientific approach to dealing with mentally retarded children, Stark Young's concluding article in *I'll Take My Stand* affirmed, "The Southern family sense, often onerous to aliens and not seldom one of our own domestic burdens, is nevertheless a good trait."[21] Yet, as shown by the regional response to eugenics, there was a growing inclination to follow the North and West in laying these burdens upon the state.

The southern sense of family responsibility reached far beyond immediate relatives to a vastly extended family network. In *I'll Take My Stand,* Young wrote of "our Southern family instinct, the home, the sense of parents, the endless cousins, uncles, and aunts, the nostalgia for one's own blood."[22] Another Agrarian idealized the old South as a place where "[f]amily, bloodkinship, clanship, folkways, custom, [and] community" supplied the basic human needs.[23] This extended sense of kinship and family responsibility influenced the region's response to eugenics in subtle ways. It provided a broader network of relatives to assume and assert responsibility for individuals who might otherwise be subject to eugenic remedies in state institutions. More critically, accepting eugenic explanations for individual disabilities carried serious implications for members of the extended family who shared common bloodlines.

Further, in the North and the West eugenic concerns typically focused on ethnically distinct immigrants who could be viewed as "Others" by the predominantly White, middle-class supporters of eugenics.[24] This could not happen in the South, which attracted few foreign immigrants.[25] The Agrarians hailed the purity of White southern bloodlines, with Young writing, "Our traditions of family involve the fact that so many of our families came from the British Isles, with Scotch clannishness plentiful enough, and remained unmixed with other bloods, as did the French and Spanish of Louisiana, for a long time."[26] Similarly, Odum's review of regional characteristics noted "the homogeneity of the white people with overwhelming ratios of native born and of prevailing early American stocks."[27] Regional pride in these pure Anglo-Saxon or French bloodlines, which reached mythic proportions in some quarters, predisposed southern Whites not to fear a eugenic taint among their own stock, whereas strict racial segregation and the assumption of White supremacy diminished their concern regarding African Americans.

Southern legislators and public officials, who would have had to enact or enforce eugenic programs, shared this sense of family relationship and responsibility. This was reflected in campaign rhetoric and political biographies from the era, which typically emphasized a politician's family. For example, Alabama regularly published a volume entitled *Official and Statistical Register* that, among other entries, contained biographical sketches of all state legislators and key state officials. Each sketch consisted of three paragraphs. The first paragraph, which was usually the longest, dealt exclusively and extensively with the individual's ancestors. The second presented the official's educational qualifications; vocational, political, and military background; religious activities; and club memberships. The final paragraph discussed the individual's spouse and offspring. The identity and personal accomplishments of all individuals appeared in the context of their lineage. Thus, the 1935 *Register* sketch for Governor Bibb Graves, a leading opponent of eugenic legislation, began by discussing his parents, one of whom descended from "Benjamin Bibb, a native of Wales who came to America during the Colonial period." The sketch then identified other notable ancestors, including two Revolutionary War soldiers and two former Alabama governors. By the time Graves's own achievements were listed, they seemed to flow naturally from his ancestry.[28] Similar details appeared about all 141 state legislators and dozens of other state officials. Some equivalent publications from other southern states paid even more attention to pedigree.[29]

Even though this emphasis on genealogy could have prejudiced southerners against recognizing eugenic defects in the long and interconnected bloodlines of their region, it should have predisposed them to accept eugenic concepts. As the hymn at the start of this chapter affirmed: "There is power in the blood." If noble bloodlines could all but predestine Bibb Graves for the governorship of Alabama, then tainted bloodlines should predetermine degeneracy. Southern eugenicists appealed to this sense of heredity, but always confronted southerners' regional pride in their own heritage. "The notion in general of kin and family," according to Stark Young, was "the source of so much proud and tender emotion" that it shaped the southern character. Reflecting on ancestors, he wrote of southerners' love of their parents, and of "those who brought them in to the world and loved them, and those yet further back, this line of hopes and struggles and love." Turning to descendants, Young added, "A man's love of these dead is only another love that is also in him: when his blood runs in other veins, not yet born." Writing of this love of one's own children, which he extended to encompass grandchildren and succeeding generations, he added, "The nature and course of such love as parents give, no matter what imperfections may appear, is like no other."[30] Eugenic remedies to social problems violated these intergenerational family ties and denied a parental love that existed, according to Young, "no matter what imperfections appear."

Of course, the vision of the distinctively southern family espoused by the Agrarians represented an ideal rather than a reality. Even they admitted "the melancholy fact that the South itself has wavered a little and shows signs of wanting to join up behind the common or American industrial ideal."[31] Old southern values need not control new southern practices, as Tindall, Woodward, and other historians have found.[32] "The Agrarians of Nashville seemed a gesture toward the past," the historian Michael O'Brien observed, "but Odum was the future."[33] And Odum's research revealed a progressive movement in southern family patterns toward the national norm.[34] Eugenics appeared in the South as part of that progressive movement, much as it did elsewhere.[35]

Southern Religion

During the early twentieth century, regional religious patterns represented an increasingly distinctive characteristic of the South. While America was rapidly becoming a more secularized country, Odum reported in 1936, "the great changes in the religious life of the nation are less marked in the Southeast than anywhere else in the nation." In particular, he found "that the region reflects a greater influence of the church than other regions; a greater place for religion in the ideology of the people; a greater influence of ministers; a greater protestantism, especially of Baptists and Methodists; a greater influence in education and politics and race."[36] Odum's findings, which he based on both federal census data and his personal sense of the region, presented a telling picture.

The 1926 federal census of religious bodies reflected the peculiar religiosity of the South. Nearly two-thirds of the region's adults claimed membership in some church, as compared to barely one-half of the adults in America as a whole. Further, church membership was more homogeneous in the South than in other regions. In five of the six states constituting the Deep South, approximately two-thirds of all White church members belonged to churches affiliated with the evangelical Southern Baptist Convention, and most of the remainder belonged to the similarly evangelical Southern Methodist Church. For African Americans in those states, church membership was even more concentrated in Black Baptist and Methodist denominations. Only Louisiana stood apart, with fully one-half of its church members following Roman Catholicism; but even in that state, nearly all of the rest were Baptists or Methodists. Comparative data from earlier periods offered by the 1926 census suggested that, if anything, southern church membership was both increasing and becoming more homogeneous. Not only had the total number of church members in the South risen by nearly a quarter during the preceding two decades, but the Southern Baptist Convention had become the fastest-growing major denomination in the country.[37] On the basis of these and other statistics, Tindall concluded that "[t]he South was indeed a bastion of evangelical Protestantism."[38]

Statistics alone, however, cannot convey the sense of religiosity that pervaded the region during the early twentieth century. A prominent English observer noted in 1910, "The South is by a long way the most simply and sincerely religious country that I was ever in."[39] Two decades later, the Vanderbilt Agrarians maintained a similar view of southern religiosity, which they hailed as a part of rural traditionalism.[40] In a 1934 response by progressive southern academics to the Vanderbilt Agrarians, the Wake Forest College theologian Edwin McNeill Poteat agreed that "the religious South exhibits a more homogeneous quality than any other section. And for that reason is more alive even though that vitality can under violent stimulation run all the way from personal hysterics to social madness."[41] The historian Charles W. Ramsdell put the issue more bluntly in his part of the response by identifying religious fundamentalism as a peculiarly southern trait.[42]

Perhaps owing to his own fundamentalist upbringing, Odum left a more detailed picture of southern religious life than did any other secular commentator of the era.[43] Southerners, he maintained, "were inclined to be intemperate in their religion." By this Odum meant that they professed a distinctly " 'Southern' Christianity [that] was the index of all Christianity," and that "upon all questions, political, financial, educational, scientific, and technical, the judgment of religion and the scripture was likely to be invoked."[44] Odum clearly had the 1925 Scopes trial and the ongoing opposition to Darwinian evolution in mind when writing these comments, but such attitudes also inevitably influenced the regional response to eugenics. Further, Odum observed that whereas in other regions of the country the social and economic classes tended to stratify into different denominations, in the South, Whites from all classes went to the same churches and belonged to the same evangelical denominations.[45] This shared commitment to a conservative faith unified the response of southern Whites to new ideas. "Everywhere among the leading people on the one hand, and the dominant middle class on the other, the religious test was apt to be an important one," Odum concluded.[46]

This did not mean that religion never served as an agent of change or reform in the South. Indeed, southern Protestant churches occasionally became the focal point of powerful social movements, such as the crusades for prohibition and against evolutionary teaching that mobilized White congregations early in the century, and the civil rights movement that emerged from the Black church fifty years later.[47] Beyond this, although Odum was clearly correct in his overall judgment that "the church has done little with reference to the tenant and the laborer in the way of programs," it did as much as any other major institution in the South at the time.[48] A handful of progressive southern church leaders championed a variety of social causes ranging from child-labor laws to prison improvement, and a spirit of religiosity pervaded the reform-minded Southern Sociological Congress and the interracial movement.[49] Yet, to a greater extent than in the North, social reform was subject to the judgment of religion, and that judgment involved biblically orthodox standards. Elsewhere, eugenics enthusiasts tended to be irreligious or to be liberal Protestants who did not impose such narrow judgments.[50] These groups also existed in the South, and they supplied many of the region's leading eugenicists. However, to a greater extent in the South than in the North or the West, eugenics encountered a culture informed by the tenets of evangelical Christianity.

Odum maintained that the tenets of southern Protestantism were most clearly expressed in the region's religious hymns. "It was not a matter of belief in concrete creeds; it was rather a matter of feeling about it," he wrote. Much of the feeling was expressed through hymns. "They were sung at church, at home, at music classes. These songs, to [southern] children, came to be part of their parents' personalities and part of the environmental pattern under which they grew up," he noted. "This picture of the religious South could not be presented without giving a large place to this powerful psychological force of religious song."[51]

According to Odum, one of the strongest themes running through these hymns was the power of Christ's blood sacrifice to redeem individual believers.[52] "Alas, and did my Savior bleed? And did my Sovereign die? / Would He devote that sacred head for such a worm as I," began an old favorite.[53] A new hymn from that era added, "Are you washed in the blood, / In the soul-cleansing blood of the Lamb?"[54]

These popular hymns, which resonated throughout the South, emphasized the dominant message of evangelical Protestantism: salvation and sanctification solely by God's grace through Christ's death. This was graphically presented in the refrain "Oh! precious is the flow that makes me white as snow; / No other fount I know, Nothing but the blood of Jesus."[55] Such salvation was available to everyone—men and women, White and Black, lowly degenerates and lofty aristocrats—for, as one hymn declared, "All Thy people are forgiven, Thro' the virtue of Thy blood."[56] The process not only forgave past sin but also enabled Christians to live holy and meaningful lives. This message ran through a popular hymn, quoted at the beginning of this chapter, that Odum cited as representative of regional beliefs.[57] Its first verse opened with the offer of salvation: "Would you be free from the burden of sin? There's pow'r in the blood." Later verses affirmed that this "wonder-working power" can make you "free from your passions and pride" and "whiter, much whiter than snow."[58] The concept of salvation and sanctification for all, solely by divine grace, challenged eugenic doctrines of fixed, inherited degeneracy and superiority.

Regional notions of kinship mixed with these religious concepts to create a sense of an extended church family that reached throughout homogeneous southern communities, and even beyond. Members of the same church often called each other "brother" or "sister." These religious ties carried responsibilities. "Awake, O Christians, from thy sleep, And heed thy brother's call! / He cries to thee across the deep, Where darkest shadows fall," began one Baptist missionary song.[59] Another hymn, which appeared in Southern Baptist hymnals when most congregations in that denomination practiced strict racial segregation, proclaimed, "Join hands, then, brothers of the faith, Whate'er your race may be: / Who serves my Father as a son is surely kin to me."[60] Even though the concept of religious brotherhood did not overcome doctrines of White supremacy, it offered a sense of extended kinship that stood at odds with eugenic proposals to segregate or sterilize defective individuals: in the words of a beloved hymn, "His blood can make the foulest clean."[61]

The New South

Family and religion constituted two distinctive features of traditional southern society. Other commonly recognized regional characteristics, such as poverty, agrarianism, disease, White racial supremacy and ethnic homogeneity, rigid social and economic class divisions, sectional pride, skepticism toward science, and the restricted role of women outside the home, also affected the area's response to eugenics. However, the extent of these differences should be kept in perspective. As Wilbur Cash concluded, the South was something less than a nation apart.[62] Further, both Odum and the Vanderbilt Agrarians agreed that, by the 1930s, the region was becoming more like the rest of America.[63] In the leading series on southern history, Woodward named his comprehensive study of the period 1877–1913 *Origins of the New South,* while Tindall used the title *The Emergence of the New South* for his history of the years 1913–45. Although neither author particularly liked the vague and shopworn term, both accepted the concept of a "New South" that was increasingly responsive to progressive economic, political, and social changes modeled on national standards.[64] What began as " 'wavering' in the Southern ranks" soon became "a pell-mell rout," according to Woodward, as "regiments and armies deserted 'to join up behind the common or American industrial ideal.' "[65] For some proponents of a New South and progressivism, eugenics offered a remedy for intractable regional social problems.

If the meaning of the term *New South* is somewhat vague, then the definition of *progressivism* is downright slippery. The latter term generally referred to the various reform efforts launched around the turn of the century to combat the manifold ills associated with increasing industrialization and urbanization. "Never before had the people of the United States engaged in so many diverse movements for the improvement of the political system, economy, and communities," the historians Arthur S. Link and Richard L. McCormick observed. "Yet in the goals they sought and the remedies they tried, the reformers were a varied and contrary lot."[66] Some progressives fought to protect the oppressed and disadvantaged through such means as child labor laws; the improvement of prisons, asylums, and schools; or the prohibition of alcohol. Others focused on "good government" issues such as direct primary elections, the establishment of expert public agencies, or woman's suffrage. Further groups of reformers sought to rationalize and regulate economic competition through antitrust, labor, and railroad-rate restrictions. Still others aimed at improving the quality of urban life by, for example, sanitation measures, hospital construction, and consumer protection laws.[67] No common goals, means, or ideology bound these reformers together.

Despite these basic differences, a characteristic form marked progressive reforms. Even though progressivism followed on the heels of populism, and the two movements overlapped in certain respects, progressivism never shared the populist impulse of working-class or agrarian revolt. Rather, progressive reformers for the most part lived in urban areas and, as Link and McCormick observed, hailed from a "'new middle class' of physicians, businessmen, scientists, engineers, and social workers." Progressive reforms characteristically reflected a "belief in interventionism" and "relied upon organization, the application of scientific (or social-scientific) expertise, and the value of efficiency and rationality" to solve the pressing social, political, and economic problems of the day. Thus, individual progressive reform movements typically began with the formation of a rational or scientific solution to a pressing problem, proceeded to the organization of a public-education campaign to promote voluntary acceptance of the solution, and concluded with the imposition of laws to compel conformity with it. Elaborating on this pattern, Link and McCormick noted that a "familiar scenario during the period was one in which progressives called upon public authorities to assume responsibilities for interventions which voluntary organizations had begun."[68] Eugenicists splendidly fit the progressive mold.[69]

The picture of urban, industrial, progressive reform contrasted sharply with the image of rural, agrarian, southern traditionalism. Perhaps that was why the Agrarians resisted progressivism and Odum championed it. Yet, as consistently found by historians ranging from Arthur Link in the 1940s to William Link in the 1990s, progressivism existed in the South despite the distinctive features of southern society, and it took much the same form there as it did elsewhere.[70] This ongoing tradition of New South progressivism gave eugenics an entrée into what would otherwise have been hostile territory.[71]

Progressivism took root in the South before the turn of the century as part of the New South campaign, and big-city newspapers served as the mouthpiece for both movements.[72] A logical connection existed here. The New South movement promoted industrialization and urbanization, which in turn intensified the need for progressive reforms. Urban newspapers expanded in circulation and influence as their cities gained population, and they naturally championed the interests of their metropolitan readers. Census data identified the extent of these demographic trends. The South remained the most rural region of the country throughout the Progressive Era, with more than three-fourths of its people living outside urban areas, but the southern cities that were industrializing grew dramatically. Atlanta's population grew from less than 90,000 in 1900 to more than 200,000 in 1920, for example, while Birmingham's numbers jumped from less than 40,000 to nearly 180,000.[73] "Within the little islands of industrialism scattered throughout the region," Woodward observed, "was rising a new middle-class society."[74]

In the New South, as elsewhere in the country, this urban middle class served as an impetus for reform. "The Southern counterpart of a Northern progressivism developed nearly all traits familiar to the genus," Woodward found in his study of turn-of-the-century developments. "Southern progressivism was essentially urban and middle class in nature, and the typical leader was a city professional man or businessman, rather than a farmer."[75] Extending this analysis into the early twentieth century, the historian Dewey Grantham found that "[a] series of progressive movements unfolded in the Southern states as hundreds of politicians, newspaper editors, educators, and members of the emerging professions cast themselves in the role of reformers."[76] Even though southern Protestants generally preferred personal pietism to a social gospel, liberal ministers from urban, middle-class churches took the lead in many reform efforts throughout the South, as did some members of the other two traditional professions, law and medicine.[77]

Southern progressives, like those from other regions, split into countless separate movements with differing specific goals and remedies. Yet, perhaps even more than elsewhere, progressives in the South were moderate reformers who generally sought increased social order and control as a means of taming the restless cities, rationalizing business practices, and promoting the general welfare. "Although Southern progressives were a rather disparate collection of social reformers," Grantham noted, "[t]hey shared a yearning for a more orderly and cohesive community."[78] This led them to renounce southerners' traditional penchant for minimal government. Whether it involved building roads, schools, and hospitals, enforcing child-labor and temperance laws, or providing public health and welfare services, southern state and municipal governments sudden-ly became a focal point for positive social action.[79] "Out of two decades of progressive ferment," Tindall concluded, "the great fundamental residue of the progressive era in Southern government was a firm estab-lishment and general acceptance of the public service concept of the state."[80] Eugenicists throughout the Deep South welcomed and encour-aged this development, firm in their belief that the state could perform no greater public service than to compel the sexual segregation or steriliza-tion of the mentally retarded and the mentally ill.

Despite their obvious impact on certain issues, however, progressives probably had less influence in the South than they did elsewhere. Conser-vative and reactionary populists successfully vied with them for control of southern statehouses even during the periods of their greatest strength. As late as 1934, a leading southern progressive acknowledged the re-gion's "relative backwardness in social progress as evidenced by legisla-tive enactments," which he described as being particularly deficient in such key areas of progressive concern as the protection of children, workers, women, mothers, and the elderly.[81]

At least in part, the relative weakness of progressivism in the South was attributable to the comparatively small size of the region's urban middle class and the feebleness of its professional organizations and edu-cational institutions. Elsewhere in the country, for example, progressives relied heavily on the scientific and social-scientific expertise provided by leading universities. This approach proved less effective in the Deep South, which could not boast any institutions in the elite American Asso-ciation of Universities, and where Odum could lament "the small num-ber of people in each state, active in the control of state policies, who know or care what a first-class university is or should be."[82] Further, as Odum also observed in 1936, "[u]ntil very recently there was nowhere in the whole region a college or university science building or laboratory equal to many of the high school laboratories in the larger and better school systems of the country."[83] This hobbled southern eugenicists, who could not call upon as much local scientific and social-scientific expertise as could their counterparts in the North and the West.[84] Indeed, southern eugenicists were cast in the role of missionaries preaching a foreign gospel in hostile territory, because even eugenicists who hailed from the South typically stood apart both as members of the region's small profes-sional class or its beleaguered progressive minority and as zealots of a new, scientific doctrine that had originally developed elsewhere and that still mostly flourished outside the region. The response of the Deep South to eugenics, therefore, must be approached in the context of the wider eugenics movement and not as an indigenous development.

CHAPTER TWO

Eugenic Seeds

"We greatly want a brief word to express the science of improving stock . . . especially in the case of man," the English scholar Francis Galton wrote in 1883. "The word eugenics sufficiently expresses the idea."[1] By giving a popular name to theories that he had already begun developing from the evolutionary concepts of his cousin Charles Darwin, Galton founded a movement that swept throughout Europe and North America during the ensuing half century. Even though Galton was a singular scholar in many respects, his eugenic theories both developed from the scientific ideas of his day and fit neatly into the larger social context.

Galton pursued a remarkable variety of interests before he focused his attention on the study of human heredity beginning in the mid-1860s. His academic study of mathematics at Cambridge University and his vocational training in medicine at King's College provided a background for his later statistical examination of human characteristics. The wealth that he inherited from his father at the age of twenty-two allowed him first to broaden his familiarity with various racial types through extensive world travels that included explorations of parts of Africa unknown to Europeans, and then to settle into the life of a Victorian gentleman scientist in London. Galton brought back from his travels a firm conviction that there was a natural hierarchy of the human races that placed Anglo-Saxons above all others.[2] His cousin's masterpiece *On the Origin of Species,* which appeared in 1859, stimulated Galton to investigate how the human species had developed through variation, selection, and inheritance, which were the driving forces of Darwinian evolution.[3] He welcomed an evolutionary explanation for human development because, as he wrote to Darwin, it "drove away the constraint of my old superstition" and allowed the acceptance of a purely secular faith in progress.[4] Traditional spiritual beliefs in a fallen creation and human redemption through divine grace gave way to a materialistic view of humanity rising through evolutionary development. With the advent of eugenics, Galton hoped, "what Nature does blindly, slowly, and ruthlessly, man may do providently, quickly, and kindly."[5]

Galton devised the word *eugenics* from the Greek for "well born," thus showing a fascination with the sources of natural ability rather than a preoccupation with the causes of human degeneration. His earliest publications on the topic, an 1865 article titled "Hereditary Talent and Character" and an 1869 book titled *Hereditary Genius,* systematically examined the family backgrounds of eminent men and women, leading to his conclusion that talent and genius tended to run in families. Accordingly, he proposed that the government encourage men and women of hereditary fitness to marry each other and to bear many children— proposals that became known as "positive eugenics."[6] Although he later suggested that the unfit might be segregated into monasteries and convents where they could not reproduce their kind, such efforts at "negative eugenics" never became as much the focus of attention for Galton as they did for many later eugenicists.[7]

Pioneering the genealogy of degeneracy was left to a New York social reformer, Richard L. Dugdale. He became interested in the issue when, during an 1874 inspection of conditions at a jail in rural New York State for a prison reform organization, he found that six of the prisoners were related. Struck by this finding, Dugdale launched an investigation into the lineage of their family, which he called the Jukes, in an effort to uncover the causes of crime. Using prison records, relief rolls, and court files, he traced the family tree "with more or less exactness through five generations," back to six sisters, two of whom had married the sons of a Dutch colonist named Max. Dugdale found that, over the years, more than half the 709 people connected to this family by blood or marriage were criminals or prostitutes, or were on relief, and that this had cost the public more than $1.3 million.[8] The publication of Dugdale's findings in 1877 created a sensation and eventually led to a series of other eugenic family studies that traced the degeneration of socially misfit rural White families in the Northeast and the Midwest.[9]

Although the early work of Galton and Dugdale laid a foundation on which later eugenicists built, the time was not yet quite ripe for the eugenics movement to flourish. In retrospect, reasons for this can be gleaned from the scientific presuppositions that informed this pioneering work. Galton followed Darwin in accepting a "blending" view of heredity, which maintained that each inherited characteristic of an offspring would be a blend of the traits of its parents and their ancestors. Indeed, Galton's own research reinforced this viewpoint, which inevitably suggested that successive generations would regress toward the norm of the initial breeding population.[10] According to such a view, the challenge was not how to pull inferior families up to the norm, but rather, how to keep superior families from falling back to it. According to Galton, only the constant inbreeding of natural talent through positive eugenics offered hope for a better future. Discouraging reproduction by the unfit, which later became the central thrust of the eugenics movement, initially did not appear to be as critical as encouraging the fit to intermarry and breed.

The blending view of inheritance, which was widely accepted in the late nineteenth century, posed a serious problem for Darwinian evolution. It suggested that random inborn variation, no matter how beneficial, would tend to regress in later generations toward the norm of the species, and therefore could not serve as the source for the evolution of new species. To deal with the problem, Darwin and most late-nineteenth-century evolutionary scientists (though not Galton) increasingly accepted the inheritance of acquired characteristics. This view, which was most forcefully advanced by American proponents of neo-Lamarckian evolution, maintained that an individual plant's or animal's adaptation to environmental changes could be passed along to its descendants. This could account for the evolution of new species if enough individuals were adapting in similar ways to the changed environment. At the same time, however, it undercut eugenics by suggesting that the environment played a significant role in heredity.[11]

Dugdale subscribed to this view. "Environment tends to produce habits which may become hereditary, especially so in pauperism and licentiousness," he wrote in *The Jukes*.[12] Further, he added, "The tendency of heredity is to produce an environment which perpetuates that heredity: thus, the licentious parent makes an example which greatly aids in fixing habits of debauchery in the child. The correction is change of the environment."[13] In particular, the way to break a chain of hereditary degeneracy in humans, Dugdale suggested, was to remove the children of social misfits from their families and give them vocational training in a healthy environment. Eugenic restrictions on reproduction would be unnecessary from this perspective because, as Dugdale maintained, "where the environment changes in youth, the characteristics of heredity may be measurably altered."[14]

By the turn of the century, however, the scientific theories that limited the eugenic implications of Galton's and Dugdale's work began to crumble. First, the German cytologist August Weismann challenged the neo-Lamarckian view of the inheritability of acquired characteristics with his theory of a hereditary germ plasm that was fixed at birth and not changeable by environmental influences. Second, the rediscovery of Mendelian genetics in 1900 suggested that hereditary information was transmitted in such a way that, for any given unit characteristic and according to certain regular patterns, the traits of either parent could dominate in an offspring without any blending. Thus, if, as Galton and Dugdale suggested, there were superior and inferior hereditary human characteristics, and if, as Weismann and Mendel added, their impact on succeeding generations could not be altered by environmental influences or blending, then negative eugenics appeared to offer the proper means to deal with serious inherited defects.[15]

The eugenics movement thus accompanied the triumph of nature over nurture as the accepted means for explaining human character traits. The new movement promptly pressed the early work of Galton and Dugdale into its service. For example, the Eugenics Education Society, which promoted negative eugenics in Great Britain, recruited an elderly Galton to serve as its honorary president.[16] Similarly, the leading American eugenics organization, the Eugenics Record Office, distributed and revised Dugdale's work.

This revised research on the Jukes revealed much about the transformation that had occurred in social thought. Whereas Dugdale's original book had categorized individual family members by their actions or lifestyle, such as licentiousness, criminality, or poverty, a 1915 revision focused on their mental ability. The new work, which located an additional 2,000 Jukes, including 1,258 living family members throughout the Northeast, concluded that "over half of the Jukes were or are feebleminded."[17] This finding was crucial for eugenicists because they viewed "feeblemindedness," which included various levels of mental retardation, as an inherited unit characteristic. As the eugenicist Henry Herbert Goddard explained before the revisions appeared: "If the Jukes family were of normal intelligence, a change of environment would have worked wonders and would have saved society from the horrible blot. But if they were feeble-minded, then no amount of good environment could have made them anything else than feeble-minded."[18] Accordingly, the revised study recommended permanent sexual segregation and sterilization for all the Jukes, whereas Dugdale had prescribed vocational training in an improved environment for the younger Jukes.[19] In doing so, the 1915 study reflected the means and objectives of the fully matured American eugenics movement.

Eugenic Methods

Even though eugenics was born in Britain, the principal legal methods of negative eugenics developed primarily in the United States.[20] Eugenicists, who were instinctively elitist, never placed as much hope in the use of ed-

ucation to discourage dysgenic unions as they did in its use to encourage
eugenic ones. Instead, for negative eugenics, they turned to four different
methods of legal restriction: marriage laws, sexual segregation, involuntary sterilization, and limits on immigration. The first three of these
methods required the enactment and enforcement of legislative programs
by the various state governments, which became the primary legal objective of the American eugenics movement during the period 1895–1945.
Typically, these three methods built upon each other as a series of overlapping and increasingly intrusive steps toward the achievement of national eugenic improvement.[21]

To the extent that laws restricting dysgenic marriages represented a
first step in eugenics reform, they were a step that many eugenicists
skipped over. States had regulated marriage long before the eugenics
movement came into existence. Well-entrenched laws in many states for-
bade marriage by persons who were underage, closely related by blood,
or of different races. Most states also maintained that a marriage involving a mentally ill or mentally retarded partner was either automatically
void or voidable by either spouse on the traditional contract-law grounds
that the mentally disabled partner lacked the legal capacity to enter into
a binding contract. By the early twentieth century, some sexual hygiene
or public health reformers were calling for laws to limit or prohibit marriage by persons infected with venereal disease. Although eugenicists
generally agreed that all of these laws helped their cause, the laws were
not strictly eugenic in their intent or impact. "When the law prevents
marriage on account of insanity, feeble-mindedness, or other hereditary
defects, it obviously has a eugenic value," two prominent American eugenicists, Paul Popenoe and Roswell Hill Johnson, explained, "but in so
far as it concerns itself with venereal diseases, which are not hereditary, it
is only of indirect interest to eugenics."[22]

Building on this long tradition of state oversight of marriage, some eugenicists sought strictly eugenic restrictions on who could marry. In 1896
Connecticut became the first state to comply, when it decreed that "no
man and woman either of whom is epileptic, imbecile, or feeble-minded"
could "inter-marry, or live together as husband and wife, when the
woman is under forty-five years of age."[23] Most northern and western
states quickly followed suit, so that by 1914 more than half of the states
had imposed new restrictions on the marriage of persons afflicted with
mental defects. Only South Dakota and Nebraska went as far as Popenoe wanted, however, by establishing central registries for all their mentally defective residents and precluding any listed individual from obtain-
ing a marriage license unless one of the wedding partners was sterile.[24]
As a region, only the Deep South, which had typically mandated fewer

restrictions on marriage than had other regions, imposed no such limits other than conventional ones based on the ability to enter into a contract.[25] Of course, every state in the Deep South maintained strict antimiscegenation statutes throughout the period, but these laws predated eugenics and were of only incidental interest to eugenicists because social barriers effectively limited interracial wedlock in the region.[26]

Despite the inevitable popular interest in eugenic marriage restrictions, many leading eugenicists dismissed them as hopelessly ineffective. For example, Goddard observed that the feebleminded so lacked any sense of morality that marriage was not a prerequisite for procreation.[27] A Saint Louis psychologist did not include marriage restrictions in the comprehensive package of eugenic reforms that he drafted for the Missouri legislature because, as he explained to a local women's group demanding such restrictions, "the enactment of such a bill would not prevent reproduction on the part of the unmarried feeble-minded girls and many similar statutes in other states were almost dead letters because they were not generally enforced."[28] After warning "that the denial of a marriage license will by no means prevent reproduction among the antisocial classes of the community," Popenoe and Johnson concluded, "it is a mistake for eugenists to let legislation of this sort be anything but a minor achievement, to be followed up by more efficient legislation."[29] The universally acknowledged spokesperson for the American eugenics movement, the Carnegie Institution of Washington biologist Charles B. Davenport, who also headed the Eugenics Record Office, left no doubt about what that more efficient legislation would entail. "No cheap device of a *law* against marriage will take the place of compulsory segregation of gross defectives," he asserted in 1913.[30]

When eugenicists spoke of segregation, they had something quite specific in mind. "Segregation," Popenoe and Johnson explained, "as used in eugenics means the policy of isolating feebleminded and other antisocial individuals from the normal population into institutions, colonies, etc., where the two sexes are kept apart."[31] Davenport put it more bluntly when he advised that "the proper action in the case of imbeciles or the gross epileptics who wish to marry is not to decline to give them a marriage license, but to place them in an institution under State care during at least the entire reproductive period."[32] This advice, of course, was not limited to those who wanted to marry, but included any such individuals who might reproduce their kind, with or without the benefit of a formal marriage.

The rudimentary infrastructure for implementing such a policy existed in many parts of the country long before eugenicists came on the scene. The movement to build state mental health hospitals, then typically called "insane asylums," began before the Civil War as a humanitarian reform to improve the care and treatment of those suffering from severe mental disease. "By the 1870's," the medical historian Gerald N. Grob noted, "mental hospitals had assumed the form that they would retain in succeeding decades," which included the entire eugenics era.[33] This form typically involved a massive, remote building housing hundreds or thousands of male and female patients in an authoritarian, custodial environment. "In general, there were significant regional differences among hospitals," Grob added. "The South provided a lower standard of care as compared with other sections." Indeed, throughout most of the Deep South, each state had only one public mental health hospital, which typically dated from before the Civil War, enforced racial segregation, and expended significantly less money per patient than did its northern counterparts.[34]

The mid-nineteenth-century movement to build state institutions for the mentally ill was followed by one to build custodial colonies or training schools for persons afflicted with inborn mental retardation. These facilities, designed to house the "village idiot" rather than the raving "lunatic," sprung up first in the Northeast shortly before the Civil War and gradually spread westward. This process was well under way before eugenics became a factor. It did not reach the Deep South prior to 1900, however, probably both because of the agrarian nature of southern life, which made the need for such facilities less apparent, and because of the lack of state financial resources to construct and maintain them. "Nearly all the early schools," the mental hygiene reformer Albert Deutsch noted in 1937, "were founded on the belief that most feebleminded children could be trained and improved to a degree that would warrant sending them back to the community as self-supporting citizens."[35] In his 1877 study of the Jukes family, Dugdale saw such institutions as offering a means of permanently breaking the cycle of hereditary degeneracy though environmental reform. By the early 1900s, eugenicists saw them as offering a different type of permanent solution for the same problem.[36]

State hospitals for the mentally ill and schools or colonies for the mentally retarded offered ready-made institutions for sexual segregation once fixed hereditarian ideas of mental disease and retardation took hold. "At first," Deutsch noted, "the ideal underlying institutional custody of the feebleminded was to protect the inmates from the dangers of society. The turn of the century witnessed a complete revolution in the custodial ideal; the main object now was to protect society from the menace of mental defectives."[37] The new objective generated increased public support, leading to the construction or enlargement of institutions for the mentally retarded throughout the North and the West, and eventually to the opening of the first such institutions in the Deep South. By 1906, Alexander Johnson, an officer of the National Conference of Charities and Corrections, could report regarding his influential association of social workers, "I believe that every member will agree that the segregation and even permanent detention of at least a great majority, if not all of the feebleminded, is the proper procedure."[38]

Alexander Johnson's brother-in-law, H. H. Goddard, who as research director for the prestigious Vineland Training School for Feeble-Minded Children in New Jersey became the leading architect of eugenic remedies, described the ideal plan for segregation. "Determine the fact of their defectiveness as early as possible, and place them in colonies under the care and management of intelligent people who understand the problem"; Goddard wrote in 1913, "train them, make them happy; make them as useful as possible, but above all, bring them up with good habits and keep them from ever marrying or becoming parents."[39] As he saw it, his plan encountered three difficulties, all of which were surmountable. First, the mentally retarded must be identified, which he proposed doing through the public schools.[40] To facilitate this process, Goddard introduced the Binet-Simon tests for what soon became known as a person's "intelligence quotient," or "IQ," into the United States from France in 1908. Using these tests, Goddard claimed that he could scientifically quantify the mental capacity of any individual. Further, he attempted to gradate the mentally retarded into three levels of increasing mental deficiency: high-grade "morons," middle-grade "imbeciles," and low-grade "idiots."[41]

Once identified, mentally retarded children needed to be institutionalized. This posed a problem because, according to Goddard, the majority "are not of so low intelligence that every one, the parents included, is convinced of their defect and is willing to have them placed in separate colonies." In fact, Goddard found that most parents refused to relinquish their children, owing to "their parental love" and the fact that many of the higher-grade defectives "are trainable to do errands and simple work which brings in a few pennies to the family treasury." As a result, he concluded in a classic testimony to the conflict between governmental and parental control over the family, "[u]ntil we come to the point where society is driven to the extreme of making laws requiring the forcible taking away of these children from their homes and placing them in the colonies, the matter will be an insurmountable difficulty."[42]

Lastly, the states needed to build enough institutions to house all the mentally retarded. Even as early as 1913, Goddard recognized that this represented an enormous and costly undertaking. He calculated that simply housing the estimated fifteen thousand "feebleminded" schoolchild-

ren of New York City would require thirty large institutions, which was
twenty-six more than then existed in the entire state. "As is often true,
however, the difficulty is not really as great as it appears," Goddard opti-
mistically proposed. "It is only necessary to show . . . that the increased
cost will be largely offset by the saving" in reduced welfare and prison
expenses.[43] Further, Goddard believed that these costs would quickly diminish as the supply of new retarded children was cut off by the prevention of procreation by known "defectives."[44] Finally, he hoped that these
institutions could "become partly self-supporting or even completely
self-supporting" through the labor of their residents.[45] Vineland's superintendent, E. R. Johnstone, elaborated on how this could happen. "The
colony should be located on rough uncleared land," he advised. "Here
the unskilled fellows find happy and useful occupation, waste humanity
taking waste land and thus not only contributing toward their own support, but also making over land that would otherwise be useless." Once
the land became productive, it could be sold for a profit, and the colony
moved to a new tract. In the meantime, the colony could largely live off
its own farming and handicrafts.[46]

Of course, it never worked out as Goddard and Johnstone hoped.
With every new count, the estimated number of mentally retarded children in every state increased far beyond the capacity of the available facilities, and none of these institutions ever became self-supporting.[47] By
1918, Popenoe and Johnson acknowledged that the objection "against
segregation is that of expense."[48] A decade later, when the American Eugenics Society tried to justify such expenditures by calculating that
$25,000 spent on segregating the original Jukes for life would have saved
the state more than $2 million in later costs, it immediately added that
sterilizing the initial Jukes would have cost less than $150.[49] Even though
eugenicists continued to support segregation, its inherent limitations inevitably drove many of them to favor sterilization as well.[50]

Early eugenicists appreciated the efficiency of surgically preventing reproduction by persons suffering from hereditary defects, but they lacked
an acceptable means to carry out this remedy. Both euthanasia and castration were suggested, but neither gained much popular support.[51] At
most, the emergence of hereditarian explanations for criminal behavior
revived interest in castrating rapists and other violent criminals, though
the primary arguments for such a penalty still focused on its direct deterrent effects rather than its indirect eugenic benefits. These deterrent effects included both the inhibition of initial criminal activity as a result of
potential criminals' fear of losing further sexual capacity and pleasure,
and the prevention of subsequent criminal acts by removing past offenders' sexual passion and desire.[52] Indeed, at the time some southern physicians saw this approach as an enlightened alternative to lynching for de-

terring what one of them characterized as "assaults on women and children by the animalized negroes."[53] The physical and psychological impact of castration on its victims, however, made its use on anyone other than "animalized" criminals appear unacceptably inhuman to the general public. For example, popular outcry ended an experiment with eugenic castration at the Kansas State Home for the Feeble-Minded in the 1890s after forty-four boys and fourteen girls were mutilated. Similarly, an early proposal to asexualize the mentally retarded in Michigan was defeated by the state legislature in 1897.[54]

Fortuitously for the eugenics movement, new surgical techniques for sexual sterilization were developed in Europe shortly before the turn of the century. Vasectomy offered a safe and simple means of terminating a man's ability to reproduce without inhibiting his sexual desire or pleasure. Salpingectomy provided a similarly effective but somewhat more dangerous sterilization procedure for women.[55] The significance of these developments for eugenics was immediately recognized. In an 1899 article announcing his pioneering research with vasectomy, the Chicago surgeon A. J. Ochsner wrote, "It has been demonstrated beyond a doubt that a very large proportion of all criminals, degenerates, and perverts have come from parents similarly afflicted." After observing that the castration of criminals "has met with the strongest possible opposition because it practically destroys the possibility of the future enjoyment of life," Ochsner offered sterilization as a socially acceptable alternative. "This method would protect the community at large without harming the criminal," he claimed. "The same treatment could reasonably be suggested for chronic inebriates, imbeciles, perverts and paupers."[56]

Eugenicists needed little encouragement. An Indiana reformatory promptly launched a eugenic sterilization effort that began in 1899 as a voluntary experiment with prisoners but rapidly expanded until 1907, when the state enacted America's first compulsory sterilization statute.[57] That law mandated the sterilization of certain "confirmed criminals, idiots, rapists and imbeciles" whose condition was pronounced incurable by a committee of three physicians.[58] Fifteen other states in the North and the West, including such progressive trend-setters as California, New Jersey, New York, Michigan, and Wisconsin, followed suit over the next decade. "The general advantage claimed for sterilization," Popenoe and Roswell Johnson explained in 1918, "is the accomplishment of the end in view without much expense to the state, and without interference with the 'liberty and pursuit of happiness' of the individual."[59] At least for these avid eugenicists, depriving individuals of the ability to procreate a mentally ill or mentally retarded child did not infringe on their liberty or happiness.

Despite the confident assurance of eugenicists that sterilization was a harmless procedure that did not deprive degenerates of anything worth having, constitutional challenges dogged the early sterilization laws. Seven of the first sixteen statutes were struck down by state or federal courts for violating individual rights of equal protection, due process, or freedom from cruel and unusual punishment.[60] These decisions so hobbled the enforcement of all the early sterilization laws that only the California program, which was repeatedly revised and reenacted, lived up to eugenicists' expectations.[61] Even Indiana's pioneering program was shut down, first by a hostile governor in 1913 and finally by court order in 1920.[62]

The situation changed dramatically in 1927, however, when the United States Supreme Court upheld Virginia's model eugenic sterilization statute in the landmark case *Buck v. Bell.* "We have seen more than once that the public welfare may call upon the best citizens for their lives," wrote the Court's only surviving Civil War veteran, Oliver Wendell Holmes. "It would be strange if it could not call upon those who already sap the strength of the State for these lesser sacrifices, often not felt to be such by those concerned, in order to prevent our being swamped with incompetence." Writing for a majority of the Court that ranged from the conservative chief justice William Howard Taft to the liberal associate justice Louis D. Brandeis, the progressive Holmes concluded, "Three generations of imbeciles are enough." Only the arch-conservative Roman Catholic jurist Pierce Butler dissented.[63] The decision in *Buck v. Bell* fueled a resurgence of eugenic sterilization lawmaking that led to the enactment of new statutes in sixteen states during the late 1920s and early 1930s, including the first general sterilization laws in the Deep South.[64] More important, confidence in their constitutionality contributed to the increased utilization of such laws. The annual average number of operations performed under compulsory sterilization statutes in the United States jumped tenfold, from 230 during 1907–20 to 2,273 during the 1930s. Although the number of operations gradually declined thereafter, it did not become insignificant until the 1960s, by which time the total number of individuals sterilized exceeded 60,000.[65]

Not all eugenicists favored sterilization. It never became popular among British eugenicists, for example, and in the United States, Charles Davenport remained lukewarm to the idea. For them and others, segregation represented a more acceptable policy.[66] A 1913 article by Goddard suggested the reasoning that led many American eugenicists from an initial acceptance of segregation to an eventual advocacy of sterilization. "If the individuals that are selected for the operation are never to go out into the world, the operation will be of no very great benefit to society," Goddard observed. "But it is true that many institutions for the feeble-minded have inmates that could go to their homes . . . if they were safe from the danger of reproduction." Then, he reasoned, "others could take their places, could be trained to work, sterilized and sent to their homes to be fairly comfortable in those homes. In this way . . . the burden of caring for so many people for their entire lives in colonies would be, to a certain extent, relieved." Following this logic, Goddard and many fellow eugenicists concluded, "it is not a question of segregation *or* sterilization, but segregation *and* sterilization."[67]

Davenport's chief assistant at the Eugenics Record Office, H. H. Laughlin, emerged as the chief national proponent of sterilization laws. From 1910 to 1939, he tirelessly compiled, analyzed, and distributed material on judicial, legislative, and administrative aspects of eugenic sterilization.[68] As early as 1914, he outlined a "conservative sterilization program" for America that aimed at cutting off "the lowest one-tenth of the total population." If the program began promptly, Laughlin estimated, this would "require the sterilization of approximately fifteen million (15,000,000) persons during [the first] interval." After the initial bottom 10 percent was sterilized during the first interval, the effort would focus on the next lowest group. "The infinite tangle of germ-plasm continually making new combinations will make such a policy of decimal elimination perpetually of value," he concluded.[69]

Even this was not sufficient for Laughlin and other radical eugenicists, however. "As a final factor, the federal government must cooperate with the states to the extent of excluding from America immigrants who are potentially parents and who are by nature endowed with traits of less value than the better ninety percent of our existing breeding stock," Laughlin wrote. "Every nation has its own eugenical problems, and in the absence of a world-wide eugenical policy, every nation must protect its own innate capacities."[70] During the early 1920s, while state sterilization laws hung in limbo owing to constitutional concerns, Laughlin concentrated on this issue as "Expert Eugenical Agent" for a congressional committee that drafted new national legislation restricting the entry of non-Nordic immigrants into the United States. Although southern members of Congress generally supported this legislation, which became law in 1924, it never aroused as much passion in the Deep South as it did in the Northeast and on the West Coast, perhaps because so few foreign immigrants lived in the region.[71] Yet it completed the panoply of eugenic methods. "The social problem in the South is the same as that in the North," Davenport asserted. "Both sections alike must not be content merely to bow their heads before the oncoming storm, but must take positive measures to increase the density of socially desirable traits in the next generation—by education, segregation, sterilization, and by keeping out immigrants who belong to defective strains."[72]

The National Movement

Despite its grandiose aspirations and notable achievements, the American eugenics movement never attracted a broad following. A few hyperactive experts such as Davenport, Laughlin, Popenoe, and Goddard provided a remarkably large proportion of its apparent scientific substance. A somewhat larger circle of distinguished professionals, including the Harvard University biologists Edward M. East and William E. Castle, the New York author Madison Grant, the paleontologist Henry F. Osborn, of the American Museum of Natural History, the University of Wisconsin sociologist Edward A. Ross, and the inventor Alexander Graham Bell added their vigorous support. Leading biologists generally endorsed, or at least did not publicly oppose, the movement during its formative years, and their attitude was shared by many prominent American psychologists and sociologists. Their professional associations typically followed suit, most notably the American Breeders' Association, which became the American Genetics Association in 1913. A handful of elite philanthropists and foundations, particularly the Carnegie Institute of Washington, the widow of the railroad magnate E. H. Harriman, the California financier E. S. Gosney, and the Rockefeller Foundation, provided a disproportionate share of the movement's financial backing.[73] But these national leaders could not claim credit for the enactment of individual state laws, especially in the Deep South, where none of them lived or worked. That role fell to local activists.

State campaigns for eugenics legislation typically followed the pattern set by other progressive reform efforts of the period. In his study focusing on early campaigns in the North, the historian Mark Haller found that "eugenics at first was closely related to the other reform movements of the Progressive Era and drew its support from many of the same persons. It began as a scientific reform in an age of reform."[74] This observation says little about the ideology of eugenics, however, because progressivism attracted followers from all parts of the political spectrum. In fact, eugenicists ranged from conservative elitists such as Davenport through liberals such as Jordan to such radical leftists as the geneticist Hermann J. Muller. At the national political level, eugenics doctrines were endorsed by three very different presidents from the era: Theodore Roosevelt, a progressive Republican; Woodrow Wilson, a liberal Democrat; and Calvin Coolidge, a conservative Republican. Rather, the eugenics movement was characteristically progressive because it involved middle-class professionals applying scientific expertise to solve pressing social problems through governmental intervention.[75]

Eugenics naturally appealed to the progressive mind. "Eugenics is that science which studies the inborn qualities—physical, mental and spiritual—in man, with the view to their improvement," its proponents declared at a major eugenics conclave. "Obviously, it is closely parallel, in essential nature, to the improvement of domestic plants and animals."[76] In short, applying recent developments in genetics and evolutionary biology, eugenicists offered a means to breed better people just when rising middle-class progressives were seeking to cope with an apparent increase in the number of urban paupers, criminals, and mentally ill or retarded persons. Surely, the progressive response called for the application of scientific expertise to the problem. "In the United States during the opening decade of the century, it became the hallmark of good government to shape public policy with the aid of scientific experts," the historian Daniel Kevles noted. "Eugenics experts aplenty were to be found in the biology, psychology, and sociology departments of universities or colleges, and among superintendents of state mental institutions."[77] These local experts on mental disease, mental retardation, crime, and human degeneracy provided much of the impetus behind the enactment of state eugenics legislation.[78]

In some states, such experts, acting alone against little organized opposition, easily secured the passage of eugenic segregation or sterilization laws.[79] On the basis of his review of the movement, Haller observed that "the legislative victories of eugenics arose more from expert testimony before legislative committees than from public demands. Support came chiefly from state boards of charity, institutional superintendents, professors, and others whose readings and interests kept them abreast of the latest findings in psychology, criminology, and the study of the feebleminded."[80] Legislators eager for solutions to problems of crime and dependency often welcomed the ideas of these experts, especially when the ideas were as inexpensive as sterilization.

In other states, these experts were joined by a broader coalition of eugenics enthusiasts who were commonly interested in both positive and negative eugenics. Kevles found that these individuals "were largely middle to upper middle class, White, Anglo-Saxon, predominantly Protestant, and educated. The movement's leaders tended to be well-to-do rather than rich, and many were professionals—physicians, social workers, clerics, writers, and numerous professors." He also found that, at the state and local levels, many of the leaders were women. These individuals and their civic, social, and religious organizations engaged in a wide variety of activities promoting eugenics. They sought to educate themselves, their friends, and the public about the importance of eugenic breeding practices through lectures, publications, exhibits, and even contests offering prizes for the fittest families or babies.[81]

For many of these socially superior enthusiasts, encouraging their own eugenic unions though education naturally spilled over into discouraging dysgenic unions by others; and the methods of doing so included the enactment of legal restrictions. For example, a society "lady" once wrote Davenport, "I want to help along Eugenics. I have a brother in the legislature and I have urged him to introduce a sterilization bill and one requiring a medical certificate before marriage. Now, is there any other law that you can suggest that he should get through?"[82] The historian Donald Pickens suggested that the American birth control movement also attracted educated, upper-middle-class women into the campaign for eugenic sterilization. Certainly, that drew the movement's founder, Margaret Sanger, to the cause—and she brought along many of her wealthy female followers.[83] Politically active local women's organizations often made a decided difference in the battle for state eugenics legislation.[84] In this respect and in many others, the Deep South was no exception.

A 1912 report by the Eugenics Section of the American Breeders' Association concluded, "The laws already enacted have usually been put through by some very small energetic group of enthusiasts, who have had influence in the legislatures. In at least two of the States it was chiefly the work of a physician. In one, of a woman."[85] The observation aptly characterized the entire movement. Despite massive efforts to educate the general public about eugenics through popular books, articles, pamphlets, lectures, and exhibits, few outside the narrow professional and upper-middle classes actively joined the cause. Of course, the subject matter under discussion—sex, crime, race, insanity, sterilization—excited widespread interest and comment, but this did not necessarily make converts. Membership in the American Eugenics Society rarely exceeded one thousand, and local eugenics groups retained a decidedly elitist cast.[86] "Although eugenics was a reform in the middle of a reform era, at bottom its outlook was necessarily elitist," the historian Carl Degler reasoned. "Thus eugenics could hardly spawn grass-roots organizations."[87] As Haller concluded, "Eugenics remained primarily a movement of specialists rather than a popular crusade."[88] This was reflected in the California experience, which served as a model for eugenicists in other states.

The California Experience

By the time eugenics reached the Deep South, proponents of the cause could refer to years of experience in other states to bolster their calls for action. At the time, no state was cited more often than California. As early as 1913, for example, a member of the legislative committee of the Medical Association of Georgia commented that California had adopted a eugenic sterilization statute, and urged Georgia to follow suit.[89] Fifteen years later, the superintendent of a Louisiana mental health hospital referred to the results of this California law in support of similar legislation for his state: "This operation has been successfully performed on five thousand cases in California, without one bad result to the patients operated upon."[90] By 1931, the head of South Carolina's State Training School for the Feeble-minded could underscore his call for stricter eugenics restrictions by observing that California "has on record over 6000 state institutional cases and several thousand private cases of eugenical sterilization."[91] Three years later, Alabama's state health officer, a rabid eugenicist, repeatedly referred to the more than "8500 operations successfully performed under the California law" in his campaign for involuntary sterilization in the Heart of Dixie.[92] The number had reached 10,801 by 1937, when Atlanta's progressive newspaper, the *Constitution,* cited it in an editorial favoring eugenics legislation for Georgia.[93] "The Georgia law is largely patterned after the one in California," the equally progressive *Augusta Chronicle* assured readers in its editorial endorsement of the measure.[94] California's experience with eugenics provided more than simply a pattern for southern eugenicists to emulate, however, it also offers a frame of reference for appreciating the distinctive response of the Deep South to the issue.

California provided a peculiar model for southern eugenicists to invoke because that state then differed so starkly from those of the Deep South. California was a relatively young state, without traditional folkways, whereas the southern states were both relatively old and steeped in tradition. While the South stagnated, California was America's fastest-growing state in terms of population, even though comparatively few of its people were natives. Approximately 60 percent of them had migrated from other states or countries, which was more than four times the percentage of newcomers in any state in the Deep South except Florida.[95] So many of California's recent immigrants had come from Asia or Mexico that severe racial cleavages were emerging, as reflected by the adoption of a strict antimiscegenation statute targeted against "Whites" marrying "Mongolians" as well as "Negroes" and "mulattoes." Further, relatively more Californians than southerners were single, divorced, or childless. Indeed, for its native White population California had the lowest fertility rate of any state in the nation, whereas the South had the highest of any region.[96]

Other factors also distinguished the Golden State from the American South. California stood at or near the top of all national statistical indicators of per capita income, wealth, and education, whereas southern states defined the bottom. For example, average personal income in California reached $1,085 in 1929, as compared to only $287 in Mississippi and $364 for the South as a whole. Despite its massive farm and mine output, California was largely urban and industrial by the early twentieth century; the Deep South remained rural and agricultural. Finally, only about one-third of Californians regularly attended church during the period, as opposed to two-thirds of all southerners.[97] The image emerges of a dynamic, mobile, unattached populace, ready to accept change, willing to experiment with new ideas, and able to pay for progressive reforms.

With its ample resources, California had built five mental health hospitals and a large "Home for the Feebleminded" by the turn of the century. These institutions housed a larger proportion of the total population than did their counterparts in any other state. This resulted from a multitude of complex factors, but had two obvious immediate causes. First, California consistently had the highest rate of mental illness in the nation.[98] Traditionally, this was attributed to the rapid influx of pioneers from all regions of the nation and the world seeking their fortune on the frontier in the Golden State. "On a people of such heterogeneous elements," the state board of health reported in 1873, "exposed to all the evils incident to changes of climate, habits, and modes of life, isolated, without sympathy, and deprived of all home influences, the shock attendant upon the sudden acquisition of wealth, with its unbounded hopes, its sudden reverse and short-lived triumphs, is well-calculated to break some link in reason's chain and throw into confusion even the best balanced properties of mind."[99] Second, California institutionalized a significantly greater proportion of its mentally ill residents than did any other state, because of both its liberal commitment policies and the lack of family or community alternatives.[100]

Both the absolute number and the percentage of Californians committed to state mental health hospitals steadily mounted throughout the late nineteenth and early twentieth centuries, becoming far higher than the corresponding figures for any other state. The total reached 6,073 persons, or 1 Californian in 270, by 1905, shortly before the enactment of the state's first sterilization statute.[101] California was more than a half century old by now: a "frontier thesis" could not account for the situation forever. State mental health officials began seeking new solutions to the problem as California taxpayers grew restive under the ever-increasing cost of traditional methods.[102]

Eugenics had a popular champion in California, Luther Burbank. The venerable horticulturist was one of the most famous and respected Californians of the era. He had developed an unprecedented number of new commercial varieties of fruits, vegetables, and flowers through his gifted application of traditional plant-breeding techniques. "During the course of many years of investigation into the plant life of the world, creating new forms, modifying old ones, adapting others to new conditions, and blending still others, I have constantly been impressed with the similarity between the organization and development of plant and human life," he wrote in a 1906 popular magazine article, which he reprinted in a small book dedicated to America's public-school children. "The crossing of species is to me paramount. Upon it, wisely directed and accompanied by a rigid selection of the best and as rigid an exclusion of the poorest, rests the hope of all progress."[103]

As a proponent of neo-Lamarckian evolution, Burbank believed that better plants and human beings could be cultivated by improving the environment, and that these enhancements were passed along to future generations. Indeed, he wrote, "In child-rearing, environment is equally essential with heredity." But he immediately added, "Mind you, I do not say that heredity is of no consequence. It is the great factor, and often makes environment almost powerless."[104] Burbank viewed this as particularly true for the mentally retarded, whose treatment raised "the hardest question of all" for him. "In the case of plants in which all tendencies are absolutely vicious there is only one course—they must be destroyed," he declared. "In the case of human beings in whom the light of reason does not burn, those who, apparently, can never be other than a burden, shall they be eliminated from the race?" No, Burbank answered, he was not prepared to accept euthanasia. "But it is as clear as sunlight that here, as in the case of plants, constant cultivation and *selection* will do away with all this, so that in the grander race of the future these defectives will have become permanently eliminated from the race heredity."[105] In this popular publication aimed particularly at schoolchildren, Burbank only explicitly endorsed prohibiting "in every State in the Union the marriage of the physically, mentally and morally unfit," but he also generally advocated "the best and broadest state aid" for these "unfortunates," which implicitly included their eugenic segregation in state institutions and did not preclude their sterilization.[106]

By the time Burbank rendered this advice to the public in 1906, the experts in charge of California's mental health institutions generally had accepted both hereditarian explanations for mental defects, and eugenic remedies for their prevention. For example, the same year that Burbank published his article on eugenics, the State Board of Charities and Corrections of California observed, "Physicians are generally agreed that feeble-mindedness is generally inherited, and that a feeble-minded mother especially will bear feeble-minded offspring. This fact . . . shows the importance of segregating from the community all feeble-minded women of child-bearing age."[107] The board soon requested added facilities specifically for this purpose, which the state legislature provided, along with funding that greatly increased the capacity for segregating the mentally retarded generally.[108] The state Commission in Lunacy, led by General Superintendent F. W. Hatch, took an even more active role in the California eugenics movement. After reporting to the commission in 1906 that heredity and alcoholism constituted the two principal causes of mental illness, Hatch began promoting a surgical solution for the problem.[109] Three years later, thanks largely to his efforts, California became the second state to authorize the involuntary sterilization of mentally ill and mentally retarded persons in public institutions.[110]

At a time when eugenic sterilization aroused stiff resistance elsewhere, Hatch's proposal passed the state legislature virtually without comment or opposition.[111] Three factors contributed to this result. First, Hatch's role in drafting the measure gave it an official imprimatur.[112] Second, it was introduced into the legislature by the senator who represented the district containing the California Home for the Care and Training of Feeble-Minded Children and who consistently championed that facilty's improvement.[113] Finally, the bill was not overtly eugenic. It simply provided for the sterilization of any patient at a state facility for the mentally ill or mentally retarded when officials determined that it would benefit the patient's "physical, mental or moral condition."[114] Even though this did not expressly authorize eugenic sterilization solely for the benefit of society, Hatch applied the law broadly. Within four years of its enactment, California sterilized 568 persons at its mental health institutions, thus performing more such operations than were performed during the period under all seven eugenic sterilization statutes then on the books in other states.[115] "We have found that it does many patients much good," Hatch reported in 1912, "while in others there has been little effect on the mental condition but generally some improvement in the general health." Apparently this was sufficient for Hatch to invoke the law. He did try to obtain permission from the patient's relatives if possible, but acknowledged that "we operate without consent" in some cases.[116] A year later, however, Hatch returned to the legislature for broader authority.

California's second sterilization law, as enacted in 1913 and revised in 1917, dropped the requirement that operations benefit the patient. Under the new law, the state lunacy commission could order the sterilization of any patient at a state mental health institution "who is afflicted with mental disease that may have been inherited and is likely to be transmitted to descendants [or who suffers from one of] the various grades of feeble-mindedness." The operation would occur prior to the patient's release from custody and did not require consent. Reaching beyond institutional walls, the law also directed state mental health hospitals to perform outpatient sterilizations without charge on "any idiot" upon the written request of the parent or guardian.[117] This legislation also passed with little comment or opposition. Indeed, the 1913 bill reached the floor of the state Senate when its sponsor was presiding over the body and was therefore precluded from making a speech. When no other senator spoke up, the sponsor simply observed, "Gentlemen, this is a good bill. I hope you will pass it." This they did, by a vote of twenty-one ayes to four nays.[118]

Hatch used social and financial arguments in support of his new legislation, in addition to scientific and medical ones. "Those who study the subject closely realize that mental defectiveness is the foundation upon which is gradually built up much of our mental troubles, much of our crime and delinquency, much of the retrogression from sober, law-abiding citizens into shiftless ne'er-do-wells, into inebriety and dependency," he asserted. The social danger came primarily from "the higher class of mental defective," Hatch explained, rather than from those whose condition was obvious. "From this class many of our drunkards, our drug users, our sexual offenders, and our repeating offenders come," he claimed without citing any specific evidence. "The problem is particularly difficult among high grade feeble-minded girls. How best can they be protected and prevented from bringing forth their kind?" Segregation offered a partial solution, Hatch noted, but cost too much. "Another greater hope is in sterilization," he concluded. "Sterilization prevents procreation and makes it safe, so far as future generations are concerned, to liberate many." Such measures were justified because, as he explained it, "[t]here is nothing more certain in inheritance than the statement that feeble-minded will bring forth feeble-minded."[119]

Once the new laws passed, Hatch unleashed a eugenic sterilization campaign unmatched in American history. During the second decade of the twentieth century, California sterilized more than twenty-five hundred patients in its state institutions, which constituted four-fifths of the national total for such procedures.[120] This number kept climbing into the 1920s, as several state institutions, including one for mentally retarded children, followed a strict policy of sterilizing all fertile patients prior to their release.[121] The running tally of eugenic sterilizations for California neared four thousand in 1925, shortly after Hatch's death, and by 1927 exceeded five thousand, which was then four times the total for the entire rest of the world. Even though other states began catching up thereafter, California continued to lead all others in the annual number of eugenic sterilizations until 1950.[122] Despite Hatch's special concern about unconfined "feeble-minded girls," the program actually sterilized slightly more males than females, and twice as many people afflicted with mental disease as people suffering from mental retardation. African Americans and foreign immigrants were sterilized at nearly twice the rate, per capita, as the general population, but this apparently reflected the higher commitment rates of these groups rather than a practice of targeting them for sterilization within institutions.[123]

Ultimately, about 20,100 patients were involuntarily sterilized in California state institutions, which represented three times the number involuntarily sterilized in any other state, and nearly one-third of the national total.[124] Even this would not have satisfied Hatch, who once called for the "sterilization of confirmed criminals, habitual drunkards, and drug habituates, epileptics, sexual and moral perverts."[125] But no American state went further. On the basis of his exhaustive investigation of the California program, Popenoe concluded that the adoption and administration of the state sterilization law formed "a permanent monument to Dr. F. W. Hatch."[126]

Of course, Hatch could not have conceived and implemented such a far-reaching and widely known public policy alone. He obviously enjoyed the acquiescence of the general public, which Burbank's early endorsement of eugenics undoubtedly facilitated. Indeed, in marked contrast to the "much controversy and difference of opinion" that surrounded the issue elsewhere, a 1930 mental health survey found that "[t]he law has been quite generally accepted in California."[127] More critically, active support came from academic experts and civic leaders throughout California. For example, Stanford University's president, the eminent biologist David Starr Jordan, was a leading eugenicist. Further, when the Pasadena philanthropist E. S. Gosney formed the Human Betterment Foundation to promote eugenic sterilization in 1928, two dozen prominent Californians joined his effort, including distinguished professors from all of the state's premier universities, progressive business and religious leaders, and the president of the influential *Los Angeles Times*.[128] Finally, the State Board of Charities and Corrections of California, which served as an independent oversight agency, wholeheartedly endorsed the effort. "From the viewpoint of prevention," the board reported in 1916, "the most important part of California's program for the insane, as for feeble-minded, is sterilization." Not only did the procedure benefit the patient and society, the board maintained, but "[f]or those with the inheritance and the future to which children of the insane are liable, it is better not to be born."[129] According to these experts, everyone profited from eugenic sterilization.

California offered a model that eugenicists in the Deep South and elsewhere sought to emulate. One committed advocate, backed by a handful of experts, had quickly led the state through an ambitious segregation effort to a comprehensive sterilization program. No popular movement ever developed, but none was needed. In a state of strangers, who lacked extended family ties and a shared tradition, the issue was left to mental health officials. They accepted the promises of a new science to deal with an unprecedented social problem, and the people followed. No other soil would ever prove so fertile for eugenic seeds, at least not in the United States—certainly not in the Deep South.

CHAPTER THREE

Sowing the Seeds

Eugenic ideas filtered slowly into the Deep South. Long after such ideas became popular in the North and the West during the first decade of the twentieth century, they remained largely unknown in the South. None of the early books or articles on eugenics were written by southerners, and none of the early leaders of the American eugenics movement lived in the region.[1] The southern press reported little about this emerging national issue before World War I, and editorialized even less. Perhaps this was because eugenic theories were first articulated by scientists and academics, and in the Deep South there were relatively few of them to speak out.

By any measure, higher education lagged in the Deep South. At the turn of the century, the entire region had about half as many professors as did the state of Indiana, and less than one-twelfth as many graduate students enrolled in all of its schools as were enrolled at the University of Chicago. The annual income of all the region's colleges and universities then totaled approximately $850,000, which was significantly less than that of Harvard University alone. Some prominent "public" institutions, such as the University of Mississippi, received no state funds at the time, while many others benefited from merely nominal state appropriations. Only one university in the Deep South had an endowment exceeding $1 million in 1900, as compared to thirty colleges and universities in the nation as a whole.[2] That singular school, Tulane University, was the only institution in the region to satisfy the minimal academic standards for colleges then established by the Carnegie Foundation for the Advancement of Teaching. The standard requiring that entering freshmen have completed four years in high school proved particularly troublesome for southern institutions. The lack of secondary schools throughout the South forced most colleges in the region to provide a basic education before they could even begin to offer advanced training.[3] Conditions began to improve in the 1920s with an increase in state and private support, but the total per-student income of colleges and universities in the region remained a fraction of that received anywhere else in the country.[4]

Scientific research suffered in this environment. At a time when leading American universities were building research-oriented science departments, southern institutions showed little initiative. In 1900, the total value of the scientific apparatus at all the colleges and universities in the Deep South was less than that at any one of a half-dozen top institutions in the North.[5] Turn-of-the-century efforts to develop engineering departments at even the strongest southern schools fell far behind achievements in the Northeast, the Midwest, and California.[6] The pure sciences fared even worse. For example, no university in the Deep South offered a Ph.D. degree in chemistry during the first third of the twentieth century.[7] In 1910, the president of Randolph-Macon College found "no [southern] university well enough equipped to do genuine research work, and twice as many professional and polytechnic schools as are needed, and none of them able to give our people the advantages that northern and western institutions offer."[8] Despite uncovering some evidence of progress a quarter century later, Howard Odum concluded that "[t]he South is, however, unsuccessful in holding its scientists of superior talent, approximately four-fifths having left the region of their birth," with relatively fewer immigrating to replace them.[9]

Research programs in the biological sciences, which initially boosted eugenics in other places, showed little promise in the South despite the region's reliance on an agricultural economy. Such research increasingly was centered in well-funded genetics and experimental biology programs at major universities, medical schools, and agricultural experiment stations. Because of the meager resources of institutions in the Deep South, none of them could hope to keep pace with developments elsewhere, and few even tried.[10] During the early twentieth century, only the University of Georgia attempted to develop a modern experimental genetics program with state funds, while Tulane used large donations from the Rockefeller Foundation to build a nationally recognized medical research facility.[11] But these stood out as exceptions from the norm. The annual state support for all agricultural experiment stations in the region was less than the support that Ohio, or any one of a number of other northern states, provided to its stations.[12] Southern research biologists simply never enjoyed a position from which they could significantly promote eugenics, even if they had been so inclined. Characteristically, no scientist in the Deep South ever served as an officer or a council member of the prestigious American Genetics Association during the period of its eugenic activity, and the only southerner named to its larger advisory committee during the era was a Florida Agricultural Experiment Station researcher who did not specialize in human genetics.[13]

The other academic disciplines that effectively introduced and promoted eugenics elsewhere were also relatively weak in the Deep South. Of the two hundred top social scientists born in the South, Odum found that nearly nine out of ten had left the region to attend graduate school, with half of those never returning to work in the South. "According to the field of specialization," Odum wrote, "the loss is least with the historians, greater among the economists, psychologists, and political scientists, and quite high among sociologists, anthropologists, and statisticians."[14] Significantly, the specialists most likely to leave the South included those most involved with championing eugenics. Tulane's Clarence Nixon glumly concluded in 1934 that "the relative backwardness of the South in research, whether scientific or social, regional or general, has been greater than potential resources justify."[15]

Even though southern scientists and academics did little to introduce eugenics to the region, national experts could directly reach southerners through books and journals. Many leading eugenicists, including such biologists and social scientists as Davenport and Goddard, tried to influence broad popular audiences through national publications. Some of this certainly reached the South, but it was probably less than reached other parts of the nation. On average, southerners simply could not and did not read as much as did people in any other region of the country. The vast majority of people in the Deep South did not have access to local public libraries, and even the region's best university libraries were wholly inadequate for research.[16] "Except for school textbooks, the southern states are the leanest book market in the United States," the Carolina educator Edgar W. Knight observed in 1929. "As readers of the leading national magazines they rank at the bottom, and as readers of newspapers the country at large makes about a three-fold better showing than the southern states."[17] Specific figures suggested that Californians were ten times as likely as Mississippians to read national magazines, and the difference was nearly as great for people in Alabama, Georgia, and South Carolina. Within the region, only Floridians read books and magazines at anything approaching the national rate.[18] "The southern literate whites, taken as a whole, are largely a non-reading public," Nixon concluded.[19] In large part, the burden of introducing eugenics to the Deep South fell on state mental health officials and local physicians, with the aid of national expertise. Lacking the initial spur of local scientists and academics, southerners were not as fast off the mark as their counterparts in other parts of America.

Mental Health Officials

"I am called sometimes down in Alabama the 'Head Crazy Man of the State,' because I am at the head of about twenty-two hundred insane persons," Superintendent James T. Searcy of the Alabama Insane Hospitals reported to the First National Conference on Race Betterment in 1914. "My following is increasing faster than any other one class of people in the state." Searcy was the only representative from the Deep South at this major eugenics conclave, but the story he told was similar to those told by the other participants. His patient population was rising at a rate about three times greater than the growth rate of his state's population, and he placed the blame on civilization. In civilized society, "we have been taught to value all human life alike," Searcy explained. "All our social work runs on these principles. Those who are defective and deficient reap quick advantage of these opportunities and live to adult life. Then they multiply themselves." He offered a straightforward eugenic remedy to this growing social problem: "The keynote of this Conference should be to deny that all are alike valuable; to show that there are grades in excellencies and in deficiencies; and to show that the hereditary multiplication of the deficient and defective ought to be discouraged in every way."[20] Although such rhetoric was standard for the national scientific, medical, and civic leaders who participated in the conference, here it was voiced by a prominent southern alienist.

Searcy presented similar arguments in a 1911 address to the annual meeting of the Medical Association of the State of Alabama (MASA) that was promptly reprinted in the prestigious *Southern Medical Journal*.[21] Because he was the dean of southern mental health officials and past president of the MASA, Searcy's views carried weight. He had not always espoused eugenics. Indeed, as late as 1904 he held to a neo-Lamarckian view of the mind that offered hope for correcting hereditary deficiencies and defects through mental exercise and effort.[22] Despite his age, the septuagenarian Searcy had changed with the times in adopting the new eugenic dogma. Perhaps his background predisposed Searcy to hereditarian thinking, for he was both the son of a prominent Alabama physician who had headed the state mental health hospital's board of trustees for three decades, and the father of three physicians. The formal discussion following Searcy's address suggested that MASA members were not yet ready to confront this issue. It focused on a secondary reference to the aggravation of mental deterioration by drug use rather than on the talk's primary eugenic theme. Nevertheless, a younger generation of southern mental health officials soon pursued the main issue.

William D. Partlow, Searcy's top assistant and later his successor at the Alabama Insane Hospitals offered a case in point. In 1907, Partlow espoused the neo-Lamarckian view: "To reduce the frequent appearance of insanity the initial cause of degeneracy must be removed. To do this, measures or remedies must be applied one or more generations in advance of the expectation of results."[23] By the time of a 1915 talk by

Searcy on the causes of mental illness and mental retardation, however, Partlow had begun his conversion to the new view. "In fifteen years' time I have learned never to dissent from Dr. Searcy or disagree with anything he says," Partlow noted in response to Searcy's talk.[24] Even though Partlow's own presentation to the MASA that year maintained that both "heredity and environment" helped to "determine the mental life of an individual," he agreed to serve with Searcy on a new MASA Committee on Mental Hygiene organized to promote eugenics. At the next MASA annual meeting, after reporting the committee's findings "that in the majority of cases feeble-mindedness is directly hereditary," Partlow offered a purely eugenic prescription: "Then how shall we avoid the increasing numbers of cases of feeble-mindedness? By segregation and possibly by sterilization during the productive period."[25] Thereafter, Partlow was a strict eugenicist. He founded and led the new Alabama Society for Mental Hygiene, which championed a state institution for segregating the mentally retarded; he lobbied for giving that institution's superintendent broad powers to sterilize its residents; and he liberally used those powers when he assumed that position. For the next quarter century, Partlow's name became virtually synonymous with that of eugenics in Alabama.[26]

Local mental health officials also took the lead in introducing eugenics elsewhere in the Deep South. For example, the first published call for eugenics by a Louisiana public official appeared in the 1912–14 biennial report of the South Louisiana Hospital for the Insane. "In keeping with the trends of the time," Superintendent Clarence Pierson wrote, "I recommend unhesitatingly the establishment at as early a date as possible of 'a colony' for the exclusive care of the epileptic and feeble-minded of the State. Their segregation is as urgent as was the segregation of the State's criminal insane." To remove any doubt as to the purpose of this segregation, he also endorsed, "a law on eugenics, as applied to inmates of insane hospitals and the penal institutions, permitting sterilization of certain classes of inmates."[27]

Not to be outdone, Superintendent John N. Thomas of the Louisiana Hospital for the Insane soon added a plea for eugenic sterilization to his biennial reports. "It is my belief that if incurable mental defectives, those showing positive hereditary taints, were sterilized, in the course of three generations insanity would diminish over fifty per cent," he claimed in a 1916 report.[28] During the 1920s, he drove home his pleas with a poem, which read in part:

> Oh, why are you men so foolish—
> You breeders who breed our men
> Let the fools, the weaklings and crazy
> Keep breeding and breeding again. . . .

This is the law of Mendel,
     And often he makes it plain,
Defectives will breed defectives
     And the insane will breed insane. . . .
Oh, you wise men take up the burden,
     And make this your loudest creed,
Sterilize the misfits promptly—
     All not fit to breed.[29]

Acknowledging a secondary role played by alcohol in mental deterioration, Thomas neatly summed up his position in 1917, "My idea would
be, if it can be done, to castrate men and take out the ovaries in women
and stop whiskey."[30]

Eugenics was first brought formally to the attention of the Mississippi
State Medical Association (MSMA) by a staff physician at the state mental health hospital in Jackson, J. N. Fox. Beginning in 1913, Fox started
urging eugenic restrictions on marriage and breeding in order to combat
an "appalling" increase in mental illness and mental retardation. "It is a
well-known fact that when two feeble-minded persons mate, their offspring is sure to be feeble-minded also," he told physicians assembled for
the MSMA annual meeting. "It is also well-known that these mental
weaklings are very prolific, and when allowed to go at will, that a line of
law-breakers, such as murderers, sexual perverts, pyro-maniacs and
thieves are brought into the world to become a burden and a menace to
the state."[31]

Superintendent J. M. Buchanan of the East Mississippi Insane Hospital agreed with Fox's diagnosis but felt that his remedy, eugenic marriage
restrictions and segregation, did not reach far enough. "'Love laughs at
locks and bars,' and the same may be said of laws, for it is to be remem-
bered that we are dealing with human beings possessed of uncontrollable
appetites," Buchanan argued in a 1912 article that favored compulsory
sterilization. Even the sterilization of confirmed criminals, the insane,
and the mentally retarded was inadequate because "there is a danger
from any form of nervous instability," he added. "I have seen both men
and women in the hospital with which I am connected be improved and
carried home, where children with an insane diathesis would be born.
The bringing into being of such children would have been prevented by a
slight surgical operation."[32]

The same year that Buchanan's article appeared, the staff at Georgia's
sole state mental health institution heard a presentation entitled "Sterilization: The Only Logical Means of Restricting the Progress of Insanity
and Degeneracy." This institution housed more than 3,200 patients at
the time, which made it the largest facility of its kind in the world.[33] The

following year, after reviewing the background of all 1,108 patients admitted in 1912, one of the institution's physicians concluded that "[h]eredity is the greatest pre-disposing etiological factor in insanity and that it exists in all types of insanity."[34] Officials at the facility then began recommending the enactment of a compulsory sterilization law for Georgia, which they continued doing until they achieved this goal a quarter century later.[35]

Between 1910 and 1920, a steady drumbeat of eugenic fear-mongering issued from southern alienists. Indeed, the only top mental health official from the region to take a public stand against eugenics during the period was Superintendent C. F. Williams of the South Carolina State Hospital for the Insane. In a 1916 address to his state medical association, Williams rejected the "popular idea of hospitals for the insane [as] a place for the segregation of the mentally afflicted, rather than a place for scientific treatment in the hope of restoring to normal the alienated."[36] Until his retirement in 1945, he remained deeply skeptical of the "army of popular lecturers," as he once called it, that promoted simplistic biological explanations for mental disorders without acknowledging environmental factors.[37] Williams's published objections to eugenics relied solely on the lack of supporting scientific evidence for the theory, especially as applied to specific types of mental illness. His confident hope that mental illness could be cured, however, rested less on any current medical views of rehabilitation than on his deep Christian faith in redemption, which his chief assistant and successor at the state hospital once described as Williams's "child-like faith in his Supreme Master."[38]

By 1920, despite Williams's dissent, the leaders of most state mental health institutions in the Deep South espoused hereditarian explanations and eugenic remedies for mental illness and retardation. In doing so, they followed national trends in their profession. "The subject of eugenics is now attracting wide attention, and many societies of scientific men are making research regarding the question of heredity," Mississippi's Buchanan explained in 1912. "These societies of eugenics are trying to teach us, under the Mendelian law, how we may do for the human race, what Burbanks [sic] is doing in plant life."[39] Also in 1912, before any state in the Deep South provided a separate institution for the mentally retarded, Superintendent Ira M. Hardy of the new North Carolina School for the Feeble-Minded appealed to national trends in promoting such facilities during a speech to a meeting of the Southern Medical Association in Florida. "The progress already made in this direction by some of the more advanced Northern and Western States of the Union is unparalleled," Hardy reported. "Happily, now that State care and [sexual] segregation of mental defectives is in the ascendancy of sociological progress, we may look forward to the ages to come when these ills will have been so well prevented that there will be no need for them or for dependent, custodial or penal institutions."[40] For eugenicists such as Hardy, preventing reproduction through sexual segregation was the key to achieving this objective, but the general public could also support "state care" for afflicted individuals in modern training facilities without subscribing to the underlying eugenic rationale.

Hardy's hopeful tone helps account for the acceptance of eugenics by southern mental health officials. For years, they had faced a steady increase in their patient population without any adequate explanation or prospect of relief. "This alarming increase is attracting attention everywhere," Searcy observed in a comment typical of the second decade of the century. "It cannot be explained by a greater willingness and greater facilities in sending patients to the hospitals; nor by a more liberal admission of all kinds; nor by returns of relapsing cases. These reasons prevailed ten years ago as much as now. There is no alternative but to recognize a large gradual increase of persons so mentally deficient and defective that they come within the jurisdiction of State care."[41] This explanation justified the continued expansion of state mental health facilities and an enlarged role for alienists, especially if they could offer the public a plausible solution to the perceived problem of growing social dependency and degeneracy. "From time immemorial insanity has been looked upon with suspicion and these unfortunates have been treated as beings possessed with demons, instead of individuals with sick minds," Mississippi's J. H. Fox wrote in 1915. "We know now that there is an underlying cause for every case. . . . Modern medicine has taught us that the prerequisite to a nature of efficiency is an inheritance of germ-plasm from our ancestors that will produce a brain capable of development into the highest grade of usefulness."[42]

Earlier reports from mental health facilities in the South and elsewhere typically attributed individual cases of mental illness to such causes as stress, grief, alcohol and drug use, and religious hysteria. Alienists could do little to remedy the larger social factors increasing the incidence of these causes and could offer few effective treatments for the afflicted other than rest and restraint. "It is not infrequent that we have patients admitted to the hospital, the cause of their insanity being ascribed to such conditions as domestic trouble, grief over the death of a friend, business worries, love affairs, etc.," J. F. Messelyn of South Carolina's state mental health hospital reported in 1917. "We have now, however, come to realize the fact that emotion alone is rarely ever sufficient to cause a disturbance of the normal brain to such an extent as to produce a true psychosis, and if a true anamnesis can be obtained, we usually find that those individuals possess a nervous condition tainted by heredity."[43] About this same time, the new superintendent of Florida's mental health hospital in Jacksonville liked to dramatize the inheritance of "insanity" by telling the story of a patient periodically allowed to go home. Upon visiting the patient's home after he took charge of the institution, the superintendent "found that the insane man has a wife and eleven children, several of whom are coming along in their father's footsteps and are defectives."[44]

With hereditarian explanations came eugenic remedies and treatments that increased the social role and the power of mental health officials. "Feeble-mindedness is a very general and comprehensive term, applicable in a general way to most of the shortcomings of private and public life," Hardy told his southern audience in 1912. "The first step in the policy of the prevention and mitigation of dependency, degeneracy and crime is to provide adequate institutions of the kind outlined to receive the unfortunate persons who are so urgently in need of permanent care." Hardy acknowledged that segregating such defectives beginning in childhood would be costly and would cover many more individuals than those then categorized as mentally ill, but he stressed that "an added tax for their segregation would be an apparent, rather than a real, increase, for through segregation of defectives the number of criminals, the number of prisoners, the cost of public trials, the demand upon private and public charities, would be largely decreased."[45] Of course, the new programs would all fall into the domain of mental health officials rather than that of the prisons, courts, and social service agencies.

Using such arguments, state mental health officials throughout the Deep South promoted the establishment of state institutions for the mentally retarded. Typically, officials from existing state mental health hospitals assumed control of these new facilities. For example, after proposing such an institution for his state, the superintendent of the East Louisiana Hospital for the Insane wrote, "In order to carry out this recommendation, and to save large expenses for the establishment of a separate and distinct institution elsewhere it will be necessary to appropriate sufficient funds to build a certain class of building [here] for the accommodation of this class of patients."[46] Similarly, after successfully lobbying for a state "home" for the mentally retarded in Alabama adjacent to the state's main mental health hospital, Partlow managed to hold the superintendency of both institutions, even though they were managed by separate boards. This gave him total power over eugenic sterilization within the new facility, under a law providing that "if after consultation the superintendent of the home and the superintendent of the Alabama Insane Hospitals deem it advisable they are hereby authorized and empowered to sterilize any inmate."[47] For fifteen years, Partlow used this power to sterilize every patient released from the new facility.[48]

Given the limited state funds available in the Deep South for any public services, mental health officials recognized that they could not secure the establishment of eugenically segregated institutions for the mentally retarded without the help of powerful allies. Further, imposing radical new eugenic restrictions on marriage or reproduction would require more clout than they had. In 1910, for example, Partlow dismissed a proposal to sterilize habitual criminals with the comment "[T]he criminal would out-vote us when we vote on such a measure as that."[49] Soon, however, his Committee on Mental Hygiene was calling on the medical community to rally behind even broader eugenic measures. "Every doctor knows of instances of the wastefulness of allowing feeble-minded paupers, criminals and prostitutes to have children of the same kind as themselves," it reported to the MASA. "The members of no other calling in life, gentlemen, are in such a strategic position for convincing the people of the State and your representatives and Senators . . . of the saving of taxes which will be effected by preventing the feeble-minded from reproducing their kind."[50] Similar calls to the medical community were issued by mental health officials in other southern states.[51] Throughout the Deep South, every state medical association and countless individual physicians answered the call.

The Medical Community

"Another subject that demands the careful attention of the medical profession to-day is the care of the feeble-minded children," J. S. Ullman declared in his 1915 presidential address to the MSMA. "Dr. J. H. Fox of the staff of the Jackson Insane Asylum, has been urging some action on this matter for several years, and I suggest that the Association take some steps in the matter." In particular, Ullman endorsed eugenic segregation and sterilization, though he added that "the method is not so important, but in some way or other society must end these animalistic blood-lines, or they will end society."[52] Thereafter, the MSMA actively fostered eugenics in Mississippi.[53]

A standard pattern of eugenic activism by the medical community emerged in the states of the Deep South. Typically, southern physicians joined the cause much later than their colleagues in other parts of the country, and, as in Mississippi, they did so primarily at the urging of state mental health officials. Within the region, private physicians in Alabama and Georgia took the largest part in introducing eugenics—but even in those states, it took the pleas of mental health officials to engage the active support of the medical community.

Alabama began its long flirtation with eugenics at the dawn of the century, before any other state in the Deep South. In 1901, John E. Purdon, speaking on behalf of a regional medical society, addressed the annual meeting of the MASA on eugenics. After reporting the "proven fact" that criminality, insanity, epilepsy, and other alleged manifestations of degraded nerve tissue were hereditary, Purdon asserted that "it is essentially a state function" to restrain "the pro-creative powers" of the unfit. Focusing in on the measures that he had in mind, Purdon declared, "Emasculation is the simplest and most perfect plan that can be adapted to secure the perfection of the race." Acknowledging that the proposal, "at its first suggestion, must inflict a tremendous shock upon the ordinary members of the work-a-day world," Purdon assured the assembled physicians that "[n]o one who calmly and dispassionately considers what is here advanced can fail to perceive that the goodness, the greatness, and the happiness of all upon the earth, will be immeasurably advanced, in one or two generations, by the proposed methods."[54]

Purdon stressed the physician's role in this campaign for Alabama's eugenic future. "I need not say that the part played by the members of the medical profession in this coming revolution will be very important," he observed, especially the role of the medical "experts in nervous disease and criminology" who would "assist in adjudicating doubtful claims to survival."[55] At least some Alabama physicians accepted the challenge. In response to a MASA presentation on mental degeneracy in 1907, one physician asserted, "People who have hereditary taints ought not to be allowed to get married." Another added, "The potentially degenerate, those who are criminals, should be relieved of the possibility of procreating. In other words, the organs which generate such individuals should be removed." Partlow held back, however, cautioning, "I do not believe that any measure so stringent as to require castration or an ovariotomy in those who show marks of degeneracy could ever be enforced in this country."[56] Accordingly, Alabama's medical community did not become politically involved with eugenics until 1910, when Birmingham's influential local medical society petitioned the MASA to endorse state legislation "by which the operation of vasectomy may be legally performed on habitual criminals in accord with such laws as now obtain in the states of Indiana, Connecticut, Utah, and California, to the end that this criminal menace to society may be minimized by the removal of the power of such criminals to propagate their kind."[57]

After the MASA failed to act on this resolution because of some members' disagreement with a purely hereditary explanation for human behavior, Walter H. Bell of Birmingham took the floor at the 1911 annual meeting "to urge the doctors to prepare the people for this advanced step." He observed, "There is no subject upon which medical men are so universally agreed as upon the hereditary nature of most of the social diseases," and broadly defined the hereditarily unfit to include "any person who would produce children with an inherited tendency to crime, insanity, feeblemindedness, idiocy, or imbecility." The appropriate treatment in all such cases, Bell avowed, was compulsory vasectomy for men and "Fallopian section" for women.[58] When Birmingham's medical society resubmitted its sterilization petition in 1912, it resolved that the proposed law should reach beyond habitual criminals to "include such feeble-minded and hopelessly diseased persons as may be under the care of state institutions."[59] Once again, the MASA deferred action, on the grounds "that it involves a very important subject, one to which there are several sides."[60] The stand-off continued until 1915, when, after state mental health officials sanctioned eugenics, the MASA endorsed a limited proposal for the sexual segregation of mentally retarded children.[61]

A similar interplay between private physicians and public mental health officials promoted eugenics in Georgia. In 1913, soon after alienists began discussing eugenics at the state's mental health institutions, the *Journal of the Medical Association of Georgia* introduced its readers to the topic in an article on the general practitioner's role in public health. Describing eugenics as "the science of trying to breed a better race of men and women," the author admonished physicians, "If you have given this subject no special attention, I commend it to you. It is one that is attracting a great deal of attention at present among thoughtful men and women, and it bears a close relation to the public health."[62]

The Medical Association of Georgia (MAG) responded to this call by including three addresses on eugenics in the "scientific program" for its annual meeting later that year.[63] In the first talk, an Atlanta physician posited hereditary causes for the increasing number of confirmed idiots, imbeciles, epileptics, criminals, and mentally retarded persons. After describing traditional practices of institutionalization, which did not incorporate eugenics measures designed to prevent breeding, he asked, "If our laws are just in confining these unfortunates and criminals for the protection of society, why should it not be our duty when they become a ward of the commonwealth to render them sterile so as to lessen the burden of future generations?" He clearly acknowledged this duty by urging the association to endorse passage of a state law compelling eugenic sterilization. Such a law, he asserted in a bold proclamation of the eugenicist's dream, could help guarantee "to the child of the future the priceless heritage of physical perfection and masterful mind."[64] The other two addresses discussed segregation as an alternative to sterilization, and hereditary causes for insanity. In the discussion following the final presentation, two state mental health officials urged general practitioners to support eugenics legislation. A third declared, "The day is past for us to be satisfied with making a diagnosis of insanity, treating all cases alike, and trusting to the Lord to make the treatment work." For these Georgia alienists, eugenics represented the enlightened response to mental illness, and no one present verbally dissented.[65]

A similar view of eugenic progress marked MAG president W. B. Hardman's banquet address at the association's 1914 annual meeting. The address endorsed a wide variety of progressive reforms aimed at enhancing public health and promoting preventive medicine. Answering the rhetorical question "What is the medical gospel of the twentieth century?" Hardman intoned, "It is the gospel that is calling for eugenic laws, so that the creature of the future may be a better specimen of manhood and womanhood; that there may be fewer inebriates and cripples, that our alms houses, hospitals, penitentiaries, chain gangs and asylums may have fewer inmates, and that our streets may be free of beggars and perverts." According to Hardman, other elements of this gospel condemned the sweatshop, appealed for clean cities, preached temperance, and called forth the Pure Food Act; but eugenics held the greatest promise. With this address, the MAG responded to the appeal of state mental health officials by going on the record in favor of eugenics.[66]

The basic chorus was repeated in Louisiana, albeit in somewhat muted tones. Shortly before Louisiana alienists began promoting eugenics in their official reports, a prominent local physician commented at a 1910 meeting of the Southern Medical Association, "[T]he medical departments of Tulane University are alive with the importance of this movement."[67] Focusing on the eugenic sterilization of rapists, a female physician from New Orleans then added, "we ourselves, for the sake of our own people should try to establish or have enacted a law protecting our sisters and our descendants from the possibilities to which they have been exposed."[68] Local medical journals soon began discussing the general topic. For example, the New Orleans Medical and Surgical Journal first broached the topic in a 1914 editorial, which reported that a national mental health association had identified "hereditary influences" as a major cause of mental retardation and insanity. The editorial went on to reprint the association's recommendation "that all known dangerous defectives be kept under restraint; that reciprocal marriage laws be passed by the various States; that the principles of heredity and sex life be taught in the schools."[69] A year later, the national uproar following a Chicago surgeon's refusal to treat seriously handicapped newborns prompted the journal to comment, "Euthanasia is as yet a dream, and so is eugenics, and both will be, perhaps, until people are fair-minded enough to see that a hopeless life can avail nothing for itself or others."[70]

The Louisiana State Medical Society (LSMS) squarely addressed the issue at its 1917 annual meeting, when a presentation on mental retardation by the New Orleans public health officer and future LSMS president Joseph A. O'Hara took a strongly eugenic tack. After discussing the "'Mendelian' law" governing mental illness and retardation, O'Hara declared, "We should begin at once by seeing that the constituted authorities adopt methods for the prevention of mental abnormalities—by segregation and sterilization of defectives and degenerates, and supervision of marriage." Noting that twenty-one northern and western states provided eugenically segregated "colonies" for the mentally retarded, he admonished Louisiana to do likewise.[71] In the ensuing discussion, one local physician noted that "[a] general concert of action on the part of physicians, together with leading citizens and politicians, will ultimately result in the establishment of just such institutions right here in Louisiana." A state alienist, John Thomas cautioned that segregation alone was impractical. "You could establish a chain of buildings from the Mississippi River to the State of Texas, and, if well maintained and managed, you would fill them up in the course of time," he declared in a comment that seemed obvious to him but must have shocked many of those present. "The proper method, as we all know, would be castration and ovariotomy."[72]

Another discussant brought these two views together, observing, "A law has been passed in one of the States to the effect that no person can be discharged from an institution for the insane or the feeble-minded until that person consents to an operation which will sterilize him or her." This, he suggested, was the proper approach. "The question must be one of education," the physician added. "The responsibility for this rests upon the medical profession. Our Representatives and State Senators should be educated along these lines. A campaign of education is very essential before we can expect to accomplish any of these things which are taking place in other States."[73] These Louisiana physicians acted with dispatch. Within a year, their state legislature approved the construction of a state colony for the mentally retarded, and the medical community turned its attention toward securing authority for the forced sterilization of eugenically unfit patients within that colony and other state custodial institutions.

The timing and pattern of eugenic activism by the medical community was similar in all the states of the Deep South. During the second decade of the century, the need to sexually segregate or sterilize the mentally retarded became a popular topic at medical conventions throughout the region. The physicians assembled in Jacksonville, Florida, for the 1912 meeting of the Southern Medical Association (SMA) heard a typical plea.

"There is no issue so vital to the nation today as the rearing of the human thoroughbred," one speaker declared. "The time is fully ripe at least for negative eugenics, i.e., the prohibition of parenthood to the unfit."[74] The "unfit" often included the mentally ill and the epileptic as well as the mentally retarded, and reports of progress along these lines elsewhere in the country were invoked to spur action. For example, a Florida physician advised colleagues at the 1918 annual meeting of the Florida Medical Association, "The epileptic and feeble-minded have much in common." Among other similarities, both "transmit their defects from parent to child [and] have an unusually high birth rate." His solution was segregation: "More than half the states in the union have made appropriate provisions for the indigent epileptic population within their borders, and only sixteen remain that have not provided the necessary facilities to care for and train their feeble-minded. Florida does not have the distinction of being on the honor role in either count."[75]

At that time, he could have added, neither did any other state in the Deep South; but such comments drew a quick response. By 1920, every state in the region had begun a program of eugenically segregating the mentally retarded, with one state also authorizing their involuntary sterilization. Local physicians and state medical associations, working hand in hand with state mental health officials, played a major role in every case. Thus, for example, when legislation creating the Georgia Training School for Mental Defectives finally passed in 1919, a local newspaper reported, "The bill had, from its inception, the strong backing and support not only of the state board of health, but [of] leading specialists and physicians in the state."[76]

Though it is difficult to appreciate in retrospect, the southern medical community thought that by promoting eugenics it was doing good. "The medical profession is indeed organized to save life and foster it," the *New Orleans Medical and Surgical Journal* editorialized in 1916, "but, at the same time, the whole trend in modern thought is directed at the prevention of the causes which menace life, and there is now no greater burden carried by humanity than that which has been brought about by [mental] defectives."[77] In part because physicians then had so little to offer in the way of effective medical cures, prevention was the watchword of the day, and the weight of scientific opinion suggested that eugenics was the best means of preventing mental illness and mental retardation. "To continue a policy the results of which are so disastrous to the human family, so fatal to our race integrity, is race suicide, nay it is idiotic," a Louisiana physician declared at a 1912 meeting of the SMA. "We let these people marry and multiply. The insane, the criminal, the consumptive, the scorbutic, the syphilitic, aye, even the pauper on the poor farm marry with the sanction of the law and blessings of the church. That is sentiment; science would insist upon stirpiculture—the rational propagation of the human species."[78]

At bottom, however, many of these physicians confused their ethical obligations to the patient with broader notions of the public good. Searcy clearly did so when, at a eugenics conclave, he declared with respect to his own patients, "The keynote of the Conference should be to deny that all are alike valuable."[79] Joseph O'Hara betrayed a similar confusion before the LSMS when he argued that, without eugenic segregation or sterilization, the dysgenic effect of public health measures caused an "eclipse whose shadow overfalls all of our other good deeds."[80] Of course, a physician could believe that eugenic remedies benefited both the individual and society. For instance, a Georgia physician wrote in 1913, "It would be best for the community and a blessing for the patient or any other inmate of our insane institutions who would produce children with an inherited tendency to crime, insanity, feeble-mindedness or idiocy . . . to have the operation of vasectomy performed on the male and salpingectomy on the female."[81]

At times, however, the underlying ethical conflict became readily apparent. For example, at a 1910 MASA session on eugenics, one physician challenged the ethics of a speaker's recommendation that physicians treating a "degenerate" should warn the patient's potential suitors of the hereditary defects. "I have always felt," the speaker asserted in his own defense, "that on the moral side our code of ethics was too narrow." Another physician vigorously seconded this response by adding, "I think a good deal of our professional ethics is tommy-rot."[82] The utilitarianism that justified eugenics inevitably clashed with a deontological medical ethics that valued solely the patient's best interests, but the claims of modern science apparently demanded a response by the twentieth-century physician. "There is too much personal liberty in this country," a speaker on eugenics at a 1910 Southern Medical Association meeting concluded. "[T]he personal liberty of an individual means very little when compared to and contrasted with the welfare of society at large. The old idea of the greatest good for the greatest number is the one that has actuated us in the consideration of this or any kindred subject."[83]

Southern physicians based their arguments for eugenics squarely on the prevailing scientific theories of the day. References to Mendel, Weismann, Galton, Davenport, and Goddard permeated their statements on the subject. Expressing a sentiment that would become common within the medical community of the Deep South, an early article promoting eugenics in the *Southern Medical Journal* concluded with the exclamation "[M]ay Science and Common Sense join hands over the cradle of the unborn."[84] Of course, such appeals to scientific authority were nothing new for physicians of that era. During the preceding half century, the practice of medicine had benefited from a host of scientific breakthroughs in such diverse fields as bacteriology, cell theory, pharmacology, and radiology. Even though the full impact of these discoveries on medical treatment was not immediately realized, physicians quickly assumed the mantle of science in a fashion that enhanced their professional status.[85] Turn-of-the-century developments in genetics also offered the promise of significant medical benefits. In particular, as the *Southern Medical Journal* article declared, "The new science of Eugenics is pregnant with great possibilities for the human race."[86] Practicing physicians in the Deep South recognized that they did not fully understand the possibilities of eugenics, however, and local scientists could not provide much help because none of them were preeminent in this new field. Therefore, to legitimate and implement eugenic remedies, physicians and mental health officials throughout the region turned to national experts for assistance.

National Eugenics Expertise

"South Carolina for a hundred years or longer has occupied an enviable position as the brightest star in the galaxy of States," began one local physician's 1916 presentation in support of a segregated home for the state's mentally retarded. "There was a time when our neighbors were willing to accede to our contentions, thus disposed, they have forged ahead and to-day their great achievements require that we become more active and progressive. . . . [I]n fact, the little we have done, has been suggested by what has been accomplished by our Eastern and Western neighbors, who regard us as subjects of missionary work."[87] These comments aptly characterized the situation throughout the region. At that time, nearly every state outside the Deep South provided at least some sexually segregated housing for the mentally retarded, whereas no state within the region offered any such facilities. Further, no southern state had yet followed the lead of New York, California, Michigan, and nine other northern or western states in enacting eugenic sterilization laws.[88] Having registered such notable gains elsewhere, leaders of the American eugenics movement turned their attention to the Deep South. Meanwhile, some southern physicians, mental health officials, and civic leaders began courting this attention. The attraction was mutual, and the fruit of this intercourse significantly influenced the regional response to eugenics.

Northern and southern eugenicists interested in making a common assault on the separate problems of mental illness and mental retardation within the region had a powerful precedent. During the previous decade, after years of ignoring the problem, northern scientists and philanthropies had joined forces with southern physicians to eradicate the scourge of hookworm that had blighted the Deep South for decades. The new challenge appeared distinctly similar. In the case of both hookworm and eugenic deterioration, European scientists had first identified the problem, and northern experts had investigated it. Both conditions offered an explanation for the mental backwardness that seemed to plague poor southern Whites. Even after northern scientists definitely associated hookworm with the South, and southern physicians recognized the problem, it took a massive public health campaign funded by the Rockefeller Foundation to eradicate the disease.[89] Soon after this triumph, the problem of eugenic deterioration loomed large on the horizon, and seemed to call for a similar cooperative effort.

In some southern states, as the comments of the South Carolina physician suggested, nationally known eugenicists took the initiative in doing missionary work for their cause. Two related national organizations based in the North, the National Committee for Mental Hygiene (NCMH) and the Committee on Provision for the Feeble-Minded (CPFM), played this role in South Carolina. Founded in 1909 to promote progressive care and treatment for those suffering mental problems, the NCMH assumed a leading role in the American eugenics movement shortly before World War I, when it began conducting a series of state surveys, funded by the Rockefeller Foundation, to investigate and document the extent of mental retardation and mental illness.[90] Faced with a crisis caused by the resignation of the crusading superintendent of the South Carolina State Hospital for the Insane following a clash with the previous governor, the incoming governor, Richard I. Manning, invited the NCMH to examine conditions at the facility in 1915. During the ensuing investigation, the head of the newly created State Board of Charities and Corrections met with the eugenicist Alexander Johnson, who then served as CPFM field secretary. The CPFM, which had been established a year earlier by NCMH officials and other prominent eugenicists to educate the public about the dangers of mental retardation, promptly arranged a guided tour of Davenport's Eugenics Records Office in New York and Goddard's Vineland Training School in New Jersey for the South Carolina official, who returned home convinced of the need for eugenic segregation in his state. Thereafter, the campaign for eugenics in South Carolina was orchestrated by the Philadelphia-based CPFM, whose efforts were funded by generous grants from such northern philanthropists as Samuel S. Fels and Mrs. E. H. Harriman.[91]

Later in 1915, Johnson addressed South Carolina's State Board of Charities and Corrections about the social menace posed by the mentally retarded, and the need for eugenic segregation. Governor Manning and state legislative leaders attended the presentation. At Manning's request, Johnson returned a year later to address a joint session of the state legislature. "When a speaker from outside the state is pressed to return and address the coming session of the legislature on the care of the feeble-minded," a northern social-scientific journal crowed at the time, "there is hope for social progress."[92] On this second visit, Johnson was joined by the Vineland Training School specialist Helen F. Hill, who toured the state promoting the cause. "She could put you in stitches or wring tears from your eyes with the narration of her experiences as she traveled up and down the state," the first superintendent of South Carolina's State Training School for the Feeble-minded observed.[93] "Literature was distributed, stereoscope slides were shown, speeches and addresses were made all over the State," the superintendent later recalled, "so that, by the work of these 'propagandists' the way was paved for a bill that was to ask the Legislature to establish an institution for the care of the State's Mental Defectives."[94] The South Carolina Medical Association (SCMA) then endorsed the project after Johnson and Hill succeeded in stirring up widespread interest in it.[95]

When the legislature failed to complete action on the issue promptly, the CPFM primed Manning for further effort with a personalized inspection of Vineland and, in 1918, sent Johnson back for a third visit to the state. Once again, Johnson addressed a joint session of the legislature, but this time his efforts were rewarded by passage of a measure creating a State Training School for the Feeble-minded, the first such institution in the Deep South.[96] Soon after this facility opened, the NCMH returned to conduct a comprehensive survey of mental retardation throughout the state, leading to its recommendation that eugenic segregation be practiced more widely.[97] Although NCMH experts conducted this work, local physicians and state mental health officials were drawn in as advisers to approve the recommendations.[98]

Missionary work by northerners and national organizations also helped introduce eugenics in Florida. The Pittsburgh social worker Marcus C. Fagg carried an interest in eugenics with him when he moved to Jacksonville in 1910 as superintendent of the Children's Home Society of Florida, a private child-welfare agency. His arrival also gave the society a closer relationship with the National Conference on Charities and Correction, which actively promoted eugenics at the time. By 1913, Fagg was calling on the state to provide "permanent institutional care" for mentally retarded and epileptic children.[99] He played a major role in persuading the 1915 legislature to authorize a commission of physicians, mental health officials, and other interested citizens to study the need for a eugenically segregated institution for epileptic and mentally retarded children.[100] To document the necessity for prompt action, the commission released an interim report two years later asserting that at least one thousand Floridians suffered from epilepsy and mental retardation and stating its "belief that this number would be increased by a material percentage if a more careful and scientific study of the statistics were made."[101]

The Russell Sage Foundation of New York, under the direction of the progressive reformer Hastings Hart, then stepped forward to conduct an expanded survey of the state's public welfare needs. During previous visits to Florida, Hart had helped to establish the guiding principles of the Children's Home Society.[102] Now his organization assumed a larger role in shaping Florida's social service policies. The foundation's survey concluded "that the most acute and pressing social problem at the present time is the problem of the feeble-minded, and especially feeble-minded girls of child bearing age." Assuming the mixed humanitarian and eugenic stance that characterized Hart's work, the survey recommended, "The State of Florida should take immediate steps to protect these unfortunate children, not only as a matter of humanity toward this helpless and innocent class, but also as a matter of protection to the community."[103]

The final reports of both the commission and the foundation endorsed eugenic segregation. "The most appropriate method of providing for the feeble-minded is the colony plan," the foundation's report explained, because it allows them to "lead natural and happy lives while they can be so protected as to prevent them from multiplying their kind."[104] In this context, the adjective *natural* clearly referred to the pastoral setting of the ideal colony rather than to the physical activities permitted residents. At the commission's request, the state House of Representatives heard an appeal from Alexander Johnson before voting on the commission's recommendations.[105] In Florida as in South Carolina, this missionary work by national experts led the state medical association to accept the gospel of eugenics.

Elsewhere in the Deep South, state medical and mental health leaders endorsed eugenics prior to the intervention of outside organizations, but the subsequent support of these groups materially advanced the cause. This was most apparent in Georgia, where the Medical Association of Georgia and state alienists began championing eugenics as early as 1913. Three years later, the Georgia legislature followed the example of its Florida counterpart by authorizing a citizens' commission to study the issue of eugenically segregating the mentally retarded. The commissioners immediately turned to outsiders for help. "The Commission," they wrote in a letter to the governor, "realizing that the problem before it was one in which it needed the assistance of experts, got in touch with the National Committee for Mental Hygiene, who [sic] most generously volunteered to make the survey of Georgia without cost to the state." Not only did the NCMH use its expertise and Rockefeller Foundation funds to conduct a comprehensive survey of the staggering social and economic toll that it attributed to mental retardation in Georgia, but it also wrote the commission's final report, which advocated eugenic segregation.[106]

After debating the issue of eugenic sterilization in Alabama for more than a decade, the Medical Association of the State of Alabama worked with the state board of health in 1914 to form a committee of local physicians to collect "needful data in regard to 'defective children,' with a purpose to urge upon the state legislature the proper provision for the care of such 'defectives.' " That committee began by seeking the advice of mental health leaders from across the nation, including the NCMH.[107] Speaking for the committee at the 1915 MASA annual meeting, C. M. Rudolph urged the establishment of a state residential school for mentally retarded children. "Segregation seems to be the solution for the care of defectives," Rudolph concluded. "Segregate the defectives of one generation to prevent the multiplication of their kind in the next."[108]

When making his presentation to the MASA, Rudolph shared the podium with Searcy, Partlow, and the NCMH's leading spokesman on eugenics, Thomas W. Salmon. The four presented a united front in support of eugenic segregation, with Salmon having the additional objective of launching an Alabama state affiliate of the NCMH. Partlow, for one, was impressed by Salmon's participation. "I feel that we should congratulate ourselves on having him present," Partlow told the MASA, "and [should] be governed to a large extent in our beginning movements by his very able advice and counsel."[109] Partlow also agreed to chair a new MASA committee charged with organizing a mixed professional and lay Alabama Society for Mental Hygiene, and subsequently performed yeoman's work as the society's secretary and chief spokesperson. This society served as the NCMH's affiliate within Alabama by distributing NCMH literature, orchestrating support for a NCMH survey of Alabama's "defectives," and otherwise popularizing the cause of eugenic segregation and sterilization.[110]

When legislation to create the "Alabama Home" for the mentally retarded finally came up for a vote in 1919, the NCMH field representative Thomas H. Haines was on the spot in Montgomery praising Partlow's "vision of the great waste, both economic and social, which Alabama is sustaining by the entire absence of care and supervision of mental defectives," and urging local physicians "to lead the people in this eugenic and economic movement."[111] In a letter to the governor after the bill passed, Haines expressed "a great satisfaction in my part in pushing for the successful end now attained . . . in the plan for the state care of the feeble-minded."[112] At the same critical time, Hastings Hart dropped by for a hasty survey of state institutions calculated to underscore the need for a eugenically segregated facility for Alabama's "feebleminded children."[113]

The NCMH also played a supporting role in Louisiana, as did other national organizations. Salmon added his voice to those of local physicians and alienists by delivering a series of lectures on eugenic segregation in Louisiana and Alabama in 1916. He took this occasion to join W. H. Slingerland of the Russell Sage Foundation to present the case before the New Orleans meeting of the Southern Sociological Conference, an influential regional association of social reformers that had already displayed more than a passing interest in eugenics. "Louisiana has not found it possible to provide any special institutions for the feeble-minded and epileptics," Slingerland told the conference. Thanks largely to the work of local eugenicists, he added, "[t]he need is now recognized by all intelligent citizens."[114] To heighten this level of recognition, the NCMH followed up by conducting a survey to estimate the number of mentally retarded individuals already cared for at public expense in existing institutions. Nevertheless, it took a promotional campaign by the CPFM two years later, highlighted by an illustrated lecture by the association's executive secretary before the state House of Representatives, to secure passage of Louisiana's first eugenic segregation statute.[115]

During that same year, 1919, Haines acted as "Scientific Advisor" to the Mississippi Mental Hygiene Commission at the request of the state's flamboyant governor, Thomas G. Bilbo, a bombastic progressive with a vicious streak of racism.[116] Mississippi medical and mental health leaders had already endorsed the creation of a separate institution for the mentally retarded, but Haines arrived at a crucial moment to promote the project by means of a mental hygiene survey and a series of lectures. "Mississippi expects such an institution to be provided by the Legislature in 1920," Haines told the Mississippi State Medical Association, "and she expects the physicians of the State, with their vision of the problems, to lead in this movement." In case the physicians did not yet share his vision, Haines went on to describe some of the mentally retarded residents that he had seen in the state's prisons, poor farms, and orphanages. "In a county poor farm in Mississippi there is one imbecile white woman of about forty years who has more children than she can count, both white and black," he noted in a typical description of eugenic degeneracy calculated to inflame his all-White audience. "She has not the common sense of an ordinary seven-year-old girl, yet she is highly sexed. The community has entrusted her with the management of her life and really aided her, at the expense of tax payers, in producing these children who can be nothing but parasites all their lives long."[117]

Haines's message was simply "that the way to prevent much of the crime, immorality and degeneracy of the community today is to *prevent this class of persons from propagating.*" At the time, he recommended that the prudent approach "is to segregate the feeble-minded and keep them segregated during the reproductive periods of their lives. Something can be done in educating the public in regards to sterilization, but public opinion is not ready for this as a general policy, and, furthermore, we need a state institution in order to manage the sterilization successfully."[118] The MSMA promptly responded to Haines's address by forming a state affiliate of the NCMH, which drafted the legislation creating the state's first such institution. Bilbo endorsed this legislation and Haines's work in his 1920 farewell address to the legislature. Legislators then invited Haines to speak before the state Senate.[119] Ultimately, Mississippi danced to Haines's two-step tune by first opening an institution to segregate the mentally retarded and later authorizing their sterilization at that facility.

Mississippi ended up as the last state in the Deep South to take this first step. In a remarkable burst of activity that overcame decades of lethargy, legislation creating facilities for the eugenic segregation of the mentally retarded passed in every state of the region during the three-year period 1918-20. This outburst was not spontaneous, however. Developments in the science of eugenics provided the justification for action. State mental health officials, local physicians, and national experts then introduced these concepts into the Deep South during the second decade of the twentieth century. But a broader coalition of forces was required to embed them into public policy throughout the region.

CHAPTER FOUR

First Growth

Thomas Haines's 1919 address to the Mississippi State Medical Association reflected a strategic redefinition of eugenicists' immediate goals in the Deep South. When southern mental health officials and physicians had first begun promoting eugenic remedies earlier in the decade, they had most often advocated sterilization. This coincided with the enactment of compulsory sterilization statutes in sixteen northern and western states during the ten years preceding America's entry into World War I.[1] During and after the war, however, growing concerns about the constitutionality of these statutes, coupled with a sense of popular discomfort about the procedure, led to a lull in sterilization activities. For a time, national eugenics leaders shifted their attention to segregation and immigration restrictions as the favored means of purifying America's bloodlines.[2] Sterilization had not made much headway in the South prior to the war anyway, and now crusading national experts advised local physicians and mental health officials first to seek facilities for eugenically segregating the mentally retarded. Even though "public opinion is not ready" for sterilization, Haines had told the MSMA, "[a] state colony for the feeble-minded is an imperative necessity in Mississippi." According to Haines, the state could later transform the colony into a place "to manage the sterilization successfully."[3]

Southern eugenicists readily accepted this strategy. In Alabama during 1910–14, for example, eugenicists within the Medical Association of the State of Alabama had repeatedly failed to secure that organization's endorsement for a sterilization statute.[4] In 1915 a special committee of MASA members working on behalf of the state board of health investigated the issue further. This committee consulted extensively with Haines's superior at the National Committee for Mental Hygiene, Thomas Salmon. It ultimately recommended a comprehensive program of eugenic segregation that did not expressly include sterilization. In reporting this recommendation to the MASA, the committee member

C. M. Rudolph observed, "Some of you may ask, why not sterilize the feeble-minded and thus prevent them from procreating their kind? That, I feel, in connection with certain cases, would be a step in the right direction, but public sentiment is so strongly against it, that I fear it will be at best only a partial remedy." While clearly favoring sterilization as an ideal, Rudolph accepted segregation as a more immediately realizable means by which, in his words, "society is protected from many crimes, and future generations of feeble-minded persons can be materially decreased."[5] This approach gained the MASA's prompt endorsement.

South Carolina's governor, Richard Manning, who also worked closely with the NCMH on this issue, appreciated the same political calculus. "The feeble-minded must be kept from propagating themselves," he told the South Carolina State Conference on Charities and Corrections in 1916. "Two methods of doing this have been most frequently mentioned, namely, sterilization and segregation. The former, though legalized in several States, has not been welcomed by public opinion to any very considerable extent. Segregation, on the other hand, is practical so far as it goes."[6] Southern eugenicists had not retreated from their support for compulsory sterilization. By the end of the decade, however, they recognized that institutional segregation offered both an attainable alternative for curtailing reproduction by the mentally retarded and a possible stepping stone toward the public acceptance of sterilization.

Because sexually segregated training colonies for the mentally retarded offered immediate benefits to their patients, southern legislators and civic leaders could approve of establishing such facilities without necessarily endorsing eugenics. For many southerners, the thought that eugenic segregation might also benefit society in the long run simply cinched the argument. "Instead of being a liability to the community by his crimes, immoralities and further production of other defectives, by proper custodial care in a well organized colony the feeble-minded person may be converted into an asset," Haines told the MSMA. "He will not produce when left to his own devices. He steals, burns, murders and leads the life of a wanton. But when put into training adapted to his needs, while yet a child, he learns the joys of labor such as he can perform, and he is able to produce much of the food, shelter and clothing which he needs."[7] This idyllic vision of humanitarian colonies for the eugenically unfit was more appealing than the purely utilitarian arguments for compulsory sterilization.[8] Once these facilities were founded, however, they never became as self-supporting as originally hoped. Eugenicists then would argue that, with sterilization, these institutions could release their trained residents without further danger or cost to the community, and make room for the next generation of mentally retarded children.[9]

Thus, segregation offered a means to restrict breeding by those who were segregated, and to facilitate their future sterilization.

Haines's address incorporated one other element that was characteristic of eugenics advocacy in the Deep South during the years 1915–20. Not only did it promote segregation rather than sterilization and highlight the benefits of such a course to the individual as well as to society, but it also employed statistics and case studies from a statewide mental hygiene survey to demonstrate the urgent need for action.[10] "To carry out a successful educational campaign in any state or community, it is highly desirable to conduct some sort of survey," Haines confided to fellow social workers at the time. "It is not necessary to make a census of feeble-minded of a state," he explained; it is simply necessary to survey enough jails, almshouses, and asylums to "bring to light large numbers of feeble-minded upon whom the state is spending money" and to uncover "striking instances of familiar immorality and criminality." This supposedly scientific evidence allowed eugenicists to appeal not only to alienists and physicians but also to the general public, especially to upper-middle-class women. "Such facts can be obtained in Florida, Maine, or Oregon, but if one is working in Florida, it is important to get the facts in that state," Haines advised. "Outside of points of local color, which should always be sought and used, it is possible to point the argument, when speaking to a woman's club, for instance, by emphasizing the inhumanity of the neglect of feeble-minded women."[11] By thus broadening the base of support for sexual segregation, this strategy enabled eugenicists to reap their first fruits in the Deep South.

State Mental Hygiene Surveys

Haines made standard use of survey data in his address to the MSMA. He began by recounting the worst-case example of a mentally retarded murderer languishing in a county jail without understanding either his crime or his conviction. "During my visits to thirty-six jails and seven convict farms of Mississippi I have seen other feeble-minded murderers," Haines continued, without ever explaining how he had determined the mental status of these inmates. "I have seen in all forty-nine feeble-minded prisoners among the 248 in these jails." Extrapolating from these figures to cover the other jails and convict farms in the state, he concluded "that there are two or three hundred feeble-minded delinquents passing through the courts of Mississippi every year." The situation in local poor farms appeared even more desperate in Haines's report. "I have visited thirty poor farms in Mississippi. In these poor farms were 310 inmates at the time of my visit. Of these, 102 were feeble-minded, 11 were epileptic, 37 insane, and 23 blind." This last statistic underscored Haines's bias.

Earlier in his address, he had lumped together mental retardation, epilepsy, and mental illness as related manifestations of hereditary degeneracy even though there was then inadequate scientific evidence for doing so, but he never offered any justification for adding blindness to his tally of dysgenic woe. Further, Haines extrapolated from these figures "that there were about 170 feeble-minded persons in county poor farms in the state."[12]

Haines deliberately conducted the NCMH survey of Mississippi as a means to promote eugenic remedies, rather than as an objective scientific investigation.[13] His case studies and figures highlighted the physical and moral danger that the mentally retarded posed to society owing primarily to their crime and dependency. Accordingly, he sought them out in jails and poor farms rather than in stable home or workplace settings. This approach inevitably emphasized the ongoing economic cost borne by taxpayers. Indeed, after simply assuming that similarly large numbers of the mentally retarded crowded Mississippi's other penal and welfare institutions, Haines concluded that "the cost of maintenance of the feeble-minded, and the properly organized colony for the same, would be considerably less than the present cost of maintenance of these persons in our jails, penitentiaries, poor farms and orphanages." Of course, in Haines's view, the colony plan carried the further benefit of preventing these persons from propagating their kind. "It is as important to prevent the birth of a defective, who is destined to be a criminal or a prostitute," Haines declared in an inflammatory analogy, "as it is to prevent the infection with syphilis."[14] In this fashion, survey data evidenced the social and economic need for segregation.

Not all mental hygiene surveys from the Deep South were as slipshod as the NCMH survey for Mississippi, but some earlier local efforts bordered on the haphazard. In 1914, for example, an Alabama board of health committee used a particularly inexact method to calculate the number of mentally retarded children within its state. It began with the "generally accepted" estimate that 1 of every 300 persons was mentally retarded, which allocated a total of 7,100 such people to Alabama. Then it attempted to conduct its survey in conjunction with an annual state census of public school students, but applied too late. As an alternative, it sent letters to all Alabama physicians asking for a count of their "feeble-minded" patients between the ages of six and eighteen years, even though this classification of mental retardation was then somewhat new and was not accurately defined in the letter. In a move certain to compromise the responses, the letter expressly urged support for the establishment of a eugenically segregated institution for such patients. Nevertheless, the committee concluded, "Our method of taking the census proved to be extremely successful" because the finally tally—1,540 afflicted children—was in agreement with the initial estimate. "Thus, you see, our census is almost correct," the committee observed in a dizzying display of circular logic, "since there must be quite a number below the age of 6 years, and a larger majority above the age of 18 years."[15] Despite these gross methodological flaws, proponents used the committee's figures to document the urgent need for eugenic segregation.[16]

A year later, the Florida legislature authorized a citizens' commission dominated by physicians and mental health officials to investigate the need for a state institution to segregate epileptics and the mentally retarded. Like its Alabama counterpart, this panel equated numbers with need. At its first meeting, the commission decided to conduct a census to gauge the extent of the problem. It asked all county school superintendents to count the number of epileptic and mentally retarded students within their schools. Unfortunately, some superintendents never responded to the commission, and other responses were incomplete. The commission sought similar information from penal and social service institutions and engaged a field agent to test schoolchildren and inmates in a few counties, but ultimately conceded that "the field, in our opinion, [is] by no means covered."[17]

Rather than analyzing responses with the statistical tools then available, the commission simply tallied the total. "There are over one thousand known cases of feeble-mindedness and epilepsy existing in the State of Florida," the commission advised the legislature in an interim report, and suggested that many more would be found by a "more complete and scientific study of the situation." Of course, the reliability of this minimum figure rested on the ability of school personnel in a largely rural state, and in an era when IQ tests had only recently been introduced, to diagnose individual cases of mental retardation—in most instances, without the assistance of psychologists. Nevertheless, the results satisfied the commission. "The need of a State institution," it reported, "to properly care for these and all other cases of a similar nature that may be found proper wards of our State, is *unquestioned,* and we most respectfully urge the proper steps be taken to enact such legislation."[18]

If the findings of this commission helped move the Florida legislature toward authorizing a segregated colony for epileptics and the mentally retarded, then a 1918 follow-up survey of the state's social welfare needs conducted by the Russell Sage Foundation provided the final push in that direction. Although it, too, lacked specificity, the survey found that Florida "had many feeble-minded adults at the State Prison Farm and the State Insane Hospital." For a composite total, the surveyors, led by Hastings Hart, simply assumed "that there are at least as many feeble-minded as there are insane. Florida is already taking care of 1600 insane patients, and doubtless has at least that many feeble-minded." It then extrapolated from that figure: "If Florida has 1600 feeble-minded people, probably 400 of them are women of childbearing age." This struck at the heart of the matter. Asserting that "the chief preventative of feeble-mindedness is the care and segregation of feeble-minded girls during the child-bearing period," the survey concluded that "Florida ought to make immediate institutional provision for at least 500 of this class."[19] After the state commission charged with investigating this matter adopted the foundation's survey in its final report, the legislature acted.

The resulting legislation testified to the significance of this survey research. After noting that the survey "has been searching and exhaustive and shows an alarming state of facts," the statute's preamble stated that "there can be no doubt but that there should be established and created in this State an Institution for the care of the Epileptic and Feeble-Minded, where they can be segregated and more economically cared for than through the numerous charitable institutions now burdened with these unfortunates."[20] These legislative findings aped the findings of the survey. Both the survey and the preamble asserted that so many of the inmates, patients, and wards in Florida's public institutions were mentally retarded that the state could save money by caring for the retarded in a partially self-supporting "Farm Colony" suited to their needs and abilities. Further, of course, the facility would reduce the propagation of future degeneracy and dependency though eugenic segregation. Thus, the legislation directed that the colony be organized and managed "to the end that these unfortunates may be prevented from reproducing their kind, and the various communities and the State at Large relieved from the heavy economic and moral losses arising by reason of their existence."[21]

Here Hart's survey had a particular impact on the Florida legislation. Many eugenicists viewed the degenerate male with at least as much alarm as the degenerate female, because men could conceive more children and could more easily force their will on their partners than could women. Hart, however, primarily feared the "feeble-minded girl," whom he deemed "always a child" and "vastly more dangerous to the community than the feeble-minded boy."[22] Accordingly, his Florida survey denounced mentally retarded females of child-bearing age as "the most acute and pressing social problem at the present time."[23] The legislature carried this fear into public policy by prescribing that the colony's admissions standards give "preference, first, to girls and women of child-bearing age."[24]

The most comprehensive mental hygiene survey prepared in conjunction with the establishment of a state institution for the mentally retarded in the Deep South covered Georgia. This survey, like the others, was conceived and executed to promote eugenics legislation. It originated in a 1918 resolution that unanimously passed both houses of the state legislature.[25] The resolution began by noting, "Statistics that are available, but incomplete, show there are many persons in Georgia, minor and adults, who are feeble-minded and as such are a menace to the schools and to the communities in which they reside." It prescribed a eugenic solution to this problem by adding that most states "make special provision for the care, detention and training of the feeble-minded and for the prevention of the evils resulting from their neglect and their being allowed at large to marry and perpetuate and increase the serious tendencies of their unhappy condition." This resolution then directed a special citizens' commission to investigate "the numbers and condition of the feeble-minded persons in Georgia . . . and make such recommendation as may seem to them suitable to relieve the State of the menace of the uncared-for feeble-minded who are such a fertile source of crime, poverty, prostitution, and misery."[26]

Concluding that this assignment called for expertise beyond its ability, the commission turned the entire task over to the NCMH, which had volunteered to conduct the survey. The NCMH sent the eugenicist V. V. Anderson to Georgia for six months to manage a team of researchers. They conducted a state-of-the-art eugenic survey. Indeed, the leading social-scientific journal of the day hailed the Georgia mental hygiene survey as "one of the finest examples of its kind."[27] Rather than attempt a statewide census of the mentally retarded, the NCMH researchers examined the mental condition of those already in Georgia jails, almshouses, orphanages, and other public institutions. "In this way," they stated at the outset of their report, "we studied the relationship of Feeblemindedness to pauperism and dependency, to adult crime, vagrancy and prostitution, to juvenile vice and delinquency, and finally to education."[28] Naturally, they found ample evidence of what they called "the positive and close relationship of Feeblemindedness to much of society's most serious social problems."[29]

Once they limited the scope of the survey to public institutions, the NCMH researchers made every effort to follow scientific procedures. They identified a representative sample of public institutions, and then examined each individual in those facilities. "In no instance did we assume that one individual, rather than another, in jail, reformatory, prison, court, orphanage or school needed an examination," they reported. "[I]n no instance did we rely upon personal opinion or general observation to tell us who should, or should not, be examined."[30] For each individual, a complete personal case history was collected and a psychiatric examination given. Using the most recent advances in psychological testing, the researchers gauged the IQ of each subject.

The results captured the state's attention. The litany of statistics presented in the NCMH report enumerated the terrible impact of mental retardation in Georgia. "Feeblemindedness" apparently afflicted 40 percent of those in almshouses, 17 percent of a "run of the mine" sample of cases in juvenile courts, 24.1 percent of all inmates at the State Reformatory for Boys, 27 percent of all inmates at the Georgia Training School for Girls, 34 percent of the inmates in two typical county jails, and 42.8 percent of the women at the State Prison Farm.[31] Researchers also examined "122 immoral women and girls" caught in the state's judicial or penal systems to link the issue of mental health with that of prostitution, and found that 43.5 percent of these women suffered from mental retardation and another 10.6 percent were afflicted with psychopathic personality, epilepsy, or mental disease. "Are we not acting stupidly," the report asked regarding these mentally retarded persons, "in returning to the community girls whose future immoral conduct we can predict with as much certainty as we can predict that on a hot summer day most people will be found on the shady side of the street?"[32]

Despite the impersonal tone and scientific methods adopted by these NCMH researchers, an undercurrent of eugenic advocacy ran through their report. Surprised by their finding that "feeblemindedness" afflicted less than one in five men at the State Prison Farm, they simply assumed that "[u]ndoubtedly, the able bodied mental defectives [had been] placed out on the chain gang" and had thereby evaded the census. Of course, this convenient assumption reinforced the idea of putting the mentally retarded to work in farm colonies. Similarly, researchers gave the worst possible reading to the finding of mental retardation among 3.5 percent of students in three representative public school districts. Not only did these few students "greatly hinder the proper training of normal children," but the survey described them as "the 'grist' of our future courts, jails, reformatories and State prisons, and . . . the very backbone of the vast and grim procession of paupers, criminals and prostitutes of tomorrow."[33]

These findings led to the researchers' inevitable recommendations, wrapped up in scientific garb. "In the hard facts presented in foregoing tables, there is no sentiment," the report concluded. "We have shown that mental deficiency forms the very root of crime, prostitution, hereditary pauperism and the like conditions for which the State is spending vast sums of money. These problems are preventable, in that the one sensible, ready and efficient measure that can be carried out is to dam the stream near its source." That measure was eugenic segregation in a farm colony where a "large proportion of the Feebleminded can be usefully and profitably employed." This would be less expensive than the inappropriate existing forms of institutionalization, the report advised, and would "do much toward the prevention of insanity, pauperism and criminality in the coming generation."[34]

Georgia quickly acted on these recommendations. Describing the NCMH survey as a "masterly piece of work," the citizens' commission adopted the NCMH report as its own and transmitted the researchers' recommendations to Governor Hugh Dorsey.[35] The governor expressed similar satisfaction with the survey, and submitted the report to the legislature with his endorsement. "Suitable provision for the proper care and training of these unfortunates would not only be economy," Dorsey observed, "but would also save them, in many instances, to [sic] themselves and to society."[36] By then, the NCMH survey had generated widespread public support for a eugenically segregated state home for the mentally retarded. Researchers cultivated this response by presenting their findings before state conventions of teachers, attorneys, county officials, labor unions, and business groups. They also sent material to every school superintendent, Rotary Club, and newspaper in the state. Their efforts paid off. A flurry of newspaper editorials used survey statistics to call for prompt legislative action. It was perhaps even more critical for the final victory, however, that the NCMH findings helped galvanize the support of the Georgia Federation of Women's Clubs, which reportedly "pushed the movement through every individual club in the state." "As a result," one observer wrote, "when the legislature met there was little further work to be done, as practically every legislator met the commission with the statement that he had already been approached time and time again by his constituents and realized the need for the bill and would vote for it."[37]

Data from mental hygiene surveys served a similar function throughout the Deep South; Georgia simply had the most comprehensive initial survey.[38] The haphazard census in Alabama and the slipshod surveys in Florida and Mississippi proved equally serviceable in securing legislation. Everywhere, promoters adopted and adapted findings from other southern states to document the need for eugenic segregation.[39] And everywhere, women's organizations rallied to the cause.

Women's Organizations

Through individual activities and club work, some women played a significant role in southern state and local politics long before women gained the right to vote in 1920.[40] A 1919 field report from a national public health organization testified to this fact. "To anyone not conversant with conditions in the south it may seem as though the position of women in politics and government is unimportant" because of the regional opposition to female suffrage, the report stated. "As a matter of fact the women of the south appear to exercise an extraordinary influence in legislation quite out of proportion to the numbers of those whose efforts are brought to bear on any particular cause."[41] The contribution of women to the movement for eugenic segregation in the Deep South stands as a striking example of this. In part, it resulted from the influence of national eugenics organizations. It also reflected the increased political and social awareness then awakening in many upper-middle-class southern females. Both factors fit the larger national, and even international, picture.

Women took part in the eugenics movement long before it reached the Deep South. The pioneering English eugenics biometrician Karl Pearson was a prominent advocate of gender equality who regularly hired a significant number of female researchers for posts at the Galton Laboratory for National Eugenics. Charles Davenport followed suit in his training and hiring of field workers for the Eugenics Record Office (ERO), which was established and maintained on a grand scale by grants from a woman philanthropist, Mrs. E. H. Harriman. Indeed, Davenport's wife was a trained biologist and served as the assistant manager of the ERO.[42] Nicole Hahn Rafter recently calculated that women constituted about seven-eighths of the students trained in ERO summer sessions during the period 1910–18, and found that several of these students later wrote some of the influential eugenic family studies that served as eugenicists' primary propaganda tools.[43] Goddard, too, employed female researchers, and once opined that "the people who are best at this work, and also I believe should do this work, are women."[44] Fittingly, a female assistant named Elizabeth Kite collected most of the data for Goddard's landmark study of the Kallikak family.[45] Many of the prominent eugenicists sent to the Deep South to promote the cause, including the Committee on Provision for the Feeble-Minded's field secretary Alexander Johnson and the NCMH psychiatrist V. V. Anderson, were accompanied there by female assistants.[46] Women also actively participated in NCMH-affiliated state mental hygiene societies in the Deep South as well as elsewhere in the country.[47]

The acceptance of women as eugenics researchers stood in sharp contrast to their general exclusion from most other types of scientific work during the early twentieth century.[48] Several factors contributed to this deviation from the norm. Goddard viewed women as superior observers of familial relationships.[49] Pearson and a fellow English eugenicist, Havelock Ellis, linked eugenics with empowering women to choose fit mates.[50] More recently, historians have suggested other factors: for instance, females could more easily elicit personal information from strangers than could males, they willingly fit into subservient roles as assistants to male scientists, and they worked for less money.[51] Whatever attracted female researchers to work in eugenics probably drew women to the field generally. The historian Daniel Kevles computed that women constituted half the members and one-quarter of the officers of the British Eugenics Education Society; played a prominent role in local eugenics groups in the United States; and provided much of the public audience for the topic in both places.[52] In her groundbreaking historical study of birth control in America, Linda Gordon found that "concern with eugenics was characteristic of nearly all feminists of the late nineteenth century," some of whom "thought women were natural eugenicists."[53]

Despite the distinctive cultural traditions that still clung to the region, these trends were followed in the Deep South. Indeed, in every southern state, "women's clubs" vied with medical associations in providing the most ready audiences for eugenicists. At the time, these clubs represented a progressive advance in the women's movement. The practice of formally organizing women's clubs began in the North primarily as a means for upper-middle-class women to get together on a regular basis for educational and social activities. The first southern women's club was formed in New Orleans during the 1880s as an organization of professional women and was designed to promote economic and political opportunities for its members as well as to serve as a social outlet. Once that club opened its membership to nonworking women, however, its political focus shifted to the promotion of reforms designed to benefit children.[54]

As women's clubs spread to nearly every city in the Deep South over the next two decades, political activism, especially on behalf of progressive children's issues, remained a top priority. Thus, the 1919 public health report observed that southern women's clubs "exercise a potent influence in securing the passage of state laws and municipal ordinances. In this respect these clubs are quite different from similar organizations in the north."[55] Soon after its founding in 1898, for example, the South Carolina Federation of Women's Clubs began campaigning for a compulsory school-attendance law.[56] The Georgia Federation of Women's Clubs adopted the same cause, and in 1916 crowed, "The compulsory school attendance measure enacted by the Georgia Assembly last August is the logical outcome of twenty years of hard work by Georgia women." That same year, this organization claimed credit for the enactment of progressive legislation restricting child labor, providing free textbooks at public schools, and establishing a training school for wayward girls.[57] The eugenic segregation of mentally retarded children represented a logical addition to this agenda.[58]

Eugenicists recognized southern clubwomen's political influence and potential interest in scientific childbearing, and cultivated the support of these women. When an Alabama board of health committee completed its investigation into the need for eugenic segregation in 1915, for example, it mailed a copy of its highly provocative report, "A Plea for Better Care for Alabama's Feeble-Minded," to the president of each women's club in the state. The only other groups targeted for this promotional mailing were legislators and newspaper editors.[59] The Florida child welfare advocate Marcus Fagg regularly spoke at women's clubs throughout his state on the need for restricting marriage and reproduction by the mentally retarded.[60] In 1919, an Emory University physician raised these same issues before an elite Atlanta "Mothers Club" in an address stating, "Mothers of Men, this is a question demanding our serious thought and more than this, our concerted action if we are to contribute our share toward the prevention and control of this unfortunate class of citizen."[61] Similarly, professional propagandists for the cause from the CPFM and the NCMH regularly addressed women's clubs during their trips to the Deep South, often with female researchers trained at the ERO making the presentations.[62]

This strategy worked. In direct response to Fagg's pleas, for example, the 1913 report of the Legislative Committee of the Florida State Federation of Women's Clubs asserted, "In order to decrease the number of feeble-minded, insane and blind, defectives of these classes must be prevented from reproducing their kind."[63] Thereafter, the Florida federation actively championed a segregated institution for the mentally retarded. As one proponent reported to the Florida Medical Association in 1918: "The Women's Clubs are asking for facts and figures regarding the subject."[64] In South Carolina, another proponent used such facts and figures to persuade the state federation of women's clubs to shift the focus of its legislative lobbying from the building of a girls' reformatory to the establishment of a eugenically segregated colony for the mentally retarded. "Mr. Johnstone of the Board of Charities and Corrections appeared before the executive board of the Federation, and stated to us that while at first he had deemed the most vital need of the State was a girls' reformatory, a more recent survey had demonstrated the greater need of an institution to care for the feeble-minded," the federation's legislative committee reported to all club members in 1916. "Your committee met with Governor Manning, Mr. Johnstone, and representative members of the House and Senate, and, after careful, deliberate consideration, it was decided to . . . work for the greater need."[65]

Johnstone underestimated these women. In 1918, the federation "used all its organizational efforts" to secure not only a State Training School for the Feeble-minded but also a girls' reformatory, and legislation for the medical inspection of schoolchildren.[66] Their efforts included a massive promotional campaign that alerted citizens to the issue by means of direct mailings to all club members and the distribution of leaflets in major communities.[67] Events unfolded similarly in other states throughout the region. Further south, for example, Florida women's clubs began by seeking an official investigation into the issue. "The State Federation of Women's Clubs," the state's leading newspaper reported in 1915, "has cause to be proud of the way in which so far its advocated measures have been received in the [legislative] committees to which they were referred. The senate committee on public health today reported favorably without amendment the bill providing for a commission of five to be appointed by the governor to look into the matter of need for an institution for the care of the epileptic and feeble-minded of the state." A sizable delegation of clubwomen attended this committee hearing, and kept the pressure on until the measure passed.[68] The governor then appointed one federation member to serve with three physicians and a businessman on this commission.[69] After this commission endorsed eugenic segregation, clubwomen joined in efforts to implement its recommendation.

During the period 1915–20, the federated women's clubs in every state of the Deep South played a decisive role in the establishment of eugenically segregated public institutions for the mentally retarded. These efforts culminated on April 2, 1920, when, as one local newspaper reported, "amid much applause from the women in the galleries who had worked so earnestly in its behalf," Mississippi's House of Representatives approved legislation making that state the sixth and last state in the region to authorize such a facility.[70] It must have been a bittersweet moment for many of these women, however, because that same body had just defeated their efforts to make Mississippi the final state needed to approve the Nineteenth Amendment.[71]

This scene of a legislature approving a campaign by women for eugenic segregation while disapproving demands for female suffrage was not unusual in that place and time. A similar mind-set led to the appointment of a woman to the Florida Commission for the Study of Epilepsy and Feeble-mindedness at a time when few females received other state appointments. This commission then hired a respected female eugenics researcher, Clara Van Norstrand, as its field agent to investigate the extent of mental retardation in selected Florida counties.[72] Southern men apparently accepted women's having a role in shaping state policies on handicapped children and eugenic childbearing, even as they rejected any general role for women in governmental decision making. Accordingly, Georgia's governor also appointed a woman to his state's committee investigating the issue in 1918, and appointed two women to the initial five-person public welfare board, which the legislature created in 1919 to monitor the state's new Georgia Training School for Mental Defectives and other social service agencies.[73]

It became a common practice throughout the region for women to hold a significant minority of seats on the boards directly controlling the new institutions for the mentally retarded. Indeed, the laws in two states required female representation on this board, while a third law encouraged it.[74] If male legislators later reneged on their promises for these institutions, women supporters of these facilities fought back. For example, when Mississippi's legislature considered repealing the law that authorized the construction of a eugenically segregated institution for the mentally retarded, a state women's club leader called on all clubwomen to lobby their legislators. "Dear women, let us fight with all the state pride that is in us to prevent this backward step," she angrily declared. "Let us pray, that with the solemn charge that is laid upon us we may walk firmly, yet softly—act intelligently, and be reasonable in all things, that we may do our women's work in the finest, most womanly way."[75]

The place of women within the management of these new institutions was especially complex in South Carolina. The legislation that created the State Training School for the Feeble-minded placed it under the jurisdiction of the mental health hospital's board of regents, which at the time included one woman. Further, the statute directed the regents to "appoint an advisory committee of three women, . . . who shall visit the institution at least quarterly and shall advise with the Regents as to its management."[76] The regents then considered appointing a woman as superintendent, until the attorney general ruled that the state law barring women from public office covered this post. "It is considered by all that a position of this kind is not at all attractive to the average man in any walk of life," the regents reasoned. "Only one having a profound sympathy for the unfortunate class which the State is trying to help is morally qualified for the place."[77] They clearly viewed this as woman's work. Frustrated in their efforts to hire a female superintendent, the regents nevertheless filled many positions at the facility with women, including the key post of staff psychologist.[78] Indeed, following the tradition of female eugenic field workers, the State Board of Public Welfare, which monitored conditions at the training school and other state social service institutions, regularly employed single women as its psychological field agents. During the 1920s, these agents conducted IQ tests at public institutions and schools across the state in an ongoing effort to identify individual cases of mental retardation.[79]

In large part, southern women assumed these positions within the eu-

genics movement at the invitation of male physicians, mental health officials, and politicians. Usually they played supportive roles advocating or
implementing policies set by men, much as occurred in South Carolina.
Befitting the site of the region's first women's club, however, some New
Orleans feminists took the lead in championing eugenics. As early as
1915, for example, Maud Loeber of New Orleans became the first female physician from the Deep South to address a major regional conference on the topic. "It is a known fact that when two imbeciles marry all
their progeny will be imbeciles, and when a normal person marries an
imbecile over one-half of their progeny will be imbeciles," she advised a
major symposium on health sponsored by the Southern Sociological
Congress.[80] By this time, another New Orleans woman attending this
conference, Jean M. Gordon, already had taken charge of the Louisiana
eugenics movement—a position she never relinquished.[81]

Jean Gordon was the youngest daughter in a socially prominent New
Orleans family. She and her two older sisters, Frances and Kate, never
married, and lived together in a comfortable home in the city's fashion-
able Garden District. While Frances tended the home, Kate and Jean pursued active careers as progressive reformers. They cut their political eye-
teeth in 1891, when they participated with a large number of prominent
Louisiana women in a successful campaign to end a notoriously corrupt
local lottery. Following this triumph, Kate became a leading suffragist,
while Jean concentrated on social reform. Kate eventually gained the
wider reputation of the two, initially as a leader of the state women's
rights movement and later as recording secretary for the National American Women's Suffrage Association. At the time, one of the few reform
movements attracting as much national attention as the campaign for
women's suffrage was the crusade against child labor. Jean latched onto
this second cause during the 1890s, which eventually led her into the eugenics movement.[82]

The road from child labor reform to eugenics took several turns for
Jean Gordon. Her persistent efforts for state restrictions on child labor,
which included organizing both a women's club investigation of the issue
and a statewide lobbying campaign, drew her to the attention of state
leaders. These efforts finally bore fruit in 1906, with the passage of
Louisiana's first child labor law and a state constitutional amendment
permitting women to serve as the factory inspectors enforcing the new
act. Gordon then became the first female factory inspector in New Orleans, which placed her in contact with many working-class children. She
quickly became obsessed with their poor mental and moral condition. At
the time, she already headed the board of the Milne Home for Destitute
Orphan Girls, a nascent entity endowed with much land but no facilities

or money. Her interests in child labor and in the Milne Home merged in 1908, when she heard Hastings Hart speak on the "problem of the feeble-minded" and the need to prevent mentally retarded females from reproducing their kind. Thereafter, she sought to establish and maintain the Milne Home as a private institution for eugenically segregating and sterilizing mentally retarded women. "To some of us had come the knowledge of the menace of the feeble-minded to our civilization," she or her sister Kate later wrote, "and knowing after long years of experience that New Orleans people learn only through actual demonstration, we gathered together this little experimental station."[83]

During the remainder of her life, Gordon dedicated most of her public service to the Milne Home and the wider eugenics movement. She almost singlehandedly raised the funds to open the Milne Home in 1919 and later served as its superintendent; actively participated in the work of the Louisiana Society for Mental Hygiene; supported legislation creating a eugenically segregated State Colony and Training School for the mentally retarded and then served on its governing board; and crusaded throughout the 1920s for a eugenic sterilization statute.[84] Even though a sincere concern for children attracted Jean Gordon to this work, deep streaks of elitism and racism undoubtedly predisposed her to a eugenic remedy. In their suffrage work, both Gordon sisters supported the additional enfranchisement only of educated White women, and viewed that as a means of diluting the strength of the male Black vote. "The question of white supremacy is one that will only be decided by giving the right of the ballot to the educated, intelligent white woman of the South," Kate Gordon once declared. "Their vote will eliminate the question of the negro vote in politics."[85] Jean Gordon fully shared this elitist and racist outlook, and once refused an invitation to a White House meeting on children's issues because Booker T. Washington was also invited. "I should have been only too glad to have attended," she later wrote, but for her policy of declining "to attend any function where [she] would be placed on equal terms with negroes."[86] The hereditarian attitudes that underlay eugenics also justified elitism and racism. In Gordon's hands, the Milne Home became a vehicle for racial purity by admitting only Whites and thereby preventing those who might weaken the White race from breeding.[87]

After opening the private Milne Home and helping to establish a similar public institution prior to 1920, Gordon continued to lead the Louisiana eugenics movement until her death in 1931. In doing so, she represented the extreme example of the role that a southern woman could play in the effort. A male physician from Louisiana acknowledged this role in 1919, when he advised his colleagues within the Louisiana

State Medical Society that the "first step" to a comprehensive eugenics reform program was the recognition "of our womanhood, of their intuitive perception, of their inspiration, of their power, and our solicitation of their active cooperation with us in the work."[88] Reflecting such cooperation, women's clubs and medical associations throughout the Deep South, acting in consort with state mental health officials and national eugenics organizations, by 1920 had secured legislation to establish a sexually segregated public institution for the mentally retarded in every state of the region.

Enabling Legislation

Once the coalition of forces supporting it became sufficiently large, legislation creating state institutions for the mentally retarded passed with little difficulty. Probably because the idea seemed good from both a eugenic and a humanitarian point of view, no organized opposition to it ever emerged within the Deep South. The legislation's proponents simply needed to overcome natural legislative inertia against new programs and competing demands for scarce state governmental resources, not principled resistance. The story was much the same throughout the region. The concept of sexually segregating the mentally retarded to prevent them from reproducing had begun gaining adherents among southern mental health officials and physicians early in the century. National advocacy organizations such as the NCMH and the CPFM then stepped in with lectures and surveys to galvanize the support of state medical associations and generate interest within other progressive groups. Women's groups proved particularly responsive to this issue, and worked together with physicians and alienists in every state to promote the legislation. Other organizations, such as the state bar, trade unions, and education associations, lent their endorsement in some states, but they never played a decisive role.[89] As the coalition of supporters broadened, soft-hearted humanitarian pleas for these institutions as havens of enlightened care to needy individuals mixed with hard-headed eugenic demands for them as a means to protect society from these same people.

Supporters in every state lobbied the governor as well as the legislature, and at a minimum obtained his consent to sign the legislation. Some governors did even more. The governors of Alabama and Georgia endorsed the proposed legislation in formal messages to their legislatures.[90] In Mississippi, Theodore Bilbo included a "Home and Colony for the feebleminded" among the list of progressive reforms that he requested from the legislature, and chaired the new facility's initial board of trustees after his retirement as governor.[91] South Carolina's governor, Richard Manning, a wealthy and well-educated progressive who hailed from a long line of state political leaders, worked closely with the NCMH and the CPFM for mental health reform during his administration and sponsored the bill creating a State Training School for the Feeble-minded. "We are progressive Democrats," Manning proclaimed upon taking office, "and we must have the courage to do justly to each and every class of our citizens even if this requires legislation hitherto untried by us." A eugenically segregated State Training School for the Feeble-minded fit splendidly into his reform program, along with compulsory school attendance and limits on child labor.[92]

The arguments that Manning made in support of his legislation exemplified those advanced by proponents of eugenic segregation throughout the Deep South. In one representative speech, he hit all the main points. Manning began with an individual case history of the type commonly featured in eugenics propaganda. Here, the story of "Jenny" illustrated how a mentally retarded White female could fall into a desolate life and propagate her deficiency "without any intention or appreciation of moral wrong on the part of the poor unfortunate girl-woman."[93] The message was already obvious: eugenic segregation in a state colony would help both the Jennys of the world and the general public. At a subtler level, Manning here shifted responsibility for Jenny's actions from the woman herself to the state.

Manning then discussed the four allegedly "fundamental conclusions" of science that underlay eugenics. "In the first place, feeble-mindedness, so far as medical science now knows, is absolutely incurable." He took this to justify permanent custodial care for the afflicted. "In the second place, a high percentage of feeble-mindedness is inherited," which suggested that eugenic segregation could alleviate the problem. "In the third place, statistics show that the feeble-minded propagate faster than normals, in fact, probably twice as fast." Manning dramatized this point with local case histories. "The State Board of Charities and Corrections had found one woman, who, according to her own count, is the mother of ten illegitimate children," he noted. "Another can stand on her doorstep and point out the homes of seven of her illegitimate children. Still another has had six children, one of whom is an idiot, another a mulatto." Even though these stories did not demonstrate that a disproportionate number of these twenty-three children were mentally retarded, they had a powerful rhetorical impact in conservative South Carolina. "In the fourth place, the number of feeble-minded is really alarming." Manning used this as an opening for a discussion of the extent of the dependency and degeneracy resulting from this source. According to Manning's figures, "fifty per cent of all the inmates of our poorhouses are feeble-minded," as were a quarter of all criminals and half the prostitutes.[94]

These scientific "facts" inevitably called for a eugenic response. After dismissing sterilization as not "welcome by public opinion," Manning recommended segregating the mentally retarded into state training colonies where they could be "happy and contented." "The humanitarian is not the only argument for State provision for the feeble-minded," he quickly added. "Any social malady that finds expression in a continual stream of persons to our charities, courts, poorhouses, and other institutions, is of great economic, as well as humanitarian, concern." Training colonies could reduce these current costs for the present generation, Manning suggested, while eliminating much of the future load for generations to come. "South Carolina must undertake to discharge its duty both in helping a great many unfortunates, and in attacking the problems of pauperism, degeneracy and crime in a fundamental way," he concluded.[95]

Manning's arguments for eugenic segregation, and others like them, were difficult to counter effectively without challenging their underlying scientific assumptions. The position taken by southern physicians and national experts virtually precluded such a challenge, and if anyone sought to make such a challenge at that time, it never received significant attention. Indeed, little opposition of any type appeared. No major newspaper in the Deep South editorialized against this first wave of eugenics legislation, while those supporting it fully appreciated its intent. "This is an instrumentality by which society protects itself and preserves its mental integrity," South Carolina's *Greenville News* wrote.[96] In Mississippi, the *Jackson Daily News* added that segregation would "put a final stop to the increase of much useless humanity."[97] A campaign brochure entitled "An Institution for Feeble-Minded of Alabama" said it all. "They do not work. They are immoral. They commit crimes. They multiply like rabbits, and their children are feeble-minded," it asserted. "This institutional care and training of the feeble-minded (1) Purifies human stock, and (2) Reduces taxes."[98]

Even though the legislation created new programs at a time of scarce resources, southern lawmakers expressed their overwhelming support for it. In response to Manning's initiative, South Carolina acted first. The measure passed the state's House of Representatives by a comfortable margin of seventy to thirty during the 1917 session, but was held over to the next year by the Senate. After a flurry of activity by administration officials and national eugenicists, the upper house approved the measure by a vote of thirty-six to two within a week of the legislators' return for the 1918 session.[99] The Louisiana legislature also acted in 1918, with a combined total of only four votes cast against the measure.[100] The results were similar the next year in Alabama, Florida, and Georgia, where only a handful of lawmakers voted no. Indeed, only one representative and no senator opposed the measure in the Sunshine State.[101] Mississippi was the last to act, and proved the most reluctant. The state's lower house had voted down a premature proposal to establish a "school for the feeble-minded" in 1916, the only such defeat in a southern state.[102] Four years of prodding by Bilbo and a NCMH survey turned the tide by 1920. Both houses of the legislature initially approved the measure by a comfortable margin in that year, but efforts to resolve minor differences between the versions passed by the two bodies broke down into a serious dispute over the facility's location shortly after Bilbo left office. His successor then narrowly salvaged the measure by making an emotional appeal before the House.[103]

During the floor debate on these measures in the various state legislatures, lawmakers did not raise principled objections to the concept of eugenic segregation. Dissenters primarily worried about cost. "I would gladly vote to supply all necessary funds to provide for the care and training of the feeble-minded under and in connection with the State Hospital for the Insane," a South Carolina representative asserted, "but I am opposed to the useless creation of new offices."[104] Similarly, a Georgia legislator declared that "he was thoroughly in sympathy with the purposes of the measure but did not know where the money could be found to carry them out." Denouncing the measure as "the entering wedge for new expenditures that might grow to millions of dollars," another Georgian complained that "it would pave the way for putting criminals in a state institution and keep them from working roads, where they belonged."[105]

In a typical response to such charges, one Georgia supporter shot back that the new program would "relieve the burden of the state rather than add to them [sic]." Another legislator defended the proposal as "a measure of conservation rather than appropriation as the state would be eventually saved large sums of money by having her mental defectives cared for."[106] Some legislators also noted the charitable features of the legislation. For example, the measure's chief legislative sponsor in South Carolina proclaimed, "In the name of humanity, I appeal to you gentlemen of the house, in behalf of those people who can not help themselves."[107] In Florida, the chief sponsor told the state Senate that "no measure before this session should appeal more to the human side of the legislature than this one."[108] No opponent attempted to resist this humanitarian plea by suggesting that some of the people covered by the legislation might want to be free, or should have a right as human beings or citizens to bear children. Despite the federal constitutional challenges then besetting eugenic sterilization throughout the country, no southern legislator questioned whether compulsory eugenic segregation might violate the Constitution. The analogy to the then-common practice of quarantining carriers of infectious diseases appeared too strong, even though here the "infection" typically required a deliberate act by the "carrier." Furthermore, in that era of Jim Crow lawmaking and strict racial segregation, southern legislators were unlikely to raise issues of a minority group's federal constitutional rights.[109]

The statutes enacted as a result of this legislative process were quite similar throughout the Deep South, and closely followed the established national pattern. Each of the new institutions was expressly and exclusively created to segregate, train, and care for a class of persons identified as "feeble-minded," except that the Florida institution could also accept epileptics.[110] The statutes defined the term *feeble-minded* much as Davenport, Goddard, and other nationally known eugenicists would define it. The Louisiana law, for example, broadly covered anyone who, through not mentally ill, suffered from an inborn mental defect "so pronounced that he is incapable of managing himself and his affairs, or being taught to do so, and requires supervision, control and care for his own welfare, or for the welfare of others, or for the welfare of the community."[111] The final phrase in this definition, which appeared in some form in all the statutes, literally invited the introduction of eugenic considerations into any determination of "feeble-mindedness." Two of the statutes went on to specify "[t]hat the greatest danger of the feebleminded to the community lies in the frequency of the passing on of mental deficiency from one generation to another, and in the consequent propagation of criminals and paupers."[112] The Georgia and Florida statutes gave this point a potentially sexist twist by providing a preference in admission to "women of child-bearing age," even though the science of the day held that fathers were as likely as mothers to transmit mental retardation to their children.[113]

The various laws contained similar procedures for determining "feeble-mindedness" and committing persons to custodial care. Most states permitted the voluntary commitment of "feeble-minded" children by their parents or guardians, subject only to the approval of the institution's superintendent. Georgia and South Carolina also allowed this request to come from certain county or school officials having custody of the child.[114] Involuntary commitment procedures were more complex, but they inevitable began with a petition to the local court. Relatives typically initiated this process for an afflicted individual. If no relative acted, and the individual lacked supervision or "was at large," any local citizen could file the petition. The local judge then decided the issue, typically on the basis of an examination of the individual by two physicians or by one physician and one psychologist.[115] Only Mississippi provided the option of a jury trial, but this involved a special jury half of whose members were physicians.[116] The Alabama statute contained a further procedure empowering the superintendent of the state mental health hospital to commit any "person confined in a poor house, jail, an orphanage or a boarding school in the State."[117]

Once committed to the custody of one of these institutions, an individual would remain there until, in the words of one typical statute, he "no longer constitute[d] a menace to himself or others."[118] All of the statutes left this determination primarily to the discretion of the facility's superintendent, though three of them permitted inmates or their families to initiate a process of judicial appeal for release.[119] Of course, the presumption existed that these individuals would remain a menace to others forever, or at least so long as they could bear children, because their affliction was incurable and hereditary. Ideally, they would come to the institution as children, receive training for manual tasks, and remain to live and work within the facility's spacious grounds. Thus the Florida statute specified that the institution must "include the three departments of asylum, school and colony co-ordinated and conducted as integral parts of a whole, to the end that these unfortunates may be prevented from reproducing their kind."[120] All of the statutes talk of training schools, residential cottages, working farms, and strict sexual segregation. Furthermore, the White founders of these state institutions demonstrated their exclusive concern with the betterment of their own race by limiting all of these facilities either by statute or practice to Whites.[121]

With the enactment of these statutes in every state of the Deep South during the period 1918–20, the region began catching up with the rest of America in implementing eugenically sound policies. The coalition of state and national eugenicists that achieved this result could not rest, however. The statutes contained inadequate appropriations to meet local needs or to match efforts elsewhere in the country. According to the mental hygiene surveys, there were in the Deep South far more people who should not breed than could fit in the new institutions. A broader program was needed. Eugenicists generally regarded sterilization as an integral part of any comprehensive eugenics program, but only the Alabama statute authorized such a procedure. Even that provision did not necessarily reflect public acceptance of sterilization within the region. The drafter of the statute, the eugenicist William Partlow, simply included the authority "to sterilize any inmate" among the powers given to the institution's superintendent, and it slipped through without generating any public comment.[122] Efforts to implement a broader eugenics agenda encountered growing resistance during the 1920s, as appeals for segregated facilities that at least promised help for afflicted individuals gave way to coarse, utilitarian arguments for sterilization.

CHAPTER FIVE

Taking Root

The opening of state institutions for the mentally retarded throughout the Deep South around 1920 fit into a larger movement for public health that was then sweeping the region. The superintendent of Alabama's state facility for the mentally retarded, William Partlow, alluded to this in an address to the Medical Association of the State of Alabama on historical developments in medicine. "Probably the greatest epoch in medical history for all time occurred about the middle of the 19th century," Partlow observed. "The notable works of Pasteur, Klebs, Hueter, Davaine, and Koch in the discovery and classification of certain living vegetable and animal organisms or germs associated with disease . . . opened up avenues and possibilities as to prevention, sanitation, and public health, giving to the world of mankind a benefaction, of which the value to human life can never be estimated."[1] The linking of particular transmittable microbes to certain dread diseases led to a variety of public health campaigns aimed at preventing specific illnesses by eliminating the causes of contagion.

Even though hereditarian explanations for mental illness and retardation relied on genetic "contagions" rather than microbial ones, the eugenics movement appeared similar to these public health campaigns at the time. "We do not hesitate to take away the liberties of a man with smallpox for the protection of society," an Emory University pediatrics professor declared in 1920, "neither should we hesitate to take away the liberties and protect the state from [the birth of] future criminals by colonizing . . . mental defectives."[2] Partlow identified a darker link between eugenics and public health in his MASA address. "Until medical science improved social, public health and sanitary conditions, nature's survival of the fittest defended the human race against the dangers of degeneracy," he noted. "Now that under the present order of a humane world, the weak are preserved as well as the strong, if we are to continue as a virile, upstanding race in body and mind, eugenics demands its share of study and attention or euthanasia may become a necessity."[3]

Propelled directly and indirectly by the successes of various public health campaigns then sweeping across the Deep South, southern eugenicists expanded their efforts throughout the region during the 1920s. The public health campaign against hookworm had offered a precedent for northern medical experts and philanthropists in their efforts to promote eugenic segregation in southern states, but hookworm did not involve a human carrier. In terms of their impact on afflicted individuals, the campaigns against tuberculosis and venereal disease offered closer analogies to the eugenics movement. Further, the simultaneous campaign to reduce infant mortality overlapped with eugenic efforts to rear better, healthier babies.

For some southern eugenicists, the antituberculosis campaign provided a model for their cause. That campaign followed the brilliant 1876 discovery of the tubercle bacillus by Robert Koch, one of the medical luminaries hailed in Partlow's address to the MASA. Further research found that consumptives transmitted the bacteria in their spittle, and often became highly contagious during the advanced stages of the disease, when they could cough up a potentially lethal infection in invisible droplets of sputum. Infected cows also transmitted the disease to humans through their milk and meat. A national campaign soon developed to identify and isolate consumptives, an approach generally accepted by the afflicted because rest and therapy in a rural sanatorium offered the best available treatment for the disease. Hundreds of tuberculosis clinics sprang up across the country during the first two decades of the new century, and most states opened sanatoria for consumptives. Many communities passed antispitting ordinances, promoted public education about the causes of tuberculosis, and required physicians to report individual cases of the disease. The Deep South initially lagged in these efforts, but strove to catch up during the second and third decades of the century, especially after the national General Federation of Women's Clubs targeted tuberculosis reform as a priority. "In calling for the support, volunteers, and money needed for a successful assault on the disease," the historian Michael Teller concluded, "tuberculosis crusaders used three basic appeals: the danger to the public from the spread of the disease, the enormous cost of tuberculosis to the nation, and humanitarian sympathy for its enormous human toll."[4]

The eugenics movement followed a similar pattern and used the same basic appeals. Both in the case of mental retardation and in the case of tuberculosis, once science had identified human carriers as the sources for an affliction that threatened the community, campaigns arose to educate the public and quarantine the carriers. Crusaders in each campaign cited public dangers, social costs, and humanitarian sympathy to justify the imposition of restrictive measures. Progressive physicians, women's groups, and voluntary organizations played a major role in both efforts. Thus in the Deep South, for example, Partlow hailed the discoveries of Koch and of Galton in the same address, the Mississippi Federation of Women's Clubs claimed credit for legislation creating a "colony of the feeble-minded" and a tuberculosis sanatorium in the same press release, and Marcus Fagg of the Children's Home Society of Florida advocated eugenic marriage laws and the erection of public sanatoria in the same list of urgent state needs.[5] As the antituberculosis campaign in the Deep South imposed increasingly comprehensive public health measures to combat the disease during the 1920s, typically by opening more clinics and sanatoria to identify and isolate consumptives, and moving from voluntary to compulsory reporting and quarantine requirements, so too southern eugenicists sought ever more restrictive programs. Indeed, by 1925 a Louisiana physician could punctuate his call for eugenic sterilization and marriage restrictions with the promise "[I]f we wage but half the fight against mental disorders that we do against tuberculosis, it would be but a short time that a notable change for the better could take place."[6]

In other respects, however, the analogy between the antituberculosis and eugenics campaigns broke down. Of course, the scientific arguments for eugenics gradually collapsed during the 1920s and 1930s, just as the effectiveness of antituberculosis measures became increasingly evident. Furthermore, highly contagious consumptives posed a direct threat of infection to innocent individuals, whereas, except in the case of rape, direct "infection" from the carrier of a eugenic defect required the willing participation of a sexual partner. In this, hereditary defects appeared analogous to venereal disease—and several features linked the campaigns against both of these scourges in the Deep South.

Like the campaigns for eugenics and against tuberculosis, the Progressive Era public health assault on venereal disease emerged in response to a new scientific understanding of the affliction. German researchers had discovered the microbe causing syphilis in 1905, and a drug for treating the disease in 1909. "If syphilis could be properly diagnosed and effectively treated," the historian Allan Brandt observed about the resulting public health campaign, "then it could be placed on the same footing by boards of health as other contagious diseases." Many cities and several states soon enacted reporting requirements, marriage restrictions, and quarantine laws covering persons afflicted with venereal disease. By 1918, thirty-two states had passed statutes mandating medical examinations for certain groups of persons (including prostitutes, inmates, and vagrants) suspected of carrying syphilis. During World War I, when the federal government pitched in with funds to build quarantine facilities for infected prostitutes, most of the new institutions were located near military bases in the South.[7] This federal wartime effort helped prod the Deep South to join the campaign against venereal disease, which largely began in the North and the Midwest. Atlanta and several other southern cities erected stockades to quarantine infected prostitutes during the war. In 1919, Alabama became the first state in the region to prohibit marriage by persons infected by venereal disease, with Louisiana following suit four years later.[8]

Proponents of the campaigns against venereal disease and for eugenics linked the two causes from the start. For example, at the turn of the century the prime mover within the medical community's effort to combat venereal disease, the New York University medical professor Prince Morrow, considered these afflictions "directly antagonistic to the eugenic ideal" because they limited the ability of otherwise fit persons to reproduce and weakened the vitality of any resulting offspring.[9] Nationally known eugenicists carried this view with them as they ventured into the Deep South. Thus, the 1919 mental hygiene survey of Georgia, conducted by the National Committee for Mental Hygiene, made a special effort to determine what it described as "the highly important relationship which feeble-mindedness bears to the whole question of prostitution and the spread of venereal diseases, a question now so prominently before the public." The survey found that more than half of the infected prostitutes examined at the Atlanta stockade suffered from "serious mental abnormalities" that rendered them eugenically unfit to reproduce healthy children even if stockade physicians cured the venereal disease. "Probably the greatest single factor in the spread of venereal disease is the feeble-minded prostitute," the survey reported on the basis of this scant evidence. According to the survey, this underscored the need for the permanent eugenic segregation of the mentally retarded.[10]

Reaching even further to link the ongoing public health efforts, in 1923 the Florida Federation of Women's Clubs commingled their concerns about venereal disease, eugenics, and tuberculosis by promoting legislation to require medical certification that any "applicant for a marriage licence is not an imbecile, or insane person, or person of feeble mind, or an epileptic, or infected with tuberculosis in an advanced stage, or infected with any venereal disease."[11] In these instances and others like them, the emerging public health campaigns of the Progressive Era cross-fertilized one another in their rhetoric and remedies.

These campaigns aligned themselves with the era's intense popular concern about infant mortality and the health of American children.

Again there was a link to recent developments in microbiology, which had identified in commercial milk products bacterial impurities that particularly harmed infants. During the 1890s a program had begun in New York City to distribute pasteurized milk at subsidized prices through stations in tenement districts. By 1910, stations in thirty mostly northern and midwestern cities provided safe milk for poor children. At that time, concerned physicians, public health experts, and other social activists organized the American Association for the Study and Prevention of Infant Mortality (AASPIM) to coordinate public and private efforts in this field. The AASPIM promoted the transformation of milk stations into complete well-baby clinics designed to help poor mothers rear healthier children, and worked closely with women's clubs to expand these programs nationwide.[12] At least in part as a result of these efforts, the Georgia Federation of Women's Clubs, for example, championed state legislation for purer milk during the years 1912–16. The federation apparently linked this objective with eugenics because, after reporting on this legislative proposal to club members, its president hailed the "scientific study of infant mortality, juvenile delinquency, feeble-mindedness . . . and everything else pertaining to the welfare of the child."[13] This clearly included eugenics.

The national infant welfare movement strongly endorsed eugenics. A historian of the movement, Richard Markel, found that every annual meeting of the AASPIM featured a session on eugenics, and that in 1911 the association recommended compulsory sterilization as a means to ensure "the prohibition of procreation to the racially unfit."[14] Responding to eugenicists' fears that efforts to reduce infant mortality might help the eugenically unfit to survive, AASPIM president L. Emmett Holt claimed that they primarily assisted children threatened by poor environment rather than poor heredity. "We must eliminate the unfit by birth, not by death," he argued in proper progressive fashion. "The race is most effectively improved by preventing marriage and reproduction by the unfit, among whom we class the diseased, the degenerate, the defective, and the criminal."[15] In the Deep South, after milk stations and well-baby clinics began spreading throughout the region in the wake of 1921 federal legislation funding such programs, supporters of the new facilities often also participated in the fight for eugenic sterilization.[16] In the minds of many progressives at the time, rearing better babies required both charitable support for the fit and eugenics for the unfit.

All of these public health campaigns developed together in the Deep South during the 1920s. Indeed, a prominent Mississippi physician later cited these four campaigns in his reminiscences of this heroic era in preventative medicine. "Political, economic and reform movements rose rapidly to prominence in the early 1900s," he recalled in a 1939 address to the Mississippi Public Health Association. "This period produced such organizations as the National Tuberculosis Association (established 1904 as the National Association for the Study and Prevention of Tuberculosis); the American Social Hygiene Association (which grew out of the American Federation for Sex Hygiene organized in 1910); the American Child Health Association (organized in 1909 as the American Association for the Study and Prevention of Infant Mortality); and the National Committee for Mental Hygiene, formally organized in 1909."[17] All four of these national organizations spawned affiliates in Mississippi and the other states of the Deep South, often with overlapping memberships. During the 1920s, southern eugenicists maintained a close tie to the NCMH and drew inspiration and ideas from the works of the other three organizations. Far from satisfied with their earlier triumphs, they turned their attention toward expanding programs to identify and sexually segregate the mentally retarded, imposing new restrictions on marriage and immigration, and securing authority to sterilize the eugenically unfit.

Expanded Programs

The new institutions for the mentally retarded opened in the various states of the Deep South during the early 1920s with high hopes but meager resources. Alabama's leading newspaper, the *Birmingham Age-Herald,* expressed these hopes in an editorial hailing the start of construction of the facility for its state. "Dreams of humanitarians are being fulfilled in the building of the home for the feeble-minded at Tuscaloosa," the editorial observed. "Thus the state of Alabama takes another step forward in the care of her wards needing and deserving help." This humanitarian dream did not focus solely on the needs of the mentally retarded, however, because the editorialist added, "Institutions such as the home for the feeble-minded are moreover a protection for the race. . . . [S]ociety runs a great risk in having them at large." The title of the editorial betrayed the newspaper's prime concern: "Home for the Feeble-Minded Protection to the Race."[18] Yet with its scant resources, the institution could offer little protection. Even though mental health surveys placed Alabama's "feeble-minded" population at more than 7,000 persons, the new facility could accommodate only 160 residents, and was filled within two months of its opening. "Other applications are urged," William Partlow noted in the institution's second annual report, "and though we as a rule declined or postponed such applications the pressure in many cases was so urgent and the appeals so acute that we yielded in sufficient numbers of cases to create two problems for ourselves:—1st, an overcrowded condition, and 2nd, insufficient classification in the dormitories."[19]

All of the public institutions for the mentally retarded in the Deep South faced similar problems. They were underfunded and overcrowded, far too small to house more than a tiny fraction of the eligible population, and largely unable to fulfill their eugenic mission. In 1922, shortly after they first opened, the total of their patient populations was only 345, as compared to the nearly 45,000 persons in such facilities nationwide. This regional total represented about one out of every thirty thousand citizens in the six states, or about one-tenth of the commitment rate for the nation as a whole, and one-hundredth of the estimated rate of mental retardation within the population. The total for the Deep South rose to 2,275 patients by the end of the decade, but this still represented only one out of every five thousand citizens, or about one-third of the national commitment rate. At no time during the 1920s did *any* Deep South state ever achieve a commitment rate that exceeded one-half of the national rate.[20] These regional differences struck Superintendent B. O. Whitten of South Carolina's new State Training School for the Feeble-Minded when he toured several northern facilities. "Such buildings!" he commented. "Such equipment! A steady flow of money for maintenance and improvements! [My] two little brick buildings near the sun-baked cotton fields were only pathetic little doll houses in comparison!"[21]

Pleas for more funds and larger facilities arose from institution officials in every southern state. In 1923, for example, the new superintendent of the Mississippi School and Colony for the Feebleminded, H. H. Ramsey, could write, "Even though at the present, we have only the nucleus of what an institution for the care and training of these defectives should be, I have unbounded faith and confidence in the future development. The people of Mississippi have never failed to rally to a just cause, and when they understand the relationship this institution bears to the prosperity and happiness of our entire citizenship, they will come to its support."[22] Ramsey lost his faith after a few years dealing with the Mississippi legislature. "Receiving additional inmates has become a physical impossibility," he reported in 1926. "To me it is a tragedy that we have a population of only 134, and a waiting list of nearly 500 and that the state continues through Legislature, after Legislature, to neglect this, its greatest vital problem . . . by withholding an investment in humanity which will not only finally pay the taxpayer a dividend in cash, but result in the purification of our blood stream, and a higher type of citizenship."[23] Southern legislatures never demonstrated a sufficient appreciation of the supposed economic and social calculus of eugenics to adequately fund eugenic segregation efforts.

As a committed eugenicist, Ramsey suffered the particular frustration of not having adequate accommodations to admit and segregate females within his institution. The enabling legislation authorized a facility for both sexes, but an early report from the Mississippi Colony noted, "Because workers are needed for the farm, at this time, only high grade imbeciles and moronic white males of the ages of 15 to 50, will be admitted."[24] Thereafter, the legislature simply did not appropriate sufficient funds to erect additional housing for females until 1928, when the always supportive Theodore Bilbo regained the governorship.[25] Ramsey tried every tack to remedy this deficiency, from evoking sympathy for mentally retarded females to arousing fear of them—but a eugenic undercurrent ran throughout. "The average defective girl has no chance in the world," he once asserted. "With her weak power of inhibition, with a developed body and retarded mind, she readily falls victim to designing persons, and aside from her own sad plight becomes a menace to the morals and health of the community."[26] Mentally retarded females became the aggressor in other accounts by Ramsey, such as when he claimed that "many a young boy is made immoral and his life ruined at the threshold of manhood by the sex advances of feebleminded girls and women."[27] Whether the unrestrained mentally retarded female was victim or villain in Ramsey's reports, the consequences were always the same: another generation of "defective illegitimates."[28]

None of the other southern institutions shared this particular limitation. Indeed, the others housed roughly equal numbers of males and females in their sexually segregated facilities.[29] Yet they all lacked adequate resources to fulfill their mission. After visiting South Carolina's State Training School for the Feeble-minded in 1922, for example, a survey team from the NCMH reported, "This institution has provision for one hundred and three patients while there are several thousand in the community who need segregation and training."[30] Similarly, Marcus Fagg greeted the opening of the Florida Farm Colony for Epileptic and Feeble-Minded by cautioning, "It is estimated by authorities that there are practically 3,000 feeble-minded in our state. The present colony will care for about 200, so you see how far we have to go."[31] The superintendent of Louisiana's State Colony and Training School estimated "that there are about 2800 feeble-minded people in Louisiana that should be in an institution" at a time when his facility could accommodate only 262 patients and had a waiting list of twice that number.[32]

Despite the pressing need to expand, none of these institutions housed more than five hundred persons at any time during the 1920s.[33] The gender restriction on admissions in Mississippi simply represented an extreme example of the conditions existing throughout the Deep South.

"The pitiful and tragic situation of the feebleminded girl should move us to do something for her sake alone," the trustees of the Mississippi Colony pleaded in 1925. "However, in providing care, supervision and proper training for her, society would be immeasurably improved by the removal of the menace of her reproduction." According to these trustees, nothing less than "the preservation of the intelligence of the race" was at stake.[34] Eugenicists in every state of the Deep South made similar appeals during the 1920s in an attempt to expand existing institutions for eugenically segregating the mentally retarded.[35]

This final comment by the all-White trustees of the Mississippi Colony betrayed a further limitation of southern efforts at eugenic segregation. They focused exclusively on "preserving" the White race, and left the other races to fend for themselves. The eugenics movement flourished during an era of strict racial segregation in the South, which forced Blacks and Whites into separate communities. In his analysis of the mental health treatment provided by southern states for African Americans at that time, Steven Noll concluded, "The policy of racial separation allowed white southerners to ignore the plight of feebleminded blacks. With control enforced by legalized segregation, there appeared little need for institutions for the feeble-minded to further control black deviants."[36] Strictly enforced antimiscegenation laws minimized the eugenic threat posed to the White race by mentally retarded Blacks. Without any compelling social-control or eugenic reason for placing mentally retarded Blacks into state institutions, and given the inadequate resources for admitting all the needy Whites, Blacks were simply excluded. Only Louisiana's State Colony and Training School made room for African Americans prior to the civil rights movement of the 1950s, albeit in racially segregated dormitories vastly inferior to the accommodations given White residents.[37] Perhaps driven by a perceived need to control the mentally ill, southern state mental health hospitals did admit African Americans into racially segregated wards throughout the Jim Crow era, and many mentally retarded Blacks ended up in these facilities as places of last resort.[38]

Although it aroused nothing akin to their fervent pleas for expanding facilities for mentally retarded Whites, a few southern eugenicists advocated the sexual segregation of mentally retarded Blacks. B. O. Whitten, the superintendent of South Carolina's State Training School for the Feeble-minded, was probably the most persistent. "The best elements of society in our State cannot advance far enough ahead to escape the influence of the weaker portion of our citizenship," he explained in 1924. "On account of the pressure from white people being stronger than from the colored we have not heretofore stressed any request for the care of negro defectives. We now feel that this should be recognized and some assistance offered without delay."[39] Fourteen years later, Whitten could still write, "The lack of facilities for white people needing the care of our Institution and the tremendous number of appeals in behalf of such individuals have overshadowed, to a considerable degree, the unpreparedness and total lack of facilities for the colored of a similar type."[40] Throughout, Whitten maintained that Blacks should receive this "assistance" in a separate institution because, as he once explained at a national meeting, "[t]radition, custom, political determination, as well as other economic and social practices have set apart the colored people from the whites."[41] On other occasions, such diverse advocates of eugenic segregation as the Georgia Department of Public Welfare and the Florida Federation of Women's Clubs endorsed separate state institutions for mentally retarded Blacks.[42] None were ever built in the Deep South.[43]

In addition to making incessant pleas for general enlargement and specific requests for facilities to segregate females or African Americans, institution officials focused their early efforts toward implementing a "colony plan" of development. The colony ideal dated from the earliest days of the eugenics movement. It envisioned placing the higher-grade mentally retarded, the "morons," in largely self-supporting agricultural colonies near the main institution, where they would be safely segregated and happily occupied at minimal cost. For "trustworthy" patients, the experience and training received in the colony setting could eventually lead to parole and reintegration into the larger community. Goddard promoted this plan at the Vineland Training School in New Jersey, and institutions throughout the country attempted to implement it during the second decade of the century, with little success.[44]

Influenced by this ideal, all of the southern institutions were located in rural or semirural settings, typically on large parcels of arable land. The Florida, Louisiana, and Mississippi institutions were initially designated as "colonies," and their enabling legislation directed them, in the words of the Louisiana statute, "to engage in agricultural, industrial and all other pursuits of life that may be beneficial or essential for the institution or the inmates thereof."[45] The other three institutions in the Deep South also experimented with the colony plan as a means to expand their impact.[46] None succeeded in this objective. The colonies never became sufficiently self-supporting to expand without state appropriations, and southern legislatures proved no more willing to spend money on farm cottages than on institutional dormitories. As early as 1920, Whitten warned, "Perhaps the idea has been a little too prominent . . . and appeared to have created the impression that the State's unfortunate incompetents could really be handled in such a way as to make them an asset to their commonwealth."[47] The vision of self-supporting farm colonies, a sort of modern-day philosopher's stone able to transmute lead into gold, may have helped sell the concept of state institutions for the mentally retarded in the first place, but it never helped them to expand.

During the 1920s, southern eugenicists not only sought to expand public facilities for segregating the mentally retarded but also attempted to implement programs for early detection of the proper subjects for eugenic segregation. "Logically," the superintendent of the Florida Farm Colony for Epileptic and Feeble-Minded observed at this time, "the first step would be to find out their numbers, where and how they are living and such facts about them as would indicate whether it was safe to leave them at large."[48] Actual proposals for conducting such efforts targeted the public schools. "The importance of public school as a social agency and of school teachers, as social workers, simply cannot be overestimated," South Carolina's State Board of Public Welfare advised in 1920. "It is during his early school years that for his own best interest, the feeble-minded child should be discovered. He should then be given institutional care."[49] Stressing that this approach would also benefit the public, the 1925 trustees' report for the Mississippi Colony darkly warned, "A large number of our future criminals, paupers and prostitutes are now mere tots in our public schools, and unless we recognize them early and make suitable provision for them the state will be hampered with a vast number of unsatisfactory citizens."[50]

Four years later, the Mississippi trustees elaborated on this idea. "With reference to the mental examination of school children we wish to point out that our compulsory school law requires every child of school age to attend," they noted. "Therefore, as a matter of economy, intelligent procedure, and justice to feebleminded children, the state should provide a small staff of competent specialists to find these unfortunate children in the public schools so that they may be transferred to the splendid school we are now building."[51] Superintendent Ramsey further explained that three "Traveling Clinics" composed of psychiatric experts "could easily cover the state every four years," testing schoolchildren. According to Ramsey, this procedure would "enable the state to assume charge of its defectives during the formative period, before they have become a menace and social liability."[52] Of course, at the time, the state offered no "splendid school" or treatment facilities to receive these charges, only a squalid colony where high-grade male "defectives" labored in the hot Gulf Coast sun to raise their own food and help build their own housing.

Mississippi never implemented this ambitious scheme, but other states in the Deep South adopted more limited versions of the same basic idea.

In South Carolina, for example, a 1922 mental hygiene survey by the NCMH recommended the development of "mental clinics" serving the school and community so that "feebleminded and mentally handicapped children could be early recognized and given proper training and supervision and, in the case of those who need it, segregation."[53] About the same time, Superintendent Whitten of the State Training School for the Feeble-minded advised the South Carolina Medical Association, "A well organized clinic is a great aid toward the discovery of cases afflicted with mental troubles, especially if conducted in connection with the public schools."[54] The State Board of Public Welfare soon hired a full-time psychological field worker to conduct mental examinations on children in public schools and institutions throughout the state. South Carolina's Department of Mental Hygiene added a traveling clinic that regularly visited major cities throughout the state. Both referred appropriate persons to the training school. "South Carolina has taken a big step forward in the last few years in the establishment of the State Training School for the Feebleminded," the psychological field worker Mary Fishburne reported in 1923. "But if we allow our defectives to remain at large, unrecognized, untaught, unskilled, uncared for, propagating their kind at will, what have we a right to expect from the future?"[55]

Comprehensive state schemes to identify the eugenically unfit served little purpose as part of a segregation program so long as existing institutions could not even hold all the persons brought in by their families or referred by local government officials. The superintendent of the East Mississippi Insane Hospital, J. M. Buchanan, acknowledged as much when he commented, "Segregation calls for an outlay of money that no state could afford, to confine all of its defectives."[56] Indeed, every public institution for the mentally retarded in the Deep South was overcrowded throughout the 1920s, and most had long waiting lists.[57] Augmented efforts to identify the eugenically unfit made perfect sense, however, as part of new measures to restrict marriages or compel sterilization. Buchanan fully appreciated this situation, and championed a comprehensive program of eugenic reforms encompassing all of these elements.[58] Many other southern eugenicists followed suit, with Ramsey commenting that one of them "hit the key-note of the whole proposition with the plan of recognition, segregation, and sterilization."[59] Indeed, a zealous Louisiana physician urged his colleagues to support "traveling psychiatric clinics," primarily as a means "for educating the communities in the need . . . to properly sterilize the feeble-minded." As he saw it, "We could not possibly get a bill before the Legislature in years on that subject, so we must get at the people in the country communities and do the work there."[60]

New Restrictions

"We had a waiting list of about 530 when the Legislature met in 1929. We added during 1929 to this already long waiting list, 135 names of very urgent cases," Superintendent John Odom of the Georgia Training School for Mental Defectives reported to the state board of health. "These feeble-minded parents continue to bring into the world children of their own type. The appeals to the different charitable organizations over the state are continually increasing, and your superintendent believes that our department should begin now to make a determined fight for laws governing the marriage of defective individuals."[61]

A tone of desperation marked Odom's report and many of the other pleas by southern eugenicists for marriage restrictions. Nationally recognized leaders of the eugenics movement had long dismissed eugenic controls on marriage as ineffective. Indeed, as early as 1913, Charles Davenport of the Eugenics Record Office pronounced that "the reproduction of the feeble-minded will not be, to an important degree, diminished by laws forbidding the issuing to them of marriage licenses. Most of them have weak sex-control. If it is easy and cheap to get married, they may do so; otherwise, they will have children without getting married."[62] Leading southern eugenicists accepted this view of the mentally retarded as a fact of life. In Mississippi, for example, Buchanan complained about the futility of such a law in one northern state. "Those who did not like it," he observed, "had little trouble in avoiding it by going to states where there was not eugenic examination in the way, and in some cases the formality of marriage was done away with altogether."[63] For example, he noted, "Valpariso, Ind., has become a Gretna Green for bordering states with eugenic laws—fourteen couples from Chicago were recently married there in one day."[64] Both Davenport and Buchanan saw custodial eugenic segregation as far more effective than marriage restrictions for controlling reproduction.[65]

Nevertheless, in the absence of adequate facilities for eugenic segregation, marriage restrictions offered some hope. "Feeble-minded persons hand on their weakness of mind to their children," South Carolina's State Board of Public Welfare advised state legislators in 1923. "For this reason persons that are of known feeble-mindedness should not be allowed to contract matrimony with one another, nor should a feeble-minded person be allowed to marry a normal one." The board immediately cautioned, however, that "we must realize that marriage laws will not completely solve this problem," and then made a pitch for expanded facilities for eugenic segregation.[66] Similarly, a Louisiana mental health official explained his support for a eugenic marriage law with the com-

ment "[B]ecause a law can not be enforced 100 per cent it does not follow that it is a poor law and it will at least serve to educate and such education may finally do some good."[67] With such tepid endorsements
from supporters, proposals for eugenic marriage restrictions made little
headway in the Deep South.

Comments made by Whitten in support of the South Carolina recommendation were even more telling. "We are still unable to appreciate the
justice or propriety of our state permitting the indiscriminate marriage
and propagation of mental defectives," he observed. "In almost every instance the propagation of this element of society results in grief and dis-
appointment to the person in question and will scarcely ever operate in
any way which can be expected to promote happiness or even Anglo
Saxon liberty."[68] This final remark about "Anglo-Saxon liberty" addressed a central issue raised by those opposed to eugenic marriage restrictions. As Buchanan noted with respect to such a statute in the North:
"Bitter opposition to the law on the grounds that it was an interference
with the private right of men and women was developed."[69]

Except as pertained to miscegenation, southern states traditionally imposed fewer restrictions on marriage than did northern states. Indeed,
even during the campaign against venereal disease, only two states in the
Deep South required a health certificate before marriage. No state in the
region ever imposed eugenic marriage restrictions, even though most
northern and western states did so at some time during the early twentieth century. Women's clubs endorsed the idea in several southern states,
just as their counterparts did elsewhere in the nation, and Marcus Fagg
persistently promoted it in Florida, but no legislation was passed.[70] The
only statutes in the Deep South directly bearing on the issue were preex-
isting restrictions in Georgia, Mississippi, and South Carolina invalidat-
ing marriage contracts entered into by "an idiot or lunatic" on the conventional grounds that such persons lacked the legal capacity to enter
into a contract.[71]

Legislative proposals to impose eugenic marriage restrictions got further in Louisiana than in any other state of the region, perhaps because
they appeared as part of broader programs to protect marital and child
health. In 1917, during the height of wartime concern over venereal disease and the ongoing public health campaign against tuberculosis and infant mortality, Joseph A. O'Hara, a leading progressive physician from
New Orleans and a future president of both the state board of health and
the Louisiana State Medical Society, called for eugenic "supervision of
marriages" as part of a comprehensive assault on mental retardation in
children. "We should begin at once," he declared, "by seeing that the
constituted authorities adopt methods for the prevention of mental ab-

normalities—by segregation and sterilization of defectives and degenerates, and supervision of marriages of tubercular and syphilitic subjects,
also alcoholics, drug addicts and cases of heredity and consanguinity."[72]
Two years later, the prominent Louisiana physician Robert Carruth delivered an impassioned address to the state medical society on the hereditary degeneration of the White race. "As a Caucasian, as an American,
as a Louisianan, I am ashamed to speak it, but these are facts that should
be known," he exclaimed. "These people—*these insane people—these
insane—are being permitted to marry among themselves;* these morons,
these imbeciles, these maniacs are *procreating their kind.* No law, I am
told, to prevent it—no law of church or State; no crystallized public
opinion to prohibit such unholy, such unclean unions." Yet when Carruth enumerated his list of recommendations to protect the race, eugenic
marriage restrictions placed second in importance behind improved education of mothers. Further, he added, only compulsory sterilization could
protect the race in extreme cases.[73]

Despite these pleas, the Louisiana legislature regularly rejected eugenic marriage bills, owing in large part to opposition from the locally
powerful Roman Catholic Church. In 1924, for example, a committee of
the state House of Representatives endorsed an ambitious scheme restricting marriages by persons afflicted with mental illness, mental retardation, epilepsy, or venereal disease, but only a lesser limitation on
prospective grooms with syphilis and gonorrhea passed into law. A special committee of the state medical society chaired by Carruth had drafted the 1924 proposal, which envisioned a "State Hygienic Marriage
Board" composed of six experts (including "one woman physician")
overseeing a network of local physicians charged with examining all ap-
plicants for marriage licenses. Any applicant found to suffer from one of
the listed conditions could only have obtained a marriage license if the
wife's age exceeded forty-five years or the afflicted person "voluntarily
submit[ted] to a sterilizing operation that will prevent the propagation of
offspring."[74] One enthusiastic supporter, a state mental health official,
predicted "that in future years the right to marry and procreate children
will be regarded as proof that the participants, while perhaps not perfect,
at least belong to the aristocracy of health."[75]

This Utopian restriction never came to pass in Louisiana. Four years
later, a similar proposal narrowly cleared the state Senate but was sound-
ly defeated by the House of Representatives.[76] Even these bills did not
simply bar marriage by the eugenically unfit, however, but also covered
persons with sexually transmitted diseases. Indeed, the newspaper coverage of the later bill described it as "designed primarily to prevent the
marriage of persons afflicted with venereal disease," and never men-

tioned its strictly eugenic features.[77] Even linked with the popular campaign against venereal disease, however, eugenic marriage restrictions failed to secure sufficient support in the Deep South to become law. The final serious attempt to secure such a statute within the region died by a vote of fourteen to twenty-one in the Florida Senate during the 1937 session, with most of the interest still focused on provisions within it dealing with venereal disease.[78]

The failure of state legislatures in the Deep South to enact eugenic marriage statutes at a time when such laws passed in most other states suggested that southern lawmakers (and, by inference, the southern public) never fully accepted eugenics. Even though many leading eugenicists questioned their effectiveness, marriage restrictions remained one of the four elements commonly discussed as part of any comprehensive eugenics program.[79] By the 1920s, southern lawmakers ostensibly had adopted only one of these four elements, eugenic segregation. Yet persuasive non-eugenic arguments helped justify the establishment of separate state institutions for the mentally retarded. Proponents certainly emphasized the eugenic benefits of these facilities—their role in preventing future generations of degeneracy and dependency. Supporters of such institutions also discussed the present criminal and moral dangers to the community posed by allowing the mentally retarded to remain at large; noted the humanitarian aspect of institutionalization for the afflicted; and observed that the state already cared for many of the potential patients in more costly and less appropriate facilities, such as mental health hospitals and orphanages. These non-eugenic factors clearly influenced southern legislators. Further, when these new facilities began costing more than expected, lawmakers refused to expand them to a size that could have a meaningful eugenic impact on the overall population, forcing them to remain much smaller than comparable institutions elsewhere in the country.

The other two elements of a comprehensive eugenics scheme made even less headway in the Deep South. Compulsory sterilization of the unfit remained a dream in the mind of most local eugenicists, who sensed that southerners would not yet accept such an "advanced" measure even though twenty-five northern and western states had enacted sterilization laws by 1925.[80] The tenor of southern support for immigration control, the final element of any comprehensive eugenics program, further betrayed the region's failure to embrace eugenics.

The imposition of ethnic restrictions on immigration topped the agenda of the national eugenics movement during the 1920s, and the enactment of the federal Immigration Act of 1924 represented its most notable achievement. Of course, nativists had opposed both foreign immigration to America and the residence of non-Anglo-Saxons in the United States long before eugenics provided any scientific basis for such prejudices. By the turn of the century, labor unions concerned about the influx of low-wage workers, and nationalistic organizations worried about foreign radicals, added their voices to those calling for immigration controls. Eugenics would offer a scientific justification for such controls if it could be demonstrated that immigrants were genetically inferior to the domestic stock or that interbreeding the two groups weakened the offspring. Although such nationally prominent eugenicists as Madison Grant instinctively believed in the superiority of the Nordic race, it took the work of the eugenics researcher H. H. Laughlin to "prove" that "recent immigrants [largely from Southern and Eastern Europe], as a whole, present a higher percentage of inborn socially inadequate qualities than do the older stocks." Laughlin based this conclusion on the national origin of persons in selected state welfare and penal institutions, and reported it to Congress in his capacity as "Expert Eugenical Agent" for the House Committee on Immigration and Naturalization.[81] Several historians credit Laughlin and this report with playing an important role in the passage of the Immigration Act of 1924, which imposed annual quotas for immigration from each European nation that were fixed at 2 percent of the number of foreign-born individuals from that nation living in the United States in 1890, before the massive influx from southern and eastern Europe.[82]

The role that members of Congress from the Deep South played in the passage of this law, however, did not reflect an acceptance or understanding of eugenics. Even though two leading historians of the eugenics movement, Hamilton Cravens and Daniel Kevles, have asserted that the House immigration committee was dominated by congressmen from the South and the West, most of its "southern" lawmakers actually came from border states.[83] Further, all the southern legislators on the committee were Democrats, at a time when Republicans firmly controlled the committee and both houses of Congress, which inevitably limited how much influence on legislation the committee's democratic members had.[84] Finally, Cravens noted, "Congressmen in the House often made blatantly racist speeches, and cited Laughlin approvingly."[85] Kevles added, "On both sides of Capitol Hill biological and racial arguments figured prominently in the floor debate on the bill."[86] Certainly members from the Deep South made their fair share of racist speeches and arguments in favor of the legislation, but none of them cited Laughlin during the floor debate or displayed the slightest interest in biological or eugenic justifications for the measure. "I am for the bill now before us," Alabama's popular congressman Jeff Busby proclaimed to a cheering House in a jingoistic statement that typified southern sentiment on the issue. "I believe we should save America for Americans, and hand our country down untarnished by foreign elements to our posterity."[87]

Members of Congress from the Deep South generally favored admitting only those foreign immigrants who would readily adopt "American" ideals and institutions. These phrases might represent code words for identifying Anglo-Saxons, but they did not reflect the purely eugenic thinking that would welcome "better" stock and fear "weaker" stock. "What I am concerned in is trying to keep pure the traditions of the early settlers of this country, wherever they came from," Congressman Allard Gasque of South Carolina explained. "I am more concerned in the perpetuation of the ideals, the ideas, the religion of the generation who lived here in 1776 and who wrote the Constitution of this great Government than where the future immigrants are to come from—whether they are Nordic stock or any other stock."[88] Representative James Aswell of Louisiana stated it bluntly: "The people of the country want the Congress to shut out and keep out all except the man who . . . is eager to become an American citizen—ready as such to support and perpetuate the institutions, not those transplanted from Europe but of this Republic."[89] Similarly, Senators Walter George of Georgia and Pat Harrison of Mississippi spoke at length about the need for Americans to limit the type and number of immigrants to those it could easily "assimilate."[90] This was old-fashioned nativism, pure and simple, not newfangled eugenics.

Indeed, most lawmakers from the region preferred closing America's borders to all foreign immigrants. Georgia's William Harris unsuccessfully offered such an amendment on the Senate floor, and a majority of the senators from the Deep South voted for it.[91] When one midwestern senator challenged the eugenic wisdom of this approach by noting, "[I]n point of literacy, the white population of Georgia is far below the white population of Norway, or of Sweden, or of Denmark, or of Germany, or of Holland, or of Switzerland," the Georgia delegation arose in defense of its White constituents.[92] Similarly, when another senator suggested that skilled immigrants from Dutch or Swedish farms could help the South break its dependency on cotton, Senator Ellison D. Smith of South Carolina replied, "We have all the institutions and all the means and the best brains and the best blood in this country to meet that task if that task were worth the meeting when met."[93] No call for positive eugenics came from these southern senators, or from Congressman Gasque, who added, "I prefer a closed-door period and I believe a majority of this House does, and I am sure a majority of this country does. I am also in favor of an amendment to this bill providing that all hyphenated Americans be deported."[94]

The most inflammatory nativist rhetoric heard in the Senate came from the Alabama demagogue Tom Heflin. Foreign immigrants carried crime and communism to America, according to Heflin, took jobs from American workers, and undermined the American way of life. To dramatize the threat, he graphically and repeatedly described "the murder of an American boy walking along the street with his father, approached from the rear, stabbed in the back and murdered by this fiendish foreigner, who stated that the reason he killed him was that he wanted to see how deep he could drive a dirk in his back."[95] In defense of American institutions, Heflin also thrice told a story "about the arrest of a negro in New York . . . by an Irish policeman, and he was astounded to hear the negro speak Yiddish; the Irishman spoke Yiddish, and they took the negro to a judge who also tried him in Yiddish." Heflin then warned his Senate colleagues, "[W]e are coming to a pitiful pass in this great country when it is unpopular to speak the English language, the American language."[96] An avowed White supremacist with close ties to the Ku Klux Klan, Heflin blindly denounced foreign immigration without putting any sophisticated eugenic gloss on his arguments.

Alabama's other senator, Oscar Underwood, expressed quite a different viewpoint when he unsuccessfully opposed an amendment shifting the basis of the quota from the 1910 census to the 1890 census. The shift, which eugenicists favored, did not significantly affect the total number of Europeans eligible for immigration, but it greatly increased the allocation for the Nordic nations at the expense of the countries of southern and eastern Europe. Underwood saw the overall legislation as needed to protect American labor, but viewed this shift as unnecessarily discriminatory. "The great body of European immigration comes from the same source," Underwood reasoned in opposition to prevailing eugenic doctrines. "There may be some dissimilar racial characteristics. But they belong to the white blood, to the Caucasian race, and it is more opportunity that has made the division than it is racial characteristics."[97] This amendment temporarily split the southern lawmakers on an issue of profound importance to eugenicists, though they came together to unanimously support the legislation's final passage.[98]

Southern lawmakers could enthusiastically support immigration control without necessarily embracing eugenics, however. Indeed, many of them backed traditional Know-Nothing positions that defied eugenic reasoning. Their constituencies encouraged this. Because so few immigrants, and so few persons of southern or eastern European descent, lived in the Deep South, nativist politicians from the region could more easily present such foreigners as abstract threats to the established order than as sources of eugenic contamination. "Many of you know that in some great States of this Republic people who do not know anything of

American ideals, who *know nothing* of the pulpit and the schoolhouse and what it stands for in the United States, absolutely control and dominate politics," Congressman Percy E. Quin of Mississippi declared on the House floor. "They hold the power politically in the presidential electoral college of the United States. They can name the President of the United States."[99] The White ethnic homogeneity of the Deep South made it politically safe in the region to oppose immigration. Busby admitted as much when he announced, "I have one county in my district which, according to the 1920 census, has only one foreign-born person. From this county I have received a petition from the citizens for me to support this bill."[100] Of course, this also made immigration control less of a concern for local eugenicists. Visiting eugenicists from the Northeast often were struck by the lack of foreigners in the Deep South, and typically omitted any mention of limits on immigration from their comprehensive eugenic plans for the region.[101] When local eugenicists failed to adopt the issue, it remained largely in the hands of traditional nativists and nationalists.

Sterilization during the 1920s

Even though immigration control never became a major issue for southern eugenicists during the 1920s, the enactment of eugenic segregation statutes did not deter them from considering other remedies for dealing with native-born "defectives." At the beginning of the decade, for example, B. O. Whitten of South Carolina advised, "The prevention of propagation is our greatest problem; even greater than providing for those already among us. This evil can be checked to a large extent by some of the following methods: asexualization; compulsory segregation . . . ; regulating marriage of the mentally weak; special registration of births in families where mental defectiveness exists; education of the people."[102] Marriage regulation and birth registration never gained a foothold in the Deep South, whereas facilities for compulsory segregation failed to attain a sufficient size to fulfill the demands of eugenicists or the needs of the region's mentally retarded population. That left asexualization (or sterilization) and education, with these two methods blurring together in certain respects.

By "education of the people" Whitten meant informing the general public about the need for imposing eugenic remedies, especially sterilization, on the "unfit."[103] Of course, eugenicists everywhere sought to encourage the "fit" to breed by educating them about their civic responsibility to increase their reproduction rate, and southern eugenicists did their part on this front.[104] Eugenicists placed less faith in the ameliorative effects of advising the "unfit" against breeding, however, except perhaps indirectly through informing them about birth control. By the 1920s, many eugenicists reasoned that, since "superior" Americans already received birth control information from private physicians, the establishment of public birth control clinics would serve a eugenic purpose by distributing such information to the masses. Margaret Sanger, the central figure in the American birth control movement during this period and a committed eugenicist, put it succinctly when she wrote, "More children from the fit, less from the unfit—that is the chief issue of birth control."[105] Some southerners supported the birth control movement for this reason. In 1927, for example, the Alabama eugenicist J. P. McMurphy urged his MASA colleagues to endorse legalized birth control by warning, "[T]he more intelligent classes already procure birth control, while the less intelligent, who lack the knowledge to restrain their births, are breeding so prolifically that they impede the general standards of human excellence of the race."[106] Similarly, a Louisiana physician argued in 1929, "Birth control is coming; it is here in some localities, and if we have to control the birth rate, why not control it with the unfit rather than with the fit?"[107]

Robert Carruth carried this reasoning a step further in his address on race degeneration before the Louisiana State Medical Society. He discussed the issue of legalized birth control only with regard to dysgenic unions in which the man insisted on having sexual intercourse. In such a situation, Carruth viewed birth control as the woman's "sacred personal right," but only insofar as it allowed her "to refuse passively to become a party with [her partner] to the crime of thrusting upon the world what she has reason to believe, what she has been told by her medical advisor, what she herself may have learned by sad experience, may be a gibbering idiot." According to Carruth, however, this would not resolve the problem posed by persons so "wholly and irremediably unfit" that they would not practice restraint. "Neither marriage laws nor medical advice control this unfortunate class," he warned. "I can suggest no better way than sterilization."[108] Thus, for some southern eugenicists, as for Sanger in the North, acceptance of voluntary birth control overlapped with support for compulsory sterilization.[109] Of all the eugenicists in the Deep South who endorsed both procedures, however, only William Partlow had the power to act on his convictions throughout the 1920s.[110]

One provision buried deep in the 1919 legislation creating the Alabama Home for the mentally retarded empowered Partlow, as the facility's superintendent, "to sterilize any inmate"; the only limitation imposed was the concurrence of the nearby superintendent of the Alabama Insane Hospitals.[111] This clause, which did not appear in early drafts of the measure, gave the two superintendents unfettered discretion over sterilization decisions within the institution, without any of the procedural protection typically required by compulsory sterilization laws in other states.[112] The idea of adding the provision probably originated with Partlow himself. He had supported eugenic sterilization for years and, in 1919, shepherded the overall proposal through the legislature in his dual capacities as chairman of the MASA's Committee on Mental Hygiene and chief assistant superintendent of the Alabama Insane Hospitals.[113] Whether or not Partlow inserted the provision in the legislation, he certainly knew how to utilize it when he assumed the superintendency of the new facility.

From its inception, the Alabama Home, which an appreciative state legislature renamed in Partlow's honor in 1927, maintained a strict policy of sexually segregating all inmates during their stay and sterilizing them upon their discharge.[114] This was done, Partlow explained in purely eugenic terms, to "serve the State and society by looking to the future."[115] By 1932, the total number sterilized at the Partlow State School since its founding reached 129 persons, with somewhat more than half of those being male.[116] The following year, Partlow broadened the sterilization policy to include "some of the delinquent boys who we fear might escape," which helped push the total figure to 158.[117] According to Partlow, these sterilization practices enabled the institution to implement a liberal discharge policy without endangering society, and thereby to treat (and sterilize) more patients.[118] An informational flyer distributed by the facility put it bluntly: Patients would "not be released except on condition of sterilization before discharge on account of the fact that the children of the feeble-minded would themselves certainly be feeble-minded."[119] Partlow later added, "We have made no exceptions except profound idiots in whom we regard from mental deficiency and physical malformation no possible chance of reproduction."[120]

By 1915, mental health officials and prominent physicians from every state of the region had publicly endorsed eugenic sterilization. At most, the campaign for eugenically segregated institutions for the mentally retarded represented a supplement to, rather than a substitute for, the earlier objective. Southern eugenicists remained keenly interested in sterilization during the 1920s, especially as they saw it used in conjunction with eugenic segregation at the Partlow State School and similar institutions in the North and the West. For example, Whitten kept discussing the issue in South Carolina and, in 1925, the oversight board for his facility formally proposed "legalizing the sterilization of institutional cases unfit for propagation."[121] Louisiana and Mississippi mental health leaders regularly recommended the procedure in their official reports throughout the decade.[122] In the "Heart of Dixie," Partlow set his sights on a broader sterilization program for his state after he became superintendent of the Alabama Insane Hospitals in 1923, a post he held for three decades while remaining the head of the Partlow State School. As he stated it at the time, "a program of sterilization of the insane, mental defective, repeating criminal, drug and alcoholic addicts would go a long way in the right direction."[123] He secured the MASA's support for this approach in 1928, when its president recommended sterilizing "all convicted criminals and insane cases committed to the State insane asylum." In a classic eugenic affirmation, the MASA president concluded, "It is not humane to allow the insane to propagate his species to the injury of himself and the public."[124] By the early 1920s, however, a series of court rulings against sterilization statutes in other states hamstrung efforts to pass such laws everywhere.

The logjam began to break in the mid-1920s, when Harry Laughlin devised model legislation designed to avoid the constitutional problems plaguing earlier laws. After the U.S. Supreme Court upheld Virginia's new sterilization statute in 1927,[125] the flow of new legislation turned into a flood that for the first time included numerous bills before legislatures in the Deep South. Within days of the Supreme Court decision, comprehensive sterilization proposals surfaced in the Alabama and Florida legislatures.[126] Legislation also appeared in the Georgia House of Representatives during its next session.[127] Like the Virginia law, these three bills covered patients at state mental health hospitals as well as institutions for the mentally retarded, which reflected eugenicists' ongoing worries about hereditary mental illness, as well as their newer hysteria over mental retardation. Caught in the excitement of the moment, sponsors hastily offered these measures without sufficiently organizing local support. As a result, the Alabama and Georgia bills never came to a vote in either chamber, whereas the Florida legislation passed the state's House of Representatives too late in the session for it to receive consideration in the Senate.[128] Better-organized efforts followed in each of these states during the 1930s. For the moment, however, Louisiana and Mississippi took center stage in the drive to enact eugenic sterilization legislation in the Deep South.

Louisiana became the site of protracted legislative skirmishes over sterilization between 1924 and 1932, during which time determined proponents led by the unstoppable Jean Gordon and the state mental health establishment clashed with the immovable opposition of the locally powerful Roman Catholic Church. Years before the issue surfaced in the Louisiana legislature, the Catholic Church had emerged as the first major organization in America to oppose eugenic sterilization. This stance reflected both the church's historic opposition to birth control on the grounds that it violates the "natural law" linking sexual activity with procreation, and its religious commitment to the sanctity of all human life regardless of eugenic "fitness." Social factors and self-interest reinforced this stance in the United States, where church membership included large numbers of immigrants and the poor, two groups often targeted for eugenic restriction.[129]

Given the fact that Louisiana contained the only large concentration of Roman Catholics in the Deep South, it seemed an odd site for the region's first comprehensive sterilization bill. Yet New Orleans was then the South's most cosmopolitan city and the home of Tulane University, which boasted of having the best medical school in the region. Furthermore, administrators at Louisiana's two state mental health hospitals had advocated the enactment of a sterilization statute for more than a decade. "The operation is simple, safe and effective and if Louisiana was to enact such a law and enforce it, within three generations insanity would, I think be reduced fifty percent in the state," Superintendent John Thomas of the Louisiana Hospital for the Insane maintained in 1922. "If some members of the legislature . . . would introduce such a bill, I will help him formulate a law that will meet requirements and stand the test of the courts."[130]

At Gordon's request, the freshman state senator Julius G. Fisher stepped forward in 1924 to introduce legislation providing for "the eugenical sterilization of inmates of State hospitals for the insane, of inmates of institutions for the feebleminded and of inmates of institutions for epileptics."[131] Senate committee amendments trimmed the proposal to the point where it only covered "persons committed in any public or private institution for the care of the feeble minded by the courts or legal guardians." Even though this left out patients at Thomas's mental health hospital, it still included residents at Gordon's private Milne Home, at a time when most compulsory sterilization statutes in other states only applied to patients at public institutions. Further, the authority to compel a patient's sterilization was entrusted solely to "the responsible head of the institution," acting with simply the "co-operation and advice" of the local coroner, the institution's physician, and a psychologist. For the Milne Home, this meant Jean Gordon. The legislation omitted many standard procedural devices designed to protect patients, such as notice to the family, and hearings.[132] Nevertheless, it sailed through the state Senate by a two-to-one margin. "Breeding of incurable feeble minded has become so rapid the asylums are being overloaded and the tax burden becoming increasing heavy because of it," a proponent argued on the Senate floor. "The operation merely sterilizes both male and female without otherwise affecting the normal sex inclinations."[133]

Such explanations of the measure, coupled with the prospect of its imminent passage by the House of Representatives, stirred a prompt response from the local Catholic clergy. "The proponents of this act apparently believe that such a law will bring about a reduction in taxes and the practical elimination in time of the feeble minded," Archbishop John W. Shaw of New Orleans sneered. "And then we should have the millennium of supermen and superwomen as perfect specimens of the human animal, bred and reared according to the latest eugenic rules." He countered this elitist vision with a biting environmentalist explanation for social ills, stating that "if the poor were properly housed and protected against the profiteer who is fattening on their life's blood by charging exorbitant prices for the barest subsistence, we would not hear so much talk about the feebleminded being a menace to society." Shaw then turned his attack against the Gordon sisters. "And the pity is that women should be numbered among the champions of such unnatural legislation," he declared. "But what can we expect of women who have abandoned the sanctuary of the home, and are fast becoming the arch–home wreckers, unlike their gentle sisters of other and happier days, who were noble home makers."[134] Following the archbishop's lead, priests throughout the state denounced compulsory sterilization as immoral mutilation and urged their parishioners to stand against the bill. This had a significant political impact in a state where half the voters were Catholic.

Gordon fought back in a dramatic appeal before the House committee considering the bill. "If something of this sort is not done soon, our nordic civilization is gone," Gordon proclaimed in classic eugenic style, "and race preservation is the highest form of patriotism." Drawing on her experience at the Milne Home, she then told of "feebleminded" women producing "idiot" sons and "prostitute" daughters. One such daughter, Gordon declared, "is today in Charity hospital in New Orleans, and, I hope, dying as the result of a criminal [abortion] which is the only reason there is not a third generation of feeble-minded persons already started." She then read a series of endorsements collected from prominent Louisiana physicians, including the president of the state medical society and two Tulane professors. "Shout from the housetops that I am in favor of this most needed legislation," one physician wrote. Another described the measure as vital "for maintaining the purity of the white race in Louisiana." Directly challenging Catholic opponents of the bill, the Tulane gynecologist S.D.M. Clark added, "This issue is not a clerical but a scientific one. The operation in not mutilation, simply sterilization."[135]

The leading progressive newspaper in New Orleans, the *Times-Picayune,* pitched in with a series of editorials defending the legislation. Denying charges that it represented "some wild eugenic scheme to breed a race of supermen," one editorial described the measure as "simply a step to protect the community and the human race against the . . . unfit." Noting the logical connection between eugenic segregation and sterilization, another editorial asked why no one objected to shutting up "these unfortunates" in institutions, but now some opposed performing "a painless minor operation" that could lead to the same results at lower cost and with less restrictions. "Which is the greater hardship? Which is the greater deprivation of 'inalienable human rights'?" the *Times-Picayune* asked.[136]

These efforts on behalf of the bill failed. With Gordon watching from the wings of the chambers, the entire House of Representatives voted to kill the measure by a slender four-vote margin. Both of the physicians then serving as state representatives supported the proposal, with one literally pleading for its passage, but key Catholic lawmakers rose in opposition. "Let nature take its course," one leading opponent declared on the House floor, adding his opinion that sterilization was "fundamentally wrong."[137]

Gordon rose to the challenge of this defeat with her characteristic resolve. Two years later, she returned to the next session of the state legislature with a new proposal for sterilizing both the mentally retarded and the mentally ill. She then brought in a leading nationally known speaker for eugenics, Judge Harry Olson, to help present the case for compulsory sterilization. "Formerly many believed that environment was everything, but science has repudiated that view today," the Chicago jurist told his New Orleans audience. "Surely the criminal is not an environmental product." Instead, he blamed criminal behavior on hereditary mental defects. "The American child of the future must be well born," Olson declared. "We must drop out of the future blood stream the defective streams at present pouring into it."[138] The local expert John Thomas chimed in with statistics and case studies about patients at the state mental health hospitals. "The figures," Thomas asserted in a talk apparently presented several times during the year, "show conclusively that the care and treatment of this unfortunate class of people is an increasing economic problem and one that reaches the hearthstone of every taxpayer. The solution to the problem lies in the hands of the lawmakers of the state."[139] Those lawmakers refused to rise to the bait. Even though Gordon's 1926 bill contained somewhat greater procedural protection than her previous one, it suffered a similar fate.

Fisher again introduced Gordon's proposal, and it sailed through the upper chamber. This bill "passed the senate by a substantial majority in 1924," Fisher explained during floor debate. "Many more states now have this law in operation and find it is effective in lowering the percentage of defective persons." Specifically, he noted that "more than 6000 persons have been sterilized in the state of California during the last three years." Now, he claimed, Louisiana should catch up with California and other progressive states.[140]

The leading Senate opponent of the bill, Grandy Cooper, interrupted Fisher at this point by asking about the mortality rate from these operations in California. When Fisher placed it at 2 percent, Cooper shot back, "Then do you realize that 120 persons have been killed in that state during these three years, all of them operated on against their wills? What right had the state to take their lives?" Later, Cooper raised a second fundamental objection to the proposal when he rhetorically asked Fisher, "And how are you going to determine just who is the proper person to sterilize?" Cooper then answered his own question by stating, "If we set the so-called mental standard even reasonably high and enforce the bill, there would not be another cotton picker born in this state—virtually all of our laborers are morons, or they would not be laborers." He obviously intended this as a backhanded objection to the bill, because he then observed that "some of this state's most useful citizens are feeble-minded." Denouncing eugenics as "a fanciful, theoretical, unproven theory," Cooper concluded, "My mind revolts at the whole theory of eugenic breeding of the human race."

The chairman of the Senate Committee on Health and Quarantine defended the proposal in purely eugenic terms. "At present there are estimated to be more than 8000 feeble-minded persons in this state, while our institutions can accommodate only about 400. For this reason the remainder must wander at large over the state, scattering the seeds of feeble-mindedness for the future generations," he stated. "Although they [could] be self-supporting, that 400 are retained in confinement because their release would be a menace to the intelligence of the unborn children." Seeking to clarify this crassly eugenic argument, one opponent asked about these patients, "And you would make them sterile and release them, bringing others in to replace them until the 8000 you refer to have been operated on?" The chairman did not flinch: "Yes, this is just what he advocated, and what was contemplated by the authors of this bill—they wanted to reach them all." To justify this approach with a specific example, he made the implausible claim that "[o]ne feeble-minded man now living in Louisiana has been found to have over 100 feeble-minded descendants, and most of them have criminal tendencies. Without injustice or injury to anyone, these might have been eliminated by the operation of this bill a few years ago." According to this Senate leader, the "Feeble-minded have no god-given right to propagate."

Louisiana's Catholic clergy held quite a different view on this point, however, and their followers waited to ambush the bill in the lower chamber. A correspondent for a local newspaper reported on the events unfolding on the House floor. "Like a bolt from the blue came the onslaught upon the sterilization bill," he observed. "The storm of opposition had gathered so quietly no one noticed its forming. Dr. Harrison Jordon of Rayville moved the [bill] be adopted, when like a shot Mr. Hebert moved that it be indefinitely postponed and Mr. Prophit laughed a broad smile from the floor."[141]

"God created these poor unfortunates just the same as he did legislators," declared Representative Julius P. Hebert, who also served as Grand Knight of the Knights of Columbus, a Roman Catholic service organization. "This is one of the most vicious measures ever introduced in the legislature," Hebert's fellow Catholic legislator R. L. Prophit added. "I hope that the House will go on record as opposed to making slaughter houses out of our feeble-minded asylums." Other opponents eagerly joined in the assault. One denounced compulsory sterilization as "morally and fundamentally wrong" and suggested, "We should kill this bill without mercy." Another described it as "humbug" and pleaded with his colleagues, "Don't make experimental white rats or guinea pigs out of these poor unfortunates." The reporter for the *New Orleans States* suggested that the fine hand of Archbishop Shaw lay behind this onslaught. Certainly the archbishop had sent an open letter to all legislators asking, "What man in Louisiana would want to feel guilty of having recklessly and wantonly voted in favor of a law that cruelly mutilated a citizen and thus robbed him of his God-given rights?"[142]

Proponents valiantly tried to stem the tide. Jordon read telegrams from national experts praising the success of eugenic sterilization in other states. A colleague decried "the vast injustice that was being done by permitting thousands and thousands of feeble-minded children to be born in Louisiana simply through the failure of the state to take precautions to see that the feeble-minded do not reproduce." Another advocate stressed "the vast economic waste to the state through the absence of a sterilization law," and noted that "the operation was simple and without danger and there is no ill effect in 98 per cent of the cases." He betrayed his own view of the mentally retarded and of the scant value of having a "defective" child by adding that, under the measure, "no one is deprived of his rights or pleasure except the right to reproduce." Outside the legislature, many state medical and mental health leaders offered their support through letters and articles.[143] The influential *Times-Picayune* appealed to lawmakers in an editorial, urging that "Louisiana should take its place with the humane and progressive commonwealths that are moving thus to relieve the coming generations of the menace of inherited insanity and feeble-mindedness and the crime and vice prolifically bred by these infirmities."[144] These entreaties failed. With Gordon again waiting in the wings of the chamber, the House defeated the bill by the slenderest of margins, forty-eight against it to forty-six for it.[145]

Curiously, the 1926 Louisiana legislature also narrowly defeated a proposal to outlaw the teaching of human evolution in public schools. This represented the only time that the same session of any state legislature ever voted on measures arising from both the eugenics and the anti-evolution movements, even though those two crusades shared the public spotlight during the 1920s, and each appeared to pit the doctrines of modern science against the commandments of traditional religion. The two movements took opposing sides in this conflict, however. The modern eugenics movement was launched by Charles Darwin's cousin Francis Galton, and sprang from a Social Darwinist world view that sought to encourage the evolutionary development of the human race through a survival-of-the-fittest mechanism. In Louisiana, as elsewhere, leading eugenicists ridiculed the anti-evolution movement.[146] For their part, leaders of the anti-evolution movement logically rejected any hope for the evolutionary improvement of the human race through eugenics, though they did not necessarily deny the influence of heredity on individual behavior. Thus, William Jennings Bryan, the most famous liberal spokesperson for anti-evolutionism, could instinctively repudiate eugenics as "brutal," while John Roach Straton, a conservative co-leader of the movement, could accept hereditarianism.[147]

The philosophical reasoning that linked evolutionism with eugenics within the thinking of movement leaders did not reach down to the votes of individual Louisiana legislators. Quite to the contrary, in both houses of the state legislature, virtually all of the lawmakers who took the allegedly proscience side by supporting eugenic sterilization also took the allegedly antiscience side by opposing evolutionary teaching, whereas those against the "science" of eugenics tended to favor the "scientific" teaching of evolution.[148] Clearly, a different dynamic than any perceived conflict of science versus religion influenced these votes. A simple breakdown along religious lines did appear, however. On the one hand, legislators representing Catholic areas generally opposed eugenic sterilization on religious grounds, while they dismissed anti-evolution lawmaking as the intrusion of Protestant fundamentalism in public education. On the other hand, legislators from Protestant districts overwhelmingly opposed evolutionary teaching as heretical, while they tended to accept pragmatic arguments for eugenics. The distinctive religious diversity of Louisiana saved it from the embarrassment of enacting either measure.

A second factor also contributed to the defeat of the 1926 sterilization bill. For the first time, a breach appeared in the ranks of state officials. Even though administrators at the two state mental health hospitals continued to support the legislation, the superintendent of the state facility for the mentally retarded provided evidence that such laws were "virtually inoperative in other states."[149] Two years later, with Gordon again promoting a sterilization bill in the legislature, a former superintendent of both state mental health hospitals testified against the measure at a Senate hearing. That physician, Clarence Pierson, who then operated a private mental health institution, explained his position before a meeting of the state medical society. "Fifteen years ago, officially and otherwise, I advocated legal sterilization as a means to gain an end," he stated. "Maturer thought however, and the experience of more capable thinkers and workers have convinced me of my error." Many experts have growing doubts "concerning heredity in its relation to mental deficiency," Pierson observed, and they have concluded that "it is quite impossible to predict with precision the type of offspring of any given mating."[150] Actually, this re-evaluation process had begun on the national level at least a half decade earlier, when some geneticists objected to the racist use of eugenics during the debate over immigration policies, but Pierson was the first prominent practitioner in the Deep South to change his position in response to this still-subtle shift.[151]

Pierson's conversion received a hostile reception within the state medical community. Leading local physicians continued to support eugenic sterilization throughout the 1920s, and the official journal of the state medical society published an article endorsing the procedure during the legislative debate over the 1928 sterilization bill. "All cases belonging to the defective development group and all cases of insanity should be sterilized to prevent propagation," the article affirmed, "because in our present state of knowledge, it seems a clear cut fact that heredity plays an important role in populating our state institutions."[152] Most of the comments following Pierson's presentation to the state medical society also attacked his position, leading to the eugenicist Robert Carruth's dramatic closing remark, "Our civilization is tottering to its fall and sterilization of the unfit is the only hope of the race."[153]

Jean Gordon attended Pierson's presentation and offered her own biting critique. "I acknowledge to over forty years that I have worked in the charities of this city, and there hasn't been a thing started here that I haven't had my share in," she noted. "I tell you we are swamped right today from the charity standpoint due to the feebleminded men and women, particularly the women." After describing various cases of hereditary degeneracy, she asked, "Have you ever seen a normal child born of a feebleminded mother?" Pierson answered his distinguished inquisitor in measured terms. "Yes, I have seen splendid normal children who have gone out and made a success, but whose mothers would be classed as feebleminded," he stated. "If we had practiced this law, some of your greatest war heroes, lawyers and literateurs [sic] would have been lost to the world."[154] Expert support for eugenic segregation was beginning to erode in Louisiana.

Thanks in part to Pierson's testimony, support for the procedure also ebbed within the Louisiana legislature. Gordon's 1928 sterilization bill fell one vote short of passage in the state Senate, and was never considered by the House of Representatives.[155] In 1930, her fourth proposal managed to clear the Senate, but failed come to a vote in the House.[156] Before she could mount a fifth attempt, the grand dame of Louisiana eugenics died from a sudden attack of appendicitis suffered while she was attending a masked ball during the 1931 Mardi Gras festivities. In describing her remarkable achievements, the Associated Press obituary noted, "Principal among them were the child labor law passed in 1908 and the proposed sterilization act for the mentally incompetent which three [sic] times was lost and which she again was planning to propose to the next legislature."[157] When a modified version of that bill was offered in the 1932 session, it lost without debate in a tie vote in the Senate.[158] No further proposals for eugenic sterilization appeared in the Louisiana legislature.[159] The institutional opposition of the Catholic Church had outlived Jean Gordon's best efforts.

During the late 1920s, as Louisiana eugenicists unsuccessfully struggled to enact a comprehensive sterilization statute, eugenicists in neighboring Mississippi quietly got the job done. The population of Mississippi was then not as diverse or cosmopolitan as that of Louisiana. The state could not boast of having a great medical school, and had fewer prominent physicians. Whereas Louisiana was the most urbanized state in the Deep South, Mississippi was the most rural. It also had the lowest percentage of Catholics of any state in the region, and the highest level of poverty. African Americans constituted nearly half of the state population, but they were effectively disenfranchised.[160] The fundamentalist Protestant tenor of state politics became readily apparent when, after the 1925 *Scopes* trial, the Mississippi legislature was the only one in the nation to follow Tennessee's lead in enacting a strict anti-evolution statute.[161] In short, White Protestants ruled Mississippi during the period, and powerful political leaders usually got their way. When Theodore Bilbo regained the governorship in 1928, political forces aligned to enact the first comprehensive eugenic sterilization law in the Deep South.

During his previous term in office, Bilbo had championed a "Home and Colony for the Feeble Minded" as part of his program of progressive reform for Mississippi. He had also deputized NCMH expert Thomas Haines to survey mental hygiene conditions within the state and to recommend a plan for improvement.[162] Haines, in turn, proposed a purely eugenic remedy for the problem of mental retardation, with sexual segregation serving as a step toward sterilization. "Something can be done in educating the public in regard to sterilization," he advised in 1919, "but public opinion is not ready for this as a general policy, and, furthermore, we need a state institution in order to manage the sterilization successfully."[163] Bilbo remained keenly interested in the new institution after he left office in 1920, going so far as to chair its initial board of trustees, but the state pulled back. Indeed, the legislature nearly closed the tiny facility in 1922, and repeatedly refused to fund its expansion. Its superintendent, H. H. Ramsey, could not even secure sufficient appropriations to admit females to the institution, a bitter frustration for any eugenicist.[164]

Increasingly, Ramsey saw sterilization as a means to extend the Mississippi Colony's eugenic impact. "Institutional segregation is probably the most practical and humane preventative of feeble-mindedness," Ramsey observed in 1924. "Sterilization, however, in selected cases, especially those sent out from the institution and continuing to present bad sex tendencies, would be an effective means of preventing the reproduction of a large number of defectives."[165] He expanded on this point in the Mississippi Colony's 1925–27 biennial report. "Hereditary imbeciles and low grade morons should not be allowed to marry and reproduce their kind. They are the promoters of pauperism, crime, prostitution, and venereal disease," he wrote. "They should be recognized as children and brought under the supervision of the state, to be trained and in such cases as would be advisable, paroled after being sterilized."[166] In the same report, the facility's trustees recommended extending this approach beyond the mentally retarded. "Sterilization should finally be made one of the requirements for release, or parole of the feebleminded, epileptic, insane or confirmed criminal cases," they advised. "Otherwise, it is easy to see that all the state's institutions dealing with defectives, dependents and criminals will have to be enlarged at frequent intervals to make it possible for the state to cope with the rapidly increasing army of abnormal and defective citizenship."[167]

Bilbo's reelection as governor provided an opportunity for the Mississippi Colony to come in from the cold. "There should be no further argument to any intelligent mind for the building and adequate support of an institution for the segregation and training of the several thousand feeble-minded children of this state," Bilbo declared in his 1928 inaugural address. "The state has spent its millions in the effort to advance our civilization, to educate and uplift our people yet our feeble-minded, epileptic, insane, paupers and criminals can reproduce without restriction, thus continuing to corrupt our society and increase tax burdens on our people."[168] At a time when the Mississippi Colony housed less than two hundred male patients, this speech literally invited a significant expansion of the facility and provided a rationale for sterilization. Ramsey worked closely with the new administration in hammering out the details of Bilbo's reform program, which combined coordinated efforts to identify mentally retarded children in public schools with expanded facilities for their eugenic segregation and training. "After training," Ramsey explained, "higher type defectives who can earn a living . . . could be sterilized and paroled, the state thus being relieved of their care and of their menace as propagators of other generations of defectives."[169]

A dutiful legislature adopted as much of Bilbo's program as the state could afford. This included enough new money for Ramsey to triple the Mississippi Colony's capacity, construct its first women's dormitory, and provide a complete mental and physical examination for all patients.[170] "The support appropriation of the school and colony for feeble-minded passed the House of Representatives Tuesday morning with a very flattering vote," one local newspaper editor observed. "It is the result of a social awakening in Mississippi reflected in our Legislature. There is evidently a growing responsibility among our people for this type of defective who must finally become both a social and economic burden to the state."[171] This "social awakening" apparently went beyond support appropriations, however, because the House passed Mississippi's first comprehensive sterilization bill by the "flattering" vote of ninety ayes to eighteen nays exactly one week later.[172]

Representative Wiley Harris, a blue-blooded lawyer from Jackson, had introduced the sterilization bill shortly after Bilbo took office. The text of the legislation echoed the language of Virginia's sterilization statute, which the U.S. Supreme Court had upheld nine months earlier, and its spirit captured the mood of the new administration. Indeed, on the very day that Harris offered his proposal, a top state official warned the Jackson Rotary Club that "imbeciles are reproducing their kind at an alarming rate, sowing their seeds of evil degeneracy on a thousand hills and bringing into the world an unfitted citizenship type that will be a burden to coming generations."[173] Harris reflected a similar viewpoint when introducing the bill. "Surely," he stated, "society owes to posterity no higher duty than by humane methods to breed out of the race such defectives as those who at once become a burden to the state and a scourge to their descendants." Cost factors favored sterilization over segregation in this context, he noted, because "it relieves society of an ever increasing economic burden, as the operation enables those who otherwise must be kept confined in colonies to be returned to the world." For Harris, these "defectives" included those "afflicted with hereditary insanity" as well as the mentally retarded, and his bill, like the Virginia statute, covered patients in both the public mental health hospitals and the state institution for the mentally retarded.[174]

With the strong support of the Bilbo administration, Harris's bill sailed through Mississippi's House of Representatives with little opposition. During the one-sided floor debate, proponents claimed that the measure would "do much toward blotting out hereditary forms of insanity" and would "allow freedom" for patients institutionalized solely for eugenic reasons. To dramatize the potential danger from a single individual, Harris alleged that "212 persons are confined to insane asylums because they happened to be descendants of one person afflicted with an insidious form of hereditary insanity."[175] On such testimony, the House overwhelmingly approved the proposal. With the legislature rushing toward adjournment, the Senate hastily added its assent by a closer vote but with even less debate. All six physicians in the state legislature supported the measure, and no organization or interest group opposed it. Bilbo promptly signed the bill, and the first eugenic sterilization statute in the Deep South became law.[176] "There is an increasing recognition of the large and fundamental part played by feeblemindedness in the causation of poverty, pauperism, delinquency, and crime," Mississippi Colony trustees reported in response to the 1928 legislative session, "and this public understanding . . . will enable the institution to render the largest possible service to Mississippi in coping with the growing burden of social problems."[177] Compulsory sterilization now became a part of that service to the state, as eugenicists elsewhere in the region looked on with increasing interest during the 1930s.

CHAPTER SIX

Full Bloom

The 1930s represented the pivotal decade for compulsory eugenic sterilization in the United States. On the one hand, Supreme Court approval for the procedure in 1927 led to the enactment of new or revised sterilization statutes in seventeen states during the ensuing four-year period. These laws, coupled with a greater confidence in the legality of proceeding under existing statutes, fueled a surge in the number of operations actually performed. During the entire twenty-year period from 1907, when authorizing statutes first passed, to 1927, when the Supreme Court upheld their constitutionality, state institutions had sterilized only about eighty-five hundred patients, and most of these had been in California. In contrast, during the 1930s the *annual* number of such sterilizations typically exceeded twenty-five hundred, and once nearly reached four thousand, before dropping to about fifteen hundred in the 1940s and then petering out during the 1950s and early 1960s.[1] On the other hand, the historian Daniel Kevles identified the 1930s as the critical period during which a coalition of critics that undercut and ultimately destroyed the academic credibility of eugenics emerged among biological and social scientists.[2] By 1935, one of those critics, the Nobel Prize–winning geneticist and political socialist Hermann J. Muller, could denounce eugenics as "lending a false appearance of scientific basis to advocates of race and class prejudice, defenders of vested interests of church and state, Fascists, Hitlerites, and reactionaries generally."[3]

Muller's comments may have accurately characterized the diehard defenders of traditional eugenics within the elite scientific community, who should have known better by 1935, but it certainly did not apply to the rank-and-file eugenics advocates and practitioners in America. Mental health institutions in most states continued to sterilize patients at a record clip throughout the 1930s without any authoritative basis for altering those practices. Indeed, during that entire decade, the professional journal for alienists working with the mentally retarded regularly presented clinical justifications for sterilization, and leading geneticists publicly endorsed H. H. Goddard's eugenic theories of mental deficiency.[4] Further, many state medical associations continued to endorse eugenic remedies throughout the period, and only gradually recognized the growing body of biological and social-scientific evidence against those procedures. This was especially true in the Deep South, where relatively few working scientists resided to spread the word of change.[5] Some time interval inevitably exists between the formation of new scientific theories and their integration into medical or mental health practices. This lag, which had helped delay the introduction of eugenics into the Deep South, also slowed the departure of eugenics from the region.

In the early 1930s, when two dozen states actively practiced eugenic sterilization, only one jurisdiction in the Deep South had enacted a comprehensive sterilization statute.[6] Moreover, that singular law, Mississippi's 1928 enactment, did not have much impact until the mid-1930s owing to bureaucratic inefficiency and cost. Its implementation took several years at the state's two mental health hospitals, and never fully occurred at the Mississippi School and Colony for the Feebleminded despite the major role that institution's superintendent, H. H. Ramsey, had played in enacting the legislation. Inopportune timing hindered the process. The sterilization statute passed shortly before the onset of the Great Depression, along with legislation to triple the Mississippi Colony's size and replace the state's antebellum mental health hospital in Jackson. Funding for these reforms dried up just as demands for state services increased. The colony completed the construction of three new dormitories by 1929, and admitted nearly two hundred additional patients, but the legislature failed to appropriate adequate operating funds for the expansion. Soon the facility began expelling patients, many of them children with no place to go. "When all the facts are known in the case of these children," colony trustees argued, "it becomes quite apparent that to leave them unsupervised in the communities is a very real form of public extravagance. The people of the State save much more than they spend by providing for their institutional care and preventing their propagation."[7]

Ramsey recognized the eugenic role for sterilization in this fiscal context, but could not realize it under the existing law. "The chief benefit of sterilization is to be derived from the sterilization of such inmates as we can release safely from time to time to go out into the community and earn their own livelihood," he advised in 1931. "By this means the state can be relieved of their care and prevent their re-production after their release." The new compulsory sterilization law contained all the procedural safeguards of the Virginia statute, however, including the right of notice to and judicial appeal by the patient's family; and the Mississippi Colony lacked the funds to pursue any resulting court action. Indeed, the state did not even have the money to distribute printed copies of the law. "Therefore," Ramsey wrote, "at present we have chosen to proceed cautiously under its provisions and sterilize only such cases as consent from parents or guardians can be secured." This rarely occurred, he acknowledged, because the procedure caused considerable concern, "especially with those parents with less intelligence themselves," which presumably included most parents of children deemed to carry eugenic defects. Ramsey could only appeal to the legislature for a "more practical" sterilization law that would "increase its liberality of application," but he soon left the state in frustration to set up a more active and better-funded program in Utah.[8]

Ramsey's successors continued to promote eugenic sterilization, but with little impact. "I would stress the importance of a simplified Sterilization Law," one Mississippi Colony superintendent advised in his 1937 biennial report. "It is useless for me to say anything about the great expense that feeblemindedness is causing the various states—especially our own—and I think that a law on the above subject without so much red tape would eventually reduce feeblemindedness to a considerable extent."[9] No changes occurred, however, and the institution continued to rely primarily on segregation to prevent the propagation of mental retardation.[10] When a new superintendent completed a review of sexual sterilization procedures at the colony in 1945, he reported that "of the three hundred thirty three patients' records examined, only three girls and no boys had this operation performed."[11] He managed to increase the number somewhat over the next two years, and asserted that the procedure should "be more widely used," but the total never became large, and the issue soon disappeared from the Mississippi Colony's official reports.[12]

Mississippi's two state mental health hospitals managed to implement more vigorous eugenic sterilization programs than the colony did during the 1930s, apparently because the families of fewer patients objected. The huge Mississippi State Hospital reported performing only six sterilizations during the first biennium after the new law passed, and the smaller East Mississippi State Hospital performed no such operations.[13] In his next biennial report, however, Superintendent C. D. Mitchell of the larger facility announced an ambitious program under which "it is to be hoped that in the future every patient who comes to the institution before they return to their home will be sterilized in order to lessen the mental disorders which will be handed down to future generations."[14] Even though *no* mental health experts then thought that heredity caused *all* mental disorders, Mitchell wanted to sterilize every patient. The program included advance notification both to patients and to their guardians, but still managed to produce 163 sterilizations in the following biennium.[15] For the same period, 1933–35, the superintendent at the East Mississippi State Hospital reported, "We have done a number of sterilizations, which is the major procedure in controlling the increase in insanity."[16] Both institutions continued this eugenic approach for combating mental illness at a gradually declining rate until World War II, when the smaller hospital lost its only surgeon to the war effort, and the larger facility drastically reduced its use of the procedure following a change in administration.[17] Thereafter, Mississippi state mental health institutions sterilized only a few patients per year under the 1928 law, which remains in effect to this day. During the middle and late 1930s, however, the total added up to more than 500 sterilizations.[18]

Significantly, the Mississippi mental health hospitals pursued their sterilization campaign during a period of progressive reform within those institutions. For example, Mitchell instituted his sterilization program at about the same time as the Mississippi State Hospital moved from its antiquated asylum in Jackson to a modern facility in nearby Whitfield. "He has delivered the patients committed to his care from iron cages where they were chained," a colleague wrote at the time, "to a haven where the buildings are clean, safe, and well-cared for, the surroundings beautiful, and the treatment scientific and humane."[19] This scientific treatment included eugenics. "Sterilization is undoubtedly a most beneficent State Law," Mitchell wrote in 1939. "By sterilizing unstable patients we reduce readmissions by prevention of the burden of child bearing and rearing, as well as to insure the survival of the fittest by abrogating defectives of power to procreate."[20] When Mitchell's successor assumed control of the hospital two years later, he found that the "chief surgical cases have been appendectomy, tonsillectomy, and sterilization," but he signaled a turning from eugenic remedies by adding, "It is our purpose and my prayer that Mississippi's mentally ill should never be denied any ray of hope that modern medical science may support and that the maternal love of a great state can provide."[21] In his later biennial reports, the new superintendent stressed the treatment of individual patients rather than the prevention of procreation by these persons, and never again mentioned sterilization or eugenics.[22]

Further, the racist policies prevailing in Mississippi institutions during the 1930s never significantly infected eugenics practices within those facilities. Even though the chief governmental proponent of eugenics legislation, Governor Theodore G. Bilbo, was also one of the most outspoken race baiters of the era, he primarily championed eugenics at the state facility for the mentally retarded, which excluded African Americans until

1968. The Mississippi State Hospital did admit roughly equal numbers of Blacks and Whites into racially segregated wards throughout the period, but although Black patients uniformly received significantly worse treatment than did White patients and suffered appalling death rates, no evidence exists of a different sterilization rate for the two groups. Indeed, the architect of the hospital's sterilization program, C. D. Mitchell, also significantly reduced the death rate among African American patients by improving conditions in Black wards. Further, the sterilization program at the all-White East Mississippi State Hospital paralleled the program at the racially mixed Mississippi State Hospital. Black mental patients suffered barbarous treatment in Mississippi, confined full-time in wards of the old asylum that Mitchell decried as "impossible to make habitable," but compulsory sterilization was not one of their particular afflictions.[23]

While the Mississippi mental health hospitals actively implemented their sterilization programs during the 1930s, eugenicists in every other state of the Deep South sought authority for similar schemes. The effort in Louisiana essentially died with Jean Gordon in 1931, although Joseph O'Hara made some effort to revive the issue, without any appreciable effect, during his tenure as president of the state board of health in the late 1930s.[24] Compulsory sterilization bills covering mentally ill, mentally retarded, and epileptic patients in state institutions surfaced in the Florida legislature during its 1933 and 1935 sessions. Both bills received preliminary approval from legislative committees, and carried the endorsement of state mental health officials, but died without final votes in either chamber of the legislature.[25] Indeed, proponents of the later bill suffered the humiliation of withdrawing their measure from consideration on the Senate floor after opponents ridiculed it by attaching amendments limiting the procedure "to persons over the age of seventy years," requiring that the "operation may only be performed on a moonlight night . . . by a clairvoyant," and submitting the law for approval by "the female electorate of the State . . . on a cold day in July."[26]

No conclusive reasons explain why eugenic sterilization became a joking matter in Florida while it remained a serious subject elsewhere in the Deep South, but several factors contributed to the difference. By the 1930s, the promotion of tourism and retirement living in the "Sunshine State" had generated a more cosmopolitan environment in Florida than existed in other states of the region. Perhaps as a result of this, during that decade the state's federation of women's clubs became the first such organization in the Deep South to shift from endorsing the compulsory sterilization of defectives to endorsing the distribution of voluntary birth control information to all women.[27] Further, the Florida Medical Association was the first state physicians' group in the Deep South to publicize

the accumulating scientific evidence "of the demonstrable effect of environment in producing the mental defective." In fact, during the consideration of the 1933 sterilization legislation, the association sponsored a
radio broadcast stating that "too little is known considering genetic selection to formulate any policy either in *theory* or *legally* that would be
comprehensive and *humanitarian* in impact or *predictable* in results."[28]
Both of these developments followed national trends not yet otherwise
evident in the Deep South. No eugenics legislation ever passed in the region without the active support of state physicians' and women's groups.
In Florida, those groups had turned away from eugenic sterilization by
the mid-1930s, just as their counterparts in South Carolina, Georgia, and
Alabama embraced that approach.

South Carolina

South Carolina acted first among these three late entrants in the field,
and in doing so became the next-to-last American state to enact a eugenic sterilization statute. The issue had lain dormant in the state for
nearly a decade. Shortly after opening the State Training School for the
Feeble-minded in 1920, Superintendent B. O. Whitten had called for the
"sterilization of feebleminded, criminal, or insane persons coming under
state control." He easily justified this extreme position on economic
grounds. "Institutional care is certainly the proper method of caring for
a large number already here," he reasoned, but "the cost of establishing
and maintaining institutions to accommodate all persons whose propagation would be a menace to society is obviously prohibitive." Using an
objective test of the patient's best interest, Whitten cavalierly dismissed
the notion that the eugenically unfit suffered harm from losing the ability
to procreate, on the grounds that no "normal person desires to become
the father, mother, . . . or even near relative of a defective." Therefore, he
asserted, "[w]ith the simplicity of the operation now in use, few people
would object to the removal of this danger among those who are obviously afflicted if they had a fair conception of the results of their being
left free to propagate." Having thus presumed the consent of "normal"
rational persons, even though his patients were neither "normal" nor
fully rational, Whitten "hoped that our state will not be as far behind in
passing certain laws regulating the procreation of the mentally afflicted
as it was in passing one to establish an institution to care for a few of the
thousands already in our midst."[29]

To Whitten's dismay, South Carolina lagged just as far behind in imposing eugenic sterilization as it had in commencing eugenic segregation.
The state's senior mental health official, Superintendent C. F. Williams of
the South Carolina State Hospital, contributed to this delay. In response

to a 1925 request from the hospital's governing board, Williams reviewed the impact of sterilization laws in other states, from which he concluded that insufficient scientific justification and constitutional authority existed for sterilizing the mentally ill.[30] Thereafter, throughout his tenure in office, which extended to 1945, Williams hesitated to endorse compulsory sterilization and continued to accept "environmental" explanations for mental illness, even though he acknowledged that clinical physicians generally held a different viewpoint on these matters.[31] "I can be of very little assistance to you," he once replied to a physician soliciting support for eugenics legislation, "for I doubt seriously if sterilization has a place in the field of psychiatry except in a very few selected cases."[32] Because of Williams's position and the constitutional concerns that dogged compulsory sterilization until the *Buck v. Bell* decision in 1927, Whitten did not immediately press the issue further.[33]

During the early 1930s, however, Whitten and other South Carolina eugenicists took the offensive. "I have kept silent for several years, hoping that I might speak out of the fullness of experience," Whitten declared in a 1931 address on sterilization to the South Carolina Medical Association. "At least, I have had fifteen years observation, commingled with a bit of study, upon which to base opinion." The intervening experience and study did not alter Whitten's basic opinion on the issue but simply provided him more examples with which to promote the cause. "I believe 90,000 is a conservative estimate of the number of people in our state who have not more than 70 percent of normal intelligence," he told his SCMA colleagues. "A disproportion of delinquents and an overwhelming number of dependents are recruited from their ranks. . . . The Utopian plan of institutionalizing all such undesirable citizens during their ages of reproduction offers a pleasing answer but no logical solution, because of the prohibitive cost." For Whitten, "selective sterilization" offered the only realistic answer. "Justice Holmes of the United States Supreme Court said: 'Three generations of imbeciles are enough.' We have on record four generations of imbeciles in South Carolina and three generations of them are now at the State Training School," the superintendent noted as he related various case histories of familial mental and social degeneracy, leading to his call for the state medical community to "register an opinion with reference to a form of legislation that would, in time, mitigate some of the conditions cited and promote eugenical development of the human race in our state."[34]

The discussion following Whitten's address offered support for his proposal. "I think we should take to heart this message which Dr. Whitten has brought to us this morning and immediately begin work upon the General Assembly. You know the history of such legislation in our state is that you have to pave the way and work carefully for several years," one experienced physician from the state's capital city commented. "You have to use propaganda in order to sufficiently influence the legislature. ... I hope you will all go back home and begin this propaganda now."[35] Actually, Whitten had already drafted a comprehensive sterilization bill, but failed to find a sponsor for it during the 1931 session. "The Legislature is somewhat timid about this subject and would really like to know the attitude of the medical profession," Whitten concluded from this experience.[36] He failed again the following year but, in 1933, managed to secure a sponsor—the 39-year-old attorney-legislator Shepard K. Nash, a New Deal progressive. The process of "propaganda" and persuasion ultimately took two more years.

Whitten's bill, which eventually passed without alteration, did not simply apply to patients at his facility. It broadly empowered the superintendent of each state mental health, penal, and eleemosynary institution to petition the state board of health for authority to sterilize "any inmate of such institution who is afflicted with any hereditary form of insanity that is recurrent, idiocy, imbecility, feeble-minded[ness] or epilepsy." After notice and a hearing, the board could authorize the operation upon finding that the inmate "is or would be the probable parent of socially inadequate offspring . . . and that the welfare of such inmate and of society will be promoted by such sterilization."[37] Eugenicists typically maintained that only the welfare of society should justify compulsory sterilization. Whitten did not intend a different result by requiring that the operation also benefit the inmate because, as he noted at the time, afflicted individuals "must have someone else to decide what is good for them," and the state would fulfill that role under the proposed law.[38] "Personally, I can not give whole hearted support to the measure unless I can feel that it is the best thing for the individual," Whitten explained, but immediately added, "In many cases, it isn't very hard for me to believe that it is."[39] Despite the breadth of Whitten's proposal, it quietly passed the South Carolina Senate before encountering a wall of opposition in the state's House of Representatives.[40]

Representative William R. Bradford, a small-town newspaper editor and former board member of the state penitentiary, spearheaded the opposition in the House. "It's inhuman," he declared during the floor debate, "the state has no right to butcher its citizens." One proponent tried to counter by explaining that the measure "would help relieve the overcrowding crisis at the insane hospital and penitentiary," but such practical argument could not overcome Bradford's moral outrage.[41] The character of Bradford's objections was reflected in various editorials that he wrote at the time. In one, he questioned a hereditary explanation for intelligence by citing "an elaborate study of many school pupils by experts." He claimed that the study "indicates that the average pupil is just about average, no matter what happened to his folks beforehand." This he saw as "just about as sensible folks suspected before we had so much research."[42] In another, he challenged the eugenicists' fatalistic view of mental illness with evidence that insanity "is a disease and should have medical treatment: between 25 and 40 per cent of those treated are recovered or improved"; and he added the warning "Most of us are a little off at times."[43] Marshaling his arguments in this folksy manner, Bradford won support. His motion to kill the sterilization bill passed by a two-to-one margin. Whitten received a personal rebuke in the process, when one legislator suggested that the superintendent should be the first person sterilized under the measure.[44]

A similar scenario unfolded the following year. Nash again introduced Whitten's bill, and it quickly passed the Senate without discussion.[45] This time it carried the endorsement of various women's clubs, but that was not enough to overcome the determined opposition in the House of Representatives. Indeed, even Whitten admitted retreating before this opposition for fear that pushing the issue "was going to jeopardize my opportunity for getting a special appropriation" through the legislature.[46] "The primary blocking to a Sterilization Law in South Carolina seems to be largely a negative apathetic attitude," Whitten explained. "Those who approve it by virtue of experience and observation allow dignity and professional decorum to inhibit their making postulations publicly, not wishing to emulate or even refute certain articles subtly released to the Associated Press by men of ability and eminence." Whitten could not understand his opponents, and dismissed them as irrational. "In the minds of many," he observed, "there are obscure reasons, not well defined or understood, why sterilization should not be performed." Religious scruples clouded the reasoning of some opponents, Whitten suggested, while "too much thinking" led others to elevate "morals to a plane far exceeding the defective's ability to attain."[47]

The next session provided a better opportunity for passing the sterilization bill. Several key opponents, including Bradford, did not seek reelection for 1935, and two physicians who favored eugenics entered the legislature that year. One of those physicians, a former pathologist at the South Carolina State Hospital named R. G. Blackburn, introduced the measure in the House of Representatives.[48] Prior to the final House vote, the SCMA formally endorsed the measure for the first time, and delegates at the annual convention of the South Carolina Federation of Women's Clubs designated it "a major legislative measure toward which to work" during the legislative session. "In South Carolina," Whitten commented at the time, "the Federated Clubs are becoming very much interested in the matter. I have about decided that the women, the [progressive] preachers and the social workers will be the main sources of my support of the Bill."[49] With the backing of these recognized forces for liberal reform, and the active support of officials from the State Training School, Blackburn finally secured House passage of the legislation during the closing days of the session.

Blackburn's arguments on the House floor stressed the economics of eugenics. "One hundred years ago the State hospital was built and at first it had only a few patients; now it is the largest institution in the state, is overcrowded, with an enormous waiting list. Appropriations for its support and for the school for the feeble-minded make up a considerable part of the state supply bill," he declared. "I believe you are taking from the normal child in order to support the unfortunates." The problem lay in heredity, Blackburn explained. "Inmates leave the institution and go home; they beget children who in turn take the place of their parents, and they constitute a menace to the social welfare of the state." Compulsory sterilization offered a solution. With it, he estimated, "[a]fter 20 years [the length of a generation], admissions to the State hospital would begin to fall off, and in 40 years, you would save 40 per cent in appropriations to the hospital and the school for the feeble-minded."[50]

Blackburn then faced the two questions that had torpedoed previous sterilization bills in the House. "Are insane children sometimes born to sane parents?" one colleague asked. "Yes, but if you prevent the feeble-minded from reproducing, you will cut down on the number of insane," Blackburn replied with care. "Is it possible for insane parents to bear sane children?" another legislator asked. "Possible, but not probable," Blackburn responded, and then turned the question aside by reading a series of eugenic case histories prepared by Whitten, leading to the conclusion, "Nearly all of the children at the state training school are offspring of low mentality parents."

Whitten had rehearsed these answers with Blackburn, and probably planted the questions, to address the persistent objections that sterilization laws were both overly inclusive *and* not inclusive enough. Certainly twenty-eight years of sterilization had "not precluded the existence of a Dillinger in Indiana," Whitten conceded, and there occurred "the possible prevention by sterilization of intelligent children being born to defective parents." He preferred to respond, "Come with me to the Institution and let us study the problem deliberately where we can mingle theories with actualities." Blackburn attempted to mimic this approach by introducing case histories from the State Training School into the House debate. Whitten initially opposed using this type of public argument on the grounds that it was too exploitative of the patients, but he eventually accepted it as necessary. "We have never considered . . . that sterilization was a cure-all," he confided to colleagues shortly before the floor debate. "We know that the laws of heredity do not operate that way. But in dealing with propaganda we are always so likely to allow the press to present it in a way that the public will get its biggest kick out of the reading."

Not every legislator accepted Blackburn's arguments. "No one has proven that insanity is hereditary," one opponent protested. "The medical community is divided on the question." Another lawmaker cautioned, "We better stop and think. We are legislating major operations on women—God forbid it." Whitten had considered these objections, and found them wanting. "Science may not illuminate all nebulous corners of this baffling subject," he commented at the time. "However, I am convinced that there is a good deal of science in preventing the propagation of dependents and delinquents." Apparently the majority of House members agreed, because they approved the bill by a margin of seventy-one to nineteen.

The measure then moved to the Senate, which had approved identical legislation twice in the preceding two years. A freshman senator with a grand future, Strom Thurmond, quickly guided the bill through the Medical Affairs Committee before another freshman, the physician S. F. Brasington, assumed that responsibility on the Senate floor.[51] In the rush toward final adjournment of the session, the Senate approved the familiar measure with little discussion. Brasington simply commented that the legislation "would do considerable good toward decreasing the amount of inheritable insanity and feeble-mindedness," and reassured his colleagues that "the operation needed to bring about the desired effect was simple and could be performed without detriment to the health of the patient." When one opponent denounced the bill for taking away a patient's "God-given right to bear children," Brasington shot back that it applied "only to persons in institutions who have no right to reproduce." In this exchange, these senators had mixed up natural and legal rights in a manner that typified the eugenics debate of the era. After another lawmaker reminded the Senate of Whitten's support, the bill sailed through on a vote of thirty-three ayes to four nays.[52] "A bill to legalize the sterilization of mental defectives was one of the last measures passed by the general assembly," the Associated Press reported a week later. "It was signed today by Governor Johnson along with the education bill."[53]

Whitten had attained his legislative objective, and the following year his peers from across the country elected him president of the American Association for the Study of the Feeble-Minded, the professional organization for experts in his field. During his presidential address, Whitten reminisced about his efforts in South Carolina. "The campus on this 1190-acre tract of land, carved in gullies and studded with trees, has been changed into a veritable flower garden," he mused. "Dormitories increased from two to fourteen, including [a farm colony of] four small units for stable, older imbeciles located some distance from the main campus."[54] Now, sterilization completed this picture of the ideal eugenics facility.

South Carolina institutions did not rush to use the new statute, however. At first, a technical glitch in the law delayed its implementation for two years. Thereafter, Williams continued to drag his feet. In an official letter affirming his willingness to enforce the new law at the state mental health hospital, Williams allowed, "I feel that the general public, even the profession, has been misled by certain eugenic arguments," and he advised a state health official, "I do not believe I would go too strong on the sterilization program."[55] Indeed, only one patient at that large facility underwent the procedure prior to the superintendent's retirement a decade later, and that involved the special case of a mentally retarded female sent to the hospital solely for sterilization by county welfare officials who had obtained prior approval from the state board of health. Even Whitten's State Training School reported performing only seventy-six eugenic sterilizations during this initial ten-year period, in addition to an unspecified number of therapeutic ones, with all but eight of these operations performed on women.[56]

Whitten had always advocated "selective," rather than "mass," sterilization in theory, and the moderate total numbers for his institution suggest that he followed this approach in practice.[57] He also stood out among early southern eugenicists in expressing greater concern about the sexual activities of mentally retarded females than about those of mentally retarded males, and this too carried over into his sterilization practices. For example, in discussing the need for compulsory sterilization, Whitten once observed, "Our experience with girls on parole has been that overtures are made from men who are not considered defective. With the more fastidious group of girls, this has an overpowering effect." Without making any parallel comment about "boys on parole," he then added, "Another group seems to possess a biological tropism,—they are drawn to any man regardless of cleanliness, manner of approach or motive, with no consideration whatever of consequences."[58] Earlier, he had commented, "It is significant that society has a certain code of ideals for young girls to which boys are not even expected to aspire. . . . We have no inclination to challenge any part of this situation."[59] This viewpoint could account for the disproportionate number of females sterilized at the State Training School during the years that followed. Finally, this initial sterilization effort excluded African Americans because Whitten's institution then only admitted Whites. In the meantime, the campaign for the enactment of sterilization laws in the Deep South shifted to Georgia and Alabama.

Georgia

Although the idea had rumbled around the state for at least two decades, the Georgia legislature first seriously considered compulsory sterilization of the eugenically unfit in 1935. In doing so, the assembly responded to a campaign much like those waged since the beginning of the eugenics movement. Analyzing the early campaigns, a 1912 report by proponents of eugenic sterilization concluded that the first sterilization laws "have usually been put through by some very small energetic group of enthusiasts," with the chief credit going to women and physicians.[60] This report could have been resubmitted twenty-five years later to cover events in Georgia, where physicians, experts at state mental health institutions, and an energetic group of women took advantage of Depression Era interest in progressive reforms to spur consideration and passage of America's last eugenic sterilization law.

Eugenics first gained a secure foothold in Georgia during the second decade of the twentieth century. At that time, officials of both the state's huge mental health institution at Milledgeville and the Medical Association of Georgia endorsed eugenic sterilization prior to focusing their efforts in the field on securing a public facility for eugenically segregating the mentally retarded.[61] The state federation of women's clubs joined in this later effort, and remained actively involved in promoting that facility, the Georgia Training School for Mental Defectives at Gracewood, after it opened in 1921.[62] All three of these groups displayed an ongoing interest in compulsory sterilization during the years that followed.[63] Indeed, the federation regularly included the distribution of "study leaflets" on mental hygiene and eugenic sterilization among its "suggested projects for Georgia clubs."[64] For its part, the MAG formally endorsed the enactment of a eugenic sterilization statute and periodically published articles suggesting basic scientific support for eugenics.[65] One such article, appearing in the MAG's journal during the 1930s, cited Goddard, Burbank, and a host of statistics on mental retardation to support its call for sterilizing everyone not "capable of reproducing normal offspring."[66]

A surprisingly potent additional force, a social action committee of the prestigious women's Junior League organization of Augusta, joined the mental health experts and physicians campaigning for a sterilization law during the 1930s. The committee, led by Nora Nixon, gravitated toward the eugenics movement gradually, beginning with its operation of well-baby clinics and a milk station for needy children during the early years of the depression. The squalid conditions they encountered when delivering milk to destitute households in and around their relatively prosperous, medium-sized city shocked these society ladies, most of whom were young. To reduce the number of unwanted children among the poor and uneducated, they opened Augusta's first birth control clinic. In doing so, the women eagerly studied the work and writings of national birth control pioneers, especially Margaret Sanger, whom the women "worshipped like a god," and the philanthropist-physician Clarence J. Gamble, whom they periodically contacted for support.[67] Both Sanger and Gamble participated actively in the national eugenics movement. Sanger wrote frequently about limiting reproduction by the unfit; Gamble promoted and distributed model sterilization laws.[68]

Nixon, whose husband was a prominent lawyer and whose father was a trial-court judge and a progressive candidate for the Democratic gubernatorial nomination in 1936, appreciated the role of legislation in addressing social problems.[69] She first became committed to eugenics through her efforts to improve the care of patients at Gracewood, where she recalled finding "feeble-minded persons living in appalling conditions." Observing that these patients generally had mentally retarded parents, she asked her father about the legality of sterilizing them as Sanger urged. He told her about lectures on the issue at the University of Georgia, which she eagerly attended.[70] Sensitized by her experiences and inspired by Sanger and the university lectures, Nixon turned her sights on a sterilization law for Georgia. Other Junior League committee members backed her efforts.

The medical community welcomed the women to the fray. At a time when other members of the Augusta Junior League would literally cover their ears when the activities of Nixon's committee were discussed, physicians associated with the state medical school in Augusta offered moral support and technical assistance. The medical school's dean, G. Lombard Kelly, allowed the women to set up birth control and eugenics exhibits at the school. He also arranged for the school to take over the operation of the birth control clinic when the Junior League could no longer maintain it.[71] Further help came from Augusta's most prominent physician and civic leader, Eugene E. Murphey. By the 1930s, Murphey had taught and practiced medicine in Augusta for nearly forty years. He served as president of the city's board of health and was a close confidant and adviser of local political leaders.[72] An advocate of modern medical techniques and of progressive reform generally, Murphey used his position as a board of health officer to commend the Junior League's activities and to endorse the enactment of a state sterilization law.[73]

Utilizing their prominent social position and the support of the local medical community, Nixon and her fellow committee members met with lawmakers and arranged the presentation of talks on birth control and sterilization to civic groups throughout the state. The talks sometimes featured such national crusaders as Gamble's top field worker, Edna Rankin McKinnon, the sister of America's first female member of congress.[74] "For the past few months, the lay public have been actively engaged in presenting our plea on sterilization of the mentally deficient," the MAG's legislation committee reported in 1934. "It appears, in the present light, that they may prepare the minds of the legislators better than we have done. Many talks on the subject have been given before organizations all over the state, and the voters seem ready to demand that a suitable bill be passed."[75] This report referred to the work of the Augusta Junior League. That work, building on years of advocacy by mental health experts and physicians, set the stage for the 1935 legislative sessions, during which Georgia lawmakers first considered a sterilization bill seriously.

The question of how to respond to the Great Depression bitterly divided Georgia's political leaders in 1935. Governor Eugene Talmadge, a bombastic and reactionary populist, eschewed Roosevelt's New Deal solutions, saying, "It is not the purpose of the State to support its people."[76] "So adamant was Gene over any type of progressive legislation," his biographer noted, "that he reportedly told a federal agent, 'The way to handle a relief program was like Mussolini was handling it in Italy, namely, to line these people up and take the troops and make them work.'"[77] Yet Talmadge could not run for reelection, and by 1935 legislative leaders were positioning themselves for the next campaign by embracing progressive reform. As Talmadge's biographer observed, "The powerful voices in the house, [the floor leader, Roy] Harris, [the Speaker, E. D.] Rivers, and [the Speaker pro tem,] Ellis Arnall, wanted to give Georgia some of the benefits of the New Deal legislation."[78] All three would advance politically after the 1936 election, with Rivers elected governor, Harris assuming the Speaker's chair, and Arnall becoming an assistant attorney general on his way to the governorship in 1942. The Georgia historian Numan V. Bartley later concluded, "E. D. Rivers and Ellis Arnall provided Georgia with almost a decade of progressive and innovative leadership."[79] Their progressive innovations included eugenics.

Arnall sponsored the sterilization bill in 1935, at the suggestion of Nora Nixon.[80] Arnall's original proposal called for the appointment of "one surgeon and one alienist of recognized ability" to examine the physical and mental condition of the "inmates" at all state and county institutions for "criminal, insane, feeble-minded and epileptic persons." Whenever these two experts and the local institution's superintendent agreed that "procreation is inadvisable" for a particular inmate, the bill provided that "it shall be lawful to perform such operation for the prevention of procreation as shall be decided safest and most effective," subject to limited rights of judicial appeal by the inmate and his or her family.[81]

A House of Representatives committee narrowed Arnall's bill to cover only "patients" at any state custodial institution who "would be likely, if released without sterilization, to procreate a child, or children, who would have a tendency to serious physical, mental, or nervous disease or deficiency." Patients would be sterilized upon the recommendation of their institution's superintendent, subject to the approval of a three-member State Board of Eugenics. Decisions could be appealed to the court for a jury trial. Sterilization would be by "a vasectomy for males, and salpingectomy for females, or some similar operation that would not unsex the patient or inmate."[82] The amended bill purportedly was patterned after California's landmark law, but included somewhat greater procedural safeguards.[83]

The amended bill was overshadowed during the session by other progressive reforms introduced by Arnall, Harris, and Rivers, including legislation for old-age pensions, slum clearance, free public-school textbooks, a seven-month minimum school year, restrictions on child labor, and increased funding for educational and social programs.[84] Nevertheless, the legislature did not overlook the bill. Backed by the chairman of the state medical board and by the physicians' lobby, the measure generated little debate as it passed the House of Representatives by an overwhelming vote of 117 to 29. One of the few negative floor comments came from an Atlanta lawmaker who protested against "trying legislation on something that ought to be left to God to take care of."[85] In explaining the bill's easy passage after years of inaction, the progressive *Augusta Chronicle* noted, "The very intelligent campaign for a sterilization law in Georgia which was conducted by a number of prominent young Augusta women did much toward educating the members of the Legislature and the people of Georgia generally as to the great necessity for such a law in this state." The *Chronicle* went on to urge prompt Senate action "in voting for a sterilization law, which would place Georgia among those progressive states in the Union which are doing their part to stamp out insanity, imbecility, and crime."[86]

The Senate complied less than two weeks after the House vote, although with more debate. Several senators complained that the bill went too far, especially in its application to prisoners and chain-gang mem-

bers. Yet an amendment to limit sterilization to patients at the Milledgeville State Hospital failed. One physician-legislator reassured his
colleagues that "sterilization was neither painful nor harmful." After
adding only a minor amendment facilitating a patient's legal appeal
process, the Senate passed the bill by a three-to-one margin. The House
immediately agreed to the Senate amendment, sending the measure to the
governor for final approval.[87] Once again the *Chronicle* rejoiced, describing the measure as "a great and forward step for Georgia" and crediting
the "group of young Augusta women headed by Mrs. Gwinn H. Nixon
[who] did a great deal during the past two months to create sentiment in
favor of such a law."[88]

The *Chronicle's* rejoicing ended a week later, when Governor Talmadge surprisingly vetoed the sterilization bill. His only public explanation for this action came in a light-hearted remark to Adjutant General
Lindley W. Camp while signing the veto. "They made no provision in
here to except the governor and the adjutant general," Talmadge observed. "Lindley, you and I might go crazy some day and we don't want
them working on us."[89] In a phrase, the governor had personalized the
concerns that populists had always felt toward eugenics; and certainly
his poor and working-class White supporters would not object to his
veto. Yet Talmadge may not have directed his rejection specifically at
sterilization, since he vetoed every progressive measure that reached his
desk that year. In a dramatic display of executive authority, Talmadge
vetoed 163 measures that spring, including such major progressive
propositions as old-age pensions and free textbooks. His actions eventually drove the legislature to adjourn without passing a budget, which resulted in the governor's assuming total authority over state spending for
the rest of his term. Talmadge later bragged "that he threw every New
Deal bill in the trash can without even reading it."[90] If so, the sterilization measure went in with the rest.

A predictable reaction greeted this veto. The *Augusta Chronicle* editorialized, "We are sorry that Governor Talmadge has struck a blow at
progress, at social security for the future and in favor of a continuation
of such terrible conditions that will mean more and more insane, more
and more feebleminded, with criminals augmented and hospitals filled to
capacity."[91] Another leading progressive newspaper agreed. "The scientific reasons for sterilization are so well established and so sound that the
governor is flying in the face of accepted practice in vetoing the bill," the
Columbus Enquirer wrote. "The absence of such a law may cause the
parents and relatives of feeble-minded persons from other states to fly to
Georgia, because most other states now have sterilization laws or are
wisely preparing to pass them."[92] The only contrary view to be published

in a major Georgia newspaper appeared in a letter to the editor from the publicity director of the Catholic Laymen's Association of Georgia. Although the letter noted a variety of scientific objections to eugenics, it clearly reflected established Roman Catholic opposition to sexual sterilization.[93]

Talmadge's veto postponed the enactment of Georgia's sterilization law until 1937, when E. D. Rivers assumed the governorship. Arnall had not sought reelection, so responsibility for introducing the measure passed to Roy Harris of Augusta, the new Speaker of the House, who had been Rivers's campaign manager in the preceding election. With Rivers's victory over a Talmadge lieutenant in the gubernatorial election, and Harris's elevation to Speaker, control of the state government passed into the hands of the progressive, pro-Roosevelt wing of the Democratic party, and Georgia's "Little New Deal" was launched. Rivers's sweeping inaugural address set the tone. "There must be adequate provision for aged needy through old-age pensions," Rivers declared. "Adequate provisions must be made for the education of our youth; we must have a comprehensive program for the health of our people, for the blind, the crippled, the dependent children; our unfortunates of all kinds must have necessary care and support."[94] A flood of progressive legislation touching on many areas of social concern followed this speech, with much of it introduced by Harris. "Rivers promoted the legislation and constitutional amendments that permitted Georgia to share in New Deal programs," the historian Numan Bartley later concluded.[95]

The reform of state eleemosynary institutions featured prominently in the Rivers-Harris program. A week before his inauguration, Rivers summoned state lawmakers to Milledgeville for an inspection of the state hospital. Rivers then called for "immediate and urgent action" to improve the "deplorable condition" of the aged and overcrowded facility.[96] Two weeks later, a thirty-five-member legislative committee termed conditions at the hospital "unbelievable" and recommended a massive construction program to expand and modernize facilities.[97] Four years and $10 million later, their efforts provided one of the lasting achievements of the Rivers administration. "The state hospital at Milledgeville stood as an indictment of neglect against the State Government," Rivers declared in his final message to the state legislature. "The housing of these mentally sick people in Georgia under such conditions was a stigma on the fair name of this State that this administration has wiped out forever." Other state eleemosynary institutions, including the facility at Gracewood, also benefited from Rivers's concern.[98] These progressive reforms also included compulsory sterilization.

Harris introduced the 1937 sterilization bill on the first day of the new session, along with several other progressive measures.[99] One leading voice for reform within state politics, the Georgia League of Women Voters, promptly endorsed many of these proposals, including the "sterilization of the unfit."[100] The Speaker's bill, identical in every respect to the sterilization measure passed by the House in 1935, reached the House floor for a vote within a month of its introduction.

A handful of representatives raised populist objections to the measure. One member asserted that a board of experts should not sterilize patients "unable to defend themselves," especially since "family jealousy often results in too many people being admitted to insane asylums who don't belong there." Another proposed that juries make sterilization decisions. Supporters moved successfully to cut off debate before it got out of hand, and after defeating a series of amendments the House passed the measure by an overwhelming margin of 123 ayes to 16 nays.[101]

Now events began to move fast. Urging prompt Senate action, the *Columbus Ledger* reasserted the progressive promise of eugenics. "Georgia can lessen the number of morons within its borders and curtail crime to some extent through enactment of the sterilization bill that has been passed by the House and sent to the Senate," the *Ledger* editorialized. "Sterilization laws now in effect in other states are working satisfactorily and in the interest of a stronger citizenship. The same would apply in Georgia under the bill now waiting action in the Senate."[102] Only a short wait remained. Without comment or debate, the Senate voted twenty-seven to one for the bill just ten days after the House action.[103] Two influential progressive newspapers traditionally friendly to Rivers then called on the governor to sign the bill in the name of progress. The Atlanta *Constitution* described "eugenic sterilization" as the "scientific and humanitarian method of checking the increase in insane, feeble-minded, physical, human derelicts."[104] Similarly, the pro–New Deal *Columbus Enquirer* described sterilization as "humane and in the interest of progress in our civilization."[105] Never one to obstruct progress, Rivers signed the bill into law a mere six weeks after its introduction.[106]

The three principal sources of support for eugenic sterilization shared in the final victory. First, state mental health officials endorsed the measure throughout the legislative process, and testified to its potential benefit.[107] Second, the MAG promoted the bill in pamphlets distributed during the 1937 session to all state lawmakers and physicians.[108] "We are to be congratulated that there is now a law in our State which permits sterilization of certain people," an article in the MAG journal reported later in the year. "While sterilization is not a panacea, it certainly is one of the most important among a number of measures in any far-sighted and humanitarian program for dealing with society's tremendous burden of mental disease, deficiency and dependency."[109] Third, the members of the Augusta Junior League had the satisfaction of seeing their objective obtained through a bill introduced by their local representative.[110] This expert and upper-middle-class core of faithful supporters, with their call for progress through the application of scientific principles, evidenced the ongoing progressive nature of the eugenic sterilization movement in Georgia. Further testimony to this effect was provided by the fact that the bill was passed during the state's Little New Deal, and by the progressive credentials of such key supporters as Arnall, Harris, and Rivers. Although nationwide scientific support for eugenics had eroded considerably by 1937, Georgia reformers were not aware of these developments.[111] For Georgians, sterilization remained a progressive reform founded on good science.

Except for the shade of scientific racism that had always darkened the eugenics movement, Georgia's belated sterilization campaign did not display a particularly racist color. Three observations support this conclusion. First, proponents never publicly advocated directing sterilization against a particular race. The *Augusta Chronicle,* for example, wrote in one of its frequent editorials on the topic, "The only way to cure conditions of degeneracy, imbecility, insanity, etc., among the lowest class of whites and negroes of this state is to sterilize the younger generation."[112] Second, the obvious target population was the patients at the Georgia Training School for Mental Defectives, who were all White. Third, by the standards of the time and place, proponents tended to be relatively liberal on the race issue. Arnall, for example, openly supported the right of African Americans to vote in the Democratic primary at a time when that was a major political issue, and later declared that "race had nothing to do with" his support for eugenic sterilization.[113] Talmadge, a self-proclaimed defender of White supremacy, was the most reactionary racist to feature prominently in the episode. Talmadge, however, vetoed the legislation.[114] Clearly, reactionary racism did not underlie the passage of Georgia's sterilization law.

America's last eugenic sterilization statute rode on a crest of progressive lawmaking in Georgia, just as such laws had done earlier elsewhere in the nation. State mental health officers and the medical community, which had supplied expert support for eugenics since 1913, remained supportive through the final victory. Then, as the scientific fallacy of eugenics became apparent nationally, and states in the North and West began reducing their use of compulsory sterilization during the 1940s and 1950s, Georgia steadily increased its commitment to the procedure.[115] But the sins of the son should not be visited on the father. Although scientific challenges to the doctrines of eugenics were mounting nationally by the mid-1930s, those challenges were not yet universally recognized and had not necessarily reached the Georgia medical community.[116] For Georgians in 1937, compulsory sterilization remained a progressive reform whose time had finally come. Neighboring Alabama almost operated on the same schedule.

Alabama

From the time that his institution opened, Superintendent William Partlow of Alabama's Partlow State School for Mental Deficients maintained a policy of sterilizing all patients released from the facility. The law authorizing the procedure, however, only applied to this one institution.[117] Partlow had long favored a more far-reaching eugenics program, however. After 1923, when he assumed the superintendency of the Alabama Insane Hospitals in addition to his responsibilities at the facility for the mentally retarded, Partlow took a particular interest in the role of sterilization in preventing mental illness and promoting public mental health. For example, in a 1928 address on ways to combat the mental stress of life in a modern industrial society, he observed, "A creed which includes high standards of living with temperance in all things for the normal, and a program of sterilization of the insane, mental defective, repeating criminal, drug and alcoholic addicts would go a long way in the right direction."[118] The Medical Association of the State of Alabama endorsed this approach the same year, when its president recommended sterilizing "all convicted criminals and insane cases committed to the State insane asylum." In a classic affirmation of eugenic principles, the MASA president concluded, "It is not humane to allow the insane to propagate his species to the injury of himself and the public."[119]

Partlow strove to generate support for an expanded state sterilization program by writing and speaking about the social and economic cost of hereditary degeneracy.[120] Reporting largely on the fruits of his own labors, he asserted in a 1934 official report, "There is a growing, popular demand for a more comprehensive sterilization law in Alabama."[121] By the following year, Partlow and his fellow eugenicists were ready to seek such a statute. The proposal reflected the big plans of a big man. By 1935, Partlow had built an empire in Tuscaloosa as superintendent first of the state institution for the mentally retarded and later also of the Alabama Insane Hospitals. He had developed a statewide power base during multiple terms presiding over the MASA and several of its key committees, and had reached beyond Alabama through an involvement in regional and national professional organizations that would culminate in his election as president of the Southern Psychiatric Association for 1936–37.[122] Partlow also had become the Deep South's leading eugenicist, and one of the few southern eugenicists who walked on the national stage. He clearly had grown frustrated with Alabama's limited sterilization program.

Although Partlow could (and did) sterilize every patient departing the Partlow State School, this only reached a small fraction of those whom he considered eugenically unfit.[123] Indeed, in this respect, Alabama's existing law covered fewer people than did any of the sterilization statutes then on the books in thirty-one other American states. Although those other statutes typically included greater procedural protection than the Alabama law, they applied to inmates at a broad range of state institutions, rather than simply a single small facility for the mentally retarded.[124] But even the efforts of these other states were inadequate for Partlow. Indeed, only the plan recently announced by Nazi Germany was sufficiently bold for some in Partlow's camp. Partlow's colleague and fellow eugenicist the Alabama state health officer J. N. Baker expressed this clearly to the state legislature early in its 1935 session, when he praised Germany's "bold experiment in mass sterilization," which he predicted would reach "some 400,000 of the population." After comparing the cost of sterilizing that many people with the cost of custodial care, he then estimated "that, after several decades, hundreds of millions of marks will be saved each year as a result of the diminution of expenditures for patients with hereditary diseases." Baker went on to call for a similar program in Alabama, and specifically to endorse legislation toward that end drafted by Partlow.[125] Endorsements for the proposal also came from the MASA, the Alabama Division of the American Association of University Women, and the Alabama Society for Mental Hygiene.[126] Partlow's two young state legislators from Tuscaloosa, Representative Aubrey Dominick and Senator Hayse Tucker, introduced the bill at the beginning of the 1935 session.[127]

Partlow's proposal would have covered more individuals and offered less procedural protection than any other sterilization program in the United States. First, it gave the superintendent of any state institution for the mentally ill or the mentally retarded unlimited discretion to sterilize any or all patients upon their release. Next, it empowered a three-member board (composed of the superintendent of the Alabama Insane Hospitals [Partlow], the state health officer [Baker], and the chief medical officer of the state prison), acting by majority vote, to sterilize "any sexual pervert, Sadist, homosexualist, Masochist, Sodomist, or any other grave form of sexual perversion, or any prisoner who has twice been convicted of rape" or thrice imprisoned for any offense. Finally, it authorized county public health committees to sterilize inmates of local custodial institutions, such as reform schools, and individuals who were either a "mental deficient of any grade" or "habitually and constantly dependent upon public relief or support by charity." In each instance, the decision to sterilize required "evidence of mental or moral degeneracy liable to be inherited," but only individuals facing sterilization by order of county health committees could appeal, and then simply to the superintendent of the Alabama Insane Hospitals (Partlow) and his staff. No right of judicial review existed: Mental health experts made all decisions.[128]

Not surprisingly, given its broad sweep, the proposal was front-page news throughout the state and, according to one observer, generated "the longest and most intense debate of the entire 1935 legislative session."[129] Its leading proponents included the state medical community and public health officials, Partlow's state legislators (who led the floor fight in both the Senate and the House of Representatives), and two major newspapers, the *Montgomery Advertiser* and the *Birmingham News*.[130]

Their arguments for the measure stressed scientific authority and common sense. "It is a rule of biology that excellence derives from excellence, that viciousness derives from viciousness," the *Advertiser* declared in one representative editorial, adding "that there is not a tenant farmer in Alabama who does not know that no exceptionally gifted man is ever born of imbeciles, and that no good man is born from a long line of vicious forebears."[131] With Partlow at his side, a University of Alabama biology professor warned in a public lecture "that the destruction of the human race is almost as certain as the dying out of the great dinosaurs of past ages, unless mankind does something about overproduction of people who are mentally and physically defective."[132] The *News* editorialized that, by adopting the bill, "Alabama will have taken a long step toward the social, mental and physical betterment of its people, which ought in time to be reflected in economic improvement for the State."[133] It later added that "the law would work no physical injury upon anyone. It would merely prevent the mentally unfit from reproducing their kind."[134] Although by this comment the *News* intended to reassure legislators and the public that sterilization did not diminish a person's sexual pleasure, it betrayed the eugenicist's typical disregard for the value of procreating a "defective" child.

Opponents of the measure focused on its broad reach and its lack of procedural safeguards. State trade-union leaders, for example, objected "that there is nothing in the bill to prevent a labor man from being 'railroaded' into an institution where he could be sterilized on 'suspicion' of insanity or feeble-mindedness."[135] The national American Civil Liberties Union (ACLU) registered its opposition to the bill's sweeping authorization for the sterilization of criminals.[136] After cautioning, "The modern science of Eugenics has yet to prove its efficacy," the state's Southern

Baptist newspaper editorialized that "the proposed bill gives too much power to the superintendent of any state eleemosynary institution."[137] In a private letter to Governor Bibb Graves, the editor of the *Alabama Herald* wrote, "[S]eeing how many elements, some in favor of sterilization, are bitterly opposed to the bill's great authority and loose language, I called Doctor Partlow on the telephone and asked him if he would be willing to save you any embarrassment by releasing the Senators he has pledged to vote for the bill."[138] When Partlow refused this request, the battle gained intensity.

The stiffest opposition came from Alabama's small Roman Catholic community, then centered in Mobile and Birmingham. Describing the bill as "the most far-reaching" legislation ever introduced in Alabama, the state's Catholic newspaper commented, "[W]e wonder what our civilization is coming to when medical, political and economic leaders of a great state such as Alabama could have their viewpoint warped to the point where they could in good conscience and without shame introduce a measure fraught with such vicious, such inhumane, such criminal possibilities."[139] Prominent Alabama Catholics, including physicians, attorneys, and educators, told their lawmakers of their opposition to the legislation in public hearings and private letters.[140] William F. Obering, a philosophy and sociology professor at a small Roman Catholic college in Mobile, helped set the tone for this resistance in a series of articles and speeches articulating the moral arguments against compulsory sterilization, which he denounced as violating "the natural rights of man."[141] The Alabama Council of the Knights of Columbus, a popular Catholic service organization, crudely expressed this position in a resolution branding the sterilization measure as "unchristian, unnatural, ungodly and therefore pagan."[142] The Mobile legislative delegation, which included the state's only Catholic legislators, raised the issue in both the Senate and the House of Representatives.[143] Some Protestants voiced similar concerns. For example, a Baptist lawmaker claimed to find "in the Bible all the warrant he required to vote against the bill."[144] Indeed, editorials in the state's Baptist and Methodist newspapers objected to the legislation, but the vociferous Catholic resistance prompted the greatest response.[145] For example, in the heat of the floor debate, one senator lashed out at the Roman Catholic Church for opposing sterilization, as it "had ever opposed scientific progress." As he began recounting various historical episodes to support this allegation, Mobile's senator reminded him that the father of modern genetics, Gregory Mendel, had been a Catholic monk.[146]

Both religious and nonreligious opponents of the sterilization bill cited the growing body of academic evidence against eugenics—evidence that was just then beginning to accumulate as leading social scientists and geneticists began turning from nature to nurture, and from simple Mendelian factors to complex genetic relationships, in their explanations of human behavior. Obering, for example, cited leading national authorities ranging from the anthropologist Franz Boas and the psychiatrist Abraham Myerson to the biologist H. S. Jennings to support the basic proposition that "the sterilization proposal as a measure of social betterment not only does not attain this objective, but is socially harmful."[147] This was not enough to overcome the support of local physicians and public health officers, however, as both houses of the state legislature overwhelmingly passed the measure and sent it to Governor Bibb Graves for his signature.[148]

Both proponents and opponents of eugenic sterilization expressed surprise when Governor Graves vetoed the bill.[149] A delegation of Roman Catholics from Mobile had visited the governor to urge him to veto it, but that had probably had little impact.[150] The popular, strong-willed Graves had first won the governorship in 1926 with the backing of the militantly anti-Catholic Ku Klux Klan, and had once served as a Grand Dragon in that racist organization. He later distanced himself from the Klan and became an ardent New Deal progressive, but this shift does not explain the veto because progressives typically favored eugenics. Graves, however, always defied simple categorization. He had the blue blood of earlier Alabama governors flowing through his veins, and a Yale law degree, but won the governorship as an outsider opposed by every major newspaper in the state. One biographer compared the man to a "colossus, his feet firmly planted on the opposite foundations of a new progressivism and a close association with the most reactionary terrorist organization ever to appear in America."[151] Perhaps as a result, Graves had a mind of his own on many matters and often played his cards close to his vest.

After the bill passed, Graves asked the Alabama Supreme Court for an advisory opinion regarding its constitutionality. The court promptly and unanimously opined that the proposal violated the due process clauses of both the state and federal constitutions. "We think that the sterilization of a person is such an injury to the person," the court wrote, "that this cannot be done without a hearing [or] notice before a duly constituted tribunal or board, and, if this is not a court, then with the untrammeled right of appeal to a court for a judicial review from the finding of the board or commission adjudging him a fit subject for sterilization."[152] Graves then convened a public hearing, at which proponents led by Partlow, and opponents led by a delegation from Mobile, presented sharply conflicting testimony regarding the scientific evidence for eugenic sterilization.[153]

Up to the last minute, Representative Dominick believed that Graves would sign the bill, and the legislator spent several days working with the governor's legal adviser preparing executive amendments designed to deal with the constitutional issues raised by the court's advisory opinion.[154] Even Partlow expressed confidence only days before the veto, when he wrote Graves, "Knowing your views and beliefs in the need for such legislation . . . I am inclined to congratulate you upon this sterilization legislation as being one of the most forward-looking, progressive and constructive measures of your present administration."[155] In the end, however, the independent-minded governor concluded "that until the scientists themselves reach further agreement and until we are in a position to supply all concerned such legal and medical and court expenses as would be necessary for the protection of their individual rights, this is not a wise policy for Alabama to adopt."[156]

Rather than attempting to override this veto simply to enact an unconstitutional statute, Dominick immediately reintroduced a virtually identical bill containing added provisions for decisions by an expert Medical Board of Sterilization and appeals to the state supreme court.[157] Again the measure passed both houses of the legislature by overwhelming margins, only to be vetoed by the governor.[158] This time, Graves penned an emotional veto message stressing the physical risks involved in sterilizing women. "We know that the enforcement of the provisions of this bill as to girls and young women will entail major operations upon many thousands," he wrote. "Those who will die are innocent and pure, have committed no offense against God or man, save that in the opinion of experts they should never have been born." Eugenic segregation, Graves maintained, was the better, albeit more costly, way to protect society.[159] After counting the votes of the administration loyalists who were committed to back the governor, Dominick gave up the fight without attempting to override the veto.[160]

A clue to explain Graves's action may lie in the letters that he received prior to vetoing the measure. Nearly all of those supporting the bill were from physicians and experts, whereas those opposing it came from a broad spectrum of individuals ranging from lawyers and business owners to an anonymous "Citizen of Mobile" with a husband temporarily in a state mental health hospital due to a head injury. "We are both in our twenties," the anonymous Mobilian pleaded, "and such an act [of sterilization] would simply ruin the lives of us both."[161] Twenty-five years earlier, Partlow had dismissed the idea of sterilizing habitual criminals as impractical because "maybe the criminal would out-vote us when we vote on such a matter as that."[162] Perhaps Graves appreciated this crude political calculus, especially when it involved a measure as far-reaching as Partlow's 1935 proposal. Privately, Partlow attributed the veto to the governor's "religious and political scruples," which also suggests some connection to Graves's membership in the small, devout Church of Christ denomination, and to the long-time support given the governor by organized labor, which opposed the bill.[163]

Whatever the explanation for it, the governor's veto, coupled with the state supreme court's advisory opinion, curtailed the practice of involuntary sterilization in Alabama. The 1919 statute authorizing the sterilization of inmates at the Partlow State School remained on the books, but it was undermined by the governor's strong stand and the court's position on judicial review. Shortly after his second veto, Graves assured the national ACLU that there would be no need to repeal this statute because "I do not think that the Superintendent will ever exercise the authority."[164] This was confirmed by an unrepentant Partlow in the facility's next annual report, which noted that, owing to constitutional concerns, Partlow and his staff had "positively discontinued the practice of sterilization, which will of necessity effect [sic] our previous liberal policy of granting paroles."[165] Even though Partlow persuaded his state representatives to reintroduce his compulsory sterilization proposal during the next two regular sessions of the state legislature, in 1939 and 1943, the time had passed for such legislation in Alabama.[166] Both of these bills died in committee, without ever reaching the House floor. Partlow attributed this to the "pressure of Catholic influence," but given the insignificant impact of such pressure on the House committee in 1935, something else clearly contributed to the outcome.[167]

If the letters received by Graves prior to his veto help to explain that action, then the letters that he received after the veto suggest why elected legislators might have subsequently avoided the issue. "It has been my privilege to meet oodles of county people recently, and I believe that fully ninety-five percent of them are against the Domineck [sic] Sterilization bill, being denunciatory and very bitter against it. I have heard of a lot of them term it as an attempt to Hitleresque Alabama," one typical letter reported. "Judging from the way people here talked to me as an indication, if this man Domineck, Dominick, Dominicker, or whatever his name is, ever runs for a State Office, he will be snowed under."[168] Dominick never ran for statewide office, and his sterilization bill never became state law. Indeed, after South Carolina and Georgia became the thirty-first and thirty-second states to mandate eugenic sterilization in the mid-1930s, no more such laws passed in America. The earlier statutes had all passed within the preceding three decades, creating the impression that they represented the wave of the future. But in acting when they did, South Carolina and Georgia ignored the beacons warning that the wave was about to break. Alabama's course more closely followed emerging national currents.

CHAPTER SEVEN

Bitter Harvest

The correspondence received by Alabama's Governor Bibb Graves on the sterilization bill revealed the emergence, as early as 1935, of a powerful new argument against eugenics. "In my judgment," one opponent wrote, "the great rank and file of the country people of Alabama do not want this law; they do not want Alabama, as they term it, Hitlerized."[1] Even though Nazi abuses of eugenics had barely begun in 1935, critics of compulsory sterilization in Alabama latched on to them in forecasting the grim consequences of adopting such an approach to medical or social problems. "The proposed Alabama Sterilization Law," William Obering asserted shortly after its introduction, "becomes a Declaration of Slavery versus the Declaration of Independence. The principle underlying it . . . is the principle actuating Hitlerism in Germany, with its blood purges, its shooting fests, and its deliberately planned famines. The same principle would justify the practice of euthanasia, or the painless murder of the incurably sick and insane."[2] Similarly, Alabama's Methodist newspaper warned that the "proposed sterilization bill is a step" toward the "totalitarianism in Germany today," where the "state is taking private matters—matters of individual conscience, and matters of family control—in hand, and sometimes it's a rough hand, and always it's a strong hand."[3]

Perhaps they had simply lost touch with common American notions of individual freedom, but many leading eugenicists in this country initially welcomed the Nazi sterilization campaign and predicted that it would boost their own efforts here. In Alabama, for example, the state health officer J. N. Baker advised the 1935 legislature, "With baited breath, the entire civilized world is watching the bold experiment in mass sterilization recently launched in Germany," and then projected how much money the program would save German taxpayers.[4] Baker was referring to the 1933 Nazi eugenics law, which empaneled special medico-legal tribunals to compel the sterilization of persons when, in "the experience of medical science, it may be expected with great probability that their offspring may suffer severe physical damage." The program initially targeted the mentally retarded, the mentally ill, and epileptics, though it also took in individuals suffering from hereditary blindness, deafness, serious physical deformity, and alcoholism. By 1937, the Nazi effort had sterilized nearly a quarter of a million people, before radically expanding its scope, to cover Jews, and its methods, to include euthanasia.[5]

Prior to this expansion, many American eugenicists praised the Nazi program. "To one versed in the history of eugenical sterilization in America, the text of the German statute reads almost like the 'American model sterilization law,'" Charles Davenport's Eugenics Record Office advised in 1934. "Prevention of hereditary degeneracy is the sole purpose of the new statute, which applies equally to all hereditary degenerates as specified by the law, regardless of sex, race or religion."[6] Two years later, an observer from the pro-eugenics American Committee on Maternal Health reported, "I am convinced that the [German] law is administered in entire fairness . . . and that discrimination of class, race, creed, political, or religious belief does not enter into the matter." The observer also found that "[t]he leaders in the German sterilization movement state repeatedly that their legislation was formulated only after careful study of the California experiment as reported by Mr. Gosney and Dr. Popenoe."[7] Heidelberg University even awarded H. H. Laughlin an honorary doctorate for his contributions to the field, which he accepted as "evidence of a common understanding of German and American scientists of the nature of eugenics."[8] Deep in the South, a Georgia eugenicist complained in his state medical journal that American institutions had sterilized only about twenty-three thousand patients since such efforts began. "Compare this with the fact that in Germany 58,000 people underwent the operation in one year. We, the doctors of this country, can not sit by and do nothing," he declared. "We must do it."[9]

In time, of course, even the most rabid American eugenicists recognized the devastating impact of Nazi practices on their cause. Laughlin personally felt this impact when the Carnegie Institution of Washington eased him out of his post at the Eugenics Record Office in 1939, and then closed the facility a year later, in part as a reaction to events in Germany.[10] After the Nuremberg war trials revealed the full extent of the Nazi abuses, Paul Popenoe concluded that "the major factor" in the demise of American eugenics "was undoubtedly Hitlerism."[11] But this impact occurred gradually. Despite the invocation of Hitler's name by Roman Catholic and Methodist editorialists to damn the 1935 Alabama legislation, the *Alabama Baptist,* which also opposed the bill, opined at the same time, "Fascist Germany should not, with reference to this matter, influence the legislation one way or the other."[12] Similarly, in an article generally critical of eugenics, a University of Georgia essayist noted that the "possibility that unscrupulous politicians might use a [sterilization] statute to promote tyranny . . . is not sufficient reason to keep laws from the statute books."[13] Indeed, during the 1937 debate over compulsory sterilization in Georgia, the prestigious Atlanta *Constitution* ran an editorial praising "this scientific and humanitarian method of checking the increase in insane, feeble-minded, physical human derelicts" next to one denouncing the "monstrous brutality of legalized anti-Semitism in Germany."[14] The editorialist undoubtedly knew about Nazi Germany's ongoing sterilization program because the *Constitution* occasionally carried wire-service articles on this highly publicized effort.[15]

The juxtaposition of these editorials in the *Constitution,* which appears so incongruous in retrospect, reflected a time when many educated Americans hesitated to condemn everything associated with German national socialism simply because of Hitler's obvious excesses. This tendency even undercut the immediate impact of a 1936 report issued by a special study committee of the American Neurological Association, which historians generally credit with helping to turn the tide of scientific and medical opinion against eugenic sterilization in the United States.[16] Even though that committee, which clearly deliberated under the shadow of Nazi practices, roundly condemned state-ordered sterilization and found "no sound scientific basis for sterilization on account of immorality or character defect," it left ample wiggle room for American eugenicists by "recommend[ing] sterilization in selected cases of certain diseases and with the consent of the patient or those responsible for him." These diseases included "feeble-mindedness of familial type," schizophrenia, manic-depressive psychosis, and epilepsy.[17]

Accordingly, in his review of this committee report for the leading national journal of social workers, a Vineland Training School official could quote the statement "[T]here need be no hesitation in recommending sterilization in the case of feeble-mindedness," without noting the committee's qualification that such an operation should at least require the consent of a parent or guardian.[18] Reviewing the report for Alabama physicians, J. N. Baker similarly stressed its endorsement of "selective sterilization" but downplayed its reservations as reflecting an "ultraconservatism, quite characteristic of the medical mind," that failed to adequately address the broad "social and economic" issues at stake.[19] As Baker's comments suggested, Alabama eugenicists continued to support compulsory sterilization despite developments within both German politics and American science.

Legislative Curtain Call in the South

Partlow, in particular, remained committed to securing a compulsory sterilization law for Alabama despite his setback in 1935. The following year, he warned in an address to colleagues within the Medical Association of the State of Alabama that "eugenics demands its share of study and attention or euthanasia may become a necessity."[20] In his 1937 presidential address to the Southern Psychiatric Association, Partlow reaffirmed his position "that we must look to some control of the propagation of the degenerate."[21] He persistently lobbied for state sterilization legislation during the late 1930s and early 1940s, and managed to retain the MASA's continued support for the proposal.[22] In 1945, even as victorious Allied armies uncovered the horrors of eugenics run wild at Nazi concentration camps, Partlow and his fellow Alabama eugenicists prepared to mount their final major push to enact a comprehensive sterilization law.

Eugenics leaders from outside Alabama encouraged this attempt as a step toward regaining the initiative nationwide after a string of legislative defeats in various states and a steady decline in the number of eugenic sterilizations across the country during the war years. With the closure of the Eugenics Record Office in 1940 and the demise of the Human Betterment Foundation following Gosney's death two years later, institutional leadership of the American eugenics movement passed to Birthright, an organization that had grown out of efforts by the New Jersey social worker Marian Olden to enact a sterilization statute in her state during the 1930s. Birthright's national influence increased in the 1940s, when Clarence Gamble merged his far-reaching and well-funded personal campaign to promote eugenic sterilization into Olden's expanding program.[23] Gamble had known William Partlow at least since the mid-1930s, when the Massachusetts philanthropist-physician first took his campaign to the Deep South.[24] In 1944, Rufus C. Partlow became his older brother's chief assistant at the Partlow State School, and quickly began swapping information with Gamble about the benefits of sterilizing the institution's residents. By this time, the Partlows' interest in eugenics had come to the attention of Olden, and she offered Birthright's help in enacting a state sterilization law.

The Partlow brothers, Gamble, and Olden worked closely together in laying the foundation for the 1945 legislation. On the one hand, Rufus Partlow and Gamble prepared a study of patients at the Partlow State School so that, in Gamble's words, "we could show the cost which the state has incurred by the failure to provide a means of sterilizing the discharges."[25] Both men then used the results to promote the legislation.

Gamble, for example, lobbied for the bill during a visit to the state and advised the measure's future House sponsor that more than one hundred Partlow State School residents "could be released with a good chance of maintaining themselves in the community provided that they were not fertile." This, he calculated, would save taxpayers "half a million dollars."[26] The younger Partlow reported the complete findings in the MASA journal, in an article that appeared during the height of legislative debate over the sterilization bill and included the pointed observation that "most of those who are considered for parole . . . should not leave the institution having the ability to reproduce others of their kind."[27] On the other hand, William Partlow went to work seeking a Senate sponsor by asking Olden to send "a collection of information on sterilization, including a model sterilization bill," to the powerful Senate committee chairman J. Bruce Henderson, a wealthy cotton planter and horse breeder with a graduate degree in animal husbandry. The elder Partlow already was partially incapacitated by the emphysema that took his life a decade later, but he promised Henderson in 1944, "I shall continue actively interested in the promotion of some practical sterilization legislation in Alabama."[28]

After forty years of fighting for eugenics in Alabama, William Partlow recognized who his friends and foes would be in the coming battle. "I believe the practical way is to interest the various state organizations, such as the Women's Federated Clubs," he advised Henderson, "so when the Legislature meets again and the sterilization measure may be presented we can combat some of the Catholic influence."[29] Proponents followed this strategy to the letter. Anticipating strident opposition from conservative religious groups, they packed the public legislative hearings on the measure with hundreds of supporters from mainline Protestant churches and women's associations. "Just as in the Senate hearing," one observer wrote, "those favoring the bill in the House hearing were led by Christian ministers well flanked by ladies' organizations." Neither of the Partlow brothers was religious, but Henderson, the chief Senate sponsor, served as an elder in the Presbyterian church, and support also came from some Episcopalians, Methodists, and Baptists. Further, the state federation of women's clubs and the Alabama Division of the American Association of University Women actively lobbied for the legislation, as did the local organizers for Planned Parenthood, Bernadine and Charles Zukoski, a socially prominent Birmingham couple. Physicians, psychiatrists, and biology professors from state universities added their expert testimony in support of sterilization.[30]

Partlow also outlined proponents' main arguments in a letter to Henderson. "There are certain types of mental illness which are hereditary," he observed, but "education relative to birth control" could combat these. "The large field for sterilization," he stated, "is that of mental deficiency or feeble-mindedness. In practically all instances the children of feeble-minded parents grow up with the same or lower mental level as their parents, and likewise become local or public burdens." Here Partlow added a significant new twist that reflected the increasing ascendancy of nurture over nature in American social thought. "Practically every County Welfare Department," he noted, "can testify to the fact that they often have problems through the juvenile and other courts involving single girls and young women with illegitimate off-spring, [because] the mothers being mental[ly] deficient are irresponsible." Whether the resulting "problems in delinquency, crime and dependency" arose from heredity (as eugenics claimed) or from environment (as the new social sciences claimed), Partlow suggested, "[s]terilization would provide some remedy."[31] The resulting focus on sterilizing "single girls and young women" was new for Partlow, however, given the fact that he had directed the sterilization of more males than females during earlier years at the Partlow State School.

"Alone in the midst of the gathering shadows of this stark unAmericanism," the diocesan newspaper for Alabama proclaimed in 1945, "the voice of the Catholic Church was raised to halt this march to self-annihilation." Olden was hardly less melodramatic when she complained, "Priests all over Alabama preached sermons against the sterilization bill, using as the argument that it was an opening wedge in a Hitlerian program of mutilation." Alabama Catholics, especially those from Mobile, wrote legislators and spoke out at public hearings in response to their bishop's plea to "use every means at our disposal to help defeat this bill." The bishop demonstrated one extreme means by resigning from a state cancer board to protest the medical community's support for sterilization. A prominent Roman Catholic physician demonstrated another by exaggerating the physical effects of sterilization, testifying that it deprived men of their virility. An editorialist for the diocesan newspaper focused more directly on the underlying principle at stake: "Anyone who deliberately mutilates an innocent fellow creature by excising or damaging a healthy organ of his body, violates his right to bodily integrity. It makes no difference whether the victim is normal or deficient from the standpoint of intellectual capacities; in either case he is a human being."[32]

Given the flurry that the sterilization bill ultimately created, it is ironic that the bill's introduction went unnoticed by the local press owing to the bigger news that day—Germany's surrender. The sole physician in the Alabama Senate, Thomas Jefferson Jones, joined Henderson in sponsoring the legislation, with the senator from Partlow's home town of Tuscaloosa leading the fight for it on the Senate floor. Events in Europe colored the debate: opponents compared the proposal to the Nazi eugenics law, while proponents defended it as "humanitarian" and "economic." Senator Vincent Kilborn, a Catholic lay leader from Mobile, filibustered against the bill for three days by offering a series of dilatory floor amendments. When the Senate finally passed the measure by a two-to-one margin, a weary Kilborn could barely whisper, "I believe the Senate has voted in complete disregard of religious rights." Reflecting this religious factor, senators voting against the bill tended to attend Catholic or small fundamentalist churches, whereas those voting for it mostly attended the large Southern Baptist, Methodist, and Presbyterian denominations whose members dominated state political and economic affairs.[33]

The victory did not last long, however. The House health committee killed the bill barely a week later. The fatal committee vote came after a heated public hearing attended by a large delegation of Roman Catholics opposed to the measure, and a deal in which one key Roman Catholic state representative agreed to support other health legislation in exchange for the defeat of the sterilization bill. "Today, the world stands aghast and stunned at the disclosure of the frightful atrocities of the Nazi," an opponent of the bill declared before the committee vote. "Like this Alabama legislation, Hitler, too, decided to start by legalized sterilization, to purify the race. But he was also logical, and so ended up by wholesale mass slaughter." Eugenicists totally rejected the implication of such reasoning, but it proved effective political propaganda.[34]

The 1945 vote in the state Senate represented the last hurrah for eugenicists in Alabama. Efforts by William Partlow to generate interest in a sterilization bill during the 1947 legislative session failed when the Alabama Federation of Women's Clubs "dropped the drive."[35] Two years later, Birthright described Alabama as one of the few places where eugenic sterilization legislation could still pass despite strong Catholic opposition within the state, but even repeated visits to the state by the organization's medical director did not produce a bill.[36] A final sterilization proposal covering only patients at the Partlow State School surfaced during the 1951 legislative session, but it never received a hearing, and no further bills appeared. The state federation of women's clubs and a short-lived Alabama League for Human Betterment jointly instigated the 1951 effort, but infighting between the two groups undermined their effectiveness.[37] William Partlow died three years later. Alabama had finally ended its long flirtation with eugenic sterilization. This marked the end of eugenic lawmaking in the Deep South, but it left three of the states with compulsory sterilization laws in force, which created a potential for future abuses.

Sterilization Practices

The number of eugenic sterilizations dipped in the Deep South during World War II, just as it did nationwide. Philip Reilly attributed this national trend more to "the shortage of civilian physicians" than to any immediate repudiation of practices associated with Nazi Germany.[38] This historical analysis generally accorded with events in Mississippi, where the sterilization program at one of the state's two mental health hospitals was ended by the loss of the institution's only physician to the war effort. The de-emphasis of sterilization at the other hospital beginning in 1941 left only the small state institution for the mentally retarded pursuing an active sterilization program. The facility actually began this program during the war, when T. Paul Haney took over as superintendent, and discontinued it in the late 1940s, after the state attorney general declared the cumbersome sterilization statute "inadequate, vague, and non-workable." During the intervening years, however, the institution accounted for most of the state's 139 eugenic sterilizations. This number did not satisfy Haney, who complained in 1947, "The [mentally retarded] group most likely to propagate more of their kind at present is not in the Institution and no plans are being made to help these people and provide the most necessary part of the [sterilization] program."[39]

Haney's comment recalled an earlier recommendation by the noted American columnist and editor H. L. Mencken, which vented eugenicists' frustrations with the existing sterilization programs in the South. Mencken complained that laws enacted to sterilize "polluters of the race" had limited impact because "they apply only to persons who are defective in some gross and melodramatic way." Turning his vitriolic wit against a favorite target, he added, "If all the lunatics in all the asylums of the country were sterilized hereafter, or even electrocuted, the sharecroppers of Mississippi alone would produce enough more in twenty-five years to fill every asylum to bursting." To remedy this situation, Mencken half-jokingly suggested that the federal government pay one thousand dollars to each man volunteering for a vasectomy. On further reflection, he more seriously proposed that some philanthropist offer a smaller bounty. "In Mississippi," he observed, "where the annual cash income of a sharecropper is said to be but $32, $50 is a large sum, and will suffice to recruit many thousands."[40]

Mencken's call "to sterilize large numbers of American freemen" expressly included "both white and black," but sterilization practices in the Deep South initially targeted Whites.[41] This resulted both indirectly from the lack of state institutions for mentally retarded African Americans and directly from southern eugenicists' overriding concern with purifying the Caucasian race. A typical example of this concern appeared throughout an article in the *Journal of the Medical Association of Georgia* during the 1937 campaign for eugenic sterilization in that state. According to the article, the "South's 'poor white trash,' so aptly named by the Negro," threatened to choke civilization "in a wilderness of weeds." Physicians must sterilize this "human rubbish," it warned, or the "time may come when it will be necessary to resort to euthanasia."[42] In his 1937 presidential address to the American Association for the Study of the Feebleminded, the South Carolina eugenicist B. O. Whitten suggested why this threat to civilization did not require the sterilization of African Americans. "The negro is the beneficiary of a civilization to which he contributed little and from which he derives much," Whitten claimed. "He is blessed by the white man's progress and security. He attends schools and is supported in many aspects of his life by institutions which he did not originate and which he can not, by himself, support."[43]

So long as southern Whites did not expect African Americans to contribute substantially to the intellectual progress of civilization, the need for eugenic improvement of Blacks lost urgency. Indeed, such improvement could upset the status quo. For example, when one Georgia state representative opposed legislation creating an institution for the mentally retarded on the grounds that it "would give judges authority to send hundreds of negro misdemeanants to this institution" rather than to the chain gangs, the sponsor replied, "Georgia courts would never be so foolish as to rob the roads of able-bodied negroes."[44] This prediction proved accurate, at least until the nationwide civil rights movement led to the integration of the Georgia Training School for Mental Defectives in 1960. Whitten's facility followed a similar course. "We may at once and briefly explain the situation with regard to our colored population. This group is not represented in our State Training School," he declared in his 1937 address. "It is considered as sound social philosophy and factual social psychology that this accepted demarcation and fairly definite separation gives the negro certain advantages, and at the same time, it assures the whites their sense of superiority and authority."[45]

One advantage that this racial separation inadvertently afforded African Americans in South Carolina, at least for a while, was a lower risk of compulsory sterilization. From 1935, when the state's sterilization law was enacted, through the end of World War II, nearly every operation performed under that law took place at the State Training School, and therefore did not impact Blacks. This pattern reflected Whitten's enthusiastic support for eugenic sterilization, coupled with the qualified opposition to that procedure displayed by Superintendent C. F. Williams of the state's mental health hospital.[46]

After a three-year lull in the mid-1940s, when South Carolina institutions reported performing no sterilizations, the annual state total began increasing following World War II, reaching a high of forty-three procedures in 1956, before dropping into the single digits during the 1960s.[47] Most of the operations performed during this second wave of sterilization in South Carolina occurred at the state mental health hospital in the years following Williams's retirement. At that time, hospital officials developed expedited administrative procedures and standard forms for ordering eugenic sterilization. For example, the hospital continued to notify the patient's representative of the pending operation, but now automatically petitioned for authority to perform the sterilization after the thirty-day notice period had expired, even if the representative did not respond. Later petitions were supported by a standardized, one-page affidavit, signed by the superintendent, stating little more than the patient's name, age, diagnosis, and number of children, together with the conclusion that the patient "is the probable parent of other offspring likewise afflicted." Interestingly, the blank forms presumed that the patient was a single mother.[48] Surviving records from this period indicate that county welfare agencies regularly asked the mental health hospital to admit local women for the sole purpose of sterilizing them and that the state penitentiary temporarily transferred at least two persons to the hospital for the same reason with the permission of the sitting governor, and later senator, Ernest F. Hollings.[49]

Unlike Whitten's State Training School, the mental health hospital admitted African Americans, including scores of mentally retarded Blacks who had nowhere else to go. Now, the racial impact of compulsory sterilization in South Carolina became quite different. During the ten years between 1949 and 1960 for which the state mental health hospital published records, 102 out of 104 surgical sterilizations were performed on African Americans. Further, the hospital only sterilized female patients. This occurred despite the fact that, throughout the period, the hospital admitted more than twice as many Whites as Blacks and somewhat more men than women.[50] American eugenicists often asserted that compulsory sterilization programs did not unequally impact racial minorities, and surviving statistics generally confirm this claim. In his history of the national movement, Reilly concluded that "only in South Carolina, which operated a small sterilization program, is there strong evidence of racial discrimination."[51] Yet this one example demonstrates the inherent risk in conferring on biased government administrators the discretionary authority to sterilize.

Of course, eugenicists never intended to exempt African Americans from sterilization programs. This was especially true for northern eugenicists, who did not have as many statutory means to control Blacks as did their southern counterparts. Mencken naturally included both races in his sterilization proposal because, living in Baltimore, he feared southern Black sharecroppers, who might migrate North, as much as he feared southern White sharecroppers, who, he said, threatened to make their region "swarm like a nest of maggots."[52] Clarence Gamble did as much as any one philanthropist could to implement the spirit of Mencken's scheme. Beginning in the late 1930s, for example, he initiated and funded a series of studies and demonstration projects in North Carolina that resulted in a greatly expanded eugenic sterilization program implemented through both state institutions and county welfare agencies. These efforts sterilized Blacks and Whites at equivalent per capita rates, even though one of his White researchers reported that "the Negroes tend to resist more than the whites which may be due to ignorance and superstition."[53] During the same period, Gamble helped establish dozens of subsidized sterilization clinics serving the poor of both races in the South and the Midwest. He also worked with Margaret Sanger to develop eugenic birth control conferences and programs in the South, including a "Negro Project" specifically targeting African Americans.[54]

"The mass of Negroes," Gamble explained in the proposal for this project, "particularly in the South, still breed carelessly and disastrously, with the result that the increase among Negroes, even more than among Whites, is from that portion of the population least intelligent and fit." The plan included hiring African American ministers and physicians to promote birth control throughout the South. "There is great danger that we will fail because the Negroes think it a plan for extermination," Gamble warned. "Hence let's appear to let the colored run it as we appeared to let [the] south do the conference at Atlanta."[55] A Gamble researcher in North Carolina concluded that no such fears existed among African Americans in that "Upper South" state, but added, "In the Deep South, it is conceivable that the attitudes of Negroes to the program there might contain more of distrust and hostility."[56] Some evidence supported this concern. For example, Savannah's Black newspaper opposed the 1935 Sterilization Act in Georgia for precisely these reasons. "To preserve the mind and body of a race there can be no successful objection to such an act, if carried out in full accord with its intent," the paper stated. "From the time of its introduction there was some apprehension relative to its impartial operation as it relates to our people. For this reason alone our objection was formed."[57]

In 1937, partly as a result of Gamble's work, North Carolina became the first state to include birth control services in its public health program. All of the states in the Deep South except Catholic-dominated Louisiana quickly followed suit, long before any northern or western

state provided such services to its poor. Of course, the southern programs served large numbers of African Americans, leading the historian
Linda Gordon to charge, "Their pioneering role in government-sponsored birth control was conditioned by the absence of large Catholic
constituencies, and stimulated by racism."[58]

These states also had greater percentages of poor Whites in their populations than did most other American states, however, and much of
southern eugenicists' rhetoric in support of birth control reflected class
bias more than racism. For example, shortly before Georgia began public
funding for birth control, an Emory University pediatrics professor declared that "[b]irth control should be taught when the economic status
precludes adequate care."[59] Similarly, when a White Louisiana physician
despairingly lamented, "As a race, *we* are surely degenerating," and then
prescribed birth control as one remedy, his obvious targets were poor
Whites.[60] A 1931 article in the South Carolina medical journal, aptly entitled "Birth Control among the Poor," brazenly expressed a class bias.
Its author, a local physician, even raised a racist objection to voluntary
birth control programs. "You have often heard the 'nigger' as the great
bugbear in the path of birth control. That they breed like rabbits, and no
desire for change," he observed. "That, with birth control [by Whites]
on one side of the hedge, and the negro on the other, spawning their millions, the Caucasian race will eventually be put out of business. I do not
'shoo' this spook lightly aside." But shoo he did, by suggesting that the
African American birth rate might also decline, especially if "young
Ham-ites" learned "legitimate preventative measures."[61] Ironically, two
decades later, it was South Carolina's mental health hospital that went
beyond voluntary means to implement a racially discriminatory compulsory sterilization program.

When considering the total number of operations on patients of both
races, however, the small program in South Carolina, and even the earlier and more vigorous effort in Mississippi, paled in comparison with the
program in Georgia, which ultimately trailed only North Carolina in
numbers during the postwar era. "The years 1949–51 saw two significant changes in eugenic sterilization programs. Most dramatic was the
marked decline in California," Reilly noted. "But events in California
were countered by the expansion of sterilization programs in Georgia,
North Carolina, and Virginia."[62] These trends persisted into the 1950s.
Indeed, during the second half of that decade, these three southeastern
states accounted for approximately three-fourths of all the compulsory
sterilizations in America.[63]

The Georgia program started later than the others, but caught up
rapidly. The late start began with the state's tardy enactment of its steril-

ization statute in 1937, and continued owing to the governor's three-year delay in activating the State Eugenics Board, which by law needed to rule on each case.[64] Wartime mobilization then reduced the numbers of surgeons available to perform operations at the state mental health hospital, helping to keep the number of operations down. The law potentially applied to persons in any state mental health or penal institution who "would be likely, if released without sterilization, to procreate a child, or children, who would have a tendency to serious physical, mental, or nervous disease or deficiency."[65] In practice, however, only the state's racially mixed mental health hospital at Milledgeville and the all-White Georgia Training School for Mental Defectives at Gracewood utilized the option.

Gracewood began implementing the law during the 1940s by adopting the practice of recommending the sterilization of all patients prior to their discharge. Parents or guardians then had ten days to file a written objection, and failure to protest was treated as an implied consent that allowed the operation to proceed without any further procedural safeguards. Apparently this approach worked. A visiting reporter observed in 1950, "The state sterilization law is preventing some future cases of inherited low mentality. A majority of students who might bear or beget children are sterilized before dismissal from Gracewood."[66] In total, the institution reported sterilizing 408 patients, nearly two-thirds of whom were female, during the period of its greatest eugenic activity, 1942–52. The sterilization rate then declined to about sixteen operations per year during the balance of the 1950s before Gracewood discontinued the practice in the 1960s. At least some of those who underwent the procedure did not fully appreciate its consequences: the superintendent reported in 1958, "We occasionally have requests from discharged [women] who have gotten married wanting to know the possibility of doing corrective surgery so that they will be able to have children."[67] Of course, salpingectomies were irreversible.

Beginning in 1949 and continuing throughout the 1950s, the number of eugenic sterilizations at the twelve-thousand-patient Milledgeville State Hospital, then the largest institution of its kind in the world, far surpassed the total at the seven-hundred-bed Gracewood facility. The Milledgeville State Hospital never sterilized more than 2 percent of its patients in any one year, but because of its huge population, the total could still exceed two hundred operations per year. Indeed, it averaged about that number throughout the decade, with vasectomies typically outnumbering salpingectomies by a two-to-one margin. Most of the sterilized patients suffered from schizophrenia, which physicians at Milledgeville viewed as a hereditary illness. Unlike earlier southern eugenicists, such as Partlow and Whitten, who boasted of their sterilization programs, Milledgeville officials did not publicize their exploits. "This attempt to weed out serious, inheritable defects from the state's population is being done by the State Eugenics Board under a 1937 law that has not attracted public notice for many years," a Georgia newspaper reported. "Furthermore, a number of officials say privately that because the program involves such highly emotional issues, they would like for it to continue to escape public notice."[68]

Any realistic hope of covering up practices at Milledgeville ended in 1959, when Georgia's leading newspaper sent a reporter to investigate conditions at the antebellum institution. His findings of squalor and of abuse of patients, presented in a series of front-page articles replete with graphic photographs, shocked readers throughout Georgia. Even a high state official admitted that the hospital was "worse than the German prison camps," with "food not fit for a dog." The list of documented abuses included the regular practice of having nurses perform surgical operations, including vasectomies and salpingectomies, on patients, without supervision by a physician. The governor responded to the resulting public outcry by appointing a physician-led advisory committee and transferring the institution from the troubled state welfare department to the well-run state health department.[69]

The newspaper exposé never actually uncovered the issue of eugenic sterilization, but the advisory committee did. The director of the health department reported to the committee that "[s]everal thousand," most of whom suffered from schizophrenia, "have been sterilized in Georgia under [the eugenics] law." He noted further, "Families and guardians frequently become greatly disturbed on being notified the person is to be sterilized," but he added that "this opposition usually disappears when they learn it merely prevents parenthood and does not interfere with other sex activity." An Emory University psychology professor on the committee responded to the revelation by noting that experts differed sharply on the hereditary nature of schizophrenia. After another member added that "this thing is highly emotional—loaded with dynamite," the full committee appointed a special subcommittee to look into the matter.[70] Even though the committee never made a specific recommendation regarding eugenic sterilization, the number of such operations performed at Milledgeville rapidly declined, at least in part for fear of lawsuits by sterilized patients or their families. By the mid-1960s, the general practice of compulsory eugenic sterilization had ended in the Deep South.[71]

Even as the advisory committee conducted the hearings that led to the end of eugenic sterilization in Georgia, other types of compulsory sterilization gained support in the state. The popular U.S. senator Herman Talmadge, whose father had vetoed Georgia's 1935 eugenic sterilization bill, now urged congressional legislation to sterilize unmarried women on welfare who repeatedly bore children. Two counties responded by formally petitioning the state legislature "to introduce a sterilization act in Georgia for the purpose of controlling illegitimate babies to irresponsible mothers." Throughout the Deep South, and elsewhere, a quiet practice of sterilizing women on welfare spread. "But," as one 1959 article reporting on this development noted, "Georgia's existing [eugenic sterilization] law has an entirely different aim—that of weeding out inheritable physical and mental defects."[72] The new practices either had purely economic purposes or, if they reflected any concern for the well-being of the potential children, then that concern focused more on environmental factors related to bad rearing than on hereditary factors related to bad birth. Nurture had replaced nature as the accepted explanation for social problems. It only remained for the states of the Deep South to confirm this shift by repealing their antiquated eugenic sterilization statutes.

Repeal

By the time southern lawmakers got around to repealing their eugenic sterilization statutes, those laws represented dead letters in the code books and an embarrassment to mental health officials. No one publicly stepped forward in their defense. By the 1970s, any delay in the repeal process resulted more from public indifference and legislative inertia than from residual support. The greatest problem lay in motivating lawmakers to act on the issue. Ironically, growing interest in population control and reproductive rights, coupled with traditional opposition to compulsory sterilization, provided the needed stimulus. All three factors contributed in Georgia, leading it to act first.

Population control had become a major political and social issue by the time of America's first "Earth Day" in 1969. It attracted both traditional eugenicists, who welcomed it as a shield from the accusations of racism that had dogged their cause since the Nazi holocaust, and a broad array of environmentalists, neo-Malthusians, and others more concerned with the quantity of human beings than with their quality. The historian Linda Gordon has traced the connection between eugenics and population control. "During the 1930s, 1940s, and 1950s academic eugenicists transformed themselves into population controllers," she noted, and went on to describe a similar metamorphosis among foundations and organizations that had once promoted eugenics.[73]

Of course, to the extent that the promotion of voluntary birth control measures represented the primary means employed by modern population controllers, many southern eugenicists did not need to undergo much of a transformation to join the new cause. In reporting the results from a 1927 survey of more than one hundred physicians from across the Deep South, for example, an article in the MASA journal noted, "[A]ll replied that birth control in some form is practiced by the majority of their patients, especially the more intelligent classes." This led the pollster, an Alabama eugenicist, to argue for the legalization of birth control information and materials on the grounds that "the more intelligent classes already practice birth control, while the less intelligent, who lack the knowledge to restrict their births, are breeding so prolifically that they imperil the general standards of human excellence of the race."[74] Reflecting this shift, between the 1940s and the 1960s Clarence Gamble refocused his attention from domestic eugenics to third-world population control, taking at least some of his southern followers in tow. Even Birthright, the principal remaining eugenics organization and a long-time advocate of compulsory sterilization statutes, transformed itself into the Association for Voluntary Sterilization (AVS).[75]

The AVS inadvertently hastened the repeal of the 1937 Georgia eugenics statute by its work for legalized sterilization. Georgia, like most other states, traditionally outlawed voluntary sterilization, along with other medical means of birth control and abortion. In 1966, as part of the national movement toward greater reproductive rights, the state legalized the sterilization of married persons so long as both spouses gave their informed consent.[76] With the support of the AVS, the Georgia legislator John H. Henderson Jr., a thirty-seven-year-old veterinarian from suburban Atlanta, sought to expand this law two years later to include unmarried adults. Betraying a population-control objective that flew in the face of reproductive rights, his proposal also empowered a parent or guardian to direct that "an unmarried minor or mental incompetent" be sterilized.[77] This additional provision brought together both opponents of birth control and supporters of reproductive rights. "The bill has drawn cries of trying to create a 'master race' and of being 'racist' and a direct attack on poor people," one Atlanta newspaper reported. "Churchmen have cried the measure can be used to force persons to submit to sterilization in order to draw welfare benefits. Attorneys and doctors have challenged the safeguards provided against abuse of sterilization."[78]

Faced with this united opposition, Henderson withdrew his bill from consideration and worked with its opponents in drafting a compromise measure that would simply legalize the voluntary sterilization of consenting adults. As part of this compromise, the legislation replaced Georgia's broad eugenic sterilization statute with a narrow one permitting the court-ordered sterilization of mentally retarded persons only with the consent of their parents or guardians and upon a showing "that such persons with or without economic aid (charitable or otherwise) from others could not provide care and support for one or more children procreated by them." With this shift from hereditarian to environmental factors as the sole justification for involuntary sterilization, eugenics lost its main foothold in Georgia law. The compromise legislation passed in 1970, without debate or significant opposition.[79]

Three years later, similar concern for the reproductive rights of the mentally retarded formally brought down Alabama's 1919 sterilization law. That statutory provision, which broadly empowered the superintendent of the Partlow State School "to sterilize any inmate," had not served as the legal basis for performing any operations since the state supreme court ruled against the proposed 1935 sterilization legislation. Sterilizations occasionally occurred at Partlow, however, even though no other statutory authority existed for performing the operation in Alabama. Following a legal complaint lodged against the practice in 1973, a federal-court panel officially declared the old statute "clearly and obviously unconstitutional" because it contained "no provision for notice, hearing, or any other procedural safeguard."[80] In 1974, the panel's chief judge issued a supplementary order proscribing any further sterilizations of minors at the facility, and strictly limiting the procedure for adults to operations performed "in the best interest of the resident," with the individual's free and informed consent.[81] These rulings clearly barred any consideration of eugenic factors for sterilizations performed at the Partlow State School.

Larger events stimulated and shaped the Partlow litigation. The plaintiffs filed their complaint shortly after a different type of forced sterilization in Alabama captured the nation's attention. According to the initial reports in the national media, a federally funded community action agency in Montgomery had sterilized four teenage daughters of an African American welfare recipient without securing their prior consent. As the story unfolded, the number dropped from four to two, and ultimately to one mentally retarded twelve-year-old girl named Minnie Relf, but the event still seemed to confirm a widespread suspicion that southern welfare programs systematically sterilized poor African Americans.[82] Within days after this story broke, an aid recipient filed a civil suit claiming that seven years earlier, under the state program developed by Gamble in North Carolina, she had been sterilized without giving her informed consent. Then, as the public outcry mounted, the press uncovered the fact that the only obstetrician treating welfare recipients in Aiken, South Carolina, required that those with more than two children consent to sterilization as part of any Medicaid-funded delivery. Local

hospital records indicated that more than half of the thirty-four such de-
liveries during the prior year had included sterilization procedures, and
that all but two of these sterilizations had been performed on African
Americans. After describing one example, the *New York Times* reported
in dramatic style, "Hers is not the only case in Aiken; it's not the only
one in the South. In fact, it is the third situation to be disclosed in recent
months in which involuntary sterilization was systematically performed
on poor black women."[83]

The *Times* added, "The disclosures are causing widespread outrage
and have prompted the filing of lawsuits and the issuance . . . of new
[federal] guidelines on involuntary sterilization."[84] Those lawsuits and
new regulations culminated in strict limits on involuntary sterilization
under federally funded programs. Even though these instances directly
involved economic and racial issues, rather than strictly eugenic ones,
they demonstrated the official repudiation of compulsory sterilization. In
its final regulation on the subject, the federal Department of Health, Education, and Welfare denounced "the sterilization of the adolescent Relf
sisters in Alabama and a case of coerced sterilization in South Carolina"
as "tragic examples of sterilization abuse."[85] Forced eugenic sterilization
could not survive in this climate, especially within programs receiving
federal funds.

Despite the events in Aiken, South Carolina did not formally repeal its
comprehensive 1935 eugenic sterilization statute for another decade. The
impetus then came from the commitment of two women to reproductive
rights. The only female member of the state Senate, Elizabeth J. Patterson, first introduced the repeal legislation in 1984, after an angry female
constituent with epilepsy complained to her about the sterilization law's
never-used provision covering epileptics. At the time, Patterson did not
know that the statute existed, even though her father, Governor Olin
Johnson, had signed it into law fifty years earlier; her brother had resided
for two decades at the state institution for the mentally retarded, by then
renamed "Whitten Village" in honor of its former superintendent; and
she had served on the state Committee for Mental Health. She checked
with that committee and with state mental health officials about the law,
and found out that they saw no need for it anymore. Indeed, the state
health department reported to her that it had not used the statute for
more than a decade, and assured her that it would never use it again.[86]

Despite these assurances, the statute offended the ambitious Patterson, who would win an upset election for Congress in 1986. Because of
her own family background, she believed that mental retardation was
not strictly hereditary. Her brother's experiences at Whitten Village suggested that close supervision and oral contraceptives adequately protect-

ed patients from unwanted pregnancies. Furthermore, her constituent's anger led Patterson to conclude that the statute did not simply represent a harmless relic. "It's definitely a slap in the face to people categorized in that legislation," she told her colleagues at the time.[87]

A final feature of the statute irritated the pro-choice Democrat. "The major problem was that it was mandatory," Patterson later recalled. "It should be a matter of choice." Therefore, she opted to go after the entire statute rather than simply addressing her constituent's concern by deleting the provision applying to epileptics. Her proposal failed to receive a hearing when first introduced in 1984, but passed without opposition during the next session of the legislature.[88] By that time, no one seemed to care much about the antiquated law except an angry constituent and a principled legislator. Reflecting similar anger but somewhat less principle, the Mississippi legislature quietly deleted epilepsy from coverage under its sterilization statute at the same time, but otherwise left the little-used law on the books as a sole surviving statutory relic of the region's eugenic past.[89]

Sifting and Winnowing

In 1991, Louisiana state representative David Duke, a former Grand Wizard in the Ku Klux Klan and a current gubernatorial candidate, introduced legislation offering payments of one hundred dollars per year to female welfare recipients who used a contraceptive device called Norplant. Duke's proposal came just four months after the federal government had approved use of the Norplant procedure, which involved inserting small capsules into a woman's upper arm during a simple operation. If left in, these capsules prevented pregnancy for up to five years by releasing progestin, a synthetic hormone used in birth control pills. Despite adverse reactions in a few women, the device appeared safer and more effective than any other form of artificial contraception. Perhaps most significant of all for Duke's proposal, government officials could easily monitor Norplant use. In short, the development offered a safe, effective means of temporarily sterilizing women.[1]

The 1991 Louisiana legislation presented certain parallels to earlier eugenic sterilization proposals. Duke offered his proposal as a way to reduce future governmental expenditures, which echoed claims once made by southern eugenicists on behalf of compulsory sterilization. Further, given Duke's Klan background and the large number of African Americans receiving welfare in Louisiana, charges of racism surrounded the Norplant bill just as they had previously dogged eugenics legislation. Finally, the very notion of a state's either offering a financial incentive to certain citizens for using Norplant or compelling them to undergo sterilization suggested that society did not value their offspring. Such thinking inevitably leads to grave consequences. Either society must accord value to all human beings, or no individual holds any intrinsic worth and the unfavored potentially suffer inhuman treatment.

Of course, society could discount the worth of certain individuals for various reasons having nothing to do with their genetic make-up, and therefore proposals to discourage their birth need not involve eugenics.

Indeed, following the pattern of eugenics lawmaking, legislation involving compulsory Norplant first surfaced in the North and the West, and some of these proposals clearly addressed environmental concerns. For example, shortly after the introduction of Norplant, the governor of California raised the possibility of requiring its use by women with a history of drug abuse. "I think to the extent you can prevent the birth of an addicted newborn, who can be terribly and irreversible damaged, God knows you want to do that," he declared.[2] A *Los Angeles Times* survey found widespread support for this position among Californians, with all segments of the population expressing overwhelming approval when asked, "Do you approve or disapprove of making the Norplant device mandatory for drug abusing women of child bearing age?"[3]

Additional parallels existed between eugenic sterilization and proposals involving compulsory Norplant. In both instances, proponents seized on a new medical breakthrough to solve a pressing social problem. Early in the southern eugenics movement, for example, William Partlow observed, "I do not believe that any measure so stringent as to require castration or ovariotomy in those who show marks of degeneracy could ever be enforced in this country," but he later expressed hope that the public would accept forced vasectomies and salpingectomies in such cases.[4] To further this acceptance, eugenicists throughout the Deep South stressed, in the words of one editorialist, that "[s]terilization does not injure the person sterilized."[5] They failed to persuade the public on this point. Nearly a century later, with the potential harm of compulsory sterilization widely recognized, Norplant appeared to offer a publicly acceptable means to achieve similar ends. For example, in an editorial entitled "Poverty and Norplant," a major northern newspaper asked, "Dare we mention them in the same breath? To do so might be considered deplorably insensitive, perhaps raising the specter of eugenics. But it would be worse to avoid discussing the logical conclusion that foolproof contraception could be invaluable in breaking the cycle of inner city poverty."[6] Of course, sterilization still represented a surer form of contraception than Norplant, yet by the 1990s the editorialist only mentioned the later option.

The authority of science played a critical role throughout. "Science can improve the human race by making the production of the mentally unfit impossible," the president of Alabama's medical association proclaimed in 1928.[7] A year later, Jean Gordon rebutted opponents of eugenic sterilization by asking, "This is a scientific question, gentlemen, is it not?"[8] Southern eugenicists rested their arguments on the authority of science, and ultimately lost the case when expert opinion turned against them. Similarly, proposals to require Norplant for women with a history of drug abuse gained support when policy makers thought that medical opinion offered little hope for the offspring of such women, but lost ground as new research came to light indicating that most drug-exposed fetuses can survive and recover.[9]

These patterns of political activity suggest that a renewed push for forced contraception, or for some more acceptable means of genetic manipulation, could follow future scientific breakthroughs linking dangerous or undesirable human traits to identifiable genes. Indeed, a leading genetics researcher declared as early as 1969, "A new eugenics has arisen, based upon the dramatic increase in our understanding of the biochemistry of heredity and our comprehension of the craft and means of evolution."[10] Of course, scientific support *now* will appear stronger for the "new eugenics" than for the "old eugenics," but the earlier theory also seemed impeccable in its day. Thus, a leading Atlanta newspaper observed in 1937, "Eugenic sterilization is now recognized by state officials, physicians, parole and probation officers, social workers, and officials of asylums, hospitals and prisons as a definite advance in modern civilization in the prevention of increase in insanity and crime."[11] Any new eugenics will enjoy similar recognition from scientific and medical experts. In theory, scientists maintain a healthy skepticism regarding their hypotheses, and seek to test and falsify them; but in practice, any prevailing scientific paradigm tends to exert a dogmatic hold on its adherents.

At least in the Deep South, values founded on traditional religion and concern for individual rights served as more effective protection against the excesses of eugenics than did any internal regulatory mechanism within medicine or science. Southern state medical associations regularly endorsed the most radical eugenic measures without regard for conventional medical ethics, which one Alabama physician bluntly dismissed as "tommy-rot" in this context.[12] Southern scientists generally followed suit, leaving it to those outside the profession (in particular, individuals who opposed eugenics on religious or individual-rights grounds) to raise scientific objections to the theory.[13] Initially, the stiffest resistance to eugenic reforms came from religious individuals and institutions, but even this diminished over time. Events in Alabama offered a case in point. Organized religion throughout the state presented a united front against eugenic sterilization bills in 1935, but many of Alabama's mainline Protestant churches came to accept such legislation by 1945, leaving only Roman Catholics and some fundamentalist Christians in opposition. Reflecting a similar shift and split, a Protestant physician in South Carolina observed at the time, "Next to the Church, I consider [eugenics] the hope of the world. What a pity that most of those little circuit-riders of the country, carting their impoverished broods from place to place, can't see it in the same light."[14] In short, religion acted more as a brake than as a barrier to eugenics in the Deep South.

Ultimately, a broadening conception of personal liberty, including civil rights for the handicapped and reproductive rights for women, provided the surest protection against compulsory eugenic programs. Governor Bibb Graves stood firmly on this ground in opposing Alabama's 1935 sterilization legislation, declaring in his veto messages, "The hoped for good results are not sure enough or great enough to compensate for the hazard to personal rights that would be involved in the execution of the provisions of the Bill."[15] A quarter-century later, increasing respect for the rights of the mentally ill and the mentally retarded helped lead to the curtailment of compulsory sterilization in Georgia and the eventual repeal of that state's eugenic sterilization statute. Growing concern for individual reproductive rights also contributed to that repeal effort, and spurred on the various legislative, judicial, and administrative actions taken during the 1970s and 1980s against compulsory sterilization programs in the Deep South.

Graves's veto messages addressed the heart of the matter. Concern for personal rights and individual freedom should control American public policy decisions. Most countries constitute little more than ancient ethnic enclaves, such as a land for the Thais or the Poles. In their loftiest rhetoric, however, Americans identify their country as the geographical manifestation of an idea: a nation conceived in liberty and dedicated to the proposition that all people are created equal and endowed with certain inalienable rights. American eugenicists forgot this ideal when they sought to impose a Nordic ethnic identity on the United States through immigration restrictions. Some southern eugenicists also became so bewitched by their cause that they denied the very notions that constitute America. "Contrary to the Constitution of the United States all men are not born equal," a prominent Georgia physician asserted. "We have no right, even if we do pride ourselves on the fact that this is a free country, to bring into the world a child who is physically or mentally unfit."[16] Similarly, an exasperated Jean Gordon exclaimed in the heat of debate, "If we are going to go on and let the feeble-minded procreate—if you all agree that procreation is 'an inalienable right'—then, I have nothing further to say. I don't agree with that[,] whether it is scientific, medical or economic."[17] Certainly, excessive individual freedom can cause adverse social consequences, but America must follow its ideals or risk losing the identity that inspired many of its noblest achievements.

If American ideals remain sound, then reserving personal decisions involving procreation to individuals should produce better results than entrusting them to the state. Thus, contrary to the beliefs of most southern eugenicists, establishing a right to voluntary sterilization could further the common good, whereas compulsory sterilization measures must ultimately hinder it. Similarly, in the future, Americans should welcome the voluntary use by individuals of expanded genetic knowledge, even as they remain deeply suspicious about its application in any government-sponsored program of "new eugenics." As if echoing the hymns from this book's opening chapter, an Alabama physician observed early in the eugenics movement, "I am an enthusiast on blood. If we want to raise good hogs we get good stock . . . and yet we are willing for our daughters to marry any kind of degenerate and then expect senators and presidents to be produced. It is impossible."[18] This observation might represent wise personal advice even as it provided a foolish basis for making public policy. If the physician wanted a great president, then perhaps he should have considered the offspring of a possibly "feeble-minded" Nancy Hanks and a seemingly "degenerate" Thomas Lincoln. Of course, as a White southerner speaking within living memory of the Civil War, he likely held an opposing view of that president's greatness—but such opinions were related to the fallout from a different story of freedom.[19]

Notes

Introduction: *Surveying the Land*

1. W. L. Funkhouser, "Human Rubbish," *Journal of the Medical Association of Georgia* 26 (1937), 197. (Hereafter this journal is cited as *Journal of MAG.*)

2. Dr. Harper, in "Discussion," *Transactions of the Medical Association of the State of Alabama* (1907), 229. (Hereafter this journal is cited as *Transactions of MASA.*)

3. Jean Gordon, in "Discussion," *New Orleans Medical and Surgical Journal* 82 (1929), 355.

4. R. McG. Carruth, "Race Degeneration: What Can We Do to Check It?" *New Orleans Medical and Surgical Journal* 72 (1919), 184–85.

5. J. M. Buchanan, "Insanity—Its Rapid Increase and Prevention Measures," *Southern Medical Journal* 5 (1912), 321.

6. Legislative Committee, "Report," in Florida State Federation of Woman's Clubs, *Manual, 1912–1913* ([Lakeland, Fla.]: n.p., 1912), 35.

7. A. Bethune Patterson, "The State's Duty to the Feeble-Minded," *Journal of the South Carolina Medical Association* 12 (1916), 375. (Hereafter this journal is cited as *Journal of SCMA.*)

8. J. P. McMurphy, "Birth Control, a Public Health Problem," *Transactions of MASA* (1927), 343.

Chapter 1: *Southern Soil*

1. E.g., Robert H. Coleman, ed., *The Modern Hymnal* (Nashville: Broadman, 1926), no. 295. (This is a Southern Baptist hymnal).

2. David L. Smiley, "The Quest for the Central Theme in Southern History," *South Atlantic Quarterly* 71 (1972), 307.

3. William Byrd, *Histories of the Dividing Line betwixt Virginia and North Carolina,* ed. William K. Boyd (Raleigh: North Carolina Historical Commission, 1929), 5.

4. Thomas Jefferson to Marquis de Chastellux, Sept. 2, 1785, in *The Portable Thomas Jefferson,* ed. Merrill D. Paterson (Harmondsworth, U.K.: Penguin, 1975), 387–88.

5. Ulrich B. Phillips, "The Central Theme of Southern History," *American Historical Review* 34 (1928), 30–43, quotation on 31. See also idem, *Life and Labor in the Old South* (Boston: Little, Brown, 1929).

6. For representative discussions of these and other factors, see Smiley, "Quest for Theme"; Carl N. Degler, *Place over Time: The Continuity of Southern Distinctiveness* (Baton Rouge: Louisiana State Univ. Press, 1977), 1–26; Frank E. Vandiver, ed., *The Idea of the South: Pursuit of a Central Theme* (Chicago: Univ. of Chicago Press, 1964); and James O. Breeden, "Disease as a Factor in Southern Distinctiveness," in *Disease and Distinctiveness in the American South*, ed. Todd L. Savitt and James Harvey Young (Knoxville: Univ. of Tennessee Press, 1988), 1–21.

7. Wilbur J. Cash, *The Mind of the South* (New York: Knopf, 1941), viii. For a recent discussion of the impact of this book, see Bruce Clayton, *W. J. Cash: A Life* (Baton Rouge: Louisiana State Univ. Press, 1991).

8. C. Vann Woodward, *The Burden of Southern History*, rev. ed. (Baton Rouge: Louisiana State Univ. Press, 1968), 15–16; George B. Tindall, "Mythology: A New Frontier in Southern History," in Vandiver, ed., *Idea of the South*, 1; and Degler, *Place over Time*, 131. See also David M. Potter, "The Enigma of the South," *Yale Review* 51 (1961), 151, which bases southern distinctiveness on collective "folk culture." Of course, some regional differences could be objectively documented and used as a basis for further perpetuating a regional state of mind. This was reflected, for example, in the use of regional differences in the manifestations of common diseases to justify the founding of a regional medical association and medical journal for the South in 1907 and 1908. See "Introduction," *Southern Medical Journal* 1 (1908), 47.

9. Smiley, "Quest for Theme," 325.

10. For a discussion of these sources, see, e.g., Michael O'Brien, *On the Idea of the South: 1920–1941* (Baltimore: Johns Hopkins Univ. Press, 1979), 14–19; and Tindall, "Mythology," 8–9.

11. "Introduction," in *I'll Take My Stand: The South and the Agrarian Tradition* (New York: Harper, 1930), ix.

12. Ibid., xv; and Lyle H. Lanier, "A Critique of the Philosophy of Progress," in *Take My Stand*, 147.

13. Lanier, "Critique," 146.

14. Howard W. Odum, *Southern Regions of the United States* (Chapel Hill: Univ. of North Carolina Press, 1936), 499. See also U.S. Census Bureau, *Abstract of the Fourteenth Census of the United States, 1920* (Washington, D.C.: Government Printing Office, 1923), 412–15.

15. Southern resistance to these three reforms on the basis of concern for traditional family structure was discussed in William A. Link, *The Paradox of Southern Progressivism, 1880–1930* (Chapel Hill: Univ. of North Carolina Press, 1992), 268–73 and 296–311.

16. W. H. Swift, "Why It Is Hard to Get Good Child Labor Laws in the South," *Child Labor Bulletin* (New York), 3 (1914–15), 73.

17. Charles W. Pipkin, "Social Legislation," in *Culture in the South*, ed. W. T. Couch (Chapel Hill: Univ. of North Carolina Press, 1934), 660.

18. Link, *Paradox of Progressivism*, 182 and 308–11, quotation on 309.

19. Odum, *Southern Regions*, 101–5, 502. See also George Brown Tindall, *The Emergence of the New South, 1913–1945* (Baton Rouge: Louisiana State Univ. Press, 1967), 254–84 and 321–24.

20. For an example of this in a modern Southern writer, see Walker Percy, *The Thanatos Syndrome* (New York: Farrar, 1987). For background on the way in which concern for the traditional family served as a basis for southern resistance to public health reforms generally, see Link, *Paradox of Progressivism*, 283–95.

21. Stark Young, "Not in Memoriam, but in Defense," in *Take My Stand*, 346.

22. Ibid., 336.

23. Donald Davidson, "Why the Modern South Has a Great Literature," *Vanderbilt Studies in the Humanities* 1 (1951), 12.

24. E.g., Daniel J. Kevles, *In the Name of Eugenics: Genetics and the Uses of Human Heredity* (New York: Knopf, 1985), 72–75. The reluctance of Canadians of this era to admit that their family members had hereditary defects is noted in Wendy Mitchinson, *The Nature of Their Bodies: Women and Their Doctors in Victorian Canada* (Toronto: Univ. of Toronto Press, 1991), 291–93.

25. Odum, *Southern Regions*, 91; and Census Bureau, *Fourteenth Census*, 98–100.

26. Young, "Not in Memoriam," 347.

27. Odum, *Southern Regions*, 15.

28. Alabama Department of Archives and History, *Alabama Official and Statistical Register, 1935* (Birmingham: Birmingham Printing, 1935), 31–32.

29. E.g., Dunbar Rowland, *Official and Statistical Register of the State of Mississippi, 1920–24* (Jackson: Hederman, 1923), 120–57 and 220–323.

30. Young, "Not in Memoriam," 347–48.

31. "Introduction," in *Take My Stand*, xi.

32. Tindall, "Mythology," 8; Woodward, *Burden of History*, 8.

33. O'Brien, *Idea of the South*, 31.

34. E.g., Odum, *Southern Regions*, 501.

35. For an introduction to eugenics as a progressive movement, see, e.g., Donald K. Pickens, *Eugenics and the Progressives* (Nashville: Vanderbilt Univ. Press, 1968).

36. Odum, *Southern Regions*, 501 and 527.

37. U.S. Census Bureau, *Religious Bodies: 1926* (Washington, D.C.: Government Printing Office, 1930), 1:42–58 and 142–75.

38. Tindall, *Emergence of New South,* 196. For analysis of this issue by other leading historians, all of whom reached a similar conclusion, see Kenneth K. Bailey, *Southern White Protestantism in the Twentieth Century* (New York: Harper, 1964); Degler, *Place over Time,* 19–23; Samuel S. Hill, "Conclusion," in *Varieties of Southern Religious Experiences,* ed. Samuel S. Hill (Baton Rouge: Louisiana State Univ. Press, 1988), 211–12; Edward L. Queen II, *In the South the Baptists Are the Center of Gravity: Southern Baptists and Social Change, 1930–1980* (Brooklyn, N.Y.: Carlson, 1991), 7–42; and C. Vann Woodward, *Origins of the New South, 1877–1913* (Baton Rouge: Louisiana State Univ. Press, 1951), 169–74.

39. William Archer, *Through Afro-America: An English Reading of the Race Problem* (London: Chapman and Hall, 1910), 73–74.

40. "Introduction," in *Take My Stand,* xiv; and Allen Tate, "Remarks on the Southern Religion," in ibid., 167.

41. Edwin McNeill Poteat Jr., "Religion in the South," in Couch, ed., *Culture in South,* 250–51.

42. Charles W. Ramsdell, "The Southern Heritage," in Couch, ed., *Culture in South,* 22.

43. See O'Brien, *Idea of South,* 18.

44. Howard W. Odum, *An American Epoch: Southern Portraiture in the National Picture* (New York: Holt, 1930), 167–68.

45. Ibid., 169. Reflecting on his own experience in a rural southern church at the turn of the century, the congressman and Southern Baptist Convention president Brooks Hays wrote, "the typical congregation covered the whole spectrum of community life." Brooks Hays, "Reflecting on the Role of Baptists in Politics and the Future of America," *Baptist History and Heritage* 11 (1976), 170.

46. Odum, *American Epoch,* 169. Confirming this observation, the historian George Marsden's analysis of developments through 1925 concluded that though the North was secularized, "evangelicalism was still a virtually unchallenged establishment" throughout the South. George Marsden, *Fundamentalism and American Culture: The Shaping of Twentieth-Century Evangelicalism, 1870–1925* (New York: Oxford Univ. Press, 1980), 179. For a study of the broad range of social and economic classes that continued to attend community churches in the South, see John A. Forrest, "The Role of Aesthetics in the Conversion Experience in a Missionary Baptist Church," in *Holding on to the Land and Lord: Kinship, Ritual, Land Tenure, and Social Policy in the Rural South,* ed. Robert L. Hall and Carol B. Stack (Athens: Univ. of Georgia Press, 1982), 80–88.

47. E.g., see Woodward, *Origins of New South,* 389–92; and Edward J. Larson, *Trial and Error: The American Controversy over Creation and Evolution* (New York: Oxford Univ. Press, 1985), 28–57.

48. Odum, *Southern Regions,* 527.

49. L. L. Bernard, "The Southern Sociological Congress," *American Journal of Sociology* 19 (1913), 91–93; "Address to the Churches," in *The New Chivalry—*

Health, ed. James E. McCulloch (Nashville: Southern Sociological Congress, 1915), 13; J. Wayne Flynt, "Southern Protestantism and Reform, 1890–1920," in Hill, ed., *Varieties of Religious Experiences,* 135–55; E. Charles Chatfield, "The Southern Sociological Congress: Organization of Uplift," *Tennessee Historical Quarterly* 19 (1960), 335; and Tindall, *Emergence of New South,* 198–99.

50. Kevles, *Name of Eugenics,* 64–68.

51. Odum, *American Epoch,* 169 and 180–81.

52. Ibid., 184–85.

53. Coleman, ed., *Modern Hymnal,* no. 255. Also quoted as representative in Odum, *American Epoch,* 185.

54. Walter Hines Sims, ed., *Baptist Hymnal* (Nashville: Convention, 1956), no. 192. (This book is a revised edition of a Southern Baptist hymnal.)

55. Coleman, ed., *Modern Hymnal,* no. 365.

56. Ibid., no. 9.

57. Odum, *American Epoch,* 180–81.

58. Coleman, ed., *Modern Hymnal,* no. 295.

59. Ibid., no. 471.

60. Sims, ed., *Baptist Hymnal,* no. 443.

61. Coleman, ed., *Modern Hymnal,* no. 185. On the impact of southern religious beliefs on racism, see Degler, *Place over Time,* 23.

62. Cash, *Mind of South,* viii.

63. Odum, *Southern Regions,* 495–531; and "Introduction," in *Take My Stand,* x.

64. Woodward, *Origins of New South,* ix; and Tindall, *Emergence of New South,* ix–x.

65. Woodward, *Burden of History,* 9.

66. Arthur S. Link and Richard L. McCormick, *Progressivism* (Arlington Heights, Ill.: Davidson, 1983), 2.

67. For an excellent overview of this issue, see Daniel T. Rogers, "In Search of Progressivism," *Reviews in American History* 10 (1982), 113–32. For a variety of interpretations of these reforms, see, e.g., Benjamin Parker DeWitt, *The Progressive Movement; a Non-partisan, Comprehensive Discussion of Current Tendencies in American Politics* (New York: Macmillan, 1925), and John D. Hicks, *The Populist Revolt: A History of the Farmers' Alliance and the People's Party* (Minneapolis: Univ. of Minnesota Press, 1931), two early works that present views of progressivism as a drive by common folk to regain control from big business and its lackeys in government. Also see Richard Hofstadter, *The Age of Reform: From Bryan to F.D.R.* (New York: Knopf, 1955), and George M. Mowry, *The Era of Theodore Roosevelt, 1900–1912* (New York: Harper, 1958), later views of progressivism as a middle-class effort to regain status and individu-

alism; Samuel P. Hays, *The Response to Industrialism, 1885–1914* (Chicago: Univ. of Chicago Press, 1957), Robert H. Wiebe, *The Search for Order, 1877–1920* (New York: Hill, 1967), and Samuel Haber, *Efficiency and Uplift: Scientific Management in the Progressive Era, 1890–1920* (Chicago: Univ. of Chicago Press, 1964), three works presenting progressivism as an attempt to solve social problems by the use of modern business, scientific, or sociological techniques; John D. Buenker, *Urban Liberalism and Progressive Reform* (New York: Scribner's, 1973), which identified the contribution of urban immigrants to progressivism; and Gabriel Kolko, *The Triumph of Conservatism: A Reinterpretation of American History, 1900–1916* (New York: Free Press, 1963), which reinterpreted progressivism as conservative reforms by business elites. For a further review of the literature, see JoAnne Brown, *The Definition of a Profession: The Authority of Metaphor in the History of Intelligence Testing* (Princeton: Princeton Univ. Press, 1992).

68. Link and McCormick, *Progressivism*, 6 and 22.

69. See Mark H. Haller, *Eugenics: Hereditarian Attitudes in American Thought* (New Brunswick, N.J.: Rutgers Univ. Press, 1963), 124; Kevles, *Name of Eugenics*, 101; Kenneth M. Ludmerer, *Genetics and American Society: A Historical Appraisal* (Baltimore: Johns Hopkins Univ. Press, 1972), 15–18; and Pickens, *Eugenics and Progressives*.

70. Arthur S. Link, "The Progressive Movement in the South, 1870–1914," *North Carolina Historical Review* 23 (1946), 172–95; and Link, *Paradox of Progressivism*, 322–26.

71. On this persistent tradition, see George Brown Tindall, *The Persistent Tradition in New South Politics* (Baton Rouge: Louisiana State Univ. Press, 1975).

72. See Woodward, *Origins of New South*, 146–47; and Dewey W. Grantham, *Southern Progressivism: The Reconciliation of Progress and Tradition* (Knoxville: Univ. of Tennessee Press, 1983), xv–xvi.

73. Census Bureau, *Fourteenth Census*, 75 and 80–83.

74. Woodward, *Origin of New South*, 150.

75. Ibid., 371.

76. Grantham, *Southern Progressivism*, xv.

77. Ibid., xvi and 14–25.

78. Ibid., xvi–xvii.

79. This is reflected in Pipkin, "Social Legislation," 646–77. See also Grantham, *Southern Progressivism*, xvii–xix and 416–17.

80. Tindall, *Emergence of New South*, 32.

81. Pipkin, "Social Legislation," 646–77, quotation on 646. See also Woodward, *Origins of New South*, 142–74; Tindall, *Emergence of New South*, 473–504; and Grantham, *Southern Progressivism*, 410–22.

82. Odum, *Southern Regions*, 241.

83. Ibid., 515–17. Despite his progressive, proscience leanings, Odum never became active in the eugenics movement. When I asked one of Odum's famous sons about whether Odum accepted eugenics, the son replied, with a characteristic twinkle in his eye, "That is why he named me Eugene." Eugene P. Odum, interview by author, Mar. 10, 1993.

84. This is reflected in the absence of articles on eugenics by contributors from the Deep South in the *Journal of Heredity*, which was the leading scientific journal for eugenics during the period. The journal's sponsoring organization, the American Breeders' Association (renamed the American Genetics Association in 1913), never had any officers or council members from the Deep South during the period of its eugenic activities. For background on this organization and its journal, see Pickens, *Eugenics and Progressives*, 52–53 and 95.

Chapter 2: *Eugenic Seeds*

1. Francis Galton, *Inquiries into Human Faculty and Its Development* (London: Macmillan, 1883), 24–25.

2. Francis Galton, *Hereditary Genius: An Inquiry into Its Causes and Consequences* (London: Macmillan, 1869), 325–37.

3. Francis Galton, *Memories of My Life* (London: Methuen, 1908), 288–89.

4. Karl Pearson, *The Life, Letters, and Labours of Francis Galton* (Cambridge: Cambridge Univ. Press, 1914–30), 1:207. See also Galton, *Hereditary Genius*, 349–50.

5. Francis Galton, *Essays in Eugenics* (London: Eugenics Education Society, 1909), 24–25. See generally Derick W. Forrest, *Francis Galton: The Life and Work of a Victorian Genius* (New York: Taplinger, 1974), 84; Mark H. Haller, *Eugenics: Hereditarian Attitudes in American Thought* (New Brunswick: Rutgers Univ. Press, 1963), 8–17; Daniel J. Kevles, *In the Name of Eugenics: Genetics and the Uses of Human Heredity* (New York: Knopf, 1985), 3–19; and Donald K. Pickens, *Eugenics and the Progressives* (Nashville: Vanderbilt Univ. Press, 1968), 23–36.

6. Francis Galton, "Hereditary Talent and Character," *Macmillan's Magazine* 12 (1865), 165; and Galton, *Hereditary Genius*, 1–2, 345, and 352.

7. Francis Galton, "Hereditary Improvements," *Fraser's Magazine* 87 (1873), 125–28.

8. R. L. Dugdale, *The Jukes: A Story in Crime, Pauperism, Disease, and Heredity*, 5th ed. (New York: Putnam, 1895), 7-15 and 69–70, quotation on 15. In conducting his investigation Dugdale was strongly influenced by the hereditarian ideas of the Italian criminologist Cesare Lombroso, but though Lombroso had clearly proposed a hereditarian basis for criminal tendencies a decade before Dugdale's work, he never conducted family studies. See Philip R. Reilly, *The Surgical Solution: A History of Involuntary Sterilization in the United States* (Baltimore: Johns Hopkins Univ. Press, 1991), 8–9.

9. Nicole Hahn Rafter, "Introduction," in *White Trash: The Eugenic Family Studies, 1877–1913,* ed. Nicole Hahn Rafter (Boston: Northeastern Univ. Press,

1988), 1–12. (This book contains many of these family studies in their entirety.) See also Carl N. Degler, *In Search of Human Nature: The Decline and Revival of Darwinism in American Social Thought* (New York: Oxford Univ. Press, 1991), 37; and Pickens, *Eugenics,* 89. In certain respects, the sensational "discovery" of mental retardation during the turn-of-the-century era paralleled the "discovery" of insanity a century earlier, which was described in Michel Foucault, *Madness and Civilization: A History of Insanity in the Age of Reason,* trans. Richard Howard (New York: Pantheon, 1965); and Daniel J. Rothman, *The Discovery of the Asylum: Social Order and Disorder in the New Republic,* rev. ed. (Boston: Little, Brown, 1990).

10. Francis Galton, *Natural Intelligence* (London: Macmillan, 1889), 83–137. See also Haller, *Eugenics,* 12; and Kevles, *Name of Eugenics,* 18.

11. See, e.g., Peter J. Bowler, *Non-Darwinian Evolution: Reinterpreting a Historical Myth* (Baltimore: Johns Hopkins Univ. Press, 1988), 72–104; Hamilton Cravens, *The Triumph of Evolution: American Scientists and the Heredity-Environment Controversy, 1900–1941* (Philadelphia: Univ. of Pennsylvania Press, 1978), 34–38; and Pickens, *Eugenics,* 38–39.

12. Dugdale, *Jukes,* 57.

13. Ibid., 65. See also Degler, *Human Nature,* 38.

14. Dugdale, *Jukes,* 55, 62, and 66, quotation on 55. About this same time, an article in a southern medical journal presented a similar view of the cause and prevention of mental illness in E. R. McIntyre, "Insanity and Some Causes Leading to It, and the Duty of the Physician Regarding Their Removal," *Southern Journal of Homeopathy* 73 o.s. [1 n.s.] (1889), 326–30.

15. For analyses of the impact of these scientific developments on the rise of eugenics, see Peter J. Bowler, "The Role of the History of Science in the Understanding of Social Darwinism and Eugenics," *Impact of Science on Society* 40 (1990), 275–77; Degler, *Human Nature,* 37–38; Haller, *Eugenics,* 58–63; Kevles, *Name of Eugenics,* 46–47, 69, and 72; Kenneth Ludmerer, *Genetics and American Society: A Historical Appraisal* (Baltimore: Johns Hopkins Univ. Press, 1972), 38–40; and Rafter, "Introduction," 8. For a purely Mendelian explanation for mental retardation in a southern medical journal from the period, see George F. Roeling, "Feeblemindedness," *New Orleans Medical and Surgical Journal* 73 (1920), 218.

16. Kevles, *Name of Eugenics,* 59; and Edward J. Larson, "The Rhetoric of Eugenics: Expert Authority and the Mental Deficiency Bill," *British Journal for the History of Science* 24 (1991), 45–60.

17. Arthur H. Estabrook, *The Jukes in 1915* (Washington, D.C.: Carnegie, 1916), 85.

18. Henry Herbert Goddard, *The Kallikak Family: A Study in the Heredity of Feeble-Mindedness* (New York: Macmillan, 1931), 60.

19. Estabrook, *Jukes in 1915,* 85.

20. For a comparison of eugenics legislation in the United States and the United

Kingdom, see Kevles, *Name of Eugenics*, 101–7; and Larson, "Rhetoric of Eugenics," 45–60.

21. For a representative discussion of these four methods by leading members of the American eugenics movement, see Paul Popenoe and Roswell Hill Johnson, *Applied Eugenics* (New York: Macmillan, 1918), 184–96. The three areas of state action were singled out for analysis in a 1914 eugenics tract. Stevenson Smith, Madge W. Wilkinson, and Louisa C. Wagoner, *A Summary of the Laws of the Several States* (Seattle: University of Washington, 1914).

22. Popenoe and Johnson, *Applied Eugenics*, 196.

23. Conn. Gen. Stat. sec. 1354 (1902).

24. Paul Popenoe and E. S. Gosney, *Twenty-eight Years of Sterilization in California* (Pasadena, Calif.: Human Betterment Foundation, 1938), 19–120. See also Popenoe and Johnson, *Applied Eugenics*, 197. The eugenicist Marian S. Olden also singled out these programs as models, and described the South Dakota effort in some detail, in Marian S. Olden, "Present Status of Sterilization Legislation in the United States," *Eugenical News* 31 (1946), 7–8.

25. For a listing and analysis of all eugenic marriage laws, see Charles B. Davenport, *State Laws Limiting Marriage Selection Examined in Light of Eugenics* (Cold Springs Harbor, N.Y.: Eugenics Record Office, 1913), table I; Mary Laack Oliver, "Eugenic Marriage Laws of the Forty-eight States" (M.A. thesis, Univ. of Wisconsin, 1937), A1–A63; Smith, Wilkinson, and Wagoner, *Summary*, 4–12.

26. Davenport, *State Laws*, 27–36, weighed the advantages and disadvantages of interracial unions from a eugenics viewpoint, and suggested that only limited restrictions were justified, which were much less than those imposed by the antimiscegenation statute in any southern state. See also Haller, *Eugenics*, 158–59. Philip R. Reilly also traced the history of antimiscegenation statutes to long before the eugenics movement, but posits a greater connection with eugenics, basing his views on the enforcement policies of Virginia's registrar for marriage. Reilly, *Surgical Solution*, 25, 72–74. Although eugenics was marked by both social and scientific racism, I could find no evidence of a direct causal link between the antimiscegenation statutes in the Deep South and eugenics. For general discussions of racism and eugenics, see Kevles, *Name of Eugenics*, 74–76; and Haller, *Eugenics*, 50–57.

27. Henry H. Goddard, *Feeble-Mindedness: Its Causes and Consequences* (New York: Macmillan, 1914), 565–66.

28. J. E. Wallace Wallin, *The Odyssey of a Psychologist: Pioneering Experiences in Special Education, Clinical Psychology, and Mental Hygiene* (Wilmington: By Author, 1955), 88.

29. Popenoe and Johnson, *Applied Eugenics*, 196.

30. Davenport, *State Laws*, 12 (emphasis in original).

31. Popenoe and Johnson, *Applied Eugenics*, 442.

32. Davenport, *State Laws*, 12.

33. Gerald N. Grob, *Mental Illness and American Society, 1875–1940* (Princeton: Princeton Univ. Press, 1983), 7. See also Albert Deutsch, *The Mentally Ill in America: A History of Their Care and Treatment from Colonial Times,* rev. ed. (New York: Columbia Univ. Press, 1949), 158–245; and Rothman, *Discovery of Asylum,* 130–54.

34. Grob, *Mental Illness,* 26. A classic but still controversial description of the structure and development of these institutions in the Northeast appeared in Rothman, *Discovery of Asylum,* 130–54.

35. Deutsch, *Mentally Ill,* 300–353, quotation on 347; and Royal Commission on the Care and Control of the Feeble-Minded, *Report upon Their Visit to American Institutions* (London: His Majesty's Stationery Office, 1908), 8:133.

36. E.g., Davenport, "Preface," in Estabrook, *Jukes in 1915,* iv.

37. Deutsch, *Mentally Ill,* 367. See also Royal Commission, *Report,* 132–33.

38. Alexander Johnson, quoted in Deutsch, *Mentally Ill,* 368. When Johnson reported to his colleagues three years earlier, he suggested the existence of more internal opposition but nevertheless affirmed, "It has long seemed to many people that the wisest course the state can take is to separate all true degenerates from society . . . [so] that they shall not entail upon the next generation the burden which the present one has borne. This is what we mean by 'segregation.'" Alexander Johnson, "Report of Committee on Colony for Segregation of Defectives," in *Proceedings of the National Conference of Charities and Corrections, 1903,* ed. Isabel C. Barrow (n.p.: Herr Press, 1903), 245–49, quotation on 248–49. Johnson served as secretary of the National Conference of Charities and Corrections from 1904 to 1913, and chaired its Committee on Colonies for Segregation of Defectives during much of this period.

39. Henry H. Goddard, *Sterilization and Segregation* (New York: Russell Sage Foundation, 1913), 4.

40. Ibid., 5.

41. H. H. Goddard, "Four Hundred Feeble-Minded Children Classified by the Binet Method," *Journal of Psycho-Asthenics* 15 (1910), 17, 26–27. An early description of Goddard's classification system as applied to residents of the California Home for the Care and Training of Feebleminded Children is in F. W. Hatch, "Report of the General Superintendent," in *Ninth Biennial Report of the Commission in Lunacy of California* (Sacramento: State Printing, 1914), 15–16. For a general discussion of Goddard's role in early intelligence testing, see Haller, *Eugenics,* 95–100; and Kevles, *Name of Eugenics,* 77–84.

42. Goddard, *Sterilization,* 6–7.

43. Ibid., 6.

44. Goddard estimated that the number of mentally retarded persons in the United States would be cut by two-thirds in a generation. Deutsch, *Mentally Ill,* 369. Popenoe and Johnson were similarly optimistic. Popenoe and Johnson, *Applied Eugenics,* 186.

45. Goddard, *Sterilization*, 5.

46. E. R. Johnstone, "Waste Land plus Waste Humanity," *Training School Bulletin* 11 (1914), 61–62.

47. Royal Commission, *Report*, 136.

48. Popenoe and Johnson, *Applied Eugenics*, 186.

49. American Eugenics Society, *A Eugenics Catechism* (New York: American Eugenics Society, 1926), 8–9.

50. For example, compare Popenoe and Johnson's 1918 view, "There are cases where [sterilization] is advisable, in states too poor or niggardly to care adequately for their defectives and delinquents, but eugenicists should favor segregation as the main policy" (Popenoe and Johnson, *Applied Eugenics*, 195), with their view in 1935, "Sterilization is only one factor, though an important one, in a complete and well-balanced system of state care for the defective and mentally diseased" (Popenoe and Johnson, *Applied Eugenics*, 2d ed. [New York: Macmillan, 1935], 153). See also Deutsch, *Mentally Ill*, 368–69.

51. E.g., Popenoe and Johnson, *Applied Eugenics*, 185.

52. Haller, *Eugenics*, 40–47.

53. John E. Purdon, "Social Selection: The Extirpation of Criminality and Hereditary Disease," *Transactions of MASA* (1901), 465. (This is a reprint of an address made on behalf of the Tri-State Medical Society of Alabama, Georgia, and Tennessee.) A similar suggestion is in Hunter McGuire and G. Frank Johnson, "Sexual Crimes among Southern Negroes," *Virginia Medical Monthly* 20 (1893), 122.

54. Haller, *Eugenics*, 48; and Ludmerer, *Genetics*, 91.

55. Haller, *Eugenics*, 48–49; Kevles, *Name of Eugenics*, 30–33; and Ludmerer, *Genetics*, 91.

56. A. J. Ochsner, "Surgical Treatment of Habitual Criminals," *JAMA* 32 (1899), 867–68.

57. H. C. Sharp, "The Severing of the Vasa Deferentia and Its Relation to the Neuropsychopathic Constitution," *New York Medical Journal* 75 (1902), 411–14; and H. C. Sharp, "The Indiana Plan," in *Proceedings of the National Prison Association* (Pittsburgh: National Prison Association, 1909), 36.

58. 1907 Ind. Acts ch. 215.

59. Popenoe and Johnson, *Applied Eugenics*, 185. The "progressive" disposition of the states that initally enacted sterilization laws was noted at the time by a southern eugenicist in A. B. Cooke, "Safeguarding Society from the Unfit," *Southern Medical Journal* 3 (1910), 16.

60. The decisions against these statutes were as follows: *Williams v. State*, 190 Ind. 526, 121 N.E. 2 (1921) (Indiana—due process); *Davis v. Berry*, 216 Fed. 413 (S.D. Iowa, 1914) (Iowa—cruel and unusual punishment, and due process);

Haynes v. Lapeer, 201 Mich. 138, 166 N.W. 938 (1918) (Michigan—equal protection); *Mickel v. Heinrichs,* 262 Fed. 688 (D.C. Nev. 1918) (Nevada—cruel or unusual punishment); *Smith v. Board of Examiners of Feeble-Minded,* 85 N.J.Law 46, 88 Atl. 963 (1913) (New Jersey—equal protection); *In re Thompson,* 169 N.Y.S. 638 (Sup. Ct. 1918), aff'd sub nom., *Osborn v. Thompson,* 169 N.Y.S. 638 (App.Div. 1918) (New York—equal protection); and *Cline v. State Board of Eugenics,* Marion County, Ore., Cir. Ct. (1921) (Oregon—due process). A eugenicist's analysis of these decisions is in Otis H. Castle, "The Law and Human Sterilization," in *Collected Papers on Eugenic Sterilization in California: A Critical Study of Results in 6000 Cases,* ed. E. S. Gosney (Pasadena: Human Betterment Foundation, 1930), 558–64.

61. See Popenoe and Johnson, *Applied Eugenics,* 192; and Harry H. Laughlin, *The Legal, Legislative, and Administrative Aspects of Sterilization* (Cold Springs Harbor, N.Y.: Eugenics Record Office, 1914), 83. Five revised versions of the California statute are reprinted in *Sterilization Laws: Compilation of the Sterilization Laws of Twenty-four States* (Des Moines: Huston, [1928]), 2–3.

62. Popenoe and Johnson, *Applied Eugenics,* 191; and *Williams v. State,* 190 Ind. 526, 121 N.E. 2 (1920).

63. *Buck v. Bell,* 274 U.S. 200, 207 (1927).

64. Kevles, *Name of Eugenics,* 111–12; and Reilly, *Surgical Solution,* 84–87.

65. Jonas Robitscher, ed., *Eugenic Sterilization* (Springfield, Ill.: Thomas, 1973), 123.

66. On British eugenicists, see Larson, "Rhetoric of Eugenics," 45–60. For Davenport, see, e.g., Charles B. Davenport et al., *The Study of Human Heredity* (Cold Springs Harbor, N.Y.: Eugenics Record Office, 1911), 28; and Davenport, *State Laws,* 36, in which Davenport writes, "This may be done by segregation during the reproductive period, or even, as a last resort, by sterilization." See also Haller, *Eugenics,* 93, 124; and Kevles, *Name of Eugenics,* 47–48.

67. Goddard, *Sterilization,* 10–11 (emphasis in original).

68. Frances Hassencahl, "Harry H. Laughlin, 'Expert Eugenics Agent' for the House Committee on Immigration and Naturalization, 1921 to 1931" (Ph.D. diss., Case Western Reserve Univ., 1970), 89–160.

69. Laughlin, *Aspects of Sterilization,* 144–45.

70. Ibid., 142–43.

71. Hassencahl, "Laughlin," 161–97; and Ludmerer, *Genetics,* 95–113.

72. Davenport, *State Laws,* 36.

73. Cravens, *Triumph of Evolution,* 49–55, 77–85, and 138–47; Degler, *Human Nature,* 43–45; and Ludmerer, *Genetics,* 9.

74. Haller, *Eugenics,* 5.

75. Arthur S. Link and Richard L. McCormick, *Progressivism* (Arlington

Heights, Ill.: Davidson, 1983), 6–8 and 22. For further discussion of the connection between eugenics and progressivism on a national scale, see Pickens, *Eugenics,* 102–30.

76. "What Eugenics Is All About," in *A Decade of Progress in Eugenics: Scientific Papers of the Third International Congress of Eugenics* (Baltimore: Williams and Wilkins, 1934), plate 3.

77. Kevles, *Name of Eugenics,* 101.

78. For the representative case of progressive Wisconsin, see Rudolph J. Vecoli, "Sterilization: A Progressive Measure?" *Wisconsin Magazine of History* 43 (1960), 195–200.

79. This occurred in California, as discussed below and in Paul Popenoe, "The Progress of Eugenic Sterilization," *Journal of Heredity* 28 (1933), 20.

80. Haller, *Eugenics,* 124.

81. Kevles, *Name of Eugenics,* 57–64, quotation on 64. Though eugenics enthusiasts were less active in the Deep South than in other places in the United States, some of their educational efforts occurred in the region. E.g., see "This Bogalusa Baby Most Perfect at Fair," *Times-Picayune* (New Orleans), Nov. 4, 1923, p. 15, col. 6, a report on a local fittest-baby contest.

82. Davenport, *State Laws,* 5.

83. Pickens, *Eugenics,* 72–83.

84. For an example of this in the case of Missouri, see Wallin, *Odyssey,* 88.

85. Bleeker Van Wagenen, "Preliminary Report of the Committee of the Eugenic *[sic]* Section," in *Problems in Eugenics: First International Eugenics Congress* (London: Knight, 1912), 477. As it turned out, implementation of these laws also rested on the support of a small group of enthusiasts, as the eugenicist Marian S. Olden observed three decades later. Olden, "Present Status," 12.

86. Kevles, *Name of Eugenics,* 59–60.

87. Degler, *Human Nature,* 42.

88. Haller, *Eugenics,* 124.

89. W. L. Champion, "Sterilization of Confirmed Criminals, Idiots, Rapists, Feeble-Minded, and Other Defectives," *Journal of MAG* 3 (1913), 113–14.

90. Jno. N. Thomas, "Report of the Superintendent for Central Louisiana State Hospital," in *Biennial Report of the State Board of Administrators of Louisiana, 1926–28* (Alexandria, La.: Wall, [1928]), 28. A year later, another Louisiana eugenicist asserted that the California total stood at 8,622 sterilizations, to which one opponent replied, "Yes . . . California is blossoming like the orange blossom that comes out on the tree." Jean Gordon and W. J. Otis, in "Discussion," *New Orleans Medical and Surgical Journal* 82 (1929), 354–55.

91. B. O. Whitten, "Selective Sterilization," *Journal of SCMA* 27 (1931), 257.

92. J. N. Baker, "Eugenical Human Sterilization," *Journal of the Medical Association of the State of Alabama* 4 (1934), 17; and idem, "Sterilization in Al-

abama," *Montgomery Advertiser,* Feb. 6, 1935, p. 4, col. 3, quotation in both sources. (Hereafter the *Journal of the Medical Association of the State of Alabama* is cited as *Journal of MASA.*)

93. "Sterilization Progress," *Constitution* (Atlanta), Feb. 23, 1937, p. 4, col. 2.

94. "Sterilization Bill Passes the House," *Augusta Chronicle,* Mar. 9, 1935, p. 4, col. 1.

95. Howard W. Odum, *Southern Regions of the United States* (Chapel Hill: Univ. of North Carolina Press, 1936), 14, 50, and 468.

96. Oliver, "Marriage Laws," 100; Davenport, *State Laws,* 28; and Odum, *Southern Regions,* 92.

97. Odum, *Southern Regions,* 46–48, 144, 240, and 526; and U.S. Census Bureau, *Religious Bodies: 1926* (Washington, D.C.: Government Printing Office, 1930), 1:44–45.

98. U.S. Census Bureau, *Tenth Census, Report on the Defective, Dependent, and Delinquent Classes* (Washington, D.C.: Government Printing Office, 1888), xii.

99. State Board of Health of California, *Second Biennial Report* (Sacramento: State Printing, 1873), 66.

100. U.S. Census Bureau, *Tenth Census,* 39.

101. State Board of Charities and Corrections of California, *Second Biennial Report* (Sacramento: State Printing, 1906), 64.

102. Ibid., 64–65; and Richard W. Fox, *So Far Disordered in Mind: Insanity in California, 1870–1930* (Berkeley and Los Angeles: Univ. of California Press, 1978), 22–27. The supposed governmental savings from eugenic sterilization for California were estimated at $2 million per year in Popenoe and Gosney, *Twenty-eight Years,* 20.

103. Luther Burbank, *The Training of the Human Plant* (New York: Century, 1907), 3–4. Burbank's work was also cited by eugenicists from the Deep South. See, e.g., J. M. Buchanan, "Insanity—Its Rapid Increase and Preventive Measures," *Southern Medical Journal* 5 (1912), 321.

104. Burbank, *Human Plant,* 47–53 and 81–86, quotation on 52–53.

105. Ibid., 55–57 (emphasis added).

106. Ibid., 57–58.

107. Board of Charities, *Second Report,* 69.

108. E.g., State Board of Charities and Corrections of California, *Third Biennial Report* (Sacramento: State Printing, 1908), 73.

109. F. W. Hatch, "Two Principal Causes of Insanity: Heredity and Alcoholism," in Commission in Lunacy of California, *Fifth Biennial Report* (Sacramento: State Printing, 1906), 41.

110. Popenoe, "Progress," 19–20.

111. Ibid., 20. Passage of the bill was not mentioned in the generally comprehensive coverage of state legislative actions provided by the *Sacramento Union* and the *San Francisco Chronicle*. For example, the *Union* report for the day that the bill passed the state assembly was entitled "It Was a Dull Day in the Assembly," and did not mention action on the sterilization bill. "It Was a Dull Day in the Assembly," *Sacramento Union*, Mar. 24, 1901, p. 2, col. 7. Only one legislator, a Roman Catholic, voted against the measure. *Journal of the Senate of California* (1909 Reg. Sess.), 1773. (Hereafter this journal is abbreviated as *Calif. Senate Journal.*)

112. Popenoe, "Progress," 20.

113. The bill was introduced by Senator Walter F. Price of Sonoma, who sponsored eight bills during the same session for various improvements at the institution. *Calif. Senate Journal* (1909 Reg. Sess.), 503.

114. 1909 Cal. Stats. ch. 720.

115. F. W. Hatch, "Report of the State Commission in Lunacy," in Commission in Lunacy of California, *Eighth Biennial Report* (Sacramento: State Printing, 1912), 21; and Hatch, "Report of Superintendent," 13.

116. Hatch, "Report of Commission," 21.

117. 1913 Cal. Stats. ch. 30; and 1917 Cal. Stats. ch. 489.

118. "Convicts May Get Citizenship Back," *Sacramento Union*, Apr. 23, 1913, p. 3, col. 4.

119. Hatch, "Report of Superintendent," 14–18.

120. H. H. Laughlin, *Eugenical Sterilization in the United States* (Chicago: Municipal Court, 1922), 52–54.

121. California Department of Institutions, *Second Biennial Report* (Sacramento: State Printing, 1924), 89; State Board of Charities and Corrections of California, *Seventh Biennial Report* (Sacramento: State Printing, 1916), 39; and E. S. Gosney and Paul Popenoe, *Sterilization for Human Betterment* (New York: Macmillan, 1930).

122. Paul Popenoe, "Eugenic Sterilization in California," *Journal of Sexual Hygiene* 13 (1927), 257; and Robitscher, ed., *Eugenic Sterilization*, 118–19.

123. Popenoe and Gosney, *Twenty-eight Years*, 6–11 and 17; Popenoe, "Sterilization in California," 325; and Paul Popenoe, "Eugenic Sterilization in California," *Journal of Applied Psychology* 12 (1928), 303.

124. Robitscher, ed., *Eugenic Sterilization*, 118–19.

125. F. W. Hatch, quoted in Laughlin, *Aspects of Sterilization*, 84.

126. Popenoe, "Progress," 20.

127. Frederick H. Allen, *Mental Hygiene Survey of the State of California* (Sacramento: State Printing, 1932), 135.

128. Popenoe and Gosney, *Twenty-eight Years*, 39–40; and Haller, *Eugenics*, 137.

129. Board of Charities, *Seventh Report*, 39.

Chapter 3: *Sowing the Seeds*

1. See, e.g., *Index-Catalogue of the Library of the Surgeon General's Office,* 3d ser. (Washington, D.C.: Government Printing Office, 1925), 5:410–11, covering 1900–1925. The relative lack of activity and interest regarding eugenics in the South during the early period was discussed in A. B. Cooke, "Safeguarding Society from the Unfit," *Southern Medical Journal* 3 (1910), 16–20.

2. U.S. Commissioner of Education, *Report, 1900–1901* (Washington, D.C.: Government Printing Office, 1902), 2:1622, 1632, 1652–71, and 1696–97.

3. Albert Bushnell Hart, *The Southern South* (New York: Appleton, 1910), 300; and George Brown Tindall, *The Emergence of the New South, 1913–1945* (Baton Rouge: Louisiana State Univ. Press, 1967), 263. Even most southern medical schools did not require a high-school degree for entrance, as noted in Christopher Tompkins, "Medical Education in the South," *Southern Medical Journal* 3 (1910), 525–27.

4. Howard W. Odum, *Southern Regions of the United States* (Chapel Hill: Univ. of North Carolina Press, 1936), 512.

5. U.S. Commissioner of Education, *Report,* 2:1631 and 1688–707.

6. See, e.g., Robert J. Norrell, *A Promising Field: Engineering at Alabama, 1839–1987* (Tuscaloosa: Univ. of Alabama Press, 1990); and Daniel J. Kevles, *The Physicists: The History of a Scientific Community in Modern America* (reprint; Cambridge: Harvard Univ. Press, 1987), 60–90 and 150–54.

7. Clarence Nixon, "Colleges and Universities," in *Culture in the South,* ed. W. T. Couch (Chapel Hill: Univ. of North Carolina Press, 1936), 235.

8. Robert E. Blackwell, quoted in C. Vann Woodward, *Origins of the New South, 1877–1933* (Baton Rouge: Louisiana State Univ. Press, 1951), 438. Also see the report on science equipment on the same page.

9. Odum, *Southern Regions,* 151. See also Nancy Smith Midgette, *To Foster the Spirit of Professionalism: Southern Scientists and State Academies of Science* (Tuscaloosa: Univ. of Alabama Press, 1991), 10–68, for an analysis of the desperate straits in which science found itself in the South during this period, together with the telling observation that no state academy of science was organized in the Deep South until the 1920s.

10. For a general discussion of these national developments, see Hamilton Cravens, *The Triumph of Evolution: The Heredity-Environment Controversy, 1900–1941* (Baltimore: Johns Hopkins Univ. Press, 1988), 15–55.

11. Ibid., 160–67; Nixon, "Colleges," 234; and Tindall, *Emergence of New South,* 265.

12. E.g., Odum, *Southern Regions,* 516.

13. The members of the American Genetics Association's executive council and advisory committee are listed in each issue of its *Journal of Heredity.*

14. Odum, *Southern Regions,* 150–51.

15. Nixon, "Colleges," 235.

16. Of all the university libraries in the Deep South, only Tulane's had more than one hundred thousand volumes at the time, and even it fell "far short of the library standards set up by the Carnegie Commission." Nixon, "Colleges," 237. See also U.S. Commissioner of Education, *Report*, 2:1699–707; and Edgar W. Knight, "Recent Progress and Problems in Education," in Couch, ed., *Culture in South*, 215–16.

17. Edgar W. Knight, "Can the South Attain to National Standards in Education?" *South Atlantic Quarterly* 28 (1929), 2–5.

18. Odum, *Southern Regions*, 528.

19. Nixon, "Colleges," 244.

20. James T. Searcy, "The Increase of Insanity," in *Proceedings of the First National Conference on Race Betterment* (Battle Creek, Mich.: Race Betterment Foundation, 1914), 167–68.

21. James T. Searcy, "The Increase of Insanity," *Southern Medical Journal* 4 (1911), 1921. Whereas early-twentieth-century alienists typically attributed most cases of mental illness to heredity, their nineteenth-century counterparts typically gave environmental explanations. For a discussion of these views, see David J. Rothman, *The Discovery of the Asylum: Social Order and Disorder in the New Republic*, rev. ed. (Boston: Little, Brown, 1990), 110–19.

22. J. T. Searcy, "Mental Abnormalities," *Transactions of MASA* (1904), 360 and 373.

23. William Dempsey Partlow, "Degeneracy," *Transactions of MASA* (1907), 224. Partlow expressed a similar view with respect to the hereditary nature of criminal behavior in "Discussion," ibid. (1910), 361.

24. W. D. Partlow, in "Discussion," *Transactions of MASA* (1915), 581.

25. W. D. Partlow, in "Proceedings," *Transactions of MASA* (1916), 33–34. Even when he held to a neo-Lamarckian view of mental illness and retardation, Partlow favored the eugenic segregation of the "insane" on the grounds that their immediate offspring would endanger society. Partlow, "Degeneracy," 225.

26. Edward J. Larson and Leonard J. Nelson III, "Involuntary Sexual Sterilization of Incompetents in Alabama: Past, Present, and Future," *Alabama Law Review* 43 (1992), 412–25.

27. Clarence Pierson, "Superintendent's Report," in East Louisiana Hospital for the Insane, *Report of Board of Administrators* [1912–14] (New Orleans: Graham, 1914), 34–35.

28. Jno. N. Thomas, "Superintendent's Report," in Louisiana Hospital for the Insane, *Report of Board of Administrators* [1916–18] (n.p., 1918), 14–15.

29. Jno. N. Thomas, "Superintendent's Report," in Louisiana Hospital for the Insane, *Report of Board of Administrators* [1920–22] (Alexandria, La.: Wall, 1922), 32–33.

30. J. N. Thomas, in "Discussion on Paper of Dr. O'Hara," *New Orleans Medical and Surgical Journal* 70 (1917), 353. Thomas described the two state mental

health hospitals and expressed a similar view on sterilization in idem, "What Louisiana Is Doing for Her Insane," ibid., 76 (1923), 148 and 153.

31. J. H. Fox, "Mental Hygiene," *Transactions of Mississippi State Medical Association* (1915), 275. (Hereafter this publication is cited as *Transactions of MSMA.*) See also "President's Address," ibid. (1915), 147; and J. H. Fox, "Feeblemindedness in the U.S. Army," ibid. (1919), 136. In 1919, Fox co-founded and served as an officer of the Mississippi Society for Mental Hygiene, a eugenics advocacy group with both lay and professional members. The superintendent of the Mississippi State Hospital for the Insane served as the society's first chair. "Mississippi Society for Mental Hygiene," *Mental Hygiene* 3 (1919), 678.

32. J. M. Buchanan, "Insanity—Its Rapid Increase and Preventive Measures," *Southern Medical Journal* 5 (1912), 323.

33. Peter G. Crawford, *But for the Grace of God: The Inside Story of the World's Largest Insane Asylum, Milledgeville!* (Augusta, Ga.: Great Pyramid Press, 1981), 68.

34. R. C. Smith [R. C. Swint], "Some Facts Concerning the Etiology of Insanity Based on a Study of the Admissions to the Georgia State Sanitarium during the Year 1912," *Journal of MAG* 3 (1913), 148.

35. E.g., J. W. Mobley, in "Discussion on Dr. Swint's Paper," *Journal of MAG* 3 (1913), 149; W. L. Champion, "Sterilization of Confirmed Criminals, Idiots, Rapists, Feeble-Minded and Other Defectives," ibid., 3 (1913), 113; and Crawford, *Grace of God,* 78.

36. C. F. Williams, "Care and Treatment of the Patients at the State Hospital for the Insane," *Journal of SCMA* 12 (1916), 119. Williams fully appreciated the growing social problems of mental illness and agreed with other southern mental health officials that preventative measures should be implemented, but viewed early detection and treatment as the appropriate response rather than eugenics. See, e.g., idem, "Mental Hygiene: A Public Health Problem," ibid., 19 (1923), 482–87.

37. C. F. Williams, "Administrative Psychiatry," in South Carolina State Hospital, *Annual Report* [1935] (Columbia, S.C.: Joint Committee on Printing, 1936), 13. In comments made at his retirement dinner, which was attended by the hospital's patients as well as by the staff and invited guests, Williams expressed his commitment to continue "work which I hope by our efforts we may be able to find remedies which will prevent mental sickness or we may be able to relieve you of your fears . . . and bring understanding to those who are confounded." Idem, untitled manuscript copy of prepared remarks, in C. F. Williams file, Department of Education and Training, South Carolina State Hospital.

38. For Williams's published comments, see, e.g., Williams, "Administrative Psychiatry," 15; and idem, "Care and Treatment," 119. Despite persistent complaints of severe overcrowding within the institution, the annual reports for the South Carolina State Hospital never advocated sterilization during Williams's thirty-year tenure as superintendent. See, e.g., C. F. Williams, "Report of Super-

intendent," in South Carolina State Hospital, *Annual Report* (Columbia, S.C.: Gonzales and Bryan, 1917), 15, which recommends that children born to patients be transferred to an orphanage so that they do not "see and mimic the actions of patients." During this period, annual reports for every other state mental health hospital in the Deep South contained some eugenic advocacy. The quote about Williams's faith appeared in Coyt Ham, "In Memoriam: Charles Frederick Williams, M.D., 1875–1948," *American Journal of Psychiatry* 105 (1948), 240. Reflecting this faith, Williams worked to erect a Christian "Chapel of Hope" at the state mental health hospital and started a clinical pastoral training program with a local seminary. William S. Hull, "C. F. Williams," *Recorder* (Columbia Medical Society), 23 (Mar. 1965), 17.

39. Buchanan, "Insanity," 321.

40. Ira M. Hardy, "Schools for the Feeble-Minded the State's Best Insurance Policy," *Southern Medical Journal* 6 (1913), 514. See also B. O. Whitten, "Contemplated Provisions for the Feeble-Minded in South Carolina," *Journal of SCMA* 16 (1920), 69, where the superintendent of South Carolina's new State Training School for the Feeble-minded points solely to institutions in the North and West as precedents for his facility.

41. James Thomas Searcy, "The Increase of Insanity," *Transactions of MASA* (1911), 244.

42. Fox, "Mental Hygiene," 273. For similar comments, see also Partlow, in "Proceedings" (1916), 34.

43. J. F. Messelyn, "A Discussion of Some of the Predisposing Influences of Nervous and Mental Disease," *Journal of SCMA* 13 (1917), 669. For a discussion of religious hysteria as a perceived cause of mental illness during the period prior to the acceptance of eugenic explanations, see Ronald L. Numbers and Janet S. Numbers, "Millerism and Madness: A Study in 'Religious Insanity' in Nineteenth-Century America," *Bulletin of the Menninger Clinic* 49 (1985), 292–96 and 313–16.

44. Hiram Byrd, in "Discussion," *Southern Medical Journal* 6 (1917), 453.

45. Hardy, "Schools for Feeble-Minded," 512 and 515.

46. Pierson, "Superintendent's Report," 35.

47. 1919 Ala. Acts ch. 704, sec. 10.

48. E.g., W. D. Partlow, "Superintendent's Report," in Alabama Insane Hospitals, *Report of Trustees* [1933] ([Tuscaloosa]: n.p., 1933), 80.

49. Partlow, in "Discussion," *Transactions of MASA* (1910), 361.

50. Thomas H. Haines, "Report of the State Committee on Mental Hygiene," *Transactions of MASA* (1917), 34.

51. E.g., Fox, "Mental Hygiene," 276–77.

52. J. S. Ullman, "President's Address," *Transactions of MSMA* (1915), 147–48.

53. See, e.g., "Minutes of the House of Delegates," *Transactions of MSMA* (1919), 12.

54. John E. Purdon, "Social Selection," *Transactions of MASA* (1901), 459 and 462–63. Purdon spoke on behalf of the Tri-State Medical Society, a forerunner of the Southern Medical Association.

55. Ibid., 463.

56. Drs. Harper, Shell, and Partlow, in "Discussion," *Transactions of MASA* (1907), 227–31.

57. "Proceedings," *Transactions of MASA* (1910), 56. This petition mimicked a resolution offered that year by a Tennessee physician at the annual meeting of the Southern Medical Association. Cooke, "Safeguarding Society," 20.

58. Walter Howard Bell, "Sterilization of the Unfit," *Transactions of MASA* (1911), 450–52.

59. "Resolution as to Vasectomy," *Transactions of MASA* (1912), 86.

60. "Report of the Board of Censors," *Transactions of MASA* (1912), 86–87.

61. "Report from Committee of Three," *Transactions of MASA* (1915), 28–40, which includes the text of the proposed statute; and C. M. Rudolph, "State Care and Training of the Feeble-Minded," ibid. (1915), 553–84, a statement by the chair of the MASA committee that drafted the proposal, preceded and followed by supporting statements by such leading state mental health officials as Searcy and Partlow.

62. C. P. Wertenbaker, "What the General Practitioner of Medicine Can Do for the Public Health," *Journal of MAG* 3 (1913), 6.

63. "The Scientific Program for the Savannah Meeting," *Journal of MAG* 2 (1913), 397–400.

64. Champion, "Sterilization," 112–13.

65. R. C. Swint, J. W. Mobley, and E. M. Green, in "Discussion," *Journal of MAG* 3 (1913), 149–50, quotation from Green.

66. W. B. Hardman, "The Medical Gospel of the Twentieth Century," *Journal of MAG* 4 (1914), 72–73.

67. Oscar Dowling, in "Discussion," *Southern Medical Journal* 3 (1910), 21. Dowling was an officer of the Southern Medical Association at this time and later served as president of the Louisiana Board of Health.

68. Isadore Dyer, in ibid., 22. Dyer's reference to "our own people" presumably referred to Whites.

69. "The Prevention of Insanity," *New Orleans Medical and Surgical Journal* 67 (1914), 378.

70. "Eugenics and Euthanasia," *New Orleans Medical and Surgical Journal* 68 (1916), 479.

71. Joseph A. O'Hara, "Feeble-Minded," *New Orleans Medical and Surgical Journal* 70 (1917), 346 and 350–51. O'Hara, a powerful ward leader within the Democratic Party, later led the Louisiana Mental Hygiene Committee, a eugenics advocacy group with lay and professional members, chaired the Louisiana Tu-

berculosis Commission, served on the board of the East Louisiana Hospital for the Insane, and presided over the state board of health during the administration of Governor Huey Long. "O'Hara, Joseph Aloysius," *National Cyclopedia of American Biography* (New York: White, 1958), 42:281–82; "Former Health Chieftain Dies," *Times-Picayune* (New Orleans), Feb. 26, 1948, p. 3, col. 7; and "Brief Illness Proves Fatal to Dr. O'Hara," *New Orleans States,* Feb. 26, 1948, p. 2, col. 1. He came to recognize an increased role for injury in causing mental illness, but continued to support eugenic measures. See, e.g., J. A. O'Hara, "Insanity Responsibility," *New Orleans Medical and Surgical Journal* 79 (1926), 44–46.

72. Thomas E. Wright and J. N. Thomas, in "Discussion," *New Orleans Medical and Surgical Journal* 70 (1917), 352–53.

73. Roy M. Van Wart, in ibid., 353–54. No one challenged Van Wart as to the content of this alleged law "in one of the States," even though no such law ever existed in the United States.

74. F. R. Harris, "Eugenics," *Southern Medical Journal* 6 (1913), 449 and 452.

75. W. Marion Bevis, "Colony Care for the Epileptic and Feeble-Minded of Florida," *Journal of the Florida Medical Association* 4 (1918), 322–27.

76. "Georgia House Wastes a Day," *Augusta Chronicle,* Aug. 2, 1919, p. 4, col. 5.

77. "Eugenics and Euthanasia," 479. Similar views were expressed by the president of the MAG in Hardman, "Medical Gospel," 72–73.

78. Fred J. Mayer, in "Discussion," *Southern Medical Journal* 5 (1912), 327.

79. Searcy, "Increase of Insanity," in *Proceedings,* 168.

80. O'Hara, "Feeble-Minded," 350.

81. Champion, "Sterilization," 113. A South Carolina physician expressed a similarly Pollyannaish view of eugenic segregation when he said of the mentally retarded, "The state should take them at an early age, train them to be useful, self-sustaining, contented and happy; segregate and exclude forever the chance of reproducing their kind." A. Bethune Patterson, "The State's Duty to the Feeble-Minded," *Journal of SCMA* 12 (1916), 376.

82. H. A. Moody, Dr. Palmer, and J. Ross Snyder, in "Discussion," *Transactions of MASA* (1916), 362–65.

83. Cooke, "Safeguarding Society," 22.

84. Harris, "Eugenics," 452. The article opened with a quote from Galton and discussed the scientific work of Mendel, Davenport, and others. Similar heavy citation of scientific authority regularly appeared in articles on eugenics by southern physicians. See, e.g., R. McG. Carruth, "Race Degeneration: What Can We Do to Check It?" *New Orleans Medical and Surgical Journal* 72 (1919), 186.

85. See, e.g., S.E.D. Shortt, "Physicians, Science, and Status: Issues in the Professionalization of Anglo-American Medicine in the Nineteenth Century," *Medical History* 27 (1983), 51–68.

86. Harris, "Eugenics," 448.

87. Patterson, "State's Duty," 374.

88. For a complete discussion of the status of eugenic measures in the various states at this time, see Stevenson Smith, Madge W. Wilkinson, and Louisa C. Wagoner, *A Summary of the Laws of the Several States* (Seattle: University of Washington, 1914). A comprehensive report on the situation with respect to eugenic segregation in 1917 appeared in Walter E. Fernald, "The Growth of Provision for the Feeble-Minded in the United States," *Mental Hygiene* 1 (1917), 50–59. A chronological listing of eugenic sterilization statutes appears in Jacob Henry Landman, *Human Sterilization: The History of the Sexual Sterilization Movement* (New York: Macmillan, 1932), 291–92.

89. For discussions of the hookworm campaign, see John Ettling, *The Germ of Laziness: Rockefeller Philanthropy and Public Health in the New South* (Cambridge: Harvard Univ. Press, 1981), 87–177; William A. Link, *The Paradox of Southern Progressivism, 1880–1930* (Chapel Hill: Univ. of North Carolina Press, 1993), 142–59; and Alan I Marcus, "Hookworm and Southern Distinctiveness," in *Disease and Distinctiveness in the American South,* ed. Todd L. Savitt and James Harvey Young (Knoxville: Univ. of Tennessee Press, 1988), 84–94.

90. See Luwellys F. Barker, "The First Ten Years of the National Committee for Mental Hygiene," *Mental Hygiene* 2 (1918), 557–60; Mark H. Haller, *Eugenics: Hereditarian Attitudes in American Thought* (New Brunswick: Rutgers Univ. Press, 1963), 71 and 126; and Gerald N. Grob, *Mental Illness and American Society, 1875–1940* (Princeton: Princeton Univ. Press, 1983), 157–59.

91. Thomas W. Salmon, "Fifty Years in Forty Days,"*Survey* 34 (1915), 13–14; Benjamin Otis Whitten, *A History of Whitten Village* (Clinton, S.C.: Jacob Press, 1967), 17–19; Haller, *Eugenics,* 127; Grob, *Mental Illness,* 159; and Leila Glover Johnson, "A History of the South Carolina State Hospital" (M.A. thesis, Univ. of Chicago, 1930), 138. Manning put forth his ambitious reform program for the South Carolina State Hospital in Richard I. Manning, *Message to the General Assembly of South Carolina on Friday, January 14, 1916* (Columbia: Bryan, 1916), 1–12.

92. "Conferences," *Survey* 35 (1915), 54. See also Haller, *Eugenics,* 127; and Whitten, *History,* 18. Johnson had spoken in the Deep South in support of eugenic segregation more than a decade earlier, but at that time he addressed a national audience of social workers simply meeting in the region. When he gave this earlier address, only three northern states had a program for eugenically segregating the mentally retarded, and Johnson could still wonder aloud "[w]hether some day or other in the future, science may so overcome sentiment that the physically and mentally unfit shall be removed, or shall be sterilized." Alexander Johnson, "Report of Committee on Colonies for Segregating of Defectives," in *Proceedings of the National Conference of Charities and Corrections,* ed. Isabel C. Barrows (n.p.: Heer Press, 1903), 249–50.

93. Benjamin O. Whitten, "Address of the President," *Journal of Psycho-Asthenics* 42 (1937), 33–34.

94. Whitten, *History,* 18. Credit for the South Carolina legislation was also given to Johnson's illustrated lectures in "Pictures the Cure for Legislative Sloth," *Survey* 37 (1917), 725–26.

95. "The Legislature," *Journal of SCMA* (1916), 365.

96. Whitten, *History,* 19; and Haller, *Eugenics,* 127–28.

97. V. V. Anderson, *Report of the South Carolina Mental Health Survey* (New York: National Committee for Mental Hygiene, 1922), 4 and 73.

98. Ibid., 3.

99. Children's Home Society of Florida, *Eleventh Annual Report* ([Jacksonville, Fla.: Children's Home Society], 1913), 6 and 9. See also Steven Noll, "Feeble-Minded in Our Midst: Florida Farm Colony, 1921–1940" (M.A. thesis, Univ. of Florida, 1985), 83.

100. Children's Home Society of Florida, *Twelfth Annual Report* ([Jacksonville, Fla.: Children's Home Society], 1914), 16–17; and idem, *Thirteenth Annual Report* ([Jacksonville, Fla.: Children's Home Society], 1915), 6.

101. *Journal of the House of Representatives of Florida* (1917 Reg. Sess.), 1345. (Hereafter this publication is cited as *Fla. House Journal.*)

102. Children's Home Society of Florida, *Twenty-sixth Annual Report* ([Jacksonville, Fla.: Children's Home Society], 1928), 2.

103. Hasting H. Hart and Clarence L. Stonaker, *A Social Welfare Program for the State of Florida* (New York: Russell Sage Foundation, 1918), 30–31. See also "Florida Surveyed for War and Peace," *Survey* 39 (1918), 698. The Russell Sage Foundation conducted similar state surveys in West Virginia, North Carolina, and Virginia. Hart's views and role were discussed in "Social Problems of Alabama," ibid., 41 (1919), 900; "H.H.H.," ibid., 45 (1921), 532; and Noll, "Feeble-Minded," 140.

104. Hart and Stonaker, *Social Welfare Program,* 31–32.

105. Senate Resolution 44, in 1918 Ga. Laws pp. 921–22.

106. Georgia Commission on Feeblemindedness, *Report* (1919), 5–9 (reprinted in *Journal of the House of Representatives of Georgia* [1919 Reg. Sess.], 205–7); and "Would Allow Keeping Liquor for Private Use," *Atlanta Journal,* July 8, 1919, p. 1, col. 5. (Hereafter *Journal of the House of Representatives of Georgia* is cited as *Ga. House Journal.*)

107. "Committee of Three," 28–29.

108. Rudolph, "Care and Training," 562.

109. W. D. Partlow, in "Discussion," *Transactions of MASA* (1915), 582–83.

110. E.g., see Partlow, in "Proceedings" (1916), 32–35; and "Report of Committee on Mental Hygiene," *Transactions of MASA* (1917), 33. The founder of NCMH, Clifford Beers of New York, attended and led the organizational meeting of this society in Tuscaloosa, Alabama. "Report of Committee Appointed to Organize a State Society for Mental Hygiene," ibid. (1916), 68. The NCMH sur-

vey of Alabama was discussed in Thomas H. Haines, "The Mental Hygiene Requirements of a Community: Suggestions Based upon a Personal Survey," in *Proceedings of the National Conference of Social Work, 1920* (Chicago: Univ. of Chicago Press, 1920), 403–4.

111. Haines, "Report," 33 and 37.

112. Thomas H. Haines to Thomas E. Kilby, Sept. 22, 1919, in Papers of Gov. Thomas E. Kilby, Alabama State Archives, Montgomery, Ala. In the letter, Haines credited Partlow with "the planning and writing of the bill."

113. E.T.D., "Social Problems of Alabama," *Survey* 41 (1919), 900. Hart conducted similar surveys in South Carolina a year earlier, when legislation creating an institution for the mentally retarded was under consideration in that state, and in Mississippi a year later. In all three cases, this coincided with campaigns to enact legislation creating state institutions for the mentally retarded. E.T.D., "Social Problems"; and "Making Social Surveys 'on High,'" *Survey* 39 (1918), 659.

114. W. H. Slingerland, quoted in Noll, "Feeble-Minded," 143.

115. Haines, "Mental Hygiene," 401–4, which discussed the NCMH survey; "Louisiana Notes," *Mental Hygiene* 3 (1919), 671; and "Session Gossip," *New Orleans States,* June 6, 1818, p. 7, col. 5.

116. *Journal of the House of Representatives of Mississippi* (1920 Reg. Sess.), 45. (Hereafter this publication is cited as *Miss. House Journal.*) For background on Bilbo, see Adwin W. Green, *The Man Bilbo* (Baton Rouge: Louisiana State University Press, 1963).

117. Thos. H. Haines, "Preventative Medicine as Applied to Mental Deficiency in Mississippi," *Transactions of MSMA* (1919), 136 and 139. A somewhat less inflammatory version of this paper was published in idem, "Preventative Medicine as Applied to Mental Deficiency in Mississippi," *Southern Medical Journal* 12 (1919), 541–44. Although it championed eugenic segregation, Haines's employer, the NCMH, did not take an official position on eugenic sterilization. For the response to Williams's inquiry to NCMH on the issue, see Edith M. Furbush to C. F. Williams, Jan. 5, 1926, in Sterilization File, Department of Education and Training, South Carolina State Hospital, Columbia, S.C.

118. Haines, "Preventative Medicine," *Transactions of MSMA,* 137–38 (emphasis in original).

119. "Minutes of House," 12; "Compulsory Education Is Again to Fore," *Jackson Daily News,* Feb. 24, 1920, p. 1, col. 1; *Miss. House Journal* (1920 Reg. Sess.), 45; and *Journal of the Senate of Mississippi* (1920 Reg. Sess.), 596. (Hereafter the latter publication is cited as *Miss. Senate Journal.*)

Chapter 4: *First Growth*

1. Jacob Henry Landman, *Human Sterilization: The History of the Sexual Sterilization Movement* (New York: Macmillan, 1932), 291–92.

2. See Philip P. Reilly, *The Surgical Solution: A History of Involuntary Sterilization in the United States* (Baltimore: Johns Hopkins Univ. Press, 1991), 50–53

and 71–87. During the six-year lull that began in 1917, only one state enacted a sterilization statute. A second wave of sterilization activity, which began in 1923, led to the passage of such laws in another thirteen states by 1931. Landman, *Sterilization,* 292–93.

3. Thos. H. Haines, "Preventative Medicine as Applied to Mental Deficiency in Mississippi," *Transactions of MSMA* (1919), 138.

4. E.g., "Report of the Board of Censors," *Transactions of MASA* (1912), 86–87.

5. C. M. Rudolph, "State Care and Training of the Feeble-Minded," *Transactions of MASA* (1915), 563.

6. Richard I. Manning, *Why Should South Carolina Make a Beginning in 1919 in Provision for the Feeble-Minded* (Columbia, S.C.:State, 1916), 2.

7. Haines, "Preventative Medicine," 141.

8. This sense of potential popular support was reflected in the publicity efforts of the 1915 MASA committee recommending a eugenic segregation plan for Alabama. It sent a pamphlet outlining its proposal to newspaper editors and women's clubs throughout the state. No such effort was ever attempted for a sterilization scheme. "Report from Committee of Three," *Transactions of MASA* (1915), 29.

9. See, e.g., "Trustees Biennial Report," in Mississippi School and Colony for the Feebleminded, *Fourth Biennial Report* (Jackson: Tucker, 1927), 11–12.

10. Haines, "Preventative Medicine," 138–40.

11. Thomas H. Haines, "Methods of Creating Public Interest in the Problems of the Feebleminded," in *Proceedings of the National Conference of Social Work, 1919* (Chicago: Rogers and Hall, 1920), 569–71.

12. Ibid., 569–71.

13. Haines set forth his customary unscientific method of, and his promotional rationale for, conducting surveys in ibid., 569–70, and tied this directly to the NCMH survey of Mississippi in Thomas H. Haines, "The Mental Hygiene Requirements of a Community: Suggestions Based upon a Personal Survey," in *Proceedings of the National Conference of Social Work, 1920* (Chicago: Univ. of Chicago Press, 1920), 401–4.

14. Haines, "Preventative Medicine," 141. The American Social Hygiene Association also used data from Haines's survey to promote its fight against venereal disease. American Social Hygiene Association, "A Report of the Control of Prostitution and the Venereal Diseases in Nine Southern States" (1919), 1—Mississippi, manuscript copy in American Social Hygiene Association Collection, Social Welfare History Archives, University of Minnesota, Minneapolis, Minn.

15. "Committee of Three," 29.

16. See, e.g., Rudolph, "State Care," 560.

17. "Florida Commission for the Study of Epilepsy and Feeble-Mindedness," *Fla. House Journal* (1919 Reg. Sess., pt. 1), 1344–45; and "Florida's Feeble-minded," *Survey* 42 (1919), 705.

18. "Florida Commission," 1345–46 (emphasis in original).

19. Hastings H. Hart and Clarence L. Stonaker, *A Social Welfare Program for the State of Florida* (New York: Russell Sage Foundation, 1918), 30–31.

20. 1919 Fla. Laws ch. 7887, preamble.

21. 1919 Fla. Laws ch. 7887, sec. 8.

22. For a discussion of Hart's views on this subject that includes these quotations from Hart, see Steven Noll, "From Far More Different Angles: Institutions for the Mentally Retarded in the South, 1900–1940" (Ph.D. diss., Univ. of Florida, 1991), 140.

23. Hart and Stonaker, *Social Welfare,* 30.

24. 1919 Fla. Laws ch. 7887, sec. 9.

25. *Ga. House Journal* (1918 Reg. Sess.), 1133.

26. 1918 Ga. Laws, pt. 4, resolution 44.

27. Robert C. Dexter, "Results in Georgia," *Survey,* 43 (1920), 650.

28. Georgia Commission on Feeblemindedness, *Report* (Atlanta: Byrd, 1919), 7.

29. Ibid., 10. The report was reprinted as "Mental Defect in a Southern State," *Mental Hygiene* 3 (1919), 527–65; and in *Ga. House Journal* (1919 Reg. Sess.), 203–64.

30. *Ga. House Journal* (1919 Reg. Sess.), 214. See also "The Feebleminded in Georgia," *Survey* 43 (1920), 467, for an analysis of the survey methods.

31. *Ga. House Journal* (1919 Reg. Sess.), 208–10, 233, and 246.

32. Ibid., 238–39.

33. Ibid., 208, 210, and 254.

34. Ibid., 257–64.

35. Georgia Commission, *Report,* 6.

36. Hugh Dorsey to Gentlemen of the General Assembly, June 26, 1919, in *Ga. House Journal* (1919 Reg. Sess.), 204–5.

37. Dexter, "Results," 650; and "Georgia," *Mental Hygiene* 3 (1919), 276–77. For a representative newspaper editorial, see "Press This Humane Bill to Speedy Enactment," *Atlanta Journal,* July 17, 1919, p. 8, col. 2. Similar editorial use of these statistics appeared in J. P. Bowdin, "Address of the President, Public Health Section, Medical Association of Georgia," *Journal of MAG* 9 (1920), 124; and W. L. Funkhouser, "Mental Hygiene," ibid., 9 (1920), 37.

38. See, Noll, "Different Angles," 147–48. Ultimately, the most extensive mental hygiene survey for any state in the region was the 1923 NCMH survey of South Carolina. This survey was conducted after the initial wave of eugenics law-making, however, in an effort to expand rather than introduce eugenic segrega-

tion in the state. See V. V. Anderson, *A Report of the South Carolina Mental Hygiene Survey* (New York: National Committee for Mental Hygiene, 1922).

39. E.g., Thomas H. Haines, "Report of State Committee on Mental Hygiene," *Transactions of MASA* (1919), 35–36.

40. See, e.g., Jacquelyn Dowd Hall, *Revolt against Chivalry: Jessie Daniel Ames and the Woman's Campaign against Lynching* (New York: Columbia Univ. Press, 1979), 159–91, which examines the role of Southern women's organizations in support of antilynching legislation; and William A. Link, *The Paradox of Southern Progressivism, 1880–1930* (Chapel Hill: Univ. of North Carolina Press, 1992), 119–20 and 134–42, which details the major role of southern women's organizations in influencing political movements to restrict prostitution and expand public education.

41. American Social Hygiene Association, "Report," 11–12.

42. See Daniel J. Kevles, *In the Name of Eugenics: Genetics and the Uses of Human Heredity* (New York: Knopf, 1985), 39 and 54–55; Garland E. Allen, "Eugenics Record Office at Cold Springs Harbor, 1910–1940," *Osiris* 2 (1986), 234–36; and Nicole Hahn Rafter, "Introduction," in *White Trash: The Eugenic Family Studies, 1977–1913*, ed. Nicole Hahn Rafter (Boston: Northeastern Univ. Press, 1988), 21.

43. Rafter, "Introduction," 20–21. The historian Garland Allen noted, "By 1917, the ERO had trained approximately 156 field workers, 131 women and 25 men." Allen, "Eugenics Record Office," 241.

44. H. H. Goddard, "The Binet Tests in Relation to Immigration," *Journal of Psycho-Asthenics* 18 (1913), 106.

45. See Elizabeth Kite, "The Killikak Family," in Rafter, ed., *White Trash*.

46. See, e.g., Benjamin Otis Whitten, *A History of Whitten Village* (Clinton, S.C.: Jacob Press, 1967), 18; Georgia Commission, *Report*, 6.

47. See, e.g., Anderson, *Report*, 2; and "Report of the Board of Censors," *Transactions of MASA* (1916), 68.

48. See Margaret Rossiter, " 'Woman's Work' in Science, 1880–1910," *Isis* 71 (1980), 381–98; and Daniel J. Kevles, *The Physicists: The History of a Scientific Community in Modern America* (Cambridge: Harvard Univ. Press, 1987), 202–7.

49. Goddard, "Binet Tests," 106.

50. See Rafter, "Introduction," 24–26 and 87; and Havelock Ellis, *The Task of Social Hygiene* (Boston: Houghton Mifflin, 1912), 46–47.

51. Rafter, "Introduction," 21; and Kevles, *Name of Eugenics*, 39 and 220.

52. Kevles, *Name of Eugenics*, 64.

53. Linda Gordon, *Woman's Body, Woman's Right: Birth Control in America*, rev. ed. (New York: Penguin, 1991), 110 and 126.

54. Carmen Lindig, *The Path from the Parlor: Louisiana Women, 1829–1920*

(Lafayette, La.: Univ. of Southwestern Louisiana, 1985), 48–52. For a general discussion of the women's club movement, see Hall, *Revolt against Chivalry*, 159–91.

55. American Social Hygiene Association, "Report," 12.

56. Bertie Iola Coley, "The Educational Program of the South Carolina Federation of Women's Clubs, 1898–1938," (M.A. thesis, Univ. of South Carolina, 1938), 25.

57. Georgia Federation of Women's Clubs, *Yearbook, 1916–17* (Greenville, Ga.: Gresham, 1916), 18–19.

58. The role that the Georgia Federation of Women's Clubs played in the 1919 campaign for eugenic segregation was discussed in Dexter, "Results," 650; "Press Humane Bill," p. 8, col. 2; "Georgia," 276–77; and Georgia Federation of Women's Clubs, *Yearbook, 1920–21* (Greenville, Ga.: Gresham, 1920), 144.

59. "Committee of Three," 29. The role played by the Alabama Federation of Women's Clubs in securing state legislation for eugenic segregation was noted in W. D. Partlow, "Report of State Committee on Mental Hygiene," *Transactions of MASA* (1920), 31; and Thomas H. Haines to Thomas E. Kilby, Sept. 22, 1919, in Papers of Gov. Thomas E. Kilby, Alabama State Archives, Montgomery, Ala. The Alabama Woman's Christian Temperance Union also backed eugenic reforms. See Mabel P. Leake, "W.C.T.U. Activities," *Birmingham New Age,* Aug. 31, 1919, p. 2A, col. 3.

60. Mrs. Frank E. Jennings, "Report of the Legislative Committee," in Florida State Federation of Women's Clubs, *Manual, 1912–13* ([Lakeland, Fla.]: n.p., 1912), 34; and Children's Home Society of Florida, *The Twelfth Annual Report* ([Jacksonville, Fla.: Children's Home Society], 1914), 16.

61. C. W. Roberts, "Boys' Rights Prenatal and Otherwise: An Address to the Mother's Club," *Journal of MAG* 8 (1919), 194.

62. See, e.g., Whitten, *History,* 18. The NCMH field representative Thomas H. Haines discussed his strategy of appealing for support to woman's clubs in Haines, "Methods," 571; and Haines, "Mental Hygiene Requirements," 404–5. He also wrote, "If one succeeds in winning the enthusiastic support of the wife of a candidate for governor, it will not be long before the given gubernatorial candidate is making one's propaganda a feature in his own campaign speeches." Haines, "Methods," 572.

63. Jennings, "Report," 35.

64. W. Marion Bevis, "Colony Care for the Epileptic and Feeble-Minded of Florida," *Journal of the Florida Medical Association* 4 (1918), 323. The ongoing efforts of the Florida federation were noted in Children's Home Society of Florida, *The Thirteenth Annual Report* ([Jacksonville, Fla.: Children's Home Society], 1915), 6; and idem, *The Nineteenth Annual Report* ([Jacksonville, Fla.: Children's Home Society], 1921), 21. See also "From Ponce de Leon's Time to Ours," *Survey* 37 (1917), 729; and "The Feebleminded in Florida," ibid., 43 (1920), 635.

65. Fannie B. Sloan, "Legislative Committee," in South Carolina Federation of Women's Clubs, *Yearbook, 1916–17* (Aiken, S.C.: n.p., 1916), 53–54; and "Minutes," in ibid., 71.

66. Coley, "Educational Program," 25 and 76. See also Noll, "Different Angles," 154.

67. Mrs. J. W. Allen, "President's Address," in South Carolina Federation of Women's Clubs, *Yearbook, 1917–18* (Aiken, S.C.: n.p., 1917), 10–11.

68. John L. McWhorter, "Federation of Women's Clubs Ably Represented at Capitol," *Florida Times-Union*, Apr. 17, 1915, p. 9, col. 4. See also C. F. Johnson, "Women Plead for Free School Books," *Tampa Morning Tribune*, Apr. 17, 1915, p. 5, col. 1; and Mrs. John W. McGriff, "Report Legislation Department, F.F.W.C.," in Florida Federation of Women's Clubs, *Manual, 1915–1916* ([Lakeland, Fla.]: n.p., 1915), 77, in which the chair of the federation's Legislative Department reported, "I spent the entire month of April in Tallahassee working vigorously for the measures, and upon my return here, our President, with her well known indefatigable zeal, made flying trips to the capital whenever her presence was needed to keep interest from flagging."

69. See 1919 Fla. Laws ch. 7887, preamble.

70. "Legislative Will Close Session Today," *Daily-Clarion Ledger* (Jackson), Apr. 2, 1920, p. 5, col. 1.

71. "House Turns Down Suffrage Again, Ninety-seven to Twenty-three," *Jackson Daily News*, Mar. 31, 1920, p. 1, col. 7.

72. 1919 Fla. Laws ch. 7887, preamble; "Florida's Feebleminded," 703; and "Feebleminded in Florida," 655.

73. Georgia Commission, *Report,* 6; and Department of Public Welfare, *Georgia's Fight against Dependency and Delinquency: Report of First Year's Work* [1920–21] (Atlanta: Dickerson-Roberts, [1921]), 2–12.

74. 1919 Ala. Acts ch. 704, sec. 2 (two women required); 1919 Fla. Laws, ch. 7887, sec. 2 (one woman required); and 1920 Miss. Laws ch. 210, sec. 4. Three women were named to the initial board in Alabama and two in Mississippi. See "The Alabama Home," in Alabama Insane Hospitals, *Report of Trustees* [1924] ([Tuscaloosa]: Hospital Print, 1924), 94; and "Committee Seeks Site for Hospital," *Commercial-Appeal* (Memphis), May 3, 1920, in Ellisville State School File (hereafter cited as "Ellisville File"), Mississippi Collection, Mississippi State University Library, Starkville, Miss. Florida ultimately did not have a separate board for its institution. See 1919 Fla. Laws, ch. 7887, sec. 2.

75. "Attacks H.B. 81," *Commercial-Appeal* (Memphis), Jan. 15, 1922, in Ellisville File.

76. 1918 S.C. Laws ch. 398, sec. 3; and Whitten, *History,* 19.

77. State Training School for the Feeble-minded [South Carolina], *First Annual Report* (Columbia, S.C.: Gonzales and Bryan, 1919), 5.

78. See Whitten, *History,* 40–55.

79. See, e.g., State Board of Public Welfare [South Carolina], *First Annual Report* (Columbia, S.C.: Gonzales and Bryan, 1920–21), 5; and idem, *Third Annual Report* (Columbia, S.C.: Gonzales and Bryan, 1923), 28.

80. Maud Loeber, "Mental Hygiene," in *The New Chivalry—Health,* ed. James E. McCulloch (Nashville: Southern Sociological Congress, 1915), 245.

81. Gordon's attendance at this conference is indicated in "Membership List," in McCulloch, ed., *New Chivalry,* 542.

82. Lindig, *Path,* 60–62 and 110–18; B. H. Gilley, "Kate Gordon and Louisiana Woman Suffrage," *Louisiana History* 24 (1983), 289–93; Kathryn W. Kemp, "Jean and Kate Gordon: New Orleans Social Reformers, 1898–1933," ibid., 24 (1983), 389–92; Glenn A. Conrad, ed., *A Dictionary of Louisiana Biography* (New Orleans: Louisana Historical Association, 1988), 1:351–52; Stella Pitts, "Devoted Sisters Served City, Fought for Woman's Suffrage," *Times-Picayune* (New Orleans), Feb. 22, 1976, sec. 2, p. 4, cols. 1–6; Era Club, *Charter and By-laws* (New Orleans: Rentschler-Nunez, 1914), 4; "Suffrage for South and State," *Daily Picayune* (New Orleans), Nov. 13, 1913, p. 5, col. 3; and "Women of Louisiana Are Working Hard Mid Unusual Surroundings—Room There for Big Thoughts!" *Times-Picayune* (New Orleans), May 28, 1916, p. 7, cols. 1–6.

83. Kemp, "Gordon," 395–97, Gordon quotation on 396 (it is unclear whether this quotation comes from Jean or Kate Gordon); Lindig, *Path,* 118 and 122–23; "Miss Jean Gordon Receives Times Picayune Loving Cup," *Times-Picayune* (New Orleans), Nov. 12, 1921, p. 1, col. 7; "Jean Gordon Dies after Forty Years of Civic Activity," ibid., Feb. 25, 1931, p. 1, col. 5; and "Louisana's Feeble-minded," *Survey,* 42 (1919), 780. At the time, the connection between the eugenic segregation of mentally retarded children and child labor reform appeared so natural that the National Child Labor Committee's agent in Alabama included legislation creating a state institution for the mentally retarded in her report of child labor reforms for 1919. Loraine B. Bush, "How Alabama Organized Her Work for Children," in *Proceedings of National Conference of Social Work, 1920,* 129.

84. Lindig, *Path,* 123; and Conrad, ed., *Louisiana Biography,* 1:351. Gordon's support for the establishment of a public institution for the mentally retarded was also reflected in the endorsement of that project made by the Era (or "Equal Rights Association") Club, a reform-oriented women's organization co-founded and led by the Gordon sisters. Era Club, "Minute Book, 1914–1919," 26, manuscript copy in Louisiana Division, New Orleans Public Library, New Orleans, La. (hereafter cited as "Louisiana Division").

85. Kate Gordon, quoted in Kemp, "Gordon," 392. Both sisters fought solely for state suffrage legislation and ultimately opposed the Nineteenth Amendment because of its implications for federal control over voting rights, which they believed could lead to federal laws on Black suffrage. See generally Gilley, "Kate Gordon," 295–302; Hall, *Revolt against Chivalry,* 21; Kemp, "Gordon," 392–94; Lindig, *Path,* 131–70; and Link, *Paradox of Progressivism,* 72 and 196.

86. Jean Gordon, quoted in Kemp, "Gordon," 393.

87. Louisiana's strict miscegenation law limited any perceived danger to the White race from eugenically unfit persons who were not classified as White by barring any "marriage between white persons and persons of color." La. Civ. Code art. 94 (1932).

88. R. McG. Carruth, "Race Degeneration: What Can We Do to Check It?" *New Orleans Medical and Surgical Journal* 72 (1919), 188.

89. See, e.g., "Press Humane Bill," p. 8, col. 2.

90. *Journal of the Senate of Alabama* (1919 Reg. Sess.), 55 (hereafter this publication is cited as *Ala. Senate Journal*); and *Ga. House Journal* (1919 Reg. Sess.), 205. See also "General Review of Session of 1919 Alabama Legislature," *Montgomery Advertiser,* Sept. 29, 1919, p. 3, col. 3, which described the bill as the "Administration's program."

91. *Miss. House Journal* (1918 Reg. Sess.), 27; ibid. (1920 Reg. Sess.), 45; and "Committee Seeks Site."

92. Richard I. Manning, quoted in W. K. Tate, "After Blease—A New Program for South Carolina," *Survey* 33 (1915), 577. See also "The Legislature," *Journal of the South Carolina Medical Association* 12 (1916), 365. For Manning's background, see Emily Bellinger Reynolds and Joan Reynolds Faunt, *Biographical Directory of the Senate of the State of South Carolina, 1776–1964* (Columbia, S.C.: South Carolina Archives, 1964), 261–62.

93. Manning, *Feeble-Minded,* 1.

94. Ibid., 2–4.

95. Ibid., 2 and 4.

96. "Building for the Future," *Greenville News,* Feb. 15, 1917, p. 4, col. 2.

97. "The Feeble-Minded," *Jackson Daily News,* Feb. 16, 1920, p. 4, col. 3.

98. *An Institution for Feeble-Minded of Alabama,* in Papers of the Partlow State School, Alabama State Archives.

99. *Journal of the House of Representatives of South Carolina* (1917 Reg. Sess.), 597 (hereafter this publication is cited as *S.C. House Journal*); *Journal of the Senate of South Carolina* (1918 Reg. Sess.), 43 (hereafter this publication is cited as *S.C. Senate Journal*).

100. *Journal of the Senate of Louisiana* (1918 Reg. Sess.), 738 (hereafter this publication is cited as *La. Senate Journal*); *Journal of the House of Representatives of Louisiana* (1918 Reg. Sess.), 698 (hereafter this publication is cited as *La. House Journal*); and "A Local Audience for the Hangman," *Survey* 46 (1918), 167.

101. *Ala. Senate Journal* (1919 Reg. Sess.), 686; *Journal of the House of Representatives of Alabama* (1919 Reg. Sess.), 2436 (hereafter this publication is cited as *Ala. House Journal*); *Journal of the Senate of Florida* (1919 Reg. Sess.), 1785 (hereafter this publication is cited as *Fla. Senate Journal*); Herbert Feikel, "Textbook Bill by Carlton Passes Senate," *Tampa Morning Tribune,* May 30, 1919, p. 2, col. 3; *Journal of the Senate of Georgia* (1919 Reg. Sess.), 834 (hereafter this

publication is cited as *Ga. Senate Journal*); and *Ga. House Journal* (1919 Reg. Sess.), 630.

102. *Miss. House Journal* (1916 Reg. Sess.), 2317.

103. *Miss. Senate Journal* (1920 Reg. Sess.), 615; *Miss. House Journal* (1920 Reg. Sess.), 1397–98, 1849–50, and 1926; "Legislators Won't Draw Any Extra Money for Session," *Daily Clarion-Ledger* (Jackson), Apr. 2, 1920, p. 3, col. 4 (according to this article, "The Governor referred to some cases he himself had seen in the jails and poor houses in different portions of the state, that were pitiful in the extreme and only by the establishment of an institution of this kind, could such people be properly cared for"); "Russell Uses Axe on Prison Reform Bill," *Jackson Daily News*, Apr. 1, 1920, p. 1, col. 1; and "Both Houses Speeding Up Adjournment," ibid., Apr. 2, 1920, p. 2, cols. 3–5.

104. *S.C. House Journal* (1917 Reg. Sess.), 598. For similar comments by other South Carolina representatives, see "Large Majority in Lower House," *State* (Columbia), Feb. 13, 1917, p. 12, col. 4.

105. "Feeble-Minded Will Have Home," *Constitution* (Atlanta), July, 9, 1919, p. 5, col. 1, the source of the first two quotations; "Would Allow Keeping Liquor for Private Use," *Atlanta Journal*, July 8, 1919, p. 1, col. 5; "Bill to Provide for Defective Children Is Passed," *Atlanta Georgian*, July 8, 1919, p. 1, col. 5; and "House Votes Home for Feebleminded," *Augusta Chronicle*, July 9, 1919, p. 3, col. 1, the source of the third quotation.

106. "Feeble-Minded Have Home," p. 5, col. 1, the source of the first quotation; and "Training School Up to Governor," *Constitution* (Atlanta), Aug. 2, 1919, p. 5, col. 3, the source of the second quotation.

107. "Large Majority," p. 12, col. 4.

108. "Textbook Bill," p. 2, col. 2.

109. On Jim Crow laws generally, see C. Vann Woodward, *The Strange Career of Jim Crow,* 2d ed. (New York: Oxford Univ. Press, 1966). An excellent discussion of Jim Crow laws in one of the states covered by this study is in Neil R. McMillen, *Dark Journey: Black Mississippians in the Age of Jim Crow* (Urbana: Univ. of Illinois Press, 1989), 5–20.

110. E.g., 1919 Fla. Laws, preamble and sec. 8. Every statute used the term *feeble-minded* to identify the target population except the Georgia law, which used the synonymous term *mental defectives.* 1919 Ga. Laws ch. 373, sec. 3.

111. 1918 La. Acts ch. 141, sec. 2.

112. 1920 Miss. Laws ch. 210, sec. 2. See also 1919 Ala. Acts ch. 704, sec. 6.

113. 1919 Ga. Laws ch. 373, sec. 3; and 1919 Fla. Laws ch. 7887, sec. 9.

114. 1919 Ga. Laws ch. 373, sec. 4(a); and 1918 S.C. Acts ch. 398, sec. 12.

115. See, e.g., 1918 La. Acts ch. 141, sec. 11.

116. 1920 Miss. Laws ch. 210, sec. 21.

117. 1919 Ala. Acts ch. 308, sec. 20.

118. 1919 Ga. Laws ch. 373, sec. 6.

119. 1919 Ga. Laws ch. 373, sec. 4(c); 1918 La. Acts ch. 141, sec. 18; and 1920 Miss. Laws ch. 210, sec. 26.

120. 1919 Fla. Laws ch. 7887, sec. 8.

121. See, e.g., 1918 S.C. Laws ch. 398, sec. 9. Louisiana operated the only southern state institution for the mentally retarded admitting any African Americans during the 1920s, and that singlar state facility only provided a limited number of beds for African Americans in a separate building. Horatio M. Pollack, "Feebleminded in Institutions in the United States," *Mental Hygiene* 10 (1926), 808. See generally, Steven Noll, "Southern Strategies for Handling the Black Feeble-Minded: From Social Control to Profound Indifference," *Journal of Policy History* 3 (1991), 130–44.

122. 1919 Ala. Acts ch. 704, sec. 10.

Chapter 5: *Taking Root*

1. W. D. Partlow, "A Debt the World Owes Medical Science," *Journal of MASA* 6 (1936), 9.

2. W. L. Funkhouser, "Mental Hygiene," *Journal of MAG* 9 (1920), 36. Similarly, an Alabama physician described eugenics as "the public health of tomorrow." J. P. McMurphy, "Birth Control, A Public Health Problem," *Transactions of MASA* (1927), 347.

3. Partlow, "Debt," 12.

4. Michael E. Teller, *The Tuberculosis Movement: A Public Health Campaign in the Progressive Era* (New York: Greenwood, 1988), 15–33, 48, 70–72, and 85–95, quotation on 33. See also Paul Starr, *The Social Transformation of Medicine* (New York: Basic, 1982), 137 and 187–97. A state-by-state compendium of tuberculosis sanatoria, clinics, and laws as of 1903 is in Philip P. Jacobs, *The Campaign against Tuberculosis in the United States* (New York: Charities Publications Committee, 1903). A first-person account of the antituberculosis "crusade" in the South appeared in Dora Lee Wilder, "The Cure of Tuberculosis by the General Practitioner," *Southern Medical Journal* 3 (1910), 424–26.

5. Partlow, "Debt," 9–12; "Attacks H.B. 81," *Commercial-Appeal* (Memphis), Jan. 15, 1922, in Ellisville State School File (hereafter cited as "Ellisville File"), Mississippi Collection, Mississippi State University Library; Marcus Fagg to Chairman of Legislation of the Florida Federation of Women's Clubs, May 24, 1922, in Archives of the Florida Federation of Women's Clubs, Lakeland, Fla. Involvement in the antituberculosis campaign could also lead individuals into the eugenics movement, as it did for Bernadine and Charles Zukoski, a prominent Birmingham, Alabama, couple. "In the beginning, we were particularly interested in tubercular women for whom it was important not to have any children until they recovered from their illness," Charles Zukoski later recalled. "That gradually evolved over the years into what is known today as Planned Parenthood of Alabama, Inc." Along the way, the Zukoskis actively lobbied for eugenic sterilization in Alabama. Becky Webster, "The Zukoski Planning Committee of

Two," *Birmingham,* Nov. 1984, 72. In Louisiana, Jean Gordon and her Era Club were actively involved in both the eugenic and antituberculosis movements. See, e.g., Era Club, "Minute Book, 1914–1919," 23, 26, 71, 83, 119, and 145, manuscript copy in Louisiana Division, New Orleans Public Library, New Orleans, La. (hereafter cited as "Louisiana Division").

6. Frank Fenwick Young, *New Orleans Medical and Surgical Journal* 80 (1928), 818.

7. Allan M. Brandt, *No Magic Bullet: A Social History of Venereal Disease in the United States since 1880* (New York: Oxford Univ. Press, 1985), 19–20, 40–41, and 84–89, quotation on 41. See also Nancy Moore Rockafellar, "Making the World Safe for the Soldiers of Democracy: Patriotism, Public Health, and Venereal Disease Control on the West Coast, 1910–1919" (Ph.D. diss., Univ. of Washington, 1990); and Daniel J. Kevles, *In the Name of Eugenics: Genetics and the Uses of Human Heredity* (New York: Knopf, 1985), 92 and 99–100.

8. Joseph P. Bowdoin, "What We Have Done in Georgia to Aid in the Control of Venereal Diseases," *Journal of MAG* 9 (1920), 88–91; *Ga. House Journal* (1919 Reg. Sess.), 238–39; and Mary Laack Oliver, "State Statutes Regulating Marriage of Venereal Diseased Persons" (M.A. thesis, Univ. of Wisconsin, 1937), 68 and 76 (appendix). A 1910 editorial in the *Southern Medical Journal* challenged southern physicians to make "war" on "the Great Black Plague" (venereal disease) with the same intensity as "focused upon the 'Great White Plague'" (tuberculosis). A.B.C., "The Great Black Plague," *Southern Medical Journal* 3 (1910), 263.

9. Prince A. Morrow, *Eugenics and Racial Poisons* (New York: Society of Sanitary and Moral Prophylaxis, [1912]), 11.

10. *Ga. House Journal* (1919 Reg. Sess.), 237–39. See also Geo. H. Preston, "Superintendent's Report," in Georgia Training School for Mental Defectives, *First Annual Report* (Atlanta: Index, 1922), 15.

11. "Needed Changes in Marriage Laws," *Florida Bulletin* 2 (Apr. 1923), 2–3.

12. Robert A. Markel, *"Save the Babies": American Public Health Reform and the Prevention of Infant Mortality, 1850–1929* (Baltimore: Johns Hopkins Univ. Press, 1990), 77–79, 124–25, and 220; and Starr, *Social Transformation,* 192.

13. Mrs. Z. I. Fitzpatrick, "Report of the President," in Georgia Federation of Women's Clubs, *Yearbook, 1916–17* (Greenville, Ga.: Gresham, 1916), 18 and 24.

14. Markel, *Save the Babies,* 116–18.

15. L. Emmett Holt, "Infant Mortality," *Transactions of the American Association for Study and Prevention of Infant Mortality* 36 (1913), 25.

16. See, e.g., Edward J. Larson, "Belated Progress: The Enactment of Eugenic Legislation in Georgia," *Journal of the History of Medicine and Allied Sciences* 46 (1991), 52–53.

17. E. A. Magiera, "Our Public Health Program," *Mississippi Doctor* 16 (1939), 19.

18. "Home for the Feeble-Minded Protection to the Race," *Birmingham Age-Herald,* July 17, 1921, p. 6, col. 1.

19. W. D. Partlow, "The Superintendent's Report," in "The Alabama Home," in *Alabama Insane Hospitals, Annual Report* [1924] ([Tuscaloosa]: Hospital Print, 1924), 94–95.

20. The figures for 1922 come from U.S. Bureau of the Census, *Feeble-Minded and Epileptics in State Institutions, 1926 and 1927* (Washington, D.C.: Government Printing Office, 1931), 5; those for 1930 are from idem, *Mental Defectives and Epileptics in Institutions, 1933* (Washington, D.C.: Government Printing Office, 1935), 14.

21. Benjamin O. Whitten, "Address of the President," *Journal of Psycho-Asthenics* 42 (1937), 34.

22. H. H. Ramsey, in "New Work to Help Feeble-Minded Persons," *Commercial-Appeal* (Memphis), Jan. 2, 1923, p. 8, col. 1.

23. H. H. Ramsey, in "Report Shows More Room Badly Needed," *Commercial-Appeal* (Memphis), Oct. 31, 1926, in Ellisville File.

24. "Submits Asylum Report," *Commercial-Appeal* (Memphis), May 20, 1922, in Ellisville File.

25. Bilbo served as the initial chair of the facility's board of trustees following his first term as governor. See, e.g., "Trustees' Report," in Mississippi School and Colony for the Feebleminded, *First Biennial Report* (Jackson: Tucker, 1921), 8.

26. Ramsey, in "New Work," p. 8, col. 3.

27. H. H. Ramsey, "Superintendent's Report," in Mississippi School and Colony for the Feebleminded, *Third Biennial Report, 1923–25* (Jackson: Tucker, 1925), 7.

28. "Trustees' Report," in Mississippi School and Colony for the Feebleminded, *Second Biennial Report* (Jackson: Tucker, 1923), 4. Superintendent J. M. Buchanan of the state mental health hospital described this situation and denounced the Mississippi legislature as "positively parsimonious" regarding the Mississippi Colony in J. M. Buchanan, "Who Is Insane?" *New Orleans Medical and Surgical Journal* 79 (1926), 263.

29. See, e.g., U.S. Bureau of Census, *Mental Defectives, 1933,* 15.

30. V. V. Anderson, *A Report of the South Carolina Mental Hygiene Survey* (New York: National Committee for Mental Hygiene, 1922), 70.

31. Children's Home Society of Florida, *Nineteenth Annual Report* (Jacksonville, Fla.: Children's Home Society, 1921), 21.

32. G.M.G. Stafford, "Mental Hygiene in Relation to General Health," *New Orleans Medical and Surgical Journal* 80 (1927), 10–11.

33. U.S. Bureau of Census, *Feeble-Minded, 1926 and 1927,* 5; and idem, *Mental Defectives, 1933,* 14. Both of these reports provide totals for the preceding years.

34. "Trustees Biennial Report," in Mississippi School, *Third Report,* 6.

35. See, e.g., Gov. Robert A. Cooper to Members of the State Assembly, in Anderson, *Report,* 4; and Department of Public Welfare [Georgia], *Report of the Third Year's Work* (Atlanta: Index, 1923), 22.

36. Steven Noll, "Southern Strategies for Handling the Black Feeble-Minded," *Journal of Policy History* 3 (1991), 133.

37. See, e.g., R. C. Tompkins, "Teaching and Care of Feeble Minded in State Institutions," *New Orleans Medical and Surgical Journal* 82 (1929), 161, which noted that "[w]ith our present facility we are only able to segregate according to sex, color and on the basis of tidiness and untidiness. On the colored wards, we are unable to separate the tidy from the untidy."

38. Noll, "Southern Strategies," 136–38. Alabama and South Carolina maintained separate mental health hospitals for African Americans. The other states of the Deep South placed mentally ill African Americans into inferior quarters within institutions that served all races. Ibid., 132; and, e.g., Brookings Institution, *Report on a Survey of the State and County Government of Alabama* (Montgomery, Ala.: Wilson, 1932), 2:143–44.

39. B. O. Whitten, "Superintendent's Report," in State Training School [South Carolina], *Fifth Annual Report* (Columbia, S.C.: General Assembly, 1924), 10.

40. B. O. Whitten, "Superintendent's Report," in State Training School [South Carolina], *Twenty-first Annual Report* (Columbia, S.C.: General Assembly, 1938), 1–5.

41. Benjamin Whitten, "Presidential Address to the American Association on Mental Deficiency, May, 1937," *Journal of Psycho-Asthenics* 42 (1937), 36. See also idem, "Report No. 2—Discussing the Question of Creating Institution for Colored, 1941," in *A History of Whitten Village* (Clinton, S.C.: Jacob Press, 1967), 104.

42. See, e.g., Department of Public Welfare [Georgia], *Biennial Report for the Years 1927 and 1928* (n.p., 1928), 81; idem, *Report for the Years 1929, 1930, and 1931* (n.p., 1931), 36–37; and Florida Federation of Women's Clubs, *Yearbook, 1932–1934* ([Lakeland, Fla.]: n.p., 1932), 6.

43. Virginia was the only state to open a separate institution for mentally retarded Blacks, and that did not occur until 1939, after the Virginia State Federation of Colored Women's Clubs backed the project. Noll, "Strategies," 139–40. During the 1950s, South Carolina temporarily set aside certain buildings at its state mental health hospital specifically for mentally retarded African Americans. See William S. Hall, "Sterilizations Performed in the Year 1955," in Association for Voluntary Sterilization Collection (hereafter cited as "AVS Collection"), Social Welfare History Archives, University of Minnesota, Minneapolis, Minn.

44. See Henry H. Goddard, *Sterilization and Segregation* (New York: Russell Sage Foundation, 1913), 5–7.

45. 1919 Fla. Laws ch. 7887, secs. 1 and 8; 1918 La. Laws ch. 141, secs. 1 and 4, quotation on 4; and 1920 Miss. Laws ch. 201, sec. 8.

46. See, e.g., W. D. Partlow, "Superintendent's Report," in Alabama Insane Hos-

pitals, *Report of Trustees* [1931] ([Tuscaloosa]: n.p., 1931), 92; State Department of Public Welfare [Georgia], *Georgia's Program in Social Welfare: Report of the Sixth and Seventh Year's Work* (n.p., 1926), 54; and State Board of Public Welfare [South Carolina], *First Annual Report* (Columbia, S.C.: Gonzales and Bryan, 1921), 15.

47. B. O. Whitten, "Contemplated Provisions for the Feeble-Minded in South Carolina," *Journal of SCMA* 16 (1920), 69.

48. "Report of Superintendent," in Florida Farm Colony for Epileptic and Feeble-Minded, *Biennial Report, 1927–29* ([Gainesville, Fla.]: n.p., 1929), 8.

49. Board of Public Welfare, *First Report*, 26.

50. "Trustees Biennial Report," in Mississippi School, *Third Report*, 6.

51. "Report of Trustees," in Mississippi School and Colony for the Feebleminded, *Fifth Biennial Report* (Jackson: Tucker, 1929), 7.

52. H. H. Ramsey, "Superintendent's Report," in Mississippi School and Colony for Feebleminded, *Fourth Biennial Report* (Jackson: Tucker, 1927), 21.

53. Anderson, *Survey*, 73.

54. B. O. Whitten, "The General Practitioner's Privilege and Responsibilities in Mental Hygiene," *Journal of SCMA* 17 (1921), 310.

55. Mary S. Fishburne, "Psychological Field Work," in State Board of Public Welfare [South Carolina], *Third Annual Report* (Columbia, S.C.: Gonzales and Bryan, 1923), 25. Regarding the work of the State Department of Mental Hygiene, see J. M. Beeler, "Nervous and Mental Disease," *Journal of SCMA* 21 (1925), 149–50.

56. Buchanan, "Who Is Insane?" 264. For a similar comment made by Buchanan before the Mississippi Colony opened, see J. M. Buchanan, "Mental Hygiene," *Southern Medical Journal* 12 (1919), 585.

57. See, e.g., Department of Public Welfare [Georgia], *Third Year's Work*, 22; and Tompkins, "Teaching and Care," 164, which presents the comments of the superintendent of Louisiana's State Colony and Training School.

58. Buchanan, "Who Is Insane?" 263–64.

59. H. H. Ramsey, "The Relationship of Feeblemindedness to the Field of General Medicine," *New Orleans Medical and Surgical Journal* 80 (1928), 757.

60. Henry Daspit, in "Discussion," *New Orleans Medical and Surgical Journal* 76 (1923), 153. The nationally known eugenics leader Thomas H. Haines had suggested this "educational" value of local clinics three years earlier in Thomas H. Haines, "The Mental Hygiene Requirements of a Community: Suggestions Based upon a Personal Survey," in *Proceedings of the National Conference of Social Work, 1920* (Chicago: Univ. of Chicago Press, 1920), 405–6.

61. John H. Odom, "Superintendent's Report," in Georgia Training School for Mental Defectives, "Biennial Report for the Years 1929–30," in State Board of Health [Georgia], *Biennial Report* ([Atlanta]: n.p., 1931), 133.

62. Charles Davenport, *State Laws Limiting Marriage Selection* (Cold Springs Harbor, N.Y.: Eugenics Record Office, 1913), 11–12.

63. Buchanan, "Mental Hygiene," 545.

64. Buchanan, "Who Is Insane?" 264.

65. Davenport, *State Laws,* 12; and Buchanan, "Mental Hygiene," 545–46.

66. Board of Welfare [South Carolina], *Third Report,* 11–12. In Alabama, the eugenicist William Partlow made similarly halfhearted arguments for eugenic marriage restrictions. E.g., W. D. Partlow, "Committee on Mental Hygiene," *Transactions of MASA* (1930), 34.

67. David H. Keller, in "Discussion," *Southern Medical Journal* 19 (1926), 197.

68. B. O. Whitten, "Superintendent's Report," in State Training School [South Carolina], *Sixth Annual Report, 1925* (Columbia, S.C.: Joint Committee on Printing, 1925), 12.

69. Buchanan, "Mental Hygiene," 545.

70. See, e.g., Florida Federation of Women's Clubs, *Yearbook, 1932–34,* 240; Bertie Iola Coley, "The Educational Program of the South Carolina Federation of Women's Clubs" (M.A. thesis, Univ. of South Carolina, 1938), 80; Children's Home Society of Florida, *Thirteenth Annual Report* ([Jacksonville, Fla.: Children's Home Society], 1915), 6; and Marcus Fagg to Chairman of Legislation of Florida Federation of Women's Clubs, May 24, 1922, 2, Archives of the Florida Federation of Women's Clubs. An address given to the Mothers Club of Atlanta endorsing such legislation appeared in C. W. Roberts, "Boys' Rights Prenatal and Otherwise: An Address to the Mothers Club," *Journal of MAG* 8 (1919), 193–94.

71. Georgia Code (1933), ch. 53, secs. 102–4, 9901, quotation at sec. 9901; Miss. Code (1927), ch. 21, sec. 1479; and S.C. Code (1933), ch. 164, sec. 8556.

72. Joseph A. O'Hara, "Feeble-Minded," *New Orleans Medical and Surgical Journal* 70 (1917), 350–51.

73. R. McG. Carruth, "Race Degeneration: What Can We Do to Check It?" *New Orleans Medical and Surgical Journal* 72 (1919), 188–90 (emphasis in original). Carruth's prominence was noted in "Funeral Rites Are Held for Dr. Carruth," *New Orleans States,* Nov. 8, 1952, p. 11, col. 3.

74. *La. House Journal* (1924 Reg. Sess.), 792; R. McG. Carruth, "Marriage Laws: Their Need, and the Cause and Cure of Their Weakness," *Southern Medical Journal* 19 (1926), 195–96, quotations on 196; and "Dr. Carruth Last Rites Set Today," *Times-Picayune* (New Orleans), Nov. 8, 1952, p. 3, col. 1.

75. Keller, in "Discussion" (1926), 196.

76. *La. Senate Journal* (1928 Reg. Sess.), 117 and 923; and *La. House Journal* (1928 Reg. Sess.), xivii and 1525.

77. "Senate Approves Re-organization of Health Board," *State-Times* (Baton Rouge), July 5, 1928, p. 13, col. 1. See also "Eugenics Defeated," *New Orleans States,* July 11, 1928, p. 4, col. 2. A 1924 Louisiana law required persons applying for a marriage license to provide a health certificate stating that they did not

suffer from venereal disease, but included no such requirement for eugenic unfitness. See La. Gen. Stat. sec. 2180 (1934).

78. *Fla. Senate Journal* (1937 Reg. Sess.), 1106; and Francis R. Bridges, "Measure Aimed at Banning Child Marriages Again Given Approval by Florida Senate," *Florida Times-Union* (Jacksonville), June 3, 1937, p. 6, col. 1, and p. 8, cols. 1–2.

79. This issue is discussed above in chapter 2, and in Kevles, *Name of Eugenics,* 96–112.

80. See, e.g., Buchanan, "Mental Hygiene," 544; and Richard I. Manning, *Why Should South Carolina Make a Beginning in 1919 in Provision for Its Feeble-Minded?* (Columbia: State, 1916), 2. A chronological listing of state sterilization statutes is in Jacob Henry Landman, *Human Sterilization: The History of the Sexual Sterilization Movement* (New York: Macmillan, 1932), 291–93.

81. *Analysis of America's Modern Melting Pot: Hearings before the House Committee on Immigration and Naturalization,* 67th Congress, 3d sess., 1922, 755, statement of H. H. Laughlin. For Grant's views, see Madison Grant, *The Passing of the Great Race* (New York: Scribner's, 1916).

82. See, e.g., Hamilton Cravens, *The Triumph of Evolution: The Heredity-Environment Controversy, 1900–1941* (reprint; Baltimore: Johns Hopkins Univ. Press, 1988), 176–78; Roy Lawrence Garis, *Immigration Restriction: A Study of the Opposition to and Regulation of Immigration into the United States* (New York: Macmillan, 1927), 240–51; Mark H. Haller, *Eugenics: Hereditarian Attitudes in American Thought* (New Brunswick, N.J.: Rutgers Univ. Press, 1963), 155; Kenneth Ludmerer, *Genetics and American Society: A Historical Appraisal* (Baltimore: Johns Hopkins Univ. Press, 1972), 65–113; and Philip R. Reilly, *The Surgical Solution: A History of Involuntary Sterilization in the United States* (Baltimore: Johns Hopkins Univ. Press, 1991), 63–66. For a detailed analysis of Laughlin's role, see Frances Hassencahl, "Harry H. Laughlin, 'Expert Eugenics Agent' for the House Committee on Immigration and Naturalization, 1921 to 1931" (Ph.D. diss., Case Western Reserve Univ., 1970).

83. Cravens, *Evolution,* 177; and Kevles, *Name of Eugenics,* 97.

84. Elmer C. Hess, *Official Congressional Directory, 68th Congress, 1st Session,* 2d ed. (Washington, D.C.: Joint Committee on Printing, 1924), 194.

85. Cravens, *Evolution,* 178.

86. Kevles, *Name of Eugenics,* 97.

87. *Congressional Record* 65 (April 11, 1924), 6124. (Hereafter, *Congressional Record* is abbreviated *Cong. Rec.*)

88. *Cong. Rec.* 65 (Apr. 12, 1924), 6269.

89. *Cong. Rec.* 65 (Apr. 11, 1924), 6158.

90. *Cong. Rec.* 65 (Apr. 16, 1924), 6464–67, statement of Senator Walter George; and ibid., 65 (Apr. 17, 1924), 6540–42, statement of Senator Pat Harrison.

91. *Cong. Rec.* 65 (Apr. 16, 1924), 6473. Nearly half of the sixteen senators supporting Harris's amendment represented the Deep South, and most of the other supporters came from south of the Mason-Dixon line.

92. *Cong. Rec.* 65 (Apr. 16, 1924), 6470, statements of Senators Reed and George.

93. *Cong. Rec.* 65 (Apr. 17, 1924), 6551, statement of Senator Simmons; and ibid., 65 (Apr. 17, 1924), 6614–15, statement of Senator Smith.

94. *Cong. Rec.* 65 (Apr. 12, 1924), 6270.

95. The story was repeated on three different days, at *Cong. Rec.* 65 (Apr. 15, 1924), 6376; ibid., 65 (Apr. 17, 1924), 6545; and ibid., 65 (Apr. 18, 1924), 6619.

96. *Cong. Rec.* 65 (Apr. 15, 1924), 6374–77, quotation on 6375; ibid., 65 (Apr. 17, 1924), 6543–45; and ibid., 65 (Apr. 18, 1924), 6619–20.

97. *Cong. Rec.* 65 (Apr. 14, 1924), 6458. On the tendency of eugenicists to equate national and racial identity, see Kevles, *Name of Eugenics,* 46–47.

98. *Cong. Rec.* 65 (Apr. 12, 1924), 6257–57, reporting the House vote on final passage; ibid., 65 (Apr. 17, 1924), 6546, reporting the Senate vote on the amendment shifting the census; and ibid., 65 (Apr. 18, 1924), 6649, reporting the Senate vote on final passage.

99. *Cong. Rec.* 65 (Apr. 11, 1924), 6161 (emphasis added to stress "Know Nothing" tie).

100. *Cong. Rec.* 65 (Apr. 11, 1924), 6124.

101. See, e.g., Anderson, *Survey,* 11. In my research, I never found any eugenicist from the Deep South who raised the issue.

102. B. O. Whitten, "Contemplated Provision for the Feeble-Minded in South Carolina," *Journal of SCMA* 16 (1920), 67.

103. Ibid., 70. See also B. O. Whitten, "The General Practitioner's Privileges and Responsibilities in Mental Hygiene," *Journal of SCMA* 17 (1921), 309.

104. See, e.g., Wm. Weston, "What May We Do for the Infant and the Child," *Journal of SCMA* 10 (1914), 480–81; and "This Bogalusa Baby Most Perfect at Fair," *Times-Picayune* (New Orleans), Nov. 4, 1923, p. 15, col. 6. For a general discussion of the issue, see Kevles, *Name of Eugenics,* 57–69.

105. Margaret Sanger, "Why Not Birth Control?" *Birth Control Review,* May 1919, 10–11. For an analysis of the relationship between the birth control and eugenics movements during the 1920s, see Linda Gordon, *Woman's Body, Woman's Right: Birth Control in America,* rev. ed. (New York: Penguin, 1990), 269–86.

106. McMurphy, "Birth Control," 342.

107. A. A. Herold, in "Discussion," *New Orleans Medical and Surgical Journal* 82 (1929), 353. A later study of birth control practices in Louisiana confirmed this physician's view that only wealthy women with private physicians readily

obtained contraceptives. Martha C. Ward, *Poor Women, Powerful Men: America's Great Experiment in Family Planning* (Boulder, Colo.: Westview Press, 1986), chs. 1 and 2. A similar view was expressed by a South Carolina physician in T. H. Dreher, "Birth Control among the Poor," *Journal of SCMA* 27 (1931), 330. For a general discussion of the relationship between the southern birth control movement and eugenics, see Gordon, *Woman's Body*, 325–30.

108. Carruth, "Race Degeneration," 189–90.

109. For a representative example of Sanger's views on sterilization, see Margaret Sanger, "The Function of Sterilization," *Birth Control Review*, Oct. 1926, 299. An example of representative southern physicians' mixing eugenic sterilization with birth control appears in "Discussion," *New Orleans Medical and Surgical Journal* 82 (1929), 353–57.

110. For Partlow's position on both issues, see, e.g., W. D. Partlow, "Pathology of Mental Rehabilitation," *Transactions of MASA* (1928), 327.

111. 1919 Ala. Acts, No. 704, sec. 10. For an official interpretation of this provision, see H. H. Laughlin to Bibb Graves, Aug. 5, 1930, in Papers of Gov. Bibb Graves (First Administration), Alabama State Archives, Montgomery, Ala.; and Lawrence H. Lee to H. H. Laughlin, Aug. 15, 1930, in Graves Papers (First Administration).

112. For example, sterilization statutes in Indiana and California, which served as early models for such laws throughout the United States, entrusted the sterilization decision to expert committees or commissions. See Reilly, *Surgical Solution*, 45–48.

113. The NCMH field representative Thomas H. Haines credited Partlow with drafting the bill. Thomas H. Haines to Thomas E. Kilby, in Papers of Gov. Thomas E. Kilby, Alabama State Archives.

114. See W. D. Partlow, "Superintendent's Report," in Alabama Insane Hospitals, *Report of the Trustees* [1932] ([Tuscaloosa]: n.p., 1932), 88; and W. D. Partlow to E. S. Gosney, Mar. 26, 1934, in AVS Collection.

115. W. D. Partlow, "The Alabama Home," in Alabama Insane Hospitals, *Report of the Trustees* [1927] ([Tuscaloosa]: n.p., 1927), 91.

116. Partlow, "Report" [1932], 88.

117. W. D. Partlow, "Superintendent's Report," in Alabama Insane Hospitals, *Report of the Trustees* [1933] ([Tuscaloosa]: n.p., 1933), 80.

118. W. D. Partlow, "Superintendent's Report," in Alabama Insane Hospitals, *Report of the Trustees* [1935] ([Tuscaloosa]: n.p., 1935), 89.

119. "Information Relative to the Partlow State School," in Papers of Partlow State School, Alabama State Archives.

120. W. D. Partlow to E. S. Gosney, Mar. 17, 1934, in AVS Collection.

121. E.g., Whitten, "General Practitioner," 309; and State Board of Public Welfare [South Carolina], *Sixth Annual Report* (Columbia, S.C.: Joint Committee on Printing, 1925), 65.

122. E.g., Louisiana Hospital for the Insane, *Report of the Board of Administrators* [1922–24] (Alexandria, La.: Wall, 1924), 15–19; and "Trustees Biennial Report," in Mississippi School, *Fourth Report, 62.*

123. Partlow, "Pathology," 324.

124. J.D.S. Davis, "The President's Message," *Transactions of MASA* (1928), 20.

125. *Buck v. Bell,* 274 U.S. 201 (1927).

126. *Ala. House Journal* (1927 Reg. Sess.), 839, House Bill no. 570, introduced June 15, 1927; "Sterilization Bill Is Given to House," *Montgomery Advertiser,* June 16, 1937, p. 10, col. 1; " 'Sterilization Bill' Given Final Reading," *Birmingham News,* June 17, 1927, p. 2, col. 5; and *Fla. House Journal* (1927 Reg. Sess.), 2890, House Bill no. 1200.

127. *Ga. House Journal* (1929 Reg. Sess.), 98, House Bill no. 206.

128. See *Ala. House Journal* (1927 Reg. Sess.), 1086; *Fla. House Journal* (1927 Reg. Sess.), 6314, which records the bill's passage; "Sterilization Bill Is Passed by House," *Tallahassee Daily Democrat,* June 3, 1927, p. 1, col. 2, which describes the last day of the session; and *Ga. House Journal* (1929 Reg. Sess.), 538, which records the bill's second reading.

129. For discussion of the Roman Catholic position on this issue, see Haller, *Eugenics,* 82–83 and 131; Kevles, *Name of Eugenics,* 118–21 and 168; and Reilly, *Surgical Solution,* 118–22.

130. John N. Thomas, "Superintendent's Report," in Louisiana Hospital for the Insane, *Report of Board of Administrators* [1920–22] (Alexandria, La.: Wall, 1922), 32. The earlier position of Louisiana mental health officials on this topic is discussed above in chapter 3.

131. *La. Senate Journal* (1924 Reg. Sess.), 458.

132. *La. Senate Journal* (1924 Reg. Sess.), 75, legislative calendar. The complete text of the Louisiana Senate legislation is in "Check on Propagation of Sub-Normal," *New Orleans Post,* June 21, 1924, p. 3, col. 1.

133. "Check on Propagation," p. 3, col. 1; and *La. Senate Journal* (1924 Reg. Sess.), 458.

134. J. W. Shaw, "Eugenical Sterilization Law," *Morning Star* (New Orleans), June 28, 1924, p. 1, cols. 2–3. For Shaw's background, see Roger Baudier, *The Catholic Clergy in Louisiana* (reprint; New Orleans: Louisiana Library, 1972), 527–35.

135. "Sterilization Bill OK'd by This Group," *New Orleans Item,* July 2, 1924, p. 1, col. 4, and p. 16, col. 5. In a later retelling of this story about the daughter suffering from the botched abortion, Gordon noted that the woman survived. "Unfortunately," she told a physicians' group, "you doctors cured her and brought her back" to the institution. Jean Gordon, in "Discussion," *New Orleans Medical and Surgical Journal* 82 (1929), 355. This episode underscores that Gordon supported the involuntary sterilization of mentally retarded women as a

means to prevent the propagation of mentally retarded offspring rather than to protect these women from the ordeal of childbirth. None of my sources stressed this second rationale for forced sterilization.

136. "Merely Another Way," *Times-Picayune* (New Orleans), June 24, 1924, p. 8, col. 2; and "Feeble-Minded," ibid., June 26, 1924, p. 8, col. 2.

137. *La. House Journal* (1924 Reg. Sess.), 830–31; "Asexualization Measure Killed," *Times-Picayune* (New Orleans), July 3, 1924, p. 1, col. 1, source of the quotation in the text; "Dry Bill Smashed," *New Orleans States,* July 3, 1924, p. 3, cols. 2–3; and "Sterilization Bill Defeated by House Vote," *New Orleans Item,* July 3, 1924, p. 7, cols. 6–7.

138. "Doctors, Not Lawyers, Due to Stop Crime, Judge Olson Declares, Blaming Heredity," *Times-Picayune* (New Orleans), Apr. 29, 1926, p. 1, col. 6, and p. 2, cols. 6–7.

139. Jno. N. Thomas, "Increasing Insanity in This Country and What Should Be Done to Prevent It," *New Orleans Medical and Surgical Journal* 79 (1926), 334.

140. The summary of the 1926 Louisiana Senate debate in this paragraph and the next two, including all the quotations therein, is compiled from "Senate Passes Sterilization in Hot Fight," *State Times* (Baton Rouge), June 15, 1926, p. 5, col. 1; Stanford Jarrell, "Bill to Sterilize Feeble Minded Passes Senate," *New Orleans Item,* June 15, 1926, p. 8, col. 7; "Sterilization Bill Passed by Senate," *New Orleans States,* June 15, 1926, p. 6, col. 8; George Vandervoort, "Senate Passes Sterilization Measure Twenty-five to Eleven," *Times-Picayune* (New Orleans), June 15, 1926, p. 9, col. 3; and *La. Senate Journal* (1926 Reg. Sess.), 375–76.

141. "Steril Bill Put to Sleep in House," *New Orleans States,* June 30, 1926, p. 6, col. 3.

142. The summary of the 1926 House floor debate in this paragraph and the next, including all the quotations therein, is compiled from ibid.; "House Members Shape Fight over Sterilization," *State-Times* (Baton Rouge), June 29, 1926, p. 5, col. 1; "House Defeats Sterilization Bill Forty-eight to Forty-six," ibid., June 30, 1926, p. 6, col. 3; and "Sterilization Bill Is Killed," *Times-Picayune* (New Orleans), June 30, 1926, p. 6, col. 3. Archbishop Shaw's letter was reprinted in "His Grace Opposes Proposed Measure on Sterilization," *Morning Star,* June 5, 1926, p. 4, col. 1.

143. E.g., John N. Thomas, letter to the editor, *Times-Picayune* (New Orleans), June 12, 1926, p. 8, col. 5.

144. "The Sterilization Bill," *Times-Picayune* (New Orleans), June 8, 1926, p. 8, col. 1.

145. "Steril Bill," p. 6, col. 3; and *La. House Journal* (1926 Reg. Sess.), 1076–77.

146. For example, the *Times-Picayune* editorialized against the antievolution bill within days after it endorsed the eugenic sterilization measure. See "The Monkey Bill," *Times-Picayune* (New Orleans), June 23, 1926, p. 8, col. 2.

147. For a representative sample of Bryan's view of eugenics, see William Jennings Bryan, *In His Image* (New York: Revell, 1922), quotation on 108. For Straton's most extensive discussion of the issue, see John Roach Straton, "Will Evolution Solve the Race Problem?" *North American Review* 170 (1908), 785–804. For a general discussion of antievolutionism during the period, see Edward J. Larson, *Trial and Error: The American Controversy over Creation and Evolution* (New York: Oxford Univ. Press, 1985), 28–81.

148. Compare the votes recorded in *La. Senate Journal* (1926 Reg. Sess.), 375–76, on sterilization legislation, with those recorded in ibid. (1926 Reg. Sess.), 597, on antievolution legislation; and the votes recorded in *La. House Journal* (1926 Reg. Sess.), 1076–77, on sterilization legislation, with those recorded in ibid. (1926 Reg. Sess.), 762, on antievolution legislation. Roman Catholic opposition to antievolution lawmaking did not necessarily translate into support for evolution. Indeed, at the same time that Roman Catholic legislators in Louisiana united to defeat the antievolution bill, Roman Catholic clergy in the state were denouncing "the absurdity of the evolutionist." See "Priest Discusses Evolution Absurdity," *Morning Star,* June 5, 1926, p. 2, col. 4.

149. "Senate Passes Sterilization," p. 5, col. 1. For evidence of the continuing support by state mental health hospital officials, see Jno. N. Thomas, "Superintendent's Report," in Central Louisiana State Hospital, *Report of the Board of Administrators* [1926–28] (Alexandria, La.: Wall, 1928), 23–25; and Thomas, letter to editor, p. 8, col. 5. Officials from both of the state mental health hospitals and the State Colony and Training School for the mentally retarded continued to view mental illness and mental retardation as directly due to heredity in most cases. See Stafford, "Mental Hygiene," 11; R. H. Bryant, "Some Observations Which May Help in a Better Understanding of the Problem of Our Mentally Ill," *New Orleans Medical and Surgical Journal* 80 (1927), 161; and Thomas, "Increasing Insanity," 330.

150. Clarence Pierson, "Are We Sufficiently Progressed Scientifically for the Legal Sexual Sterilization of Inmates of State Institutions in Certain Cases?" *New Orleans Medical and Surgical Journal* 82 (1929), 350. In this article, however, Pierson expressed his continued support for eugenic segregation and marriage restrictions (pp. 350–52). For Pierson's background, see Henry E. Chambers, *A History of Louisiana* (Chicago: American Historical Society, 1925), 8:16–17. His earlier position is noted above, in chapter 3.

151. The shift in national expert opinion is discussed in Cravens, *Evolution,* 178–86; Kevles, *Name of Eugenics,* 122–47; and Reilly, *Surgical Solution,* 111–15.

152. Frank Fenwick Young, "Mental Disorders and Society," *New Orleans Medical and Surgical Journal* 80 (1928), 818.

153. R. McG. Carruth, in "Discussion" (1929), 356.

154. Jean Gordon and Clarence Pierson, in "Discussion" (1929), 355 and 357.

155. George Vandervoort, "House Votes Down Tax on Tobacco," *Times-Picayune* (New Orleans), June 20, 1928, p. 2, col. 3.

156. *La. Senate Journal* (1930 Reg. Sess.), 181; and *La. House Journal* (1930 Reg. Sess.), 964–65.

157. Associated Press, "Orleans Womens Leader Is Dead after Operation," Feb. 25, 1931, in Jean Gordon file, Louisiana Collection, Tulane University Libraries, New Orleans, La.

158. Frank Allen, "Senate Proposal on Sterilization Loses in a Tie Vote," *Times-Picayune* (New Orleans), June 16, 1932, p. 3, col. 1; *La. Senate Journal* (1932 Reg. Sess.), 422.

159. A second sterilization bill introduced by a physician in the Louisiana senate during the 1932 session died without action. *La. Senate Journal* (1932 Reg. Sess.), 449 and 523.

160. These population data are taken from Robert Hunt Lyman, ed., *The World Almanac and Book of Facts for 1926* (New York: World, 1926), 307 and 320; and U.S. Census Bureau, *Religious Bodies: 1926* (Washington, D.C.: Government Printing Office, 1930), 1:42–48 and 142–75. The political situation of Black Mississippians is discussed in Neil R. McMillan, *Dark Journey: Black Mississippians in the Age of Jim Crow* (Urbana: Univ. of Illinois Press, 1989), 44–45.

161. Larson, *Trial and Error,* 75–81.

162. See, e.g., Theodore Bilbo, "Retiring Message," *Miss. House Journal* (1920 Reg. Sess.), 44–45.

163. Thomas H. Haines, "Mental Deficiency in Mississippi," *Southern Medical Journal* 12 (1919), 542.

164. "Attacks H.B. 81," *Commercial-Appeal* (Memphis), Jan. 15, 1922, in Ellisville File; and "Feeble-Minded Suffer," ibid., Jan. 21, 1922, in Ellisville File.

165. H. H. Ramsey, quoted in Edger S. Wilson, "The Mississippi Colony for the Feeble-Minded at Ellisville," *Commercial-Appeal* (Memphis), Dec. 21, 1924, in Ellisville File.

166. Ramsey, "Superintendent's Report" (1927), 22. Ramsey explained the scientific basis for his view that mental retardation was "transmitted by heredity" in H. H. Ramsey, "The Relation of Feeble-Mindedness to the Field of General Medicine," *New Orleans Medical and Surgical Journal* 80 (1928), 753.

167. "Trustees Biennial Report," in Mississippi School, *Fourth Report,* 12.

168. Theo. G. Bilbo, "Inaugural Address," *Miss. House Journal* (1928 Reg. Sess.), 140–41. Portions of this address closely tracked the language and content of Ramsey's report in the 1925–27 biennial report for the Mississippi Colony. Compare Bilbo, "Inaugural Address," 140–45, with Ramsey, "Superintendent's Report" (1927), 20–22.

169. "Need Vision in Dealing with the Feeble Minded," *Jackson Daily News,* Feb. 15, 1928, p. 5, cols. 1–3; and "Notes and Comments: Mississippi," *Mental Hygiene* 12 (1928), 435. Ramsey incorporated portions of Bilbo's program into

his subsequent official reports. See, e.g., H. H. Ramsey, "Superintendent's Report," in Mississippi School, *Fifth Report*, 15.

170. "Report of Trustees," in Mississippi School, *Fifth Report*, 6–7.

171. "What Our Neighbors Are Saying: Hattesburg, Miss., *American*," *Times-Picayune* (New Orleans), Apr. 3, 1928, p. 8, cols. 5–6.

172. *Miss. House Journal* (1928 Reg. Sess.), 771.

173. "Need Vision," p. 1, col. 1, source of the quotation in the text; and *Miss. House Journal* (1928 Reg. Sess.), 301. Extensive biographical information on Harris is in Dunbar Rowland, *Official and Statistical Register of the State of Mississippi, 1924–1928* (New York: Little and Ives, 1927), 216–18.

174. "Sterilization Bill Meeting with Approval," *Jackson Daily News*, Feb. 17, 1928, p. 5, cols. 7–8, and p. 7, col. 1, source of all quotations; "Capital Chat," *Daily Clarion-Ledger* (Jackson), Feb. 17, 1928, p. 12, col. 6; and 1928 Miss. Laws, ch. 294, sec. 1.

175. "In the House," *Daily Clarion-Ledger* (Jackson), Apr. 11, 1928, p. 3, col. 1.

176. *Miss. House Journal* (1928 Reg. Sess.), 771, 1067; *Miss. Senate Journal* (1928 Reg. Sess.), 1259; "Sterilization Bill Passes," *Jackson Daily News*, Apr. 10, 1928, p. 1, col. 2; and "In the Senate," *Daily Clarion-Ledger*, Apr. 25, 1928, p. 3, col. 5.

177. "Report of Trustees," in Mississippi School, *Fifth Report*, 6.

Chapter 6: *Full Bloom*

1. For compilations of these figures, see Philip R. Reilly, *The Surgical Solution: A History of Involuntary Sterilization in the United States* (Baltimore: Johns Hopkins Univ. Press, 1991), 17; and Jonas Robitscher, ed., *Eugenic Sterilization* (Springfield, Ill.: Thomas, 1973), 118–25. The upturn was noted at the time in "Eugenic Sterilizations to Date," *Eugenical News* 18 (1933), 78.

2. Daniel J. Kevles, *In the Name of Eugenics: Genetics and the Uses of Human Heredity* (New York: Knopf, 1985), 113–64.

3. Hermann J. Muller, *Out of the Night: A Biologist's View of the Future* (New York: Vanguard, 1935), ix.

4. Reilly, *Surgical Solution*, 91; David Barker, "The Biology of Stupidity: Genetics, Eugenics, and Mental Deficiency in the Inter-War Years," *British Journal for the History of Science* 22 (1989), 363–68. A 1930 survey by the association of professionals working with the mentally retarded found that 94 percent of the members responding to the survey supported eugenic sterilization. Harvey M. Watkins, "Selective Sterilization," *Journal of Psycho-Asthenics* 35 (1930), 54–55. One of the first comprehensive articles in this association's journal to question eugenic sterilization practices did not appear until 1940. See Bronson Price and Sidney C. Halperin, "Sterilization Laws—Bane or Banner of Eugenics and Public Welfare?" *American Journal of Mental Deficiency* 4 (1940), 134. (The journal had been renamed.)

5. For a general survey of support within the American medical community, see

L. P. Harshman, "Medical and Legal Aspects of Sterilization in Institutions," *Journal of Psycho-Asthenics* 40 (1935), 51–67. The particular allegiance of the region's medical community to eugenics was illustrated by Partlow's installation as president of the Southern Psychiatric Association in 1937, at which time he reaffirmed his support for eugenics. William D. Partlow, "Psychiatry Adrift with the Times," *Journal of MASA* 7 (1937), 210.

6. See Jacob Henry Landman, *Human Sterilization: The History of the Sexual Sterilization Movement* (New York: Macmillan, 1932), 289.

7. "Biennial Report of the Board of Trustees," Ellisville State School, *Sixth Biennial Report* (Jackson: Tucker, 1931), 6–7, quotation on 7. The Mississippi School and Colony for the Feebleminded had been renamed "Ellisville State School." For the condition of Mississippi mental health institutions in 1930, see Brookings Institution, *Report on a Survey of Government in Mississippi* (Jackson: Research Commission, 1930), 555–56. The absence of eugenic sterilization in Mississippi prior to the mid-1930s is noted in Landman, *Human Sterilization*, 289.

8. H. H. Ramsey, "Superintendent's Report," in Ellisville State School, *Sixth Biennial Report*, 10. See also Ellisville State School, *Seventh Biennial Report*, in *Biennial Reports of Eleemosynary Institutions* [Mississippi, 1931–33] (Jackson: Tucker, 1933), 56.

9. J. E. Brumfield, "Superintendent's Report," in Ellisville State School, *Ninth Biennial Report*, in *Biennial Reports of Eleemosynary Institutions* [Mississippi, 1935–37] (Jackson: Tucker, 1937), 93. Ramsey's immediate successor complained, "Our sterilization law is so technical that it is almost impossible to comply with it, especially when there is any complaint by either inmates or parents." A. L. Develin to Human Betterment Foundation, Jan. 9, 1933, in Association for Voluntary Sterilization Collection (hereafter, "AVS Collection"), Social Welfare History Archives, University of Minnesota, Minneapolis, Minn. The next successor lamented the inability to sterilize patients by noting, "I wish it was possible that we could have the material and facilities for doing that much for society." R. L. Halfacre to R. H. Whitfield, Jan. 9, 1935, in AVS Collection.

10. See, e.g., Ellisville State School, *Tenth Biennial Report*, in *Biennial Reports of Eleemosynary Institutions* [Mississippi, 1937–39] (Jackson: Tucker, 1939), 109.

11. T. Paul Haney, "Superintendent's Report," in Ellisville State School, *Thirteenth Biennial Report* (Jackson: Tucker, 1945), 15.

12. T. Paul Haney, "Superintendent's Report," in Ellisville State School, *Fourteenth Biennial Report* (Jackson: Tucker, 1945), 9. See, e.g., Ellisville State School, *Fifteenth Biennial Report* (Jackson: Tucker, 1949); and idem, *Sixteenth Biennial Report* (Jackson: Tucker, 1949).

13. Mississippi State Hospital, *Thirty-eighth Biennial Report* (Jackson: Tucker, 1931), 18; and East Mississippi State Hospital, *Eighteenth Biennial Report* (Jackson: Tucker, 1931). Beginning with these reports, the names of the two institutions no longer included the word *Insane*.

14. C. D. Mitchell, "Superintendent's Report," in Mississippi State Hospital, *Thirty-ninth Biennial Report* (Jackson: Tucker, 1933), 5.

15. Mississippi State Hospital, *Fortieth Biennial Report,* in *Biennial Reports of Eleemosynary Institutions* [Mississippi, 1933–35] (Jackson: Tucker, 1935), 9–10.

16. East Mississippi State Hospital, *Twentieth Biennial Report,* in *Biennial Reports of Institutions* [1933–35], 39. This institution reported performing its first two eugenic sterilizations during the preceding biennium. The superintendent noted that one of the sterilized patients later committed suicide. J. L. Hoye to E. S. Gosney, Feb. 13, 1933, in AVS Collection.

17. See East Mississippi State Hospital, *Thirtieth Biennial Report* (Jackson: Tucker, 1945), 5; and Marian S. Olden, "Present Status of Sterilization Legislation in the United States," *Eugenical News* 31 (1946), 4.

18. See Robitscher, ed., *Eugenic Sterilization,* 118, which relied on sterilization figures compiled by the Human Betterment Foundation and Birthright, for which the more detailed underlying data from each state institution are preserved in the AVS Collection. These detailed records indicated that no sterilizations were performed under the Mississippi statute during the early 1950s, after the state attorney general questioned the law's validity, but that the Mississippi State Hospital resumed performing a small number of sterilizations beginning in 1956. See W. L. Jaquith, "Sterilizations Performed in the Year 1949," in AVS Collection (annual sterilization questionnaire reply form returned from Mississippi).

19. E. A. Magiera, "Our Public Health Program," *Mississippi Doctor* 16 (1939), 17. Mitchell described these progressive reforms in treatment and his humane approach to mental health care in C. D. Mitchell, "The Modern Treatment of the Insane," *New Orleans Medical and Surgical Journal* 77 (1925), 374–76.

20. C. D. Mitchell, "Report of Superintendent," in Mississippi State Hospital, *Forty-second Biennial Report,* in *Biennial Report of Institutions* [1933–35], 13.

21. C. M. Speck, "Report of Superintendent," in Mississippi State Hospital, *Forty-third Biennial Report,* in *Biennial Report of Eleemosynary Institutions* [1939–41] (Jackson: Tucker, 1941), 11.

22. See, e.g., Mississippi State Hospital, *Forty-fourth Biennial Report,* in *Biennial Reports of Eleemosynary Institutions* [1941–43] (Jackson: Tucker, 1943), 7–57.

23. For conditions in the Black wards and Mitchell's efforts to improve them, see, e.g., C. D. Mitchell, "Report of the Superintendent," in Mississippi State Insane Hospital, *Thirty-fifth Biennial Report* (Jackson: Tucker, 1925), 33–34; and idem, "Report of the Superintendent," in Mississippi State Insane Hospital, *Thirty-seventh Biennial Report* (Jackson: Tucker, 1929), 5–6. (Mitchell wrote, "During the last two years 300 [African American] patients died which should not have died; which would have lived and been mentally restored could they have been on wards such as will be provided for them at the new hospital.") For general discussion of the treatment of mentally ill Blacks in the South during the period, see Charles E. Magnum Jr., *The Legal Status of the Negro* (Chapel Hill:

Univ. of North Carolina Press, 1940), 220–26; and E. Franklin Frazier, *The Negro in the United States,* rev. ed. (New York: Macmillan, 1953), 654–62.

24. See "Louisiana," *Mental Hygiene* 21 (1937), 510.

25. *Fla. House Journal* (1933 Reg. Sess.), 37 and 267; and *Fla. Senate Journal* (1935 Reg. Sess.), 52, 181, and 390. For the support of state mental health officials, see, e.g., Florida Farm Colony for Epileptics and Feeble-Minded, *Eighth Biennial Report* ([Gainesville, Fla.]: n.p., 1935), 7; idem, *Ninth Biennial Report* ([Gainesville, Fla.]: n.p., 1937), 13; idem, *Tenth Biennial Report* ([Gainesville, Fla.]: n.p., 1939), 12; and idem, *Eleventh Biennial Report* ([Gainesville, Fla.]: n.p., 1941), 8.

26. *Fla. Senate Journal* (1935 Reg. Sess.), 390, source of the quotations in the text; O. S. Wodrich, "Bill Providing Appropriation for Schools Passed," *Florida Times-Union* (Jacksonville), May 4, 1935, p. 12, col. 1; and "Sterilization Bill Is Killed in Senate," *Tampa Morning Tribune,* May 4, 1935, p. 4, col. 2.

27. Compare Florida Federation of Women's Clubs, *Yearbook, 1932–1934* ([Lakeland, Fla.]: n.p., 1932), 260, with "Resolution," *Florida Club Woman* 15 (Dec. 1935), 7.

28. T. Z. Cason, "What We Inherit," *Journal of the Florida Medical Association* 20 (1934), 312, a reprint of an Apr. 2, 1933, radio broadcast (emphasis in original).

29. B. O. Whitten, "Sterilization versus Propagation," *Journal of SCMA* 18 (1922), 167–68.

30. C. F. Williams to H. E. Bailey, July 23, 1926, in Sterilization File, Department of Education and Training, South Carolina State Hospital, Columbia, S.C. This file also contains correspondence with national organizations, including the National Committee for Mental Hygiene and the Eugenics Record Office, relating to Williams's investigation.

31. See, e.g., C. F. Williams, "Mental Hygiene as a Public Health Problem," *Journal of SCMA* 19 (1923), 486–87; idem, "Presidential Address," in South Carolina State Hospital, *117th Annual Report* (Columbia, S.C.: Joint Committee on Printing, 1935), 13; and C. F. Williams to Robert E. Seibels, Sept. 11, 1944, in AVS Collection. (In the last-named document, he reported that no sterilizations were performed during the preceding two years, and added the comment, "I am firmly of the opinion that it is no panacea for mental disorders and delinquency.")

32. C. F. Williams to F. N. Andrews, June 15, 1934, in Sterilization File. In this letter and others written to other physicians about the same time, Williams waffled on the issue of sterilization for the mentally retarded, and occasionally referred the correspondents to Whitten. See C. F. Williams to Albert H. Hoge, June 18, 1934, in Sterilization File; and C. F. Williams to Charles J. Lemmon, Jan. 24, 1935, in Sterilization File.

33. See, e.g., B. O. Whitten, "The General Practitioner's Privileges and Responsibilities in Mental Hygiene," *Journal of SCMA* 17 (1922), 309, which notes

constitutional concerns; and idem, in "Discussion," ibid., 26 (1932), 257, where Whitten alludes to Williams's position.

34. B. O. Whitten, "Selective Sterilization," *Journal of SCMA* 26 (1931), 256–59. The institutional name "State Training School," used in this quotation, was then the institution's full, legal name; the words "for the Feeble-minded" had been deleted from the name in 1923.

35. F. M. Routh, in "Discussion," *Journal of SCMA* 26 (1931), 259.

36. B. O. Whitten, in "Discussion," *Journal of SCMA* 26 (1931), 259. A copy of this legislation is attached to a letter sent by the head of the sociology department at the University of South Carolina to a state legislator, endorsing it. (G. Croft Williams to W. M. Manning, Dec. 18, 1931, in Sterilization File.) The legislator, a relative of both C. F. Williams and former governor Richard Manning, forwarded the correspondence on to C. F. Williams with a cover note asking, "What do you think of this?" Williams's written response avoided taking any position of the issue. W. M. Manning to "Fred," Dec. 19, 1931, in Sterilization File; and C. F. Williams to W. M. Manning, Dec. 22, 1931, in Sterilization File.

37. 1933 S.C. Senate Bill 161, sec. 1, in South Carolina State Archives, Columbia, S.C.

38. B. O. Whitten, in "Discussion," *Journal of Psycho-Asthenics* 40 (1935), 68.

39. B. O. Whitten, in "Discussion," *Journal of Psycho-Asthenics* 39 (1934), 201.

40. *S.C. Senate Journal* (1933 Reg. Sess.), 369 and 491. Whitten testified in support of the bill before at least one legislative committee, and tried to get Williams to join him. B. O. Whitten to C. F. Williams, Mar. 7, 1933, in Sterilization File.

41. "Senate Ready to Take Up Question of Beer Tonight," *Charleston Evening Post,* Apr. 11, 1933, p. 1, col. 1.

42. Wm. R. Bradford, "Editorials," *Fort Mills Times,* May 2, 1933, p. 2, col. 1.

43. Wm. R. Bradford, "Editorials," *Fort Mills Times,* Feb. 28, 1933, p. 2, col. 1.

44. *S.C. House Journal* (1933 Reg. Sess.), 1370–77; and Whitten, in "Discussion" (1934), 202. Williams played an ambiguous role in this debate by reluctantly conceding that eugenic sterilization might be appropriate in certain selected cases of mental retardation, but denying that it had any place in his own field, psychiatry. See C. F. Williams to Albert H. Hoge, June 18, 1934, in Sterilization File. When a frustrated proponent challenged Williams, "Will you tell me under what conditions you believe in sterilization?" Williams refused to answer. Mary E. Frayser to Fred Williams, Apr. 13, 1933, in Sterilization File; and C. F. Williams to Mary E. Frayser, Apr. 14, 1937, in Sterilization File.

45. "Sterilization Bill Offered by Nash," *Sumner Herald,* Mar. 15, 1934, p. 5, col. 4; "Sterilization Bill Is Passed," *Charleston Evening Post,* Mar. 21, 1934, p. 1, col. 7; and *S.C. Senate Journal* (1934 Reg. Sess.), 587, 630, and 698.

46. Whitten, in "Discussion" (1934), 201; "Women Are in Favor of Sterilization [of] Habitual Criminals," *State* (Columbia), Jan. 5, 1934, p. 7, col. 6; and *S.C. House Journal* (1934 Reg. Sess.), 1544.

47. B. O. Whitten, "Sterilization," *Journal of Psycho-Asthenics* 40 (1935), 62–64. The unidentified "men of ability and eminence" presumably included Bradford and Williams.

48. *S.C. House Journal* (1935 Reg. Sess.), 374.

49. "Minutes of House of Delegates," *Journal of SCMA* 29 (1935), 121–22; "Economy Urged by Clubwoman," *State* (Columbia), Apr. 11, 1925, p. 13, col. 8; and Whitten, "Discussion" (1934), 202.

50. The summary of South Carolina House action that appears in this paragraph and the next three, including all the quotations therein, was compiled from "Sterilization Bill Advanced to Third Reading," *Charleston Evening Post,* May 1, 1935, p. 1, col. 6; "House Approves of Sterilization," *State* (Columbia), May 2, 1935, p. 2, col. 1; "Sterilization Bill Advanced by S.C. House," *Greenville News,* May 2, 1935, p. 1, col. 2; *S.C. House Journal* (1935 Reg. Sess.), 1797–98 and 1827; and Whitten, "Sterilization," 62–64 and 68. Supplying case histories to Blackburn is discussed in C. F. Williams to B. G. Blackburn, Mar. 19, 1935, in Sterilization File. (The letter includes a case history complete with patients' names.)

51. *S.C. Senate Journal* (1935 Reg. Sess.), 1006; "Governor Asks Liquor Report Wait Few Days," *Columbia Record,* May 3, 1935, p. 2, col. 5; and "Legislature," *Greenville News,* May 3, 1935, p. 6, col. 4.

52. This summary of South Carolina Senate action, including all the quotations therein, was compiled from "Conferees at Work Today on Two Measures," *Charleston Evening Post,* May 7, 1935, p. 1, col. 6; "Jam May Block Adjournment of State Assembly," *Columbia Record,* May 10, 1935, p. 1, col. 5; "Sterilization Bill Approved in Legislature," ibid., May 10, 1935, p. 20, col. 3; "Sterilization Bill Is Passed by Legislature," *Charleston Evening Post,* May 10, 1935, p. 1, col. 3; "House Looks to Adjournment," *State* (Columbia), May 11, 1935, p. 11, col. 2; "Senate Proposes Teacher Raise on Borrowed Money," *Charleston News and Courier,* May 11, 1935, p. 2, col. 5; "Senate Moves to Speed End of Long Session," *Greenville News,* May 11, 1935, p. 10, col.7; "Senate Approves of Sterilization," *State* (Columbia), May 11, 1935, p. 6, col. 3; "Sterilization Bill Is Passed," *Greenville News,* May 11, 1935, p. 1, col. 1; "Sterilization Bill Is Passed," *Charleston News and Courier,* May 11, 1935, p. 1, col. 1; and *S.C. Senate Journal* (1933 Reg. Sess.), 1214.

53. "Legislature Quits Sine Die," Associated Press wire service article, *Charleston News and Courier,* May 19, 1935, p. 1, col. 8.

54. Benjamin O. Whitten, "Address of the President," *Journal of Psycho-Asthenics* 42 (1937), 42.

55. C. F. Williams to E. A. Hines, May 9, 1938, in Sterilization File. In this letter, and in other letters in the same file responding to physicians who favored eugenics, Williams tactfully affirmed his acceptance of "selective sterilization," but then minimized its role in combating mental illness without ever mentioning the deep religious convictions that probably underlay his position on the issue.

56. Composite figures for South Carolina are in Robitscher, ed., *Eugenic Sterilization,* 119, which relied on sterilization figures compiled by the Human Betterment Foundation and Birthright, for which the more detailed underlying data from each state (in the form of annual questionnaires collected from each state institution authorized to perform eugenic sterilizations) are preserved in the AVS Collection. Sterilization figures for the State Training School are in that institution's annual reports. See, e.g., State Training School [South Carolina], *Annual Report* [1940-41] (Columbia, S.C.: Joint Committee on Printing, 1941), 25, which lists fifteen sterilizations of females and none of males. The single sterilization among Williams's charges is discussed in C. F. Williams to J. A. Haynes, Apr. 30, 1938, in Sterilization File. (The letter describes the patient as "an idiotic Negro girl.") Williams apparently conceded a larger place for sterilization in preventing mental retardation than in preventing mental illness. See C. F. Williams to F. N. Andrews, June 15, 1934, in Sterilization File. He also approved at least one therapeutic sterilization in a case in which the patient's life would have been endangered by pregnancy. C. F. Williams, "Supplementary Data: Mrs. ———, White Female," [1942], in Sterilization File. Williams explained the technical glitch in the law in C. F. Williams to B. O. Whitten, July 15, 1937, in Sterilization File. Whitten discussed the delayed implementation of the law and therapeutic sterilizations in B. O. Whitten to [Human Betterment Foundation], Jan. 4, 1937, in AVS Collection; and B. O. Whitten, "Sterilizations Performed in State Institutions, Clinton, South Carolina, for the Year Ending December 31, 1937," in AVS Collection (annual sterilization questionnaire reply form returned from South Carolina).

57. For the theory, see, e.g., Whitten, "Selective Sterilization," 55-59. For the practice, see Whitten's response to a questionnaire from a national eugenics organization on institutional sterilization practices for patients discharged in 1949. Whitten reported that only four out of sixty such patients were sterilized, and gave various reasons for not sterilizing the others. B. O. Whitten, sterilization report, May 4, 1950, in AVS Collection.

58. Whitten, "Sterilization," 63.

59. B. O. Whitten, "Superintendent's Report," in South Carolina Industrial School for Girls, *Annual Report* [1933-34] (Columbia, S.C.: Joint Committee on Printing, 1935), 28-29. (Whitten supervised this institution for a period in addition to filling his role at the State Training School.)

60. Bleeker Van Wagenen, "Preliminary Report of the Committee of the Eugenic *[sic]* Section," in *Problems in Eugenics: First International Eugenics Congress* (London: Knight, 1912), 477.

61. J. W. Mobley, in "Discussion on Dr. Swint's Paper," *Journal of MAG* 3 (1913), 149; W. L. Champion, "Sterilization of Confirmed Criminals, Idiots, Rapists, Feeble-Minded, and Other Defectives," ibid., 3 (1913), 113; Peter G. Crawford, *But for the Grace of God: The Inside Story of the World's Largest Insane Asylum, Milledgeville!* (Augusta, Ga.: Great Pyramid, 1981), 78.

62. See, e.g., Mrs. B. M. Boylein, "Committee on Care of Feeble-Minded," in

Georgia Federation of Women's Clubs, *Yearbook, 1920–21* (Greenville, Ga.: Gresham, 1920), 144; and Mrs. W. C. Kellogg, "Gracewood School for Defective Children," idem, *Yearbook, 1931–32* (Greenville, Ga.: Gresham, 1931), 199.

63. See, e.g., Department of Public Welfare [Georgia], *Reports for Years 1932, 1933, 1934 and 1935* (Atlanta, Ga.: n.p., 1935), 34, which presents the position of state mental health officials; and Mrs. Hamilton McWhorter, "Legislation," in Georgia Federation of Women's Clubs, *Yearbook, 1933–34* (Greenville, Ga.: Gresham, 1933), 207.

64. "Suggested Projects for Georgia Clubs," in Georgia Federation of Women's Clubs, *Yearbook, 1934–35* (Greenville, Ga.: Gresham, 1934), 33.

65. The MAG's ongoing lobbying activities are reported in its journal. On this issue, see, e.g., Committee on Public Policy and Legislation, "Legislative Program," *Journal of MAG* 21 (1932), 335; and "Report of Committee on Public Policy and Legislation," ibid., 22 (1933), 248. Basic scientific support for eugenics is suggested in Tremble Johnson, "Review of *Principles of Genetics and Eugenics*, by Nathan Fasten," ibid., 24 (1935), 382–83.

66. W. L. Funkhouser, "Human Rubbish," *Journal of MAG* 26 (1937), 199.

67. Nora [Nixon] Parker, interview by author, Atlanta, Ga., Oct. 2 1990; Wallace North, interview by author, Augusta, Ga., June 14, 1989; Mrs. Joseph Bryan Cumming, interview by author, Augusta, Ga., June 12, 1989; Eleanor Hoernle, interviews by author, Atlanta, Ga., June 7, 1989, and June 15, 1989; and Gwinn H. Nixon, interview by author, Augusta, Ga., June 7, 1989. Both Hoernle and North used the quoted phrase about Sanger. Nora Nixon said of Sanger, "She did everything. She was a wonderful person." See also Eugene E. Murphey, "The Junior League," 1, in Eugene E. Murphey Papers, Manuscripts Collection, University of Georgia Libraries, Athens, Ga. The movement of these "wives of professionals" and "upper-class women's clubs" into the role of amateur organizers of a birth control clinic fit a national pattern described in Linda Gordon, *Woman's Body, Woman's Right: Birth Control in America*, rev. ed. (New York: Penguin, 1990), 251, 290, and 323; the quoted phrases in this note are from this book.

68. David M. Kennedy, *Birth Control in America: The Career of Margaret Sanger* (New Haven: Yale University Press, 1950), 114–17; Margaret Sanger, *An Autobiography* (New York: Norton, 1938), 374–75; Gordon, *Woman's Body*, 270–83 and 354; and Doone Williams and Greer Williams, *Every Child a Wanted Child: Clarence James Gamble, M.D., and His Work in the Birth Control Movement* (Boston: Harvard University Press, 1978), 178.

69. Edward J. Cashin, *The Story of Augusta* (Augusta, Ga.: Richmond County Board of Education, 1980), 251 and 259; Zell Bryant Miller, "The Administration of E. D. Rivers as Governor of Georgia" (M.A. thesis, Univ. of Georgia, 1958), 21.

70. Parker, interview; and Hoernle, interview.

71. Parker, interview; North, interview; and Hoernle, interview. For background on Kelly, see Cashin, *Story of Augusta*, 83–84; and B. Phinizy Spalding, *The His-*

tory of the Medical College of Georgia (Athens: University of Georgia Press, 1987), 164–72 and 180. Kelly later served as an officer of a national eugenics organization, the Human Betterment Federation. See Mrs. Lloyd A. Marousck to William S. Hall, in Sterilization File.

72. Spalding, *Medical College,* 113, 124, and 190; Cashin, *Story of Augusta,* 249; and Cumming, interview. Cumming called Murphey "the King of Augusta".

73. Murphey, "Junior League," 1; "Sterilization Bill," 1, in Murphey Papers; and "Re: Progress of Medicine," in Murphey Papers. Reflecting his progressivism, Murphey said, "I come before you as an avowed and ardent supporter of the new deal." "Re: Senator George," 1, in Murphey Papers.

74. North, interview; and Parker, interview; Wilma Dykeman, *Too Many People, Too Little Love: Edna Rankin McKinnon, Pioneer for Birth Control* (New York: Holt, 1974), 78–82. McKinnon's national status is discussed in Williams and Williams, *Every Child,* 114 and 283–84.

75. "Report of the Committee on Public Policy and Legislation," *Journal of MAG* 23 (1934), 304.

76. Talmadge's anti–New Deal stance is discussed in William Anderson, *Wild Man from Sugar Creek: The Political Career of Eugene Talmadge* (Baton Rouge: Louisiana State Univ. Press, 1975), 114–23; Numan V. Bartley, *The Creation of Modern Georgia* (Athens: Univ. of Georgia Press, 1983), 173–74; Sarah McCulloh Lemmon, "The Public Career of Eugene Talmadge, 1926–1936" (Ph.D. diss., Univ. of North Carolina, 1952), 211–12; and Miller, "Administration of Rivers," 11–14. The quotation is from *Ga. Senate Journal* (1935 Reg. Sess.), 1964.

77. Anderson, *Wild Man,* 120.

78. Ibid., 115–16.

79. Bartley, *Modern Georgia,* 185.

80. Arnall's law partner and fellow representative from Newnan, Ga., Stonewall Dyer, co-sponsored the bill. *Ga. House Journal* (1935 Reg. Sess.), 1838. Arnall knew Nixon's father and welcomed the opportunity to sponsor an attention-grabbing progressive measure as a way to advance his own political career. Ellis Arnall, interview by author, Atlanta, Ga., July 25, 1989.

81. 1935 Ga. House Bill 204, secs. 1–3, in Georgia Department of Archives and History, Atlanta, Ga.

82. *Ga. House Journal* (1935 Reg. Sess.), 1840–41.

83. "Sterilization Bill Passes the House," *Augusta Chronicle,* Mar. 9, 1935, p. 4, col. 1. The California law, which covered only repeat criminal offenders and persons to be released from state mental health institutions, and contained no formal legal appeal process, is reprinted in Harry Hamilton Laughlin, *Eugenical Sterilization in the United States* (Chicago: Municipal Court, 1922), 18–19.

84. Anderson, *Wild Man,* 119–120; Lemmon, "Career of Talmadge," 211–12; and Thomas Elkin Taylor, "A Political Biography of Ellis Arnall" (M.A. thesis, Emory Univ., 1959), 24–28.

85. *Ga. House Journal* (1935 Reg. Sess.), 1845; "House Votes Sterilization," *Atlanta Georgian*, Mar. 7, 1935, p. 2, col. 4, the source of the quotation in the text; "Sterilization Act Enacted by House," *Constitution* (Atlanta), Mar. 8, 1935, p. 1, col. 8; and "Sterilization Bill Vetoed," *Atlanta Georgian*, Mar. 27, 1935, p. 3, col. 2.

86. "Sterilization Bill Passes House," *Augusta Chronicle*, Mar. 9, 1935, p. 4, col 1.

87. *Ga. Senate Journal* (1935 Reg. Sess.), 1653; *Ga. House Journal* (1935 Reg. Sess.), 2675; "Sterilization Bill Passed by Senate," *Constitution* (Atlanta), Mar. 20, 1935, p. 1, col. 6, and p. 7, cols. 6–8, the source of the quotation in the text; "Sterilization Bill Is Passed by Senate," *Columbus Enquirer*, Mar. 20, 1935, p. 4, col. 4; and "Sterilization Measure in Amended Form Is Passed by Senate," *Atlanta Journal*, Mar. 20, 1935, p. 12, col. 4.

88. "Sterilization Bill Passes the Senate," *Augusta Chronicle*, Mar. 21, 1935, p. 4, cols. 1–2.

89. "Talmadge Vetoes Bill to Sterilize Criminals, Insane," *Constitution* (Atlanta), Mar. 27, 1935, p. 1, col. 6.

90. The vetoes are discussed in "Talmadge Vetoes 163 Measures and Okays Four Hundred Bills," *Times Journal* (Eastman, Ga.), Apr. 4, 1935, p. 1, col. 2; Anderson, *Wild Man*, 119–23 and 141–50, Talmadge quotation on 119; Lemmon, "Career of Talmadge," 211–12; and Miller, "Administration of Rivers," 14–16.

91. "The Governor's Veto of the Sterilization Bill," *Augusta Chronicle*, Mar. 27, 1935, p. 4, col. 1.

92. "Governor is Wrong," *Columbus Enquirer*, Mar. 28, 1935, p. 6, cols. 2–3.

93. Richard Reid, "Mr. Reid on Sterilization," *Augusta Chronicle*, Mar. 27, 1935, p. 4, col. 4. The Roman Catholic position on this issue in the 1930s was discussed in John T. Noonan Jr., *Contraception: A History of Its Treatment by the Catholic Theologians and Canonists* (Cambridge: Harvard University Press, 1965), 424–31.

94. E. D. Rivers, quoted in Miller, "Administration of Rivers," 32.

95. Bartley, *Modern Georgia*, 176. For a summary of 1937 "Little New Deal" legislation, see " 'New Deal' Measures Presented to Assembly," *Macon Telegraph*, Jan. 14, 1937, p. 1, col. 8; and Miller, "Administration of Rivers," 34–59.

96. "Solons Gather to Study Hospital Needs," *Augusta Chronicle*, Jan. 5, 1937, p. 1, col. 5; "State Hospital in Need of Aid, Rivers Asserts," ibid., Jan. 9, 1937, p. 1, col. 5, the source of the quotation in the text.

97. "Legislative Committee Makes Study Conditions State Hospital," *Milledgeville Union-Recorder*, Jan. 21, 1937, p. 1, col. 6.

98. E. D. Rivers, *Final Message to the General Assembly of Georgia* (Atlanta: State of Georgia, 1941), 27–31, quotation on 28. See also Miller, "Administration of Rivers," 162; Crawford, *Grace of God*, 84.

99. "Rivers Starts 'New Deal' Plan through Assembly," *Augusta Chronicle,* Jan. 14, 1937, p. 1, col. 8; "'New Deal' Measures Presented to Assembly," *Macon Telegraph,* Jan. 14, 1937, p. 1, col. 8; and "The Sterilization Bill," *Augusta Chronicle,* Jan. 15, 1937, p. 4, col. 1. Harris co-sponsored the sterilization bill with other members of the House delegation from Augusta.

100. "Program, 1937," *FACTS* (Atlanta League of Women Voters), 10 (Feb. 1937), 20; "State-Wide Bills," ibid., 10 (Mar. 1937), 12; and "Atlanta League Health Plan," ibid., 10 (May 1937), 9. The quotation in the text appeared in all three sources.

101. *Ga. House Journal* (1937 Reg. Sess.), 1278–84; "Vote Sterilization of State's Insane," *Savannah Evening Press,* Feb. 9, 1937, p. 1, col. 4, the source of the quotations in the text; "Attack on Harrison's Record Stirs Senate," *Atlanta Journal,* Feb. 9, 1937, p. 2, col. 2; "House Votes Sterilization," *Columbus Enquirer,* Feb. 10, 1937, p. 1, col. 1; and "House Approves Sterilization Bill," *Constitution* (Atlanta), Feb. 10, 1937, p. 11, col. 6.

102. "By Other Editors: The Sterilization Bill," *Savannah Morning News,* Feb. 17, 1937, p. 6, col. 3.

103. "Sterilization Bill Passed," *Atlanta Georgian,* Feb. 19, 1937, p. 1, col. 8; and "Sterilization of Mentally Unfit Is Voted by Senate," *Savannah Evening Press,* Feb. 19, 1937, p. 1, col. 4.

104. "Sterilization Progress," *Constitution* (Atlanta), Feb. 23, 1937, p. 4, cols. 1–2.

105. "The Sterilization Bill," *Columbus Enquirer,* Feb. 20, 1937, p. 6, col. 2.

106. "Sterilization Bill Accorded Governor's OK," *Atlanta Journal,* Feb. 24, 1937, p. 1, col. 8.

107. See, e.g., "The Sterilization Bill," *Augusta Chronicle,* Jan. 15, 1937, p. 4, col. 1.

108. "To All Members of the General Assembly of Georgia," *Journal of MAG* 26 (1937), suppl. 1; and "To All Members of the Medical Association of Georgia," ibid., 26 (1937), suppl. 2.

109. Avary M. Dimmock, "Human Sterilization," *Journal of MAG* 26 (1937), 425.

110. Hoernle, interview; and Parker, interview. Nixon, whose reform-minded husband often clashed with Harris before that opportunistic legislator began supporting progressive reforms during the late 1930s, commented that Harris "appeared to be all for [the sterilization bill] but really was not."

111. These national trends are discussed in Kevles, *Name of Eugenics,* 164–75. Arnall later maintained that he always viewed the sterilization bill as a progressive reform. Arnall, interview.

112. "The Governor's Veto of the Sterilization Bill," *Augusta Chronicle,* Mar. 27, 1935, p. 4, col. 1.

113. E.g., see Ellis Gibbs Arnall, *The Shore Dimly Seen* (Philadelphia: Lippin-

cott, 1946), 83–106; Bartley, *Modern Georgia,* 187; and Arnall, interview, which is the source of the quotations in the text. Later, in Alabama, Charles Zukoski also actively supported both eugenic sterilization and civil rights. Charles Frederick Zukoski Jr., "A Life Story" [1980], 144–90. (This document is a manuscript autobiography in the custody of Charles F. Zukoski, Birmingham, Ala.)

114. See, e.g., Bartley, *Modern Georgia,* 174 and 187–88; and Anderson, *Wild Man,* 205–14. Whereas Arnall portrayed himself as a pro-change progressive, he characterized Talmadge as a conservative populist who always opposed change. Arnall, interview.

115. Robitscher, ed., *Eugenic Sterilization,* 118–19.

116. Established scholarship posits that American geneticists gradually rejected eugenics during the 1920s and 1930s, with Daniel J. Kevles identifying a 1936 American Neurological Association report as a major event in this process, and Kenneth M. Ludmerer attributing a similar role to pronouncements from the 1939 International Genetics Congress. Kevles, *Name of Eugenics,* 166–67; Kenneth M. Ludmerer, *Genetics and American Society: A Historical Appraisal* (Baltimore: Johns Hopkins Univ. Press, 1972), 121–29; and Mark H. Haller, *Eugenics: Hereditarian Attitudes in American Thought* (New Brunswick: Rutgers Univ. Press, 1963), 179–83. This view suggests that the change in American scientific opinion on eugenics was not yet complete when Georgia enacted its sterilization law. Later scholarship reports that there was ongoing support among American geneticists for H. H. Goddard's eugenic theories of mental retardation throughout the 1930s. David Barker, "The Biology of Stupidity: Genetics, Eugenics, and Mental Deficiency in the Inter-War Years," *British Journal of the History of Science* 22 (1989), 266–68. The Medical Association of Georgia's journal did not report the mounting scientific challenge to eugenics during the 1930s, and favorably reviewed a 1935 eugenics textbook in Johnson, "Review," 183. The textbook endorsed compulsory sterilization of the feeble-minded and stated, "Geneticists . . . believe that nothing but good can come from efforts in the direction of the rapid elimination of this branch of society." Nathan Fasten, *Principles of Genetics and Eugenics* (Boston: Ginn, 1935), 345–55, quotation on 355.

117. Ala. Code (1923), sec. 1476. Partlow discussed his sterilization policy in W. D. Partlow to E. S. Gosney, Jan. 9, 1938, in AVS Collection.

118. William D. Partlow, "Pathology of Mental Rehabilitation or Mental Conservation vs. Mental Rehabilitation," *Transactions of MASA* (1928), 324. For a particularly revealing expression of Partlow's social philosophy, see idem, "The Relation of the Problem of Mental Disease and Mental Deficiency to Society," *Southern Medical Journal* 26 (1933), 1066–68.

119. J.D.S. Davis, "The President's Message," *Transactions of MASA* (1928), 20.

120. See, e.g., W. D. Partlow, "The Relation of the Problems of Mental Disease and Mental Deficiency to Society," *Southern Medical Journal* 26 (1933), 1066–68; and "Social Workers Elect Officers," *Birmingham Age-Herald,* Apr. 17, 1935, p. 3, col. 1.

121. W. D. Partlow, "Superintendent's Report," in Alabama Insane Hospitals, *Report of Trustees* [1934] ([Tuscaloosa]: n.p., 1934), 85.

122. See Thomas McAdory Owen, *History of Alabama and Dictionary of Alabama Biography* (Spartanburg, S.C.: Reprint, 1978), 4:1324; *Who Was Who in America* (Chicago: Marquis Who's Who, 1973), 5:556.

123. See W. D. Partlow to E. S. Gosney, Mar. 26, 1934, in AVS Collection. (This letter adds "epileptics" to the list quoted above.)

124. See generally Landman, *Human Sterilization*. (Landman compiled and analyzed the sterilization statutes of every state.)

125. J. N. Baker, quoted in "Sterilization in Alabama," *Montgomery Advertiser,* Feb. 6, 1935, p. 4, col. 3. Partlow claimed credit for drafting the legislation in W. D. Partlow to E. S. Gosney, Jan. 10, 1935, in AVS Collection; and W. D. Partlow to Marian S. Norton Olden, May 11, 1944, in AVS Collection.

126. See J. N. Baker, "Medical and Health Legislation in 1935," *Journal of MASA* 5 (1935), 157–58; "Report of the Committee on Mental Hygiene," ibid., 5 (1935), 27; "Sterilization Progresses," *Montgomery Advertiser,* May 11, 1935, p. 4, col. 1; William L. Truby, "Today in Both Houses of the Alabama Legislature," *Decatur Daily,* Sept. 4, 1935, p. 2, col. 4; and "History of the Alabama Division of the American Association of University Women, 1927–1946," in "A.A.U.W., Montgomery Branch Scrapbook, 1941–42," in Manuscripts Division, Alabama State Archives, Montgomery, Ala.

127. *Ala. House Journal* (1935 Reg. Sess.), 143.

128. 1935 Ala. House Bill 87, secs. 1–6, in Alabama State Archives.

129. Hugh Sparrow, "Sterilization Bill for State Up to Governor," *Birmingham Age-Herald,* June 1, 1935, p. 1, col. 3.

130. "Foes 'Run Out' on Measure to Cut Phone Tax," *Montgomery Advertiser,* Sept. 5, 1935, p. 7, col. 3; Frank Gordy, "House Spotlight Is Taken by Sterilization Measure Passed by Large Majority," *Mobile Register,* May 11, 1935, p. 1, col. 3; "Sterilization Bill Passes Senate; Up to Governor," *Montgomery Advertiser,* June 1, 1935, p. 1, col. 5, and p. 3, col. 1; "Sterilization in Alabama," p. 4, col. 3; "Sterilization Progresses," p. 4, col. 1; and William I. Truby, "House Passes Sterilization Bill," *Decatur Daily,* May 10, 1935, p. 1, col. 8.

131. "Thoughts on Sterilization," *Montgomery Advertiser,* June 5, 1935, p. 4, col. 2.

132. "Biologist Sees Control of Human Defectives Only Solution of Race," *Montgomery Advertiser,* June 30, 1935, p. 5, cols. 1–2.

133. *Birmingham News,* quoted in "Thoughts on Sterilization," p. 4, col. 2.

134. "The House Passes the Sterilization Bill," *Birmingham News,* May 11, 1935, p. 4, col. 1. The *Montgomery Advertiser* made an almost identical comment in "Sterilization Progresses," p. 4., col. 1.

135. "Some Aspects of the Sterilization Fight," *Catholic Week* (Birmingham), May 26, 1935, p. 4, col. 2 (citing the *Labor News* of Birmingham). No copies of

any May 1935 issues of this union newspaper survive in any Alabama public library or archives.

136. Lucille Milner to Bibb Graves, June 4, 1935, in Papers of Gov. Bibb Graves (Second Administration), Alabama State Archives.

137. "The Sterilization Bill," *Alabama Baptist,* July 4, 1935, p. 3, col. 7.

138. Hugh DuBose to Bibb Graves, June 3, 1935, in Graves Papers (Second Administration).

139. "Some Aspects," p. 4, col. 2.

140. Ralph Hurst, "$2000 Tax-Free Homesteads Is Urged in House," *Birmingham News,* May 10, 1935, p. 1, col. 6; "Mobilians Join in State Protest on Dominick Bill," *Mobile Press,* May 16, 1935, in William F. Obering File, Spring Hill College Library, Mobile, Ala.; "Solons Hear Opposition to Sterilization," *Catholic Week* (Birmingham), May 19, 1935, p. 1, col. 4; "Sterilization Bill Is Said to Be Illegal," ibid., Sept. 1, 1935, p. 1, col. 6; and A. L. Stabler to Bibb Graves, June 26, 1935, in Graves Papers (Second Administration). (Stabler was a Roman Catholic physician who denounced eugenics as pseudo-scientific.)

141. E.g., William F. Obering, "Authority Says Alabama Sterilization Measure Is Declaration of Slavery," *Catholic Week* (Birmingham), May 5, 1935, p. 1, cols. 4–5, p. 6, cols. 4–5, and p. 7, cols. 2–3; "Social Workers Elect Officers," p. 1, col. 5, the source of the quotation in the text; "Father Obering Attacks Alabama Sterilization Law in Birmingham," *Springhillian,* Apr. 29, 1935, p. 1, col. 4. Obering's natural-law arguments rested largely on the jurisprudence of the Federalist Era U.S. Supreme Court justice James Wilson, about whom Obering was then writing a book. See William F. Obering, *The Philosophy of Law of James Wilson: A Study in Comparative Jurisprudence* (Washington: Catholic Univ. of America, [1926]).

142. Hurst, "$2000 Tax-Free," p. 1, col. 6. The quotation is from the resolution.

143. Gordy, "House Spotlight," p. 1, col. 3; Frank Gordy, "Sterilization Bill Passes, Awaits Governor's Action; Rogers Leads in Opposition," *Mobile Register,* June 1, 1935, p. 1, col. 3; Sparrow, "Sterilization Bill," p. 1, col. 3; Truby, "House Passes," p. 1, col. 8; and William I. Truby, "Sedition Bill Veto Is Under Fire," *Decatur Daily,* Aug. 6, 1935, p. 1, col. 8.

144. "Sterilization Bill Passes Senate," p. 1, col. 5, and p. 3, col. 1.

145. "Sterilization Bill," p. 3, col. 3, from a Southern Baptist newspaper; "That Serialization Bill," *Alabama Christian Advocate,* May 23, 1935, p. 3, col. 2, from a Methodist newspaper; and "Totalitarianism," ibid., Aug. 1, 1935, p. 2, col. 3.

146. "Sterilization Bill Passes Senate," p. 1, col. 5, and p. 3, col. 1. See also Gordy, "Sterilization Bill," p. 1, col. 3.

147. See, e.g., Obering, "Authority," p. 6, cols. 4–5, and p. 7, cols. 2–3, quotation on p. 7, col. 2; "Solons Hear Opposition," p. 2, col. 4; and W. B. Palmer,

"Objecting to Sterilization Bill," letter to editor, *Montgomery Advertiser,* May 15, 1935, p. 4, cols. 5–6. The shift in scientific opinion on eugenics is discussed in Haller, *Eugenics,* 179–83; Kevles, *Name of Eugenics,* 166–67; and Ludmerer, *Genetics,* 121–29.

148. The House passed the bill by a vote of sixty-nine to sixteen. *Ala. House Journal* (1935 Reg. Sess.), 640. The vote in the Senate was seventeen to nine. *Ala. Senate Journal* (1935 Reg. Sess.), 622–23.

149. "'Sterilization' Bill Gets Veto of Governor Graves," *Mobile Register,* June 26, 1935, p. 1, col. 3; and "Sterilization Bill Killed by Veto," *Montgomery Advertiser,* June 26, 1935, p. 1, col. 5.

150. "Dominick's Bill Vetoed by Graves," *Mobile Press,* June 25, 1935, p. 1, col. 8.

151. William D. Barnard, *Dixiecrats and Democrats: Alabama Politics, 1942–1950* (Tuscaloosa: Univ. of Alabama Press, 1974), 17; and John Craig Stewart, *The Governors of Alabama* (Gretna, La.: Pelican, 1975), 174–81, quotation on 176.

152. *In re Opinion of the Justices,* 230 Ala. 543, 547, 162 So. 123, 128 (1935).

153. See Graves's veto message, in *Ala. House Journal* (1935 Reg. Sess.), 1343; "Dominick's Bill Vetoed," p. 1, col. 8; "'Sterilization' Bill Gets Veto," p. 1, col. 3; and J. L. Busby to Hugh B. DuBose, June 1, 1935, in Graves Papers (Second Administration).

154. "'Sterilization' Bill Gets Veto," p. 1, col. 3; "Under the Capitol Dome," *Alabama Journal* (Montgomery), June 25, 1935, p. 6, col. 3.

155. W. D. Partlow to Bibb Graves, June 2, 1935, in Graves Papers (Second Administration).

156. Bibb Graves, veto message, in *Ala. House Journal* (1935 Reg. Sess.), 1342.

157. *Ala. House Journal* (1935 Reg. Sess.), 1313–14; see also "Senate Approves Decision to Boost Income Tax," *Decatur Daily,* June 26, 1935, p. 1, col. 2; Hugh Sparrow, "Poll Tax Bill Is Kept Alive," *Birmingham Age-Herald,* Aug. 7, 1935, p. 4, col. 2.

158. The House vote was seventy-four to twenty-one in favor of the sterilization bill. *Ala. House Journal* (1935 Reg. Sess.), 1994–97. The Senate approved the bill by a vote of twenty-one to eight. *Ala. Senate Journal* (1935 Reg. Sess.), 1725–26.

159. Bibb Graves, second veto message, in *Ala. House Journal* (1935 Reg. Sess.), 2753–54.

160. *Ala. House Journal* (1935 Reg. Sess.), 2754, reporting the House's vote to approve Dominick's motion to table the veto override; "Foes 'Run Out'," p. 7, col. 3; and Truby, "Today," p. 2, col. 3.

161. "Citizen of Mobile" to Bibb Graves, June 26, 1935, in Graves Papers (Second Administration). The letters received by Graves on this matter are preserved in Graves Papers (Second Administration).

162. W. D. Partlow, in "Discussion," *Transactions of MASA* (1910), 361.

163. W. D. Partlow to E. S. Gosney, Jan. 9, 1938, in AVS Collection. Later, Partlow privately suggested that "the Catholics . . . persuaded the Governor to veto the bill." W. D. Partlow to Marian S. Norton Olden, May 11, 1944, in AVS Collection.

164. Bibb Graves to Lucille Milner, Sept. 10, 1935, in Graves Papers (Second Administration).

165. W. D. Partlow, "Superintendent's Report," in Alabama Insane Hospitals, *Report of Trustees* [1935] ([Tuscaloosa, Ala.]: n.p., 1935), 89. See also W. D. Partlow to E. S. Gosney, Jan. 9, 1938, in AVS Collection.

166. *Ala. House Journal* (1939 Reg. Sess.), 1643; and ibid. (1943 Reg. Sess.), 197.

167. W. D. Partlow to Marian S. Olden, May 10, 1946, in AVS Collection.

168. A. J. Beverett to Bibb Graves, July 6, 1935, in Graves Papers (Second Administration).

Chapter 7: *Bitter Harvest*

1. A. J. Beverett to Bibb Graves, July 6, 1935, in Papers of Governor Bibb Graves (Second Administration), Alabama State Archives, Montgomery, Ala. See also W. D. Palmer, letter to editor, *Montgomery Advertiser*, May 15, 1935, p. 4, col. 5. (Palmer urged, "Let Germany and other fascist nations try their political experiments.")

2. William F. Obering, "Authority Says Alabama Sterilization Measure Is Declaration of Slavery," *Catholic Week* (Birmingham), May 5, 1935, p. 7, col. 2.

3. "Totalitarianism," *Alabama Christian Advocate*, Aug. 1, 1935, p. 2, col. 3.

4. J. N. Baker, in "Sterilization in Alabama," *Montgomery Advertiser*, Feb. 6, 1935, p. 4, col. 3.

5. For a discussion of the Nazi law, see Daniel J. Kevles, *In the Name of Eugenics: Genetics and the Uses of Human Heredity* (New York: Knopf, 1985), 116–18; and Philip R. Reilly, *The Surgical Solution: A History of Involuntary Sterilization in the United States* (Baltimore: Johns Hopkins Univ. Press, 1991), 105–10, quotation on 107.

6. "Eugenical Sterilization in Germany," *Eugenical News* 18 (1933), 89.

7. Marie E. Kopp, "Legal and Medical Aspects of Eugenic Sterilization in Germany," *American Sociological Review* 1 (1936), 763 and 770. The same year, a prominent Jewish American critic of compulsory sterilization reached similar conclusions on the nondiscriminatory nature of the German program. J. H. Landman, "Sterilization and Social Betterment," *Survey* 25 (1936), 162.

8. H. H. Laughlin, quoted in Kevles, *Name of Eugenics*, 118.

9. Avary M. Dimmock, "Human Sterilization," *Journal of MAG* 26 (1937), 424.

10. Frances Hassenchal, "Harry H. Laughlin, 'Expert Eugenics Agent' for the

House Committee on Immigration and Naturalization, 1921 to 1931" (Ph.D. diss., Case Western Reserve Univ., 1970); and Kevles, *Name of Eugenics,* 199.

11. Paul Popenoe, quoted in Donald K. Pickens, *Eugenics and the Progressives* (Nashville: Vanderbilt Univ. Press, 1968), 99 n.

12. "The Sterilization Bill," *Alabama Baptist,* July 4, 1935, p. 3, col. 3.

13. Donald W. Calhoun, "The Ethical Questions Involved in Eugenic Legislation" (Univ. of Georgia Hill Essay, 1940), 11, in Georgia Collection, Univ. of Georgia Libraries, Athens, Ga.

14. "Sterilization Progresses," *Constitution* (Atlanta), Feb. 23, 1937, p. 4, cols. 1–2; and "The Jews in Poland," ibid., Feb. 23, 1937, p. 4, col. 2.

15. E.g., "Germans Estimate 189,677 Sterilized under Nazi Decree," *Constitution* (Atlanta), Mar. 25, 1937, p. 4, col. 6.

16. See, e.g., Kevles, *Name of Eugenics,* 166–67; and Reilly, *Surgical Solution,* 122–24.

17. Abraham Myerson et al., *Eugenical Sterilization: A Reorientation to the Problem* (New York: Macmillan, 1936), 4 and 177–83. With respect to the inheritance of mental retardation, the committee concluded "that in a considerable segment of feeblemindedness, heredity plays a role of importance." Myerson, *Eugenical Sterilization,* 130.

18. Anthony J. Mitrano, "Sane and Critical," *Midmonthly Survey* 73 (1937), 124.

19. J. N. Baker, in "Book Abstracts and Reviews," *Journal of MASA* 7 (1937), 101–2.

20. W. D. Partlow, "A Debt the World Owes Medical Science," *Journal of MASA* 6 (1936), 12. The relationship between the movement for eugenic sterilization and the movement for legalized euthanasia in this period merits further study, as suggested by the willingness of the pro-sterilization organization Birthright to swap mailing lists with the Euthanasia Society of America. See Birthright, Inc., "Minutes of Meeting of Executive Committee," Nov. 23, 1943, in Association for Voluntary Sterilization Collection (hereafter, "AVS Collection), Social Welfare History Archives, University of Minnesota, Minneapolis, Minn.

21. W. D. Partlow, "Psychiatry Adrift with the Times," *Journal of MASA* 7 (1937), 210.

22. W. D. Partlow to Marian S. Olden, May 10, 1946, in AVS Collection; "Committee on Mental Hygiene," *Transactions of MASA* (1939), 9; and "Report of Board of Censors," ibid. (1939), 24. Partlow secured the introduction of eugenic sterilization legislation into the Alabama Senate during this period, in 1939 and 1943, but these bills met continued opposition from Roman Catholics and died in committee. See W. D. Partlow to Marion [sic] S. Norton Olden, May 11, 1944, in AVS Collection.

23. Reilly, *Surgical Solution,* 128–37. Reilly attributed the declining number of sterilizations to the lack of surgeons resulting from the war effort.

24. Doone Williams and Greer Williams, *Every Child a Wanted Child: Clarence James Gamble, M.D., and His Work in the Birth Control Movement* (Boston: Harvard Univ. Press, 1978), 125–35 and 175–88; Charles Frederick Zukoski Jr., "A Life Story" [1980], 129; and Becky Webster, "The Zukoski Planning Committee of Two," *Birmingham*, Nov. 1984, 74.

25. Clarence J. Gamble to R. C. Partlow, July 15, 1944, in R. C. Partlow, Partlow State School Scrapbook, in custody of Ilouise Partlow Hill, Montgomery, Ala. (Hereafter this collection is cited as "Partlow Scrapbook.")

26. Clarence J. Gamble to Sidney Smyer, March 21, 1945, in Partlow Scrapbook. The impact of Gamble's visit to Alabama was discussed in Birthright, Inc., "Minutes of Meeting of Directors," Dec. 13, 1944, in AVS Collection. Above the clipping of an article reporting the passage of this legislation by the Alabama Senate, Olden wrote, "Resulting from Dr. Gamble's Jan. visit and subsequent literature sent to the legislators and Women's Clubs." Birthright, Inc., clipping file, folder 93, in AVS Collection.

27. R. C. Partlow, "A Study of 838 Inmates of the Partlow State School," *Journal of MASA* 14 (1945), 391.

28. W. D. Partlow to Marion [sic] S. Norton Olden, May 11, 1944, in AVS Collection; and W. D. Partlow to J. Bruce Henderson, May 23, 1944, in AVS Collection.

29. W. D. Partlow to J. Bruce Henderson, May 23, 1944, in AVS Collection. According to Partlow's earlier letter to Olden, the Alabama Federation of Women's Clubs already was "very much interested" in the legislation. W. D. Partlow to Marion [sic] S. Norton Olden, May 11, 1944, in AVS Collection.

30. This analysis of supporters is compiled from "AAUP Legislative Report—1945," in "AAUP Montgomery Branch, Correspondence Committee Reports, etc., 1937–1954," in Manuscripts Division, Alabama State Archives; Ilouise Partlow Hill, interview by author, Montgomery, Ala., May 7, 1992; C. F. Zukoski Jr. to James A. Simpson, Apr. 30, 1945, in James A. Simpson Papers, Alabama State Archives; Marian S. Olden, "Present Status of Sterilization Legislation in the United States," *Eugenical News* 31 (1946), 9–10; "Senate Votes for Sterilization as Foe Raises Religious Issue," *Montgomery Advertiser*, June 1, 1945, p. 1, col. 3; "Sketches of Senators," in Alabama Department of Archives and History, *Alabama Official and Statistical Register* (Wetumpka, Ala.: Wetumpka Printing, 1943), 245; and "Sterilization Bill Killed," *Catholic Week* (Birmingham), June 15, 1945, p. 1, cols. 4–5, the source of the quotation in the text. With respect to his own religious beliefs, Charles Zukoski characterized himself as "basically a humanist seeing no controlling power in the universe which affects man either for good or bad." Zukoski, "Life Story," 507. The Zukoskis' long association with Gamble was discussed in Wilma Dykeman, *Too Many People, Too Little Love: Edna Rankin McKinnon, Pioneer for Birth Control* (New York: Holt, Rinehart, and Wilson, 1974), 72–82.

31. W. D. Partlow, "Extract from Letter to a State Senator in Alabama," attached to W. D. Partlow to Marian Olden, Jan. 10, 1946, in AVS Collection.

32. This summary of Roman Catholic opposition was compiled from "Let Us Fight Sterilization," *Catholic Week* (Birmingham), June 8, 1945, p. 1, cols. 4–5, and p. 6, cols. 4–5, the source of the quotations from the diocesan newspaper and the bishop; Olden, "Present Status," 9, the source of the quotation from Olden; "Sterilization," *Catholic Week* (Birmingham), May 18, 1945, p. 4, col. 1, the source of the quotation from the editorialist; and "Sterilization Bill Killed," p. 1, cols. 4–5.

33. This summary of Senate action was compiled from Partlow, "Extract from Letter"; Frank Gordy, "Kilborn Fight Fails to Stop Bill in Senate," *Mobile Register,* June 1, 1945, p. 1, col. 1, and p. 4, col. 4; Hugh W. Sparrow, "Sterilization Measure Is Passed by Senate; House Action Awaited," *Birmingham News,* June 1, 1945, p. 1, col. 7, and p. 10, col. 8; *Ala. Senate Journal* (1945 Reg. Sess.), 419–20 and 455–64; "Let Us Fight," p. 1, cols. 4–5; and "Senate Votes," p. 1, cols. 2–3, source of the quotation from Kilborn.

34. "Let Us Fight," p. 1, cols. 4–5, the source of the quotation in the text; Olden, "Present Status," 9–10; and "Sterilization Bill Killed," p. 1, cols. 4–5.

35. Josephine F. Eddy to W. D. Partlow, June 4, 1947, in Partlow Scrapbook, the source of the quotation in the text; and W. D. Partlow to Josephine F. Eddy, June 6, 1947, in Partlow Scrapbook.

36. F. O. Butler, "Report of Field Committee and Board of Directors," 1950, in AVS Collection; and Fred O. Butler to R. C. Partlow, Nov. 25, 1949, in Partlow Scrapbook. The medical director's visits to Alabama in 1949 were also discussed in [Birthright, Inc.], "Minutes of Annual Meeting, 1949," in AVS Collection; and idem, "Minutes of Board of Directors," Dec. 9, 1949, in AVS Collection.

37. *Ala. House Journal* (1951 Reg. Sess.), 170; and F. O. Butler, "Summary of Eight Months' Work," Dec. 1, 1950, in AVS Collection. A return visit by Birthright's medical director, during which he secured the renewed support of the Alabama Federation of Women's Clubs, helped spawn this bill. Mrs. E. S. Fuller, chair, Legislative Committee, Alabama Federation of Women's Clubs, interview by F. O. Butler, in "Interviews of Interest, Sept. 27—Dec. 15, 1949," in AVS Collection; and "Dr. Butler's Interviews," Spring 1950, in AVS Collection. (The latter reference notes a presentation to the Alabama Federation of Women's Clubs and a meeting with Bernadine Zukoski.) Birthright also provided technical assistance to the Alabama League for Human Betterment in drafting the legislation. Douglas Arant to League for Human Betterment, Nov. 6, 1950, in AVS Collection.

38. Reilly, *Surgical Solution,* 95 and 129.

39. T. Paul Haney, "Superintendent's Report," in Ellisville State School, *Thirteenth Biennial Report* (Jackson: Tucker, 1945), 15 and 18; idem, "Director's Report," in Ellisville State School, *Fourteenth Biennial Report* (Jackson: Tucker, 1947), 9, source of the quotation from Haney; and Reilly, *Surgical Solution,* 136. Detailed sterilization figures for the three institutions exist in both their annual reports and in responses to the annual sterilization surveys conducted by Birthright, now in the AVS Collection. The Mississippi attorney general's ruling

is mentioned in the responses from the Mississippi State Hospital for the years 1949, 1950, 1951, and 1953; the quotation is in the response for 1953.

40. H. L. Mencken, "Utopia by Sterilization," *American Mercury* 41 (1937), 405 and 407. Mencken had all but given up on his scheme by the time of Haney's comment, as suggested by a 1947 letter from Mencken to a leading national eugenics organization that expressed his appreciation at its use of his statements in a pro-sterilization pamphlet but added, "Unhappily, I am convinced that it is now too late to turn back the tide of imbecility. . . . Here in Baltimore the burden of incompetents rises sharply and steadily. They are now at least twice as numerous, relatively speaking, as they were even twenty years ago." H. L. Mencken to Mrs. Bass, Jan. 23, 1947, in AVS Collection.

41. Mencken, "Utopia," 399.

42. W. L. Funkhouser, "Human Rubbish," *Journal of MAG* 26 (1937), 197–98. Similarly, a prominent Louisiana eugenicist wrote of "the danger to white civilization of the unlimited propagation of the unfit." R. McG. Carruth, "Marriage Laws: Their Need, and the Cause and Cure of Their Weaknesses," *Southern Medical Journal* 19 (1926), 193.

43. Benjamin O. Whitten, "Address of the President," *Journal of Psycho-Asthenics* 42 (1937), 36–37.

44. "Feeble-Minded Will Have Home," *Constitution* (Atlanta), July 9, 1919, p. 5, col. 1.

45. Whitten, "Address," 36.

46. During a visit to the state in the late 1940s, Birthright's medical director concluded that the South Carolina sterilization law was "operable." Several state mental health officials told him that the law was not used because of "the lack of interest on the part of the various superintendents and their staffs." At the time, however, he found Whitten and the State Training School staff quite supportive of the law, which suggested that opposition centered at the mental health hospital, which Williams led until 1945 and where he continued to work until 1947. Butler, "Interviews," in AVS Collection; and "Digest of Dr. Butler's Report on Field Trips," in AVS Collection. In 1944, Williams reported to Birthright, "I am firmly of the opinion that [sterilization] is no panacea for mental disorder and delinquency." C. F. Williams to Robert E. Seibels, Sept. 11, 1944, in AVS Collection. Shortly after Williams's death in 1948, the hospital's superintendent wrote to Olden that he expected "less difficulty in securing the required permission" for sterilizations in the future. Coyt Ham to Marian S. Olden, Feb. 14, 1948, in Sterilization File, Department of Education and Training, South Carolina State Hospital, Columbia, S.C.

47. For annual figures, see Jonas Robitscher, ed., *Eugenic Sterilization* (Springfield, Ill.: Thomas, 1973), 118–19. The earlier period of sterilization in South Carolina is discussed above, in chapter 6. South Carolina officials attributed the mid-1940s lull in sterilization to the absence of medical personnel caused by World War II, and to procedural difficulties with the law. Olden, "Present Sta-

tus," 4; and Coyt Ham to Marian S. Olden, Feb. 14, 1948, in Sterilization File. They also initially attributed the decline in the number of operations during the early 1960s to "a shortage of physicians and other personnel in institutions where these operative procedures are authorized." William S. Hall to Darlene M. Upmann, Apr. 25, 1961, in Sterilization File.

48. South Carolina State Hospital, "Procedures re: Request for Sterilization Operation for Patient," Dec. 3, 1953, in Sterilization File; and William S. Hall, "Affidavit Giving Facts Concerning Personal and Family History of ———," 1963, in Sterilization File, the source of the quotation in the text.

49. See, e.g., Mary T. Elam to William S. Hall, Mar. 1, 1955, in Sterilization File; and W. M. Manning to William S. Hall, Mar. 27, 1959, in Sterilization File.

50. See South Carolina State Hospital, *Annual Report* [1949] (Columbia, S.C.: State Budget and Control Board, 1949), 25; and the hospital's subsequent annual reports as follows: the 1950 report, p. 10; the 1951 report, p. 15; the 1953 report, p. 17; the 1954 report, p. 23; the 1955 report, p. 138; the 1956 report, p. 42; the 1957 report, p. 55; the 1958 report, p. 64; and the 1960 report, p. 112. Some mentally retarded African Americans simply were housed in the state mental health hospital prior to 1953. At that time, a building at the hospital set aside for mentally retarded African Americans was designated "Pineland, A State Training School," but it never gained an independent identity and served primarily to forestall racial integration at Whitten's facility. William S. Hall served as the superintendent of both the state mental health hospital and Pineland. See William S. Hall, "Sterilizations Performed in the Year 1953," in AVS Collection (annual sterilization questionnaire reply form returned from South Carolina).

51. Reilly, *Surgical Solution,* 138. Other mental health institutions in the Deep South did not use racial categories in their published sterilization statistics, and neither the Human Betterment Foundation nor Birthright asked for such a breakdown in their annual sterilization surveys. Institutions occasionally volunteered this information in their responses to those surveys, however, and that information was preserved in the AVS Collection. Except for the responses from South Carolina, no clear racial bias appeared in these responses. For example, the Mississippi State Hospital reported sterilizing forty-eight Whites and twenty-nine Blacks in 1934, whereas the Milledgeville State Hospital in Georgia reported sterilizing twenty-one Whites and twelve Blacks in 1942. Alabama only admitted and sterilized Caucasians at the Partlow State School.

52. Mencken, "Utopia," 399. Northern eugenicists typically did not single out African Americans for sterilization either, and Marian Olden once indicated that Birthright would not accept a much-needed grant that carried a condition that it fund a racially discriminatory sterilization program. Marian S. Olden to Mrs. Bradford, Feb. 12, 1947, in AVS Collection.

53. Mona Woodside, *Sterilization in North Carolina: A Sociological and Psychological Study* (Chapel Hill: Univ. of North Carolina Press, 1950), 85 and 192. This study, which promoted the program, was funded by Gamble. Woodside, *Sterilization,* ix. On Gamble's work in North Carolina generally, see Williams, *Every Child,* 128–48; and Reilly, *Surgical Solution,* 134–39.

54. For a general discussion of this work, see Linda Gordon, *Woman's Body, Woman's Right: Birth Control in America*, rev. ed. (New York: Penguin, 1990), 325–29 and 349–50; and Reilly, *Surgical Solution*, 134. In the South, to conform to prevailing practices of racial segregation, separate clinics often were opened for Blacks and Whites. See Gordon, *Woman's Body*, 326; and Zukoski, "Life Story," 130.

55. Clarence Gamble, quoted in Gordon, *Woman's Body*, 328–29. The "conference at Atlanta" was further discussed in Dykeman, *Too Many People*, 81–82. This concern for regional pride also appeared at the time in a report from the southern field representative for Gamble's organization Birthright. She wrote, "The Southern states resist overt efforts to show them that they are ignorant of what Northern states know, they resist attempts to get them to join national organizations." Elsie Wulkup, "Summary of Field Reports, 1944," Feb. 15, 1944, in AVS Collection.

56. Woodside, *Sterilization*, 86–87.

57. "The Sterilization Act," *Savannah Tribune*, Apr. 1, 1935, p. 4, col. 1.

58. Gordon, *Woman's Body*, 326. Alabama's pioneering effort in government-sponsored birth control, which occurred under the leadership of the state health officer J. N. Baker and with funding from northern philanthropy, was described in Zukoski, "Life Story," 130–32; and Dykeman, *Too Many People*, 72–78. Gordon discussed African American opposition to birth control in Gordon, *Woman's Body*, 441 and 481.

59. Funkhouser, "Human Rubbish," 199.

60. R. McG. Carruth, "Race Degeneration: What Can We Do to Check It?" *New Orleans Medical and Surgical Journal* 72 (1919), 184 and 189 (emphasis added).

61. T. H. Dreher, "Birth Control among the Poor," *Journal of SCMA* 27 (1931), 331–32. During the 1930s, *nigger, spook,* and *Hamite* were widely recognized derogatory terms for an African or African American.

62. Reilly, *Surgical Solution*, 137–38.

63. Annual statistics for all states are in Robitscher, ed., *Eugenic Sterilization*, 118–19.

64. "Sterilization Law Being Scrutinized," *Savannah Morning News*, Sept. 11, 1959, p. 5A, col. 3; and T. F. Abercrombie to E. S. Gosney, Jan. 26, 1938, in AVS Collection.

65. 1937 Ga. Laws ch. 5, sec. 3.

66. Margaret Shannon, "$1.18 a Child a Day Gracewood's Budget," *Atlanta Journal*, Mar. 27, 1950, p. 28, col. 1, the source of the quotation in the text; "Sterilization Scrutinized," p. 5A, col. 3; Jones T. Wright to F. O. Butler, June 15, 1950, in AVS Collection; and Reilly, *Surgical Solution*, 136.

67. Annual sterilization figures for Gracewood were reported in response to Birthright's annual survey, and were preserved in the AVS Collection. The quotation appeared in the response to the 1957 survey, and the policy change was

noted in the response to the 1960 survey. See Norman B. Pursley, "Sterilizations Performed in the Year 1957," in AVS Collection (annual sterilization question- naire reply form returned from Georgia); and John N. McFarland and Norman B. Pursley to Ruth P. Smith, Jan. 5, 1961, in AVS Collection.

68. Ed Rogers, "Georgia Sterilizing 225 of Its Mental Patients," *Daily Times* (Gainesville), Sept. 10, 1959, p. 6, cols. 2–5, the source of the quotation in the text; and "Dr. Venable Named State Hospital Head," *Atlanta Journal,* Sept. 10, 1959, p. 1, col. 8. Annual sterilization figures for the 1950s appeared in Mill- edgeville State Hospital, *Annual Report* [1951] ([Atlanta]: n.p., 1951), 39; and the hospital's subsequent annual reports, as follows: the report for 1952, pp. 43–44; the report for 1953, p. 38; the report for 1954, p. 38; the report for 1955, p. 36; the report for 1956, p. 33; the report for 1957, pp. 32–33; and the report for 1958, p. 32. Figures for the 1940s appear in the typed copies of the hospital's annual reports, which are available in the hospital's museum at Milledgeville. Figures for both periods appeared in the institution's response to annual steriliza- tion surveys conducted by the Human Betterment Foundation and Birthright, which were preserved in the AVS Collection. The 1950 response, for example, in- dicated that 191 sterilizations had been performed during the year, and that 2,517 patients had been discharged, and noted, "All cases are passed on by the State Board of Eugenics and consent of relatives or guardians is not required. Only one of the above cases filed an appeal with the Superior Court in Baldwin County and the Court upheld the decision of Board." F. Y. Peacock, "Steriliza- tions Performed in the Year 1950 in AVS Collection (annual sterilization ques- tionnaire reply form returned from Georgia). For a description of Milledgeville State Hospital, see Georgia Department of Public Health, *A Comprehensive Mental Health Plan for Georgia* ([Atlanta]: n.p., 1965), 21–23.

69. For a review of this episode, see "Milledgeville State Hospital," in Georgia Department of Public Health, *Annual Report* ([Atlanta]: n.p., 1959), 67–68; "Report of MAG Milledgeville Study Committee," *Journal of MAG* 48 (1959), 275–88; and William Rottersman, "Mental Illness—Responsibility and Oppor- tunity," ibid., 49 (1960), 32–33, the source of the quotations in the text. The ex- posé appeared in the Atlanta *Constitution* during March 5–11, 1959. A similar exposé of Alabama's main mental health hospital made national headlines, as noted in David J. Rothman, *The Discovery of the Asylum and Social Order and Disorder in the New Republic,* rev. ed. (Boston: Little, Brown, 1990), xvi.

70. "Dr. Venable," p. 1, col. 8; Rogers, "Georgia Sterilizing," p. 6, col. 4, the source of the quotations about numbers and emotion; and "State Checks Steril- ization of Mentally Ill," *Columbus Ledger,* Sept. 10, 1959, p. 10, col. 1; and "Sterilization Scrutinized," p. 5A, cols. 3–4, the source of the quotation about opposition.

71. See Robitscher, ed., *Eugenic Sterilization,* 118; and Georgia Department of Public Health, *A Comprehensive Mental Retardation Plan for Georgia* ([At- lanta]: n.p., 1968), 63. (The latter document requests legal protection from law- suits before performing further sterilizations.)

72. Rogers, "Georgia Sterilizing," p. 6, cols. 2–4, the source of the quotation from the 1959 newspaper article; "Sterilization Study Asked by Tift Jury," *Tifton Gazette,* Sept. 9, 1959, p. 3, cols. 7–8, the source of the quotation from the petition; and "Sterilization Scrutinized," p. 5A, col. 3.

73. Gordon, *Woman's Body,* 386–96, quotation on 396.

74. J. P. McMurphy, "Birth Control, a Public Health Problem," *Transactions of MASA* (1927), 343. For the impact of such reasoning generally, see Gordon, *Woman's Body,* 275.

75. Williams, *Every Child,* 149–73; Dykeman, *Too Many People,* 207–22 (the Zukoskis are mentioned on 211); Zukoski, "Life Story," 346–52; Webster, "Zukoski," 72, which notes the Zukoskis' tie to Gamble; and Reilly, *Surgical Solution,* 146.

76. 1966 Ga. Laws ch. 534, sec 2.

77. 1968 Ga. House Bill 255, sec. 2, on file in the Georgia State Archives, Atlanta, Ga.; and Bill Collins, "Sterilization Approved in House," *Atlanta Journal,* Feb. 17, 1970, p. 8A, col. 8, which notes AVS support.

78. Gene Stephens, "Sterilization Bill Back in Panel," *Constitution* (Atlanta), Feb. 27, 1969, p. 14, col. 1. In 1957 and 1966, opposition from church leaders led the Georgia legislature to reject proposals submitted or supported by physicians that would have legalized the sterilization of mental incompetents outside state institutions, subject to parental consent and governmental approval. "Sterilization Bill Killed after Bishop Testifies," *Constitution* (Atlanta), Feb. 20, 1957, p. 9, col. 1; "Five Doctors in House Propose Sterilizing of Mentally Ill," ibid., Feb. 12, 1965, p. 12, cols. 1–2; and "Sterilization Surgery Again Asked in House," ibid., Jan. 14, 1966, p. 16, col. 3.

79. Gene Stephens, "Teachers Pay Index, Sales Tax Increase Rejected by House," *Constitution* (Atlanta), Feb. 17, 1970, p. 8A, cols. 2–4; Collins, "Sterilization Approved," p. 8A, col. 8; *Ga. House Journal* (1970 Reg. Sess.), 2016–23, which includes the text of the compromise bill; and *Ga. Senate Journal* (1970 Reg. Sess.), 1469.

80. *Wyatt v. Aderholt,* 368 F.Supp. 1382, 1383 (M.D. Ala. 1973).

81. *Wyatt v. Aderholt,* 368 F.Supp. 1883, 1884–85 (M.D. Ala. 1974).

82. "Suit by Girls in Sterilization Is Dismissed," *New York Times,* Aug. 1, 1973, p. 14, col. 3; Reilly, *Surgical Solution,* 150–52; and Edward J. Larson and Leonard J. Nelson III, "Involuntary Sexual Sterilization of Incompetents in Alabama: Past, Present, and Future," *Alabama Law Review* 43 (1992), 439–40.

83. "Three Carolina Doctors Are under Inquiry in Sterilization of Welfare Mothers," *New York Times,* Aug. 22, 1973, p. 30, col. 1; and Nancy Hicks, "Sterilization of Black Mother of Three Stirs Aiken, S.C.," ibid., Aug. 1, 1973, p. 27, col. 1, the source of the quotation in the text.

84. Hicks, "Sterilization of Black Mother," p. 27, col. 1. For a general discussion of this episode in the historical context of the birth control movement, see

Gordon, *Woman's Body,* 431–36. Gordon noted that the AVS claimed to oppose the new federal regulations "on the grounds that they were paternalistic, deprived women of choice, and interfered with the doctor-patient relationship." Gordon, *Woman's Body,* 434.

85. *Federal Register* 42 (Nov. 8, 1978), 52146. See also *Relf v. Weinberger,* 372 F.Supp. 1196 (D.D.C. 1974); *Relf v. Mathews,* 403 F.Supp. 1235 (D.D.C. 1975); and *Relf v. Weinberger,* 545 F.2d 722 (D.C. Cir. 1977).

86. Elizabeth J. Patterson, interview by author, Spartanburg, S.C., June 1, 1993. The background information on Patterson is from Michael Barone and Grant Ujifusa, *The Almanac of American Politics, 1991* (Washington: National Journal, 1990), 1126–28.

87. "Senate Votes to Kill 1937 Sterilization Law," *State* (Columbia), Apr. 19, 1985, p. 3C, col. 1, the source of the quotation in the text; and "Senate Votes to Repeal Law," *Greenville News,* Apr. 19, 1985, p. 1C, col. 1.

88. Patterson, interview; *S.C. Senate Journal* (1985 Reg. Sess.), 1605–7; *S.C. House Journal* (1986 Reg. Sess.), 360; and 1986 S.C. Acts ch. 316.

89. 1984 Miss. Laws ch. 472. For the current law, see Miss. Code Ann., title 41, ch. 45.

Conclusion: *Sifting and Winnowing*

1. 1991 La. House Bill 1584. For a discussion of the early political reaction to Norplant, see Tamar Lewin, "Five-Year Contraceptive Implant Seems Headed for Wide Use," *New York Times,* Nov. 29, 1991, p. A1, cols. 1–2, and p. A26, cols. 1–4.

2. Daniel M. Weintraub and George Skelton, "Wilson Favors Use of Drug Control Implant," *Los Angeles Times,* May 17, 1991, p. A1, cols. 3–4, p. A28, cols. 1–3, and p. A29, cols. 1–2, quotation on p. A29, col. 2.

3. Daniel M. Weintraub and George Skelton, "Most Support Norplant for Teens, Welfare Addicts," *Los Angeles Times,* May 27, 1991, p. A1, cols. 3–4, and p. A34, cols. 1–3; the survey questions are on p. A34, cols. 2–3.

4. William Dempsey Partlow, "Degeneracy," *Transactions of MASA* (1907), 231.

5. "Thoughts on Sterilization," *Montgomery Advertiser,* June 15, 1935, p. 4, col. 2.

6. "Poverty and Norplant," *Philadelphia Inquirer,* Dec. 12, 1990, p. 18A, col. 1. For a similar comment nearly a year later, see Matthew Rees, "Shot in the Arm," *New Republic,* Dec. 9, 1991, 17.

7. J.D.S. Davis, "The President's Message," *Transactions of MASA* (1928), 21.

8. Jean Gordon, in "Discussion," *New Orleans Medical and Surgical Journal* 82 (1929), 355.

9. For such research, see, e.g., Ira J. Chasnoff et al., "Temporal Patterns of Cocaine Use in Pregnancy," *JAMA* 261 (1989), 1742–44; Bertis B. Little et al., "Cocaine Abuse during Pregnancy: Maternal and Fetal Implications," *Obstetrics and*

Gynecology 73 (1989), 157–60; and Anthony J. Hateed and Sharon R. Siegel, "Maternal Cocaine Use during Pregnancy: Effect on the Newborn Infant," *Pediatrics* 84 (1989), 205–9.

10. Robert L. Sinsheimer, "The Prospect of Designing Genetic Change," *Engineering and Science* 32 (Apr. 1969), 8.

11. "Sterilization Progress," *Constitution* (Atlanta), Feb. 23, 1937, p. 4, col. 1.

12. J. Ross Snyder, in "Discussion," *Transactions of MASA* (1910), 365.

13. E.g., Richard Reid, "Mr. Reid on Sterilization," *Augusta Chronicle*, Mar. 27, 1935, p. 4, col. 4; and William F. Obering, "Authority Says Alabama Sterilization Measure Is Declaration of Slavery," *Catholic Week* (Birmingham), May 5, 1935, p. 6, cols. 4–5, and p. 7, cols. 2–3.

14. T. H. Dreher, "Birth Control among the Poor," *Journal of SCMA* 27 (1931), 332.

15. Bibb Graves, veto messages, *Ala. House Journal* (1935 Reg. Sess.), 1343 and 2753.

16. W. L. Funkhouser, "Human Rubbish," *Journal of MAG* 26 (1937), 199.

17. Gordon, in "Discussion" (1929), 355.

18. Dr. Harper, in "Discussion," *Transactions of MASA* (1907), 229.

19. In his response to the statement by Jean Gordon quoted above, Clarence Pierson alluded to the possible loss of people such as Abraham Lincoln through the eugenic sterilization of their parents. Clarence Pierson, in "Discussion," *New Orleans Medical and Surgical Journal* 82 (1929), 357.

Note on Sources

Although numerous historical studies dealing with the American eugenics movement have appeared, they neither focus on the medico-legal aspects of the movement nor pay particular attention to developments in the Deep South. The best of these studies ably explore the broad intellectual contours of the eugenics movement but have little to say about the actual policy-making implications of this ideology. Only a few of them directly examine specific eugenic enactments, and even fewer deal with this at the state level, where most of this legislative activity occurred. No existing work attempts to present a comprehensive survey of eugenic lawmaking viewed in its historical setting. In filling this void, the present study analyzes the eugenics movement as one particularly rich point of interaction between science and society, with that analysis set in the context of parallel legal and medical developments.

Despite the novel approach of this study, I am deeply indebted to many of the existing historical books and articles examining the eugenics movement. These secondary works and the multitude of primary sources used for this study appear in the endnotes that follow the text, and they will not be repeated here at length. Readers should consult those references for material on specific topics. This "Note on Sources" is intended simply as a guide for students or scholars entering this field and as a brief overview of the major resources used in the preparation of this book.

A handful of secondary works provide an excellent introduction to eugenics for the general reader. One must begin with Daniel J. Kevles, *In the Name of Eugenics: Genetics and the Uses of Human Heredity* (New York: Knopf, 1985), for an overview of the Anglo-American eugenics movement within its scientific and intellectual context. Three earlier books also deserve mention, though they have been somewhat superseded by Kevles's work: Mark H. Haller, *Eugenics: Hereditary Attitudes in American Thought* (New Brunswick, N.J.: Rutgers Univ. Press, 1963); Kenneth Ludmerer, *Genetics and American Society: A Historical Appraisal* (Baltimore: Johns Hopkins Univ. Press, 1972); and Donald K. Pickens, *Eugenics and the Progressives* (Nashville: Vanderbilt Univ. Press, 1968). Following the publication of Kevles's seminal book, most scholarship on this topic has focused on examining narrow issues in great depth. Two of the best such books are Nicole Hahn Rafter, ed., *White Trash: The Eugenic Family Studies, 1877–*

1913 (Boston: Northeastern Univ. Press, 1988); and Philip R. Reilly, *The Surgical Solution: A History of Involuntary Sterilization in the United States* (Baltimore: Johns Hopkins Univ. Press, 1991).

Beyond these important studies dealing specifically with eugenics lie numerous volumes surveying general developments in twentieth-century American medicine, psychology, or birth control. Several of these works include material on eugenics within their overall account, and thereby present this subject in the context of broader developments. The leading book on the history of medicine and public health in modern America is Paul Starr, *The Social Transformation of Medicine* (New York: Basic, 1982). Three differing views of developments within American psychology and social-scientific thought during the twentieth century, all of which discuss eugenics, are Hamilton Cravens, *The Triumph of Evolution: American Scientists and the Heredity-Evolution Controversy, 1900–1941* (Philadelphia: Univ. of Pennsylvania Press, 1978); Carl N. Degler, *In Search of Human Nature: The Decline and Revival of Darwinism in American Social Thought* (New York: Oxford Univ. Press, 1991); and Gerald N. Grob, *Mental Illness and American Society, 1875–1940* (Princeton: Princeton Univ. Press, 1983). Eugenics appears throughout the groundbreaking study of birth control in America— Linda Gordon, *Woman's Body, Woman's Right: Birth Control in America*, rev. ed. (New York: Penguin, 1990).

The subject matter of this book also requires an introduction to southern history. No section of the United States has generated a richer body of regional analysis than has the American South. Nevertheless, though it is nearly impossible to say where to end any investigation into southern social and political history, it is easy to point out where to begin such a study. For decades, the Louisiana State University Press series on southern history has stood as the basic work in this field. The period covered by this book falls within the time span covered by two of the best volumes in this series—C. Vann Woodward, *Origins of the New South, 1877–1913* (Baton Rouge: Louisiana State Univ. Press, 1951); and George Brown Tindall, *The Emergence of the New South, 1913–1945* (Baton Rouge: Louisiana State Univ. Press, 1967). The traditional, and still unparalleled, masterpieces on southern life during the era are Wilbur J. Cash, *The Mind of the South* (New York: Knopf, 1941); and Howard W. Odum, *Southern Regions of the United States* (Chapel Hill: Univ. of North Carolina Press, 1936). A useful recent overview of progressivism in the region appears in William A. Link, *The Paradox of Southern Progressivism, 1880–1930* (Chapel Hill: Univ. of North Carolina Press, 1992).

Three types of primary sources were used to investigate ongoing eugenic activity in each state of the Deep South. First, I reviewed the publications of each state medical association for the period from 1895 to the end of eugenic activity in that state, typically around 1950. This usually included an annual "transactions" volume for the early years and a monthly "journal" for most of the period. Tulane University's remarkable medical school library contains most of these publications, but I tracked down many volumes and issues in other medical school libraries or the headquarters of the various state medical associations. I also went through the *Southern Medical Journal* from its inception, and went through several national medical and social-scientific journals, looking for articles on eugenics by authors from the region. Second, I read the publications of each state federation of women's clubs for the same period. No regional repository of these publications exists, so they had to be located on a state-by-state basis. In some states, such as Florida, the federation office maintains relatively complete records. Elsewhere, state archives or major university libraries proved to be the best sources for these largely neglected materials. Finally, I examined the annual reports for each state mental health hospital, facility for the mentally retarded, and public health board, beginning as far back as possible and continuing to the present. The Library of Congress in Washington, D.C., retains copies of many such reports, whereas each of the various state archives generally holds a complete run of them for their local institutions.

I used two additional types of primary source material to study particular eugenic statutes and legislative proposals. First, I looked through the official legislative record pertaining to each eugenics bill. This included the legislation itself, the journals of the Senate and House of Representatives for each state considering such a bill, official rosters and biographical material on legislators, and pertinent legislative voting records. Copies of many such records are preserved in the Library of Congress, but I usually relied on state archives and law school libraries in the various states. The extensiveness and quality of these official records vary greatly from state to state, with the impressive collections of the Alabama state archives at the one extreme and the scanty legislative record from Florida at the other. Second, I searched the key newspapers of a particular state for any period when eugenics legislation was under consideration in that state. This search covered all major daily newspapers, local papers from communities with state mental health facilities, and any surviving African American newspapers. Typically, the process provided me with firsthand accounts of legislative action written by capitol reporters from three to six papers, a wealth of editorial comment, insight into the surrounding political and social atmosphere, and a variety of letters to the editor; but I was able to find very little from the African American press about the pending legislation.

These basic primary source materials were supplemented whenever appropriate by other materials, on a state-by-state basis. For example, where particular individuals, such as William Partlow in Alabama or Jean Gordon in Louisiana, played a prominent part, I sought to know them thoroughly. This often involved reading whatever they published or has been published about them, examining available archival materials, and interviewing surviving friends or relatives. Similarly, I examined the archives of certain key institutions, such as the Children's Home Society of Florida. I also visited each state's original facility for the mentally retarded (all of these institutions are still operating), and most of the region's older state mental health hospitals. This served a dual purpose. My initial intent simply was to inspect the institutions' libraries, museums, and archives, and thereby to learn more about their eugenic past. Over time, however, I grew to appreciate these opportunities to see the current patients and staff, which helped me to keep this study in perspective. The specific source material resulting from these visits, together with my other primary and secondary sources, is cited in the appropriate notes.

Index

Abortion, 109, 161, 212 n. 135

African Americans, 11; eugenics applied to, 2, 38, 153–57, 162–63, 236 n. 51; excluded from eugenics programs, 9, 93–94, 131, 138; mental health treatment of, 218 n. 23, 236 n. 50. See also Segregation, racial

Alabama, 9–10; eugenics introduced to, 50, 60–64, 74; institution for mentally retarded in, 81–84, 90, 105–7 (see also Partlow State School); marriage restrictions in, 88; mental health survey of, 66–67, 71, 90; sterilization law in, 84, 105–7, 139–52, 162–63. See also Medical Association of the State of Alabama

Alabama Baptist, 147

Alabama Federation of Women's Clubs, 152, 198 n. 59, 233 n. 29, 234 n. 37

Alabama Herald, 142

Alabama Home, The. See Partlow State School

Alabama Insane Hospitals, 43, 48, 79, 105–7, 139–41

Alabama League for Human Betterment, 152, 234 n. 37

Alabama Society for Mental Hygiene, 44, 60, 140

Alcohol, as cause of mental illness, 36, 45, 47, 99

American Association for the Study and Prevention of Infant Mortality, 89, 90

American Association of University Women, 140, 149

American Breeders' Association, 30, 32, 41, 177 n. 84

American Civil Liberties Union, 141, 145

American Eugenics Society, 26, 32

American Genetics Association. See American Breeders' Association

American Neurological Association, 148, 227 n. 116

Anderson, V. V., 69, 72

Arnall, Ellis, 133–36, 138, 224 n. 80

Associated Press, 115, 127, 129

Association for Voluntary Sterilization. See Birthright, Inc.

Aswell, James, 102

Atlanta Constitution, 33, 137, 148, 238 n. 69

Atlanta, Ga., 16, 74, 88

Augusta Chronicle, 33, 134–35

Baker, J. N., 33, 140, 146, 148

Baptist, 11, 14, 141–42, 150, 152, 174 n. 45. See also Religion

Bartley, Numan V., 133, 136

Beers, Clifford, 193 n. 110

Bell, Walter, 50

Bilbo, Thomas G., 61–62, 79, 82, 92, 115–18, 122

Binet-Simon test, 25

Birmingham Age-Herald, 90

Birmingham, Ala., 16, 50, 142

Birmingham News, 141

Birth control: availability of, 160–61, 210 n. 107; Catholic opposition to, 107; and eugenics, 32, 104–5, 151; public funds for, 156–57; women's support for, 123, 131–32. See also Norplant

Birthright, Inc., 149–52, 161

Blackburn, R. G., 127–29

Blacks. See African Americans

Blindness, eugenic remedies proposed for, 65–66, 74, 147

Bradford, William R., 126–27

Brandt, Allan, 87

Brasington, S. F., 129

Bryan, William Jennings, 113

Buchanan, J. M., 45, 46, 96, 97, 98

Library of Congress Cataloging-in-Publication Data

Larson, Edward J. (Edward John)
    Sex, race, and science : eugenics in the deep South / by Edward J. Larson.
        p.   cm.
    Includes bibliographical references and index.
    ISBN 0-8018-4938-1 (hardcover : acid-free paper)
    ISBN 0-8018-5467-9 (pbk. : acid-free paper)
    1. Eugenics—Southern States—History—20th century.   I. Title.
HQ755.5.U5L37   1995
363.9'2'0975—dc20   94-28124
                                                               CIP